John James Tayler

A Retrospect of the Religious Life of England

Or the Church, Puritanism, and Free Inquiry. Second Edition

John James Tayler

A Retrospect of the Religious Life of England
Or the Church, Puritanism, and Free Inquiry. Second Edition

ISBN/EAN: 9783337077365

Printed in Europe, USA, Canada, Australia, Japan

Cover: Foto ©ninafisch / pixelio.de

More available books at **www.hansebooks.com**

A RETROSPECT

OF THE

RELIGIOUS LIFE OF ENGLAND;

OR, THE

CHURCH, PURITANISM, AND FREE INQUIRY.

BY

JOHN JAMES TAYLER, B.A.,

MEMBER OF THE HISTORICO-THEOLOGICAL SOCIETY OF LEIPSIC

"Opportunos magnis conatibus transitus rerum."—*Tacitus*, Hist. I. 21.

SECOND EDITION,

RE-ISSUED WITH AN INTRODUCTORY CHAPTER ON RECENT DEVELOPMENTS

BY

JAMES MARTINEAU, LL.D., D.D.

LONDON:
TRÜBNER & CO., LUDGATE HILL.
1876.

[*All Rights Reserved.*]

PRINTED BY TAYLOR AND CO.,
LITTLE QUEEN STREET, LINCOLN'S INN FIELDS.

ADDRESS TO THE READER.

In bringing again before the public my late father's work on "The Religious Life of England" (the first edition of which appeared in 1845, and the second in 1853), I have sought the means of giving effect to a suggestion which has been made to me, that it should be accompanied by some notice of the changes which have taken place since it was written, so as in a measure to continue the history to the present day without interfering with the character and completeness of the original work. There are but very few whom I could have asked (or indeed should have wished to ask) to render such a service, but in my father's valued friend and colleague Dr. Martineau I have found exactly the helper that I needed. If his preface should be the means of bringing the book—on its re-introduction to the public—to the notice of a wider circle than it might otherwise have reached, I know that his work of love will be better repaid than by any thanks of mine.

H. E. OSLER.

Hampstead,
  December 1, 1875.

INTRODUCTORY CHAPTER.

MODEST as are the pretensions of this volume, it occupies a peculiar, if not a unique position in English literature. The reader who, on closing it, seeks the right place for it upon his shelves, looks in vain for the class to which it belongs. It is not Theology, though treating of the deepest grounds of faith. It is not Ecclesiastical History; for it passes by incidents and personages dear to the memory of the Church, and travels freely into State affairs and the vicissitudes of secular society. It is not Biography, though abounding in exact and delicate portraiture. It is not Criticism, though it reviews and estimates a series of writers, English and foreign, from Wycliffe and Chaucer to Ewald and Strauss. It approaches most nearly to the German type of "*Cultur-Geschichte*;" yet is still marked out among productions of this kind, by its survey of all culture only in its bearing upon the changing aspects of Religion. This specialty might easily have narrowed the work of any ordinary hand. But an author who discerns the affinity of Religion with every side of human nature, and sees all faculties converging towards it in their culmination, is rendered catholic, and not exclusive, by a religious aim; being drawn by sympathy towards every form of higher aspiration, and winning an insight, denied to critical antipathy, into the inner meaning of many an outward extravagance of word or act. In no notices of English ecclesiastical literature and parties have I ever met with the breadth of conception, the unforced justice, the various appreciation of excellence, which, without any loss of fine discrimination, characterise this little volume. The late Mr. Maurice's judgments on men and systems are marked by a similar comprehensiveness of sympathy; but they rest so much more on subjective than on historical grounds, and their diffusive light is attended with so little shadow, that they do not always help the reader, and sometimes endanger his confidence by an overstrained humility and candour. An opposite defect impairs the value of Lord Macaulay's sketches of religious parties in England. Copious in research, and impartial in observation, he traced their origin, learned their language, was familiar with their habits and costumes; and, having reproduced them in imagination, flung them on the canvas of his brilliant description. But he was fair to all, because in sympathy with none; judging them simply as objective phenomena springing from past thought or passion, he looked at them, not from the interior position which gives their meaning, but from the stage which exhibits their effects. While they must all acknowledge that they receive relative justice at his hands, not one will feel that its true genius or animating idea has been adequately seized and presented by him. If, in quest of this essential key, we turn to the special Church histories in which it is offered to us, we find ourselves in the presence of partisan reporters, and we gain the truth on one side at the expense of missing it on another. The Anglican writer, accustomed to regard his Church as "National," and to identify its history with the course of English life in its religious aspects, moves in an ecclesiastical world of his own, and remains for the most part a stranger to the literature and character of other communities, knowing more of Lutheranism and Anabaptism abroad than of Independency and Quakerism at home, and treating all that does not enter the parish church as a foreign element outside the current of national history. The Nonconformist, on the other hand, cannot tell the story of his sect without seeing in it the representative of conscience, which has won from the grasp of a reluctant hierarchy the chief liberties of modern England: the genius of the established religion he finds in the Church of the Restoration: reproached with being a disaffected Englishman, he charges his opponent with being a disloyal Christian, rendering unto Cæsar the things that are God's; and though his reading is less restricted than the Churchman's to the writers of his own communion, it is rarely comprehensive enough to emancipate him from narrow formulas and open his mind to wide and genial admirations.

From all these contracting influences, the author of this book was exceptionally free. In him a pure and sensitive religious nature responded to every genuine expression of human trust and aspiration, and enabled him to recognise a sweet music and a native speech where others heard only the rude tones of a fanatic jargon. The humiliating catalogue of aberrations which his ecclesiastical erudition spread before him did not impair his conviction that the human spirit and the Divine are capable of true communion, or weaken his insistence on a free movement of thought and conscience as the condition of its attainment. But individual liberty he valued as a means of working out a spiritual *consensus* of humanity; in which the gains of the past should be enlarged by the experience of the present, yet should interpret and control it. His quick sympathy with generous popular movements born from some oppression or inspiration of the hour, was qualified by the scholar's veneration for history and tradition, and his distrust of every promised morrow that does flow naturally from the hours of to-day. This rare and happy balance of mind enables the author to guide us through the most passionate conflicts of our national history, without misdirecting an admiration or awakening a prejudice.

Since the publication of this volume, religious change in England has proceeded with marked acceleration; *so* marked, that the air is filled with vague alarms and vaguer hopes; and while, on the one hand, anxious Protestants and revolutionary prophets alike forebode for Christianity a near crisis of agony, on the other hand preparation is openly made for a reaction into mediæval faith and obedience. It is natural for a fresh and eager generation to be struck with wonder at the ferment of thought which agitates it, and to overrate the originality of its own time. It is born into currents of opinion which are relatively new, and is unconscious that the wind has ever set from the same quarter before. But, in fact, all the recent movements of belief and usage are on the lines continuously traced in the following pages, and do but express, in terms of modern life, the same ineffaceable tendencies of human nature; the same reverence for authority in its three forms, historical, spiritual, rational, and the same difficulty in bringing them all to harmony.

I. THE CHURCH.

i. *High Church.*

It is in the CHURCH alone that the principle of Tradition has room to work out any unexpected results: and during the last twenty years advantage has been taken of its Catholic origin and its elastic Rubrics, to transform its services, and to steal back, through a ritual conspicuously ornate and secretly symbolic, into the supernatural circle of sacerdotal doctrine. The issues first raised in the courts between the Tractarians and their opponents had reference to theological teaching. It was for certain published propositions that Mr. Gorham in the West, Professor Jowett at Oxford, and the Essayists Wilson and Rowland Williams in the Court of Arches, were called to account. The result plainly showed a prevailing indisposition to create needless ecclesiastical offences, or to narrow by interpretation the illogical but convenient latitude of the authoritative formulas; and the attempt to put down low doctrine by law was abandoned for a more effective policy, the embodiment of high doctrine in priestly vestments, in banners, thuribles and processions, in significant gestures, and a service of the "Altar" barely distinguishable from the mass. Hence whatever questions have recently been brought to judicial hearing have had reference, not to teaching, but to the external form of worship. Though the decisions have placed the ceremonial under some legal restraints, prohibiting the eastward position of the celebrant at the communion, and regulating the elevation of the elements and the use of lights at the altar, and though by a special Act of the Legislature new facilities have been created for enforcing the law, it may be doubted whether the sacerdotal tendency is not too deeply rooted in the history of the Church, and too widely fostered by the piety of dependent minds, to receive any serious check from such agencies. It is not uncommon, with both amiable peace-makers and contemptuous adversaries, to depreciate the significance of ritualism, by reducing it to a question about the æsthetics of worship, and pretending that it is but a new dress upon the old and familiar sanctities. But nothing can be more futile than such attempts either to justify or to condemn a symbol by expelling from it all that it means. Copes, albs and chasubles, gold crosses and altar cloths, are no more mere upholstery;—and genuflection, the lifting of the hands, the turning of the face at the communion, are no more mere gymnastics or deportment, than spoken words are mere exercises of the vocal chords, identical because audible to a sheep and to a man. Notoriously, it is the ideal significance of his favourite forms that makes the High Churchman passionately cling to them, and feel his Christian loyalty itself so involved in his fidelity to them as to justify a disregard of legal inhibition. Nor is there any uncertainty as to the scheme of theological conceptions which is thus reclaiming its old abode. It is the doctrines of the Real Presence, of the unbloody sacrifice, of Sacramental Grace, of a supernaturally endowed Priesthood, which constitute the soul and sense of this ceremonial restoration. Wherever it raises its head, the Catholic theory of Christianity is undeniably displacing the Protestant.

But we should greatly underrate the power of this reaction, if we measured it merely by the number of ritualistic churches and priests. Its indirect influence may be traced in modified habits, in a new literature, in an altered tone of devotion, pervading the whole of the Anglican community. Religious orders are established as an asylum for those who feel the call of some "Counsel of Perfection;" and the tension of sacred duty is strained or relaxed according to the rank of souls. Manuals of devotion circulate extensively, framed upon the Catholic model, and reviving the mediæval discipline of piety. And numerous Hymn-books have passed into popular use, which reproduce, in a bald and literal way, a childish ecclesiastical mythology, and in their arrangement follow the Breviaries and the Saints' Calendar. Since the High Church movement has passed, for its wider diffusion, into inferior hands, the literary descent has been marvellous, from the graceful and tender poetry of Keble, rich in ideal painting and meditative depth, to the realistic daubs, the mawkish common-place, the poor doggrel, which constitute so large a part of their present Hymnals. But so much the more does the wide acceptance of these books attest the prevalence of their characteristic ideas in a lower and larger stratum of religious society. The activity and self-devotion of the sacerdotal party have given it an importance out of all proportion to its numbers. The practice of frequent communion, the week consecrated in large towns to "Missions" of revival, the attempt at Pananglican union, have originated with its clergy, but have affected a far larger circle. No one who remembers the parochial administration of religion, the tone of the ecclesiastical newspapers, and the prevailing topics of clerical interest, thirty years ago, can fail to admit, that, through the presence of the High Church influence, a sensible change has been wrought in the general complexion of devout thought and feeling, if not of the fluctuating outer congregations of Conformists, at least of the habitual communicants.

ii. *Influence of Mr. Maurice.*

From the usual law of social antagonism it might be expected that this wave of Catholic reaction would be met by an intenser movement of Low Church Calvinism. Yet it has not been so. On the contrary, the last quarter of a century has brought no more remarkable clerical change than the softening of the severe "Evangelical" theology, and the rapid disappearance of the once swarming successors of Simeon and Venn. Several causes have compelled them to alter their voice, or to retreat from the front. The assaults of the "Tracts for the Times" *told* upon them with permanent effect, and, in the estimation of competent judges, whether on the intellectual or the spiritual side, disabled them for conducting the resistance to any Romanizing advance. Moreover, the chief need of the age was no longer the same,—the awakening of torpid and careless minds to the sense of inward discord and the means of Divine harmony. A pantheistic tendency had set in; and the danger now was of a lapse, on the part of men neither torpid nor careless, from all personal relations with God. In looking through the resources of the orthodox theology for meeting this state of mind, it was obvious that to insist on the atoning merits of the Saviour's blood would speak to no felt doubt, and could be of no avail; but that in the assumption of our nature by the Divine was a pertinent fact, rebuking all dreams of mere impersonal power. Thus the centre of gravity shifted from the Cross to the Incarnation: the interest which had been concentrated on the Death of Christ as an expiation became diffused over his whole earthly life as a manifestation of the Divine Personality; and the theology of Erskine, Maurice, and Macleod Campbell, which placed this newer conception in the intensest and most attractive light, was forced by grateful disciples out of its modest obscurity, and drew to itself the more spiritual class of minds that had hitherto given vitality to the Evangelical school. It is in this class, undoubtedly, and not in the "No-Popery" Low Church, that we are now to look for the proper Puritan counterpoise within the Establishment to the High Catholic Anglicanism.

It may seem paradoxical, yet is hardly hazardous, to say that the Maurice theology owes its power not less to its indulgence, than to its correction, of the pantheistic tendency of the age. It answers the demand of every ideal philosophy and every poetic soul for an indwelling Divine Presence, living and acting in all the beauty of the world and the good of human hearts. Its "Incarnation" is not, as in other schemes, an historical prodigy, setting its period apart, as an *Annus Mirabilis*, in vehement contrast with the darkness of an otherwise unvisited world; but is rather a revelation, by a supreme instance, of the everlasting immanence of God and his consecrating union with our humanity. The "Evangelical" preachers had worked out an "economy" of redemption which they presented as a drama introduced upon the stage of time, with acts definitely localised and dated, and affecting only a select company of observers. It was a sacred story of things that had happened on the earth, and which, now that they were accomplished, a few might apply to their salvation. The new theologians translated Christianity out of time into eternity: they read in the life and death of Christ no scheme, no plot with astonishing catastrophe; but the symbol and sample of constant Divine life with men, and of human sonship to God, disclosing relations that had for ever been and would for ever be; only adding now the glad surprise that the sigh for better life, the response of conscience to high appeals, the inward sympathy with all righteousness, are no lonely visions, but the personal communion of the Perfect with the imperfect mind. This lifting of revelation from a tale of Divine action into an objective manifestation of the Divine life and love in humanity, brings it into contact with a far higher order of affections. It delivers the heart from the intolerable shadows of Calvinism. It leaves no room for either the passionate fears or the transports of gratitude of which self is the centre. It carries the mind to the source at once of intensest action and of supreme repose in reverent surrender to a Living Inspirer of all good. The type of character formed in this school is accordingly of larger dimensions, of better proportions, and of purer elevation, than the Evangelical discipline usually produced. Both of these parties have been distinguished by a noble philanthropy, not, however, without a characteristic difference in its style and inspiration. It would be unjust to say that the Low Church leaders were indifferent to temporal objects. They have been foremost in the great struggle against slavery; in the creation of reformatories and asylums of refuge for every neglected class; in claiming needful restrictions on the hours of labour; nor are any names so frequent as theirs in the administrative lists of the Public Hospitals, the City Missions, the Evening Schools. But their care for the conditions of this life springs from their anxiety about the prospects of another. They cannot bear that any soul which has an eternal stake should be lost under degrading necessities here; and they insist on securing it the possibility of escaping perdition. It is the vision of things beyond death that quickens their eye of compassion to the shadows and the shame of life, and sends them forth as apostles of rescue. To the Maurice school the world appears under another aspect. It is not a place of banishment from Heaven, or a mere house of call on the way thither; but is itself the permanent scene of a Divine government,—of an ever-advancing " Kingdom of God," the aims of which men are to make their own, and to pursue with self-sacrificing faith. A consecration thus falls upon the earth as it is, and saves it from borrowing all its interest from another sphere. An ideal of human Society haunts the mind with the persuasion of a supreme authority, and renders intolerable to the conscience every remediable sorrow, every unrighteous institution, every unbrotherly neglect. Men possessed by this feeling care for the world on its own account, as the Republic of God committed to their charge. Every improvement in it is intrinsically welcome to them, though it convert no soul, but only shed some joy or beauty upon many. Their zeal is not all spent in individualised pity, but is kindled by large hopes of social, national, and international reform, which **may make** history less sad, and bring **the drama of the ages to an** issue nearer to the thought of God. Some of the projects suggested by this larger view have failed; but its general effect on the methods of modern benevolence is not to be mistaken.

The Maurice theology, which I have treated as **succeeding** to the Puritan spirituality in the Anglican communion, is more often classed under the general name of the "Broad Church," **with the** Rationalist divinity represented in the volume **of " Essays and Reviews."** And there is certainly a precedent for such a grouping in the application of the word "Latitudinarian" in the seventeenth century to so mixed a body of writers as to include together the logical Chillingworth and the mystical More. Yet, beyond the common desire for a wider ecclesiastical comprehension, there is little affinity between the Platonising realism and Johannine genius of Mr. Maurice, and the critical intellect and historical feeling of such writers as Baden Powell, Pattison, Jowett, or even Stanley. His distinctive work has been in the direction of religious depth; theirs, is that of mental breadth; and the two influences have for the most part worked upon minds of different order, so as rarely to meet in a blended discipleship.

iii. *Broad Church.*

Though there were liberal clergymen of eminence among his contemporaries,—Maltby, for instance, and Whately,— the "Broad Church" party **took** a fresh start from Arnold. His activity, his moral enthusiasm, his wide social influence through his pupils and their parents, **his** intense sympathy **with** the anti-Tractarian feeling, his identification with the reforming side in politics, gave an exceptional weight to his opinions, even during his life; and the shock of sorrow at his sudden death, followed by the marvellous charm of the Memoir **and** Letters soon after, immeasurably deepened and widened his personal action on his age. His ecclesiastical latitude was peculiar in its type. It did not arise from loosened orthodoxy, from flexible appreciation of beliefs other than his own, from deep experience of the difficulties of religious problems: it **was** political rather than theological, springing from his theory of the State, and his intense reluctance to break the Unity of the Nation. Citizenship and Church membership were to be co-extensive, and the duties of patriotism and piety to coalesce. This attempt to wed the compactness of the ancient Commonwealths to the complex conditions of modern society and Protestant Christendom, led immediately to consequences at variance with its whole aim. As the State was to be Christian, **Jews** and others who declined the Christian profession, were to dwell in the land as aliens. As the Public Worship was to be uniform in its basis, and, in order to express the general feeling, must address itself to three Divine Persons, the Unitarians, though deeming themselves Christians, must be lopped off, and left outside with the ξένοι of foreign faiths. By thus failing to cover cases for which it was bound to provide, the theory was shattered in its first encounter with experience.

The power of Arnold lay, however, not in his speculation, but in his life and personality; especially in that ethical nobleness and elevation which opened the hearts of a whole army of English youths to the recognition and reverence of the true and good, wherever found. The spirit thus awakened soon bore fruits in other fields than he had cultivated. Biblical scholarship was not his *forte*; and surprise has been naturally felt that, **with** all his confidence in Niebuhr's **methods of** "**divination,**" he never applied his principles **of criticism to** the Jewish and Christian records. It **was left, however, to his** pupil and biographer, in conjunction with Professor Jowett, to carry into sacred literature the careful exegesis and fine historical feeling of which **an** example had been given in the edition of Thucydides. In 1855 appeared their joint edition and version of the principal Pauline Epistles, copiously annotated, and accompanied by numerous disquisitions. The work, if compared with the best foreign expositions, may not, perhaps, stand quite in the first rank, as an interpretation of the apostle's thought. The preponderance of Classical studies in the education of the English clergy, their prevailing neglect of Hebrew and the Semitic literature, and their comparatively late and slight familiarity with the Hellenistic Greek, unfavourably affect their qualifications as commentators **on** Scripture.

Though the two eminent Editors have spared no voluntary labour and learning which could rightly modify for their task the early set of their taste and culture, yet at times the experienced reader may feel that their minds are not fully steeped and tinctured in the Pauline thought, but exhibit it through an invisible film of literary or philosophical light which, while clearing and beautifying it, suffuses it with a colour not its own. But by one capital merit the work renders a most important service to the progress of a just theology. It shows conclusively what the apostle did *not* mean; that the dogmatic statements drawn from his language overstrain his purpose,—defining more than he intended to define, universalising what he left in the particular, pronouncing on theses which were not present to his thought. The reader is so put in possession of the historical and personal situation of St. Paul as to be recalled from the abstractions of modern metaphysical divinity to the concrete scenery, the local life, the party controversies, of the apostolic age. He is familiarised with the idea of a gradual change and expansion of the apostle's own theology, and of some illusory conceptions blended with it throughout. And he is led to contemplate the marvellous crises and inward struggles of the "Man of Tarsus" in relation to analogous spiritual experiences in other ages of awakened faith. The appended Essays of Professor Jowett treat the most sensitive and entangled problems of Religion with a subtle depth and moral tenderness rarely found within the compass of so large an intellectual view, and often read like the autobiography of a mind that, in unswerving search for light, has touched the limits of thought, and shrunk from no possibility of feeling. If it be a fault to raise more questions than can be settled, to reason round them, and illumine the immense space in which they lie, without altering their suspense, it is a fault relative only to a time of too large and rambling thought, that sees everything afloat. In dealing with an age and place in the Church which narrows all piety, and crystallises all belief into dogmatic form, and can neither love nor think beyond, there is often a wise reverence in not exactly breaking the tenacious centre, but rather passing out beyond it and showing its latitude and longitude in the wide seas of thought. This service is eminently rendered by the Pauline commentaries of 1855.

Five years later there issued from the same school a book which, with far less claim to distinction, has obtained a greater celebrity,—the "Essays and Reviews." From the combination of seven writers in its production, and the prefatory statement that it was an experiment in the independent treatment of ecclesiastical topics of the time, the book was taken as a sort of party manifesto; though the absence of concerted plan was conspicuous in the very table of contents, and the writers disclaimed all joint responsibility. The panic occasioned by this idea of a rationalistic conspiracy within the Church invested the volume with an importance out of all proportion to its intrinsic power. No original Essays which seven scholarly and freshminded men would deem worth publishing could well contain less that was startling; and few, if any, of the characteristic opinions advanced were unfamiliar to readers versed in theological literature. But, when scrutinized by the keen eye of detective alarm, the pages seemed to look up with an audacious face, and to abound with suspicious oracles. Where was the glory of Revelation, if it were to be merged in the Education of the world? Where, its depositaries, if Scripture were not all authentic? Where, its certainty, if Inspiration were not infallible? Where, its authority, if the Geologists might call Moses to account? These were natural questions; and naturally, in its hour of fear, did ecclesiastical orthodoxy seek shelter from their disturbance in the Courts of Law. Dr. Lushington's remarkable judgment, that the authenticity of parts of Scripture might be called in question, also their Inspiration, but not their Canonicity, disappointed the prosecutors' hopes, and saved theological learning from being blindfolded by public law.

While the ecclesiastical waters were still heaving with this storm of the seven winds, a new wave of disturbance was advancing from the seas of South Africa, and in 1862 rolled into the Thames, to the alarm of Lambeth and Fulham, and all low-lying Church districts. In that year commenced the publication of the Bishop of Natal's commentaries on the Pentateuch; in the Introduction to which the story was told, with noble and characteristic ingenuousness, how the mind of the evangelical missionary, brought into contact with unartificial intelligence, and compelled to think in terms universally human and speak in the vocabulary of another tongue, caught by sympathy some of the fresh impressions of his scholars, and became sensible of difficulties never felt before in his own formulated beliefs. [Humorists may be allowed to see a pleasant picture in the Zulu converting the Bishop; and to enjoy their laugh when the author of a capital manual of arithmetic sets himself sums out of the statistics of Exodus, and proves that the Bible answers are impossible. But, seriously estimated, the one fact is full of moral beauty, and the other of intellectual sagacity. Cultivated minds, in proportion as they are truthful, may often expand more in having to retreat upon first principles than in working out ulterior results. And, for the testing of historical narratives, no method is more serviceable than the analysis and comparison of quantitative statements, when they are present in sufficient number to affect the complexion of the story. As successive parts appeared of the Bishop's examination of the Pentateuch, the contemptuous voices which greeted it at first fell off into silence: no competent theologians, however hostile, could withhold their admiration from the indefatigable industry which had rapidly matured his Hebrew scholarship, and mastered all the elements of the problems under his hand. The conclusions which he reached, while in general agreement with those of the most eminent European Hebraists and historical critics, were marked by important distinctive features, attesting the independence of his researches; that the Pentateuch contains a tissue of composite materials widely differing in age, primarily distinguished by the respective Divine Names *Elohim* and *Jehovah*, and combined in their present form not simply by post-Mosaic but by quite late hands; that the Elohistic portions are the more ancient and constitute a continuous history (due possibly to Samuel) stopping at Exodus VI.; that Deuteronomy belongs to the time and probably to the pen of the prophet Jeremiah; that the Levitical Law was of gradual growth, some of its provisions being earlier than Deuteronomy, others later than Ezra and Nehemiah; and that the Jehovistic monotheism of the Jews was wrought out into ultimate clearness from other worships of less pure or even strongly contrasted character.

Opinions which reduced a large portion of the Old Testament to the level of a literature not only of simply human origin, but of unhistorical contents, could not but produce great commotion in a Church accustomed to ask, in such matters, not what is true, but what is orthodox and decorous. The consequences of his insight and veracity fell upon the heretical Bishop, in the order of their readiness. It was easiest to denounce him; perhaps possible to depose him; hardest, to answer him. The first was effected at once by inhibition of his preaching in every English diocese which he entered. The second was attempted by the Bishop of Cape Town; who took on himself, as South African Metropolitan, to convene a local Synod, and, after a spurious trial, to pronounce the deprivation of the Bishop of Natal. The third was immediately promised, in the shape of an authoritative Commentary on the Bible, to be contributed, under patronage of the Speaker of the House of Commons, by a body of learned and approved Anglican divines; but was delayed in the public commencement of its performance for nine years. The ecclesiastical proceedings against Dr. Colenso being wholly null and void, he remains by decision of the supreme tribunal the legitimate occupant of his see; stripped, however, by the Society for the Propagation of the Gospel and by trustees of the Colonial Fund, of the revenues for the support of his office; in the presence of an Episcopal rival, appointed by voluntary election; and, it is to be feared, unacknowledged by most of the clergy whose labours it is his legal function to supervise. These personal troubles, endured throughout with singular gentleness and dignity, have not been lightened by his affection and fidelity towards the native population for which chiefly he has laboured and lived. An unjust and illegal punishment having been inflicted on one of their tribes and its head, for some insubordinate acts committed and avenged in panic, the Bishop stood up alone, to resist the wrong while there was hope of preventing it, and to expose and reverse it, when it was complete in Africa but unratified in England. The evidence he brought to this country convinced the Government, as it had convinced himself; and he returned, with honourable but painful success, to a baffled and exasperated community, which felt the presence of his clear-sighted equity as a mortifying reproach.

That the Colenso episode in our Church history, though seeming to leave its author in a minority of one, will not be without theological result, is evident from the complexion of the "Speaker's Commentary." On the one hand, concessions are made in it which alter the whole basis of the accepted Biblical divinity. And on the other, they are refused on grounds so weak as plainly to indicate the temporary nature of the defence. The Pentateuch can never return to its old position : and the history of Judaism has to be re-written.

Old Testament researches can only indirectly, however certainly, affect the received theory of Christianity. But, in the midst of the Colenso Controversy,—in 1866,—an anonymous writer, of large historical grasp and great literary power, stepped upon the immediate field of the Evangelical narratives, and presented the figure and work of Christ under aspects at once winning to the reverence and shocking to the orthodoxy of the traditional believer. The author of "Ecce Homo," avoiding all prejudgment of problems respecting the ontological rank and constitution of Christ's person, proposed to approach and delineate his career as an historical phenomenon, and to characterise the impression which his life has produced upon human society. The effort to clear away all media of custom and read the gospels with a fresh natural eye, is in itself commendable, and is sure, when carried out by a mind of quick moral apprehension, to open lights of beauty unmarked before. Accordingly, the author, by many skilful and delicate combinations, has brought home to himself and to others the features, so gracious, tender, and majestic, of the figure unique in history. Yet his task, under the condition of abstinence from doctrinal assumption, was an impossible one. The intended "historical" picture could only be drawn, either from the objective reality, or from reports of it carefully stripped of all distorting accretions and subjective discolouring. It is actually drawn by the artist without any such precaution. He looks, not at the life set in the clear, but at representations of it just as they stand in the Gospels; where already the image has passed into the doctrinal spectrum, and not always into the same part of it. The particular theory of Christ's nature laid down in the Nicene Creed he does not assume : but that which pervades the fourth Gospel, and that very different one which runs through the first, he does assume ; forgetting that these earlier media intercept the historical view not less than the later, and, where they vary from each other, confuse it with incongruities. Hence, while the title and the apparent purpose of the book promise us the interior study of a *human* life, and many a true pathetic glimpse is really given us, the "Homo" before long disappears, in favour of an artificial nature upon quite another scale, where our measures of sympathy are lost. To Jesus of Nazareth the author attributes forms of self-knowledge which it is difficult to adjust harmoniously in any ideal of humanity; a voluntary command of indefinite supernatural power; a foresight of his place in the ages, and the consolidation of Christendom around his name; a consciousness that the new order of society was to be formed by the power of his character, and that attachment to himself must be invited, in order to constitute it and hold it together. It has been often urged,—not surely without justice,—that the sort of self-magnifying and self-assertion in which such an inward experience must speak, must be for ever out of place in beings like ourselves. May we not add, that for us they mar the beauty of *any* nature—and all the more the higher it is—to which they are ascribed? This personal glorification is the result of no impulse of the spiritual man, but of a retrospective reverence in others. Through an uncritical working up of the evangelic materials, the author sets before us, in the person of Christ, a fictitious compound of self-forgetfulness and self-exaltation, of faith amid blinding darkness and sight of supernatural vision, of real sacrifice in utter obedience, and show-sacrifice by way of lordly example. No artistic skill in word-painting can provide middle tints to blend these incompatible elements. When you approach the figure to fling your homage before it, its feet are not upon the earth: it hangs in the air, it retreats from your embrace, and a bright cloud absorbs its reality. It is quite otherwise when the author, stepping upon secured historical ground, compares the ancient and the Christian types of civilization, and estimates the moral debt of society to the new law of life and love. With easy command of all the materials for such a comparison, he throws into the strongest relief the side of human nature which has been born beneath the eye of Christ, and has changed all the proportions of our inner and outer experience.

The enthusiasm with which the "Ecce Homo" was received is one of many signs that the age, no longer satisfied with its dogmatic instructors, is eager for any competent guide to the real human personality of Christ; and is grateful to one who can transfer that wonderful but half-faded image to the waiting canvas of modern imagination. This reverential curiosity respecting the "Son of Man," is regarded with impatience by the Low Church party, as symptomatic of failing faith in the "Son of God": and, in a moment of excitement, the benevolent nobleman who is the acknowledged head of that party, denounced the "Ecce Homo" in terms which might have been deemed intemperate, had they not been too rich in infernal imagery to be literally taken. This explosion of anger certainly did not weaken the impression of the book. The second volume, which was to give the doctrinal key to the life exhibited in the first, has not appeared. The delineation, as it now stands, accords entirely with the conceptions of the older Unitarians, especially of America: but there is nothing to exclude, though nothing to require, a higher type of doctrine.

As the "Ecce Homo" is anonymous, and is silent on the topics which divide English theological parties, the treatment of it as a Broad Church phenomenon is merely conjectural. But the intellectual mould in which it is cast, is not of the Scottish or the Nonconformist pattern: only in the Church of England could we find a New Testament criticism so immature combined with a general culture so scholarly and large: and the pure and noble English style bears the inimitable stamp of our old Universities.

The Latitudinarians of the seventeenth century found a centre of union in Lord Falkland's house. If we looked for a corresponding rallying point where we might expect to meet the modern successors of Hales and Chillingworth, we should perhaps fix our eye upon the Deanery of Westminster: only that here the High Church Archdeacon, the Low Church curate, the Presbyterian Moderator, the Independent minister, are likely also to be found. Falkland gathered together a private club, to *talk* of latitude: the Dean of Westminster lays himself out with resolute consistency to *practice* it; not hesitating to let his venerable Abbey hear the voice, now of an Oxford layman, now of a Glasgow

Professor, and now of a Nonconformist Missionary; or himself to occupy the pulpit in parishes beyond the Tweed. This courageous openness, in preaching, in writing, in the Convocation debates, and in social action, contrasts strongly with the reserve of the old latitudinarians, and has greatly strengthened the liberal wing of the Church of England. Complaint indeed is sometimes heard that its leading preachers do not define their precise theological position: while unshrinkingly rejecting popular errors, they are too reticent as to the form of faith which they preserve. The complaint proceeds from the lingering dogmatic conception of Christian Union, against which it is their purpose to protest. They insist that religious worship and fellowship might be much more comprehensive than it is, and that the obtrusion of dogmatic superfluities is a schismatic act, hurtful to piety and charity, and disguising the true spiritual affinities of men. Their own minds have passed into a region above these hindrances to sympathy; and though they may carry definition to the last refinement in the study, they would surrender themselves to common trusts and affections in the Church. The possibility of this is precisely what it is their mission to show: and to demand from them that, in its discharge, they shall tell you just where they agree and cease to agree with others, is to ask them to recant and renounce their work. The real weakness of the party lies in the false position of its clergy. In proportion as they are true labourers for the Church of the future, are they less true servants to the Church of the present. The dogmatic engagements and limitations against which they protest are precisely of the kind to which they are committed: and enough is visible of their theology to render it certain, that it would never spontaneously speak in the prayers and creeds of which they are the public organ. The subtle casuistry, the considerations of social expediency and historical development, which reconcile some of the best as well as wisest men of our time to this position, will never convince the conscience of simpler type that veracity is not paramount in worship, and that even a suspected disregard of it by the recognised guides of public morals, is too heavy a price to pay for a quickened pace of liberty and charity.

It may be doubted whether the divisions in the Church of

England have really weakened it for either action or resistance. The stimulus of new ideas is needful for the vitality of every moral institution : and these have been supplied, and scattered among groups of minds asleep before, by the development of each type of ecclesiastic life. Never probably have more recruits been enlisted and organised for Church work than during the last twenty years. And though an easy logic insists that a Church must be a failure which, pretending to be One, breaks into factions, yet the argument takes little effect upon Englishmen accustomed to free political strife without loss of national feeling. They rather respect than condemn the inevitable conflicts of opinion; and more readily sympathise with Protestant diversity than with Romanist uniformity. Though the habitual Church-goers are still not found below a certain stratum of society, yet the actual influence of the clergy is felt considerably lower; and, through their increased activity, devotedness, and kindliness, has certainly been extended of late years. On the whole, the Church is probably better secured at the present time in the affections of English people, than at any date since the Revolution.

II. Puritan Nonconformity.

Though the Anglican Church embodies in it the conservative feeling of the country, while the Nonconformist communities have sprung from the need of keener life and freer movement, it is remarkable that the religious history of England, during its recent stadia, lies almost entirely in the former. The dissenting bodies have doubtless experienced some change. But it has been for the most part silent; marking no crises, producing no striking episodes, and recording itself in no literature which will be essential to the future historian. The most conspicuous feature in it is found in an altered attitude towards the Established Church, and a more active and united interest in questions of public policy.

It is curious that John Wesley, who meant to found only a society within his own communion, should have created the only regularly organised ecclesiastical body outside that communion. The Methodists are really governed; have their senate, their hierarchy of officers, their administrative system, penetrating to every village school and chapel in the land. And this vast structure, which not only touches, but actually shapes the life of a large section of our population, subsists side by side with the Anglican Church, complete in itself, and too content with its own work to be hostile to its neighbour. Among the older bodies of Nonconformists,—the Presbyterians especially,—the effort at a collective organisation faded away after the Restoration; and they practically fell into the Independent order, subsisting only in detached societies, drawn by habit and sympathy into local groups, but each managing its own affairs. This sole survival of the congregationalist principle has naturally brought the Independents to the front rank of Nonconformity, and made its recent history in great measure a development of their ideas. Though they themselves have largely relinquished the impelling thought which moved their forefathers, it has nevertheless determined the track they have taken, and accounts for their present characteristics.

The sharp distinction which Calvinism draws between the elect and the reprobate was imported by the Independents into their conception of Christian association. A church might be called, in their view, *a club of saints*. To enter it, you must have undergone conversion, and received your call: and, to prevent the intrusion of those who were not "children of the kingdom," the approaches to it were guarded by vigilant scrutiny into the candidate's spiritual experience and faith. It was the worth of the individual soul in the sight of God, its privileged relation to Him as selected for sanctification, that qualified for admission. Within the sacred circle, all, as alike invested with this qualification, before which every difference vanished, were brethren and equals, a spiritual democracy in all that concerned their fellowship. Outside the circle, thronged the unconverted world; but mingled in the crowd there must be some, distinguishable as yet by no visible or conscious sign, who were to be heirs of grace. To find these and draw them from the multitude, the word must be openly administered to all: and, wherever it was preached, it was right that there should be, around the Church of the chosen few, the mixed congregation of the unconverted. This larger number however were present by invitation or permission, at a transaction not their own, and could be allowed no voice in affairs quite foreign to their sphere. How should "the natural man" "know the things of the Spirit of God;" for "they are spiritually discerned?" It was impossible to concede to the unredeemed world any share in governing the assembly of the regenerate. Their discipline and order were divinely prescribed in Scripture, and committed to their own members, under guidance of the Spirit of God. It is for them alone to admit to the Lord's Table, or to exclude from it, and so to define the boundary of the sacred fold.

What the Communicants are to the Congregation at large in a particular society, *that* is the whole Church in a nation to the State; the one, the living communion of the "members of Christ;" the other, the organised form of the mixed multitude throughout. To the former is reserved, by Divine right, the administration of sacred things: all other concerns which call for authoritative action are consigned to the latter. The theory which thus divides the temporal from the spiritual is not incompatible with the theocratic conception that the "Saints should rule the World," and actually assumed this form among the extreme sections of the Puritans. But it is totally incompatible with any admission that the World may rule the Saints, and has necessarily induced the attempt entirely to separate the two spheres. The Independents are in this country the hereditary representatives of this theory: and we see only a consistent carrying out of their early principles in their zealous efforts for the "Liberation of Religion from State patronage and control." They are joined in these efforts by many external allies: and the maxims set forth as substantiating their case are often political rather than theological. But it is none the less true that their present devotion to the problem of disestablishment is an historical consequence of their early theology.

The Anglican's conception of the Church was different. To him regeneration was not the indispensable condition, but the hoped-for consequence of membership. The Church was not a select association of persons already in a state of sanctification, and in whom therefore the end of the Christian dispensation had been attained; but the whole body of professed believers, united for the worship of God and administration of the means of grace. As an institution for making "saints," rather than for setting them apart when ready made, it was necessarily a mixed field, in which "the tares and the wheat" grew together; nor was it given to men to anticipate "the harvest" which would sever them from each other. When the 19th of the 39 Articles defines "the Visible Church of Christ" to be "a congregation of *faithful* men in the which the pure Word of God is preached, and the Sacraments be duly administered according to Christ's ordinance in all those things that of necessity are requisite to the same," the word "*faithful*" means no more than "*of the faith,*" i.e., avowed disciples, not persons holy and regenerate. For in the 26th Article it is affirmed that "in the Visible Church the evil are ever mingled with the good, and sometimes the evil have chief authority in the Ministration of the Word and the Sacraments," without however taking away the effect of the ordinances. That mixed body therefore which to the Independents was but the outer "Congregation," belonged to "the Visible Church" itself for the Anglican. And with this body the Nation throughout was homogeneous,—indeed identical,— as composed of professing Christians: so that it belonged to the Church, and the Church belonged to it: all Englishmen were members of it: nor was there any reason why they should not, through their State organisation, deal with its constitution and administer its affairs, as in the case of any other instrument of their common welfare. They are its constituent elements; and cannot be precluded from settling together their reciprocal duties and the rules suitable for their combined religious life.

In this view, not only do the same *persons* compose the ecclesiastical and the political body, but the *functions* of the Church cease to be withdrawn from those of the State, as a reserve foreign to its domain, and become simply a special part of them. The State, in short, is an organisation of society *for all purposes* in regard to which there is a possibility and a need of common life: and no province, marked off by a priori survey, can make good its claim of exemption from jurisdiction. It does not follow that the State would be wise to do all that it is entitled to do. Through a large portion of human action there may be no "need" of a common life; or it may adequately shape itself into due order. In other departments, there may be no "possibility" of it, and the attempt at uniformity may only intensify division. These are good reasons for delegating to the play of individual will, or for holding in abeyance, the public powers which, under other conditions, might rightly have been exercised, and at other times have rightly been exercised, by the supreme authority. The Anglican would allow it to be a fair question, whether there is any longer a sufficient unity in English religion to justify the maintenance as National of a Church which has ceased to be so. But the Independents' principle,—that even a unanimous nation must abstain from using its Government organisation for **the regulation of** Church Order, — will always be addressed to **him in vain.**

The difficulty of drawing **any boundary line** between the temporal and the spiritual provinces **of** life was rendered apparent by the attitude of **the Independents towards the** Government in its first action on **the question of** Public Education. They knew not whether to approve or disapprove: and for many years opinion among them wavered and was divided. Was education in the temporal or in the spiritual sphere? **In** this country, it was undoubtedly a religious impulse which had created the great mass of elementary schools: they were in connection either **with one of** two great Societies, supported respectively by the Church **and** by the Dissenters, or with some particular local congregation: so that the whole system was interwoven with the Christian philanthropy and devout habits of the land. This, it would seem, was not ground **on** which the Civil power was at home: if it were once let into the School, how could it be refused admission **to the** Church? Both must be voluntary institutions, or neither. Yet, on the other hand, the temporal interests of which the State was guardian **were** powerfully affected by the ignorance or the intelligence of the population: and if the **power** which had to punish **crime** chose to try its hand **rather at** preventing it, it appeared pedantic **to charge** it with overstepping its line, and to insist that it **should fold its** hands and look on till **the** evil was committed. **A small** but important minority supported the Parliamentary grants for Education. The majority denounced them, and declined all aid from them, as a betrayal of the "voluntary principle." In thus screening Education from the profaning touch of the State, they treated it as belonging to the spiritual sphere. But they have since changed their voice; and now demand that the elementary schools should be all Public and all Secular. It is only just to say that in this practical reversal of their policy, they rather correct than contradict their regulating principle. At first, some of them looked on education as a temporal, others as a spiritual, **concern**. Now, they run the dividing line of this antithesis through the midst of it, and all agree that **it is** *both* ; and, **while** jealously reserving the religious side **of it for private** duty and affection, call upon public Law **and** authority to take possession of its secular province. Thus, they are still true to their traditional conception that the World and the Church must be kept apart; and the field of neither be permitted to overlap the other's.

The Independents have too noble a history, **and, in** studying it, pass through a gallery of portraits too impressive, ever to be absorbed in the struggles of the present, or to lose their **veneration for the** learning and intellectual gifts, **which** gave **force to the** virtues of such men as Robinson and Owen. They have persistently maintained effective institutions for imparting University culture to their ministers; and of late years have encouraged the **more able** of them to prolong their studies in some one of the great schools of Germany. In Biblical theology and in Philosophy their **attainments are** carried, among the regularly trained men, considerably beyond the standard which satisfies the Church. The natural consequence has been, a very perceptible relaxation **of the** older orthodox rigour, and the introduction of a type of preaching which would have been heard with grave displeasure by the elders of even the last generation. Without any loss of the fervour and spiritual depth of an earlier age, and with unabated resort to scriptural imagery and expression, their foremost ministers no longer speak in the sense of the seventeenth century: they have put new wine into the old bottles : and the bursting has yet to come. There have been occasional instances of avowed theological change,— as Mr. Baldwin Brown's renunciation of the doctrine of eternal punishment; and occasional explosions of frightened conservatism, whether ineffectual, as in the attempt to silence the sweet flowing of "the **Rivulet**," or crowned with a fatal success, as in the removal of Dr. Samuel Davidson from the College which his learning adorned. But these conspicuous examples afford no measure of the silent movement which is shifting the whole body into a different stratum of the theological atmosphere, and lessening the interval between the Puritan and the Rationalist modes of religious thought. It is not by "disputings in the market place," but by reflection in the study and **communings** with higher minds, that true conversions are made, and the level of the spirit gains in altitude : and larger changes pass unnoticed in meditative shade than in the midday heat and brilliancy of controversy. If the Inde**pendents are too much tied to** the Past **to give** promise of **taking the lead** into the **Future, yet** they evince a ready susceptibility to the quickening powers of **the time;**—in Dr. Davidson appropriating its critical erudition and courage; in Mr. Baldwin Brown, the influence of the Maurice theology; in Mr. Picton, the operation of scientific theories; and having, through their popular forms and habits, **the ear** of a large and active-minded middle class, they may at least become effective distributors of the new thought which they absorb, and prevent the breach so often threatened between the elder and the **younger** pieties.

III. Free Inquiry.

If Religion be the first awakener of thought, Thought would seem to have played the part of an ungrateful child, and been never tired of rebellion against its parent. Every fresh start of intellectual activity, like that which has carried the natural sciences over their newest stadium, is invariably attended by an outburst of disaffection towards the contemporaneous theological beliefs. Rightly understood, this fact is neither strange nor ill-omened. The **permanent springs of religion,** —**whether in** the intuition **of Power behind phenomena,** or in the sense of authoritative Right in action, or in the recognition of Beauty in the world,—can only turn what we see and feel into something Divine : they do not create, **they** only interpret and colour the scene, without **or** within, **on** which we look: the range and contents of that scene, the order of its parts, the scheme of relations into which it is best thrown, must be determined by other faculties,— of Perception and Understanding,—commissioned to organise what *appears* not to apprehend what *is*. The moral and spiritual faith in us necessarily accepts from contemporary intelligence the *given* universe, whatever it may be; thinks in the ordinary moulds of thought; yields itself to the approved framework of abstractions; and spreads its consecration over the whole. The intellect which it had sent forward under the inspiration of wonder discovers that its picture of the world is inadequate, and works out a **new** perspective **of its structure, a new** program of its relations: and thus strips **of** their *truth* many things which lay in the imagination **under a** light of sacred beauty. That light, however, **is no** self-light which perishes with the object; but a radiance eternally abroad, ready to glorify that which succeeds to the vacated place. But, as the **substitution** takes time, so must the consecration: and a troubled interval there cannot but be, during **which the scene itself is** confused, and the rays **are unsettled, here seeming to be** quenched, there **to be pursuing the old as it** vanishes, **and not** yet reposing **on the new as it arrives.** In a little while it will **return to its rest, and** illumine **a fairer** as well as vaster **kosmos.** The function of the intellect through this process is simply corrective to the devout imagination of men. As **the** instrument of phenomenal knowledge, it is not the **source of religion; or** its **destroyer;** but the critic of its representations **and modes of conception.** In this it performs a friendly **office, indispensable to the** balance of human progress. To expect from **free** inquiry any fruits of piety, and to dread from it any triumph of impiety, are alike absurd. It **is** spiritually neutral; only, by revising the forms of theologic thought, it keeps the sanctities alive for the **front** rank **of** human minds, instead of surrendering them **to the** rear, as a monopoly of the ignorant and weak.

i. *Science and Dogma.*

The **recent** advance **of** knowledge respecting the physical history of Man has pressed much more hardly on the traditional creed than the astronomical discoveries which, in the seventeenth century, broke up the Mosaic firmament. Undeniably, the structure of Church divinity not only contains a definite anthropological theory, but rests upon it. The Redemption, which is its substance and its crown, is simply a reversal of the Fall: the Fall is a reversal of the Paradisiacal state: and this again involves the origin of Man by special creation in a manner which absolutely distinguishes him, in "his first estate," from other living beings on the earth. Parts of this scheme had long been weakened by doubts. The accessory notion that human sin was answerable for the infliction of pain and death upon the whole of animated nature was criticized on moral grounds as involving a cruel wrong to innocent creatures; and was defended, or rather explained away by Bossuet on the curious ground that, according to the Cartesian philosophy, animals were mere automata, and did not feel: they were only made to enact the symbolism of suffering, that the whole aspect of things might be in keeping with the penalty of man.* The geological record furnished an objection less easy to meet, when it exhibited the presence and the extinction of life on earth through incalculable ages before the appearance of the human race. It was possible, however, without serious sacrifice, to limit the consequences of Adam's offence to his own descendants, and let the other creatures be as they were: only, if Death already fell on them in the order of nature, it was difficult to withdraw man from the analogy, and execute him by the moral law. The researches of the last two or three decades have propagated the shock of doubt from the outworks to the very citadel of the whole system. From various sides evidences accumulated which, summed up by Lyell, Lubbock, Prestwich, Tylor, have at once enormously extended the "Antiquity of Man," and established his gradual ascent from the lowest conditions of existence; plainly exhibiting to us not the wreck, but the rudiments, of a higher nature, and leaving no room for the drama of a ruined perfection and a lost Paradise. Parallel with this line of discovery came the speculations of Darwin, carried on with a rare mastery of the methods of induction, and an entire possession of their fair and patient spirit, on the " Origin of Species," and the " Descent of Man :" which appear finally

---

* The argument is founded on a misapprehension of Descartes' doctrine of automatism, a misapprehension still constantly repeated. He did not deny that animals were *sentient*, but only that they were *self-conscious*.

to dispose of the provisional conception of spasmodic creation, and so to link together the types of terrestrial life as to draw even man into the universal relationship, and assign to him a genesis from some inferior kind. Mr. Herbert Spencer's systematic working-out of the theory of Evolution, now filling it in by happy and ingenious conjectures, now extending it by well-devised abstractions and telling analogies, has greatly confirmed its hold on the mind of an age eager for the largest generalisations. The scientific imagination of the time is accordingly occupied by a natural history of the earth reversing the order, denying the crises, changing the causes, transcending the time-measures, of the accepted story of humanity and its redemption.

Under conditions so threatening, no resource is legitimately left to the orthodox theologian but either to surrender or to deny. Either what he daily teaches is not true, or what he everywhere hears taught is fatal falsehood; and it is of the first necessity that he decide himself, and enable others to decide between the contradictories. This, however, is the course which he is least apt to take. It is not uncommon to find him, on the first shock, quickly deny, and then slowly surrender, falling in at last with the language and conceptions which he withstood at first, only not keeping the terms of an honourable submission, but slipping back into the old grooves of thought which were to be erased. More often he lives on, and takes no notice, telling the old story to the class in church which he prepares for confirmation, or spending his zeal on the pattern of a faldstool and the contents of his vestment-room, heedless of the dry rot which is crumbling the main timbers of the temple itself. The school of Mr. Maurice alone is able to make the necessary admissions. It has always, with Coleridge, repudiated the doctrine of birth-sin, and held its "Redemption" clear of the "Fall." Its theory of the relation between the human nature and the Divine has an experimental ground independent of mythology and tradition. And, beyond the rationalising circle, it is only among its disciples that we find at once the competency and the resolve fairly to weigh the pretensions of modern science, and allow every probable truth its modifying influence on theological ideas.

Unitarians are not affected by the scientific disproof of

doctrines already discarded by them. It cannot be unwelcome to them to find their moral and critical pleadings supported and crowned by conclusive physical evidence. If, however, the same evidence which justifies their heterodoxy should invalidate their Theism, or shake the foundation of their Ethics,—and no less than this is affirmed by expositors of evolution,—then they also must reconsider their position, and see whether anything remains but unconditional surrender to material development.

ii. *Science and Natural Theology.*

The writers on Natural Theology in the last century proceeded on the mechanical conception of the universe, which the discoveries of Newton and their extension by the French mathematicians had set in the ascendant. In conformity with this, they thought of all Causation as a phenomenal succession, and of the relation between God and the world as that between the first term and the second of a physical series,—this second summing up in itself the antecedents of all that follows. In order to establish the existence of God as "*First* Cause," they thus bound themselves to find a time when the system of "Second Causes" began to be. Till that was done, this system itself held the field: it could be dispossessed only on proof that it was not the first there, but once was absent, ere yet a prior Power had called it up. Accordingly the older treatises endeavour to prove that matter and its properties cannot always have been,— that the "laws of nature" which prevail among phenomena are themselves phenomena, and have had their birth,—that there is a limit to what "second causes" will account for, beyond which, as in the adaptation of organisms to their media, and the distinction of Species, and the equilibrium of the Solar system, recourse must be had to an extramundane cause. Above all, and latest of all, appeal was confidently made to the recent and apparently abrupt appearance of Man upon the earth, as inexplicable but as a result of special creation. The literature of Natural Theology has been held in great favour among Unitarians: and so far as they have allowed themselves to depend upon this line of argument, they must certainly be disturbed by the newer Science.

For there is no longer hope of finding a birth-day for "Matter," for "Laws," for "Species," for planets, or even for Man; and no longer despair of comprehending all known phenomena within the probable range of an admitted natural order. They must either relinquish their Theism, or amend its fundamental conceptions.

For the most part, however, **this emendation** has long ago taken place among Unitarians: **and God is** conceived, not as "*First* **Cause**" prefixed to the scheme of things, but as *Indwelling* **Cause** pervading it; **not excluded** by "**Second Causes,**" but coinciding with them **while** transcending them; as **the One** ever-living Objective Agency, the modes of which **must be classified** and interpreted by Science in the outer field, by conscience in the inner. This change of conception is due to the lessened prominence of Mechanical ideas and the advance of Physiology **to a** dominant position; substituting the thought **of** Life **working from** within for that of transitive impulse **starting from** without. Under this higher form of **religious** thought, **all need** entirely ceases of reaching a **Creative** epoch when the Divine "**fiat**" **first went forth,** and **prior to** which was an eternal solitude **of God;** or **of finding** tasks accomplished which are beyond **the** resources **of the** known methods of the world; or of insisting on gaps in the continuity of being which only paroxysms of Omnipotence could overleap: and the breakdown therefore **of** the old proofs on these points leaves the Theism quite unharmed. The modern Science does not even disturb **us with a new idea;** for "**Evolution**" is only *growth:* it merely raises the question *how far* into **the** field of **Nature that idea can** properly be carried,—a question surely of **no** religious significance. If, without superseding the Divine causality, we can recognise an *individual's* **cycle** of development and decline from **the embryo to** the **corpse, and** trace a *species* passing through a range **of** divergent variations, whence can any sudden difficulty spring, on our extending the process to genera differencing their members into **species, and** similarly **to larger** groups, till the continuity is complete? The Unity of the Causal Power, —which is all **that** the spreading network of analogies can establish, cannot possibly **be** unwelcome to those **who** regard it all as the working of One Mind. This **thesis of** theirs,—that **it is** Mind,—no physical knowledge can disprove, or can prove. It is intuitively given, in the very idea of Causality itself, and secretes itself behind all the phenomenal masks which in different regions that idea may assume.

iii. *Science and Ethics.*

If the foundation of Ethics is affected by **the theory** of Evolution, it must be through the derivation of the **Moral** Sentiments, by hereditary modifications of nerve and **feeling**, from unmoral conditions. It is no new thing to measure the authority of a faculty by its origin; to insist on its being intuitive (*i.e.* unmediated), if you would dignify it; to show how **it is fabricated out of** common materials, if you would disparage it. Philosophers who, like Locke, rebelled against the tyranny of pretended axioms, or, like Bentham, against arbitrary oracles of an absolute Moral Sense, have assailed the objects of their dislike with the instrument of analysis, and discredited them by displaying their elements. And if the conscience can be shown to be not even indigenous to the individual at all, but to fetch its rudiments from the struggling impulses and stored up memories of an indefinite line of ancestral brutes and savages, it may be supposed to forfeit all claim to an imperative or Divine prerogative. Here, however, there is a distinction to be observed. It is not the *process* of growth, which lowers the rank of a faculty in our estimation; but the *materials* for its growth, when they prove to be, or are alleged to be, from a level far below its own. When disinterestedness is educed from self-love weaving illusions around itself and mistaking **means for** ends; when ideas of right and wrong are explained as contrivances for extorting what we want from others; when the compunctions and peace of conscience are construed back into the fancied frowns and smiles of spectators; when the feeling of beauty is said to be composed of agglutinated pleasures of visual and auditory sensation; we certainly are dissatisfied **and** humiliated by these equations, because we had thought there was something in the whole which we know has no existence in these parts, and which, without conscious degradation, we cannot dismiss to the land of dreams. But if the elements were homogeneous with the product, instead of inferior in kind,—molecules of the ultimate mass,—there would be nothing in the mere fact of passing from an inchoate stage to gradual maturity, which could in the least impair our appreciation of the faculty as it is. Its authority is immediately known to us as a present fact, and does not vanish on our remembering that it is not a *first phenomenon*, but, like ourselves, has come to be. A natural history it must have, as the function of a growing life: and to know its natural history can take nothing from it. This holds equally, whether the evolution be short or long, comprised within the single life, or continuous through indefinite generations. And it holds equally of every faculty. Were there ground for Moral scepticism in the slow maturation of conscience, there would be no less for Intellectual scepticism in the tardy development of Reason. The Right and Wrong are assured to our knowledge by the same title as the True and False.

In this vindication of the modern view of Nature from the imputation of irreligious consequences, more, it must be owned, is saved for it than many of its adherents care to claim. It is certainly regarded, by its chief representatives, abroad and at home, as atheistical, or at least as excluding all theology. This is only natural to minds that move entirely within the scientific scheme of conceptions framed for the phenomenal world, and then force it to serve in ulterior problems where it fails. The path of Induction, which is so safe a guide through the physical and the historic fields, fades away in the skirting forests of the Infinite, and will lead no one to either the sanctuary of beauty or the temple of worship hid within the silent depths. Of this none are more aware than the men in whom the pure scientific genius appears as only one province of a larger nature and a richer culture,—men like Herschel, Oersted, Faraday: but it is hid from specialists of every kind; and above all from the typical favourites of the medical school, whose cleverness early promotes them to the public lecture-room, and enlists them in the production of our popular scientific literature. The former order of mind contains the latter, as Plato and Aristotle contained Epicurus, with much more: but, for that very reason, the latter speaks more directly home to the congenial onesidedness of an age, and the ready tendency of similar intellects.

There was much in the earlier Unitarian training to foster the simply logical and inductive intelligence, and to draw together persons in whom other gifts were quite subordinate: hence the repute of coldness and dryness which has always attached to the name. It is not surprising that, from among a people thus formed, some few, both in England and in America, should have lost their moorings of faith in the rise of the scientific tide, and been swept out to sea. There is no religious body that has not similarly lost adherents: and for a long time to come there will probably be a cloud of negative skirmishers hovering around every church and harassing its peace. But while they find its **weaknesses, they** will but consolidate its strength; and when they **have** compelled withdrawal from untenable positions, and quickened the vigilance and devotion of the whole encampment within, their work will be done, and the field of the future will be reopened for the march.

iv. *The Miracles.*

Whoever adopts the modern principle of Evolution *ipso facto* relinquishes, to the same extent, a certain portion of miracle. For special Divine acts of creation he substitutes the mediation of successive steps of law. **By** thus removing from the physical history of the world every anomalous transition, and identifying the Divine agency with the flow of natural order, he leaves the moral history **of mankind** without supporting analogies for its alleged "**signs and wonders**": and if they are still to hold their place, it will be under an increased stress, and by the unaided force of testimonial evidence. Yet it cannot be said that the growing indisposition to admit miracles has been countervailed by any enhanced appreciation of their historical proofs. On the contrary, under patient and repeated investigation, our synoptical gospels have disclosed enough **of** their age and composition to leave their testimony anonymous, and take from it any higher guarantee than belongs **to** a venerable popular tradition. The **genuine** relics which they doubtless hand down to **us from the** "sacred **year,**" **can be** distinguished only **by internal** evidence, and are mixed with questionable additions, coloured with the spirit and purpose of another generation. The fourth Gospel there will yet, no doubt, be many efforts to save as an original authority. Proceeding from a single mind, of rare spiritual depth and ideality, it will win its best readers to wish it history. But the verdict pronounced by the author of this volume, in his special treatise on the subject,* is not likely to be reversed: nor would even Mr. Matthew Arnold, who endeavours to reinstate this gospel, confide in it enough to accept the miracles which it records. The adventurous criticism of such writers as Baur, Schwegler, Volkmar, and Straatman, presents **many a false** position, many a rash sally, to the attack of **keen** opponents. It is the habit of the German Professor to overwork his case. But by even cautious students who have followed the researches of the last thirty years it is admitted that new light has been thrown on the Christian affairs of the first and second centuries; on the struggle between the Petrine and the Pauline gospel, ending in the compromise **of the Catholic** church; on the development of doctrine respecting the **person of Christ**; and on the traces which, in its successive **stages,** this history has left on the several books of the New Testament. The various attempts which **have been** made by Hase, Schenkel, Keim, and Renan, to reproduce the figure of Jesus and his work, differ in numerous and important details; but, in this difference, concur in proving that the sources are not in harmony with one another, and have not the exceptional solidity needful to sustain a supernatural weight.

The **tendencies of scientific** and of historical research being thus **in the same direction,** and meeting with no adequate counteraction from conservative resistance, a general disposition is manifested, among churches open to theologic change, no longer to lay **stress** on the miraculous elements of early Christian tradition; **to** regard them as rather weakening than strengthening **the** authority of the narrative; and to frame a conception of the origin of Christianity, which shall not be dependent on their objective reality. So well understood **is** this disposition among the liberal Protestants of France, that when M. Guizot, with his orthodox majority, determined to force on

---

* An attempt to ascertain the character of the Fourth Gospel, especially in its relation to the first Three; by the late Rev. John James Tayler, B.A., Second Edition, 1870. Williams and Norgate, London.

a secession, he had only to impose, as a condition of fellowship, a belief in the events which the Christian Festivals commemorate at Christmas, Easter, and Whitsuntide. Although the introduction of *any* fresh condition would have been resisted on constitutional grounds, yet the selection of the test was made not without knowledge of its sufficiency, if applied. It would probably have a precisely similar operation, could the experiment be tried among the confrères of M. Coquerel in England and America. In both countries there are doubtless many who are still satisfied with the unyielding historic Christianity of Priestley and of Andrews Norton, which not only maintained the miracles, but built everything upon them: nor is it many years since the author of this volume was sharply attacked by an Irish representative of the older school, for his inability to accept the reports of Christ's bodily resurrection and ascension. Even, however, among the conservative theologians, a significant silence respecting the "signs and wonders," on which they rest indicates that the old emphatic appeal to them is known to be out of keeping with the feeling of the time, and can no longer be hopefully urged. It is not surprising that Unitarians of the elder school regard this state of things with sadness and displeasure, encounter it with earnest protest, and treat it as an apostacy. Such it would actually be, had there meanwhile been no change in the philosophy of religion and the consequent logic of belief. But in virtue of such a change, miracles had already lost all special religious value, before they fell under critical doubt: and as, on declaring themselves incredible, they had already become indifferent, they could pass innocently away, and leave the disciple's allegiance precisely where it had long rested.

v. *Non-Christian Theism.*

The English conception of Revelation, born of the longing for *truth*, not for spiritual beauty, or moral perfection, has always carried in it the idea of *infallibility:* and in the studies to which it has given rise, the only question has been, where was the oracular seat, in Council, or Pope, or Bible. When the Protestant, inheriting the assumption that it was in the Scriptures, fails on personal research to find it there, he not unreasonably feels that he has been imposed upon, and flings away a Christianity which does not fulfil the promise made to him in its name. He wants well-accredited statements about Divine things, and a solution of moral perplexities, and a code or manual of duties: he is disappointed of them all; and dismisses the religion as a delusive guide. This mode of procedure is the more natural, the more he has lived under the dominant idea of an *orthodoxy,* or divinely-given creed, as an essential to right relations with God. Flung off from his old dependences, he is driven, if his mind have any depth and spirituality, to begin anew with the problems of Religion and Duty, and work them out by the reckoning of Reason and Conscience upon the data of nature and life. In this way has arisen the pure Theism of F. W. Newman and Miss F. P. Cobbe,—so noble a product of the most capable thought and truest inward experience, that if it only were an historic instead of a private gift, and could come to men as Inspiration instead of Reason, it would regenerate the world. This school has added to our literature some volumes which deserve a place among the most select " companions of the devout life." In Theodore Parker's " Discourse of matters pertaining to Religion," a cool critic may readily find, as in St. Augustine and in Pascal, the unbalanced judgments and passionate overstatements of an intense nature: but he must be *very* cool, if he is never caught up by the inspiring power of the book, and carried beyond the bounds of criticism into the sanctuary of prayer and tears. F. W. Newman's book on " the Soul," with its happy union of rational and spiritual method, has brought many a wavering mind that was " half a wreck," to safe and quiet anchorage. And though Miss Cobbe, in taking her stand on Kant's " Categorical Imperative," occupies perhaps too narrow a basis for her " intuitive morals," yet this philosophical doubt is soon forgot: for the missing data incidentally drop in; and the scheme of duty and right affection carries its own persuasion with it as it expands: and the work, in its second part, supplies the fitting prelude of thought to her later volume of devotion, the " Alone to the Alone."

What influence these writings may have had in stimulating the movement of Indian Theism, and the organisation of the Brahmo Somâj, it would be difficult to define: but of the sympathy and interaction of the Eastern and the

Western thought, in the aim at religious reform, there can be no doubt. Its mission in India is much more extensive than in England. Here, its chief function is the correction of erroneous belief, which narrows the mental horizon, and limits the natural affections. There, it rises up in protest against forms of superstition which have shaped the habits of society for ages, and set into a fixed type of civilization; which carry in them a taint of deep moral corruption; which degrade the life of women; which sanctify the exclusiveness of class; and check and baffle at every turn the hopes of social progress. In the presence and under the challenge of evils so little endurable, the Brahmo leaders fling themselves upon their work with a prophetic fervour and self-abandonment, with a sustaining enthusiasm brought from communion with God, with an heroic insistence on purity and simplicity of life, which place them in far more impressive relations to the society around them than can be claimed for their fellow-believers in the West. Theism here is a product of scepticism: Theism there is a kindling of inspiration. Here it is the clinging to a God not lost: there, the rapture of a God just found. Perhaps the happiest sign for its societies here is their fraternal interest in its representatives there. If anything can charm to rest the ever-creaking logic of distrust, and wake up some uniting harmony of spiritual affection, it may be the appreciated example of a kindred faith free of detaining doubts and kindled with Divine love.

vi. *Christian Theism.*

The ranks of English Theism have been largely recruited from the Unitarians: among whom some congregations even have been formed, which abstain from any Christian profession, and use no Christian rite. Trained in a Scripturalism as rigid as that of more orthodox believers, they were liable to the same reaction on finding that the *authority* which they had trusted was fallible. Amid the varieties of inward want, there is room for every conscientious and thoughtful experiment: and should it prove that, from the sensitive independence of the age, the spirit of Christ's religion can best take up its power by escaping from the name, it is the part of true discipleship to rejoice that the world is evangelized even under a disguise. Meanwhile, however, there are many Unitarians to whom the discovered fallibility of Scripture brings no shock, and spoils nothing that has been the object of their trust and love; who had long ceased to look out for any "external authority," or ask for foreign information respecting things Divine; who expect no help in their approach to God and ascent to higher duty, except through the hierarchy of greater and holier minds; but who see, in Jesus Christ, the supreme term in that hierarchy, the realization of life in God, the image of a pure and tender humanity made perfect in weakness and sublime in humiliation by utter self-surrender to His loftiest call. In this aspect his figure looks upon them, with the power of an objective Conscience, still clear and living, scarcely dimmed by its encumbering traditions, and unhurt by fiction because transcending it. They affect no independence of this spiritual ideal, and decline to part from it. It has rendered possible to them a consciousness of Divine relations, a faith in the resources of humanity and the uplifting presence of an Infinite Compassion, and an apprehension of the range of duty, which no private experience, no intellectual speculation would have enabled them to reach. They refuse therefore to quit the line and disown the obligations of the Christian succession; and conceive that, by identifying their religion by name with the religion of Christ, they mark at once its source and its type with exactitude and simplicity. To take a new name is to profess a new thing. But they make no pretension to render any purer worship than went forth into the night on the mountains of Galilee, and in the garden of Gethsemane; to fix any higher standard of duty than was raised in the saying "Be ye therefore perfect, as your Father in heaven is perfect;" to aspire to more gracious affections than those which for ages have brought a consecration upon the "little child," and pity upon the guilty, and prayers of forgiveness upon the persecutor's head. And so organic is the constitution of humanity, that, even if you teach the same truths to-day that have been heard and lived of old, you will teach in vain if you suppress their age and start them afresh as your own new lights. Their power is not logical and abstract, but comes through human life,—the minds that have held them, the souls they have subdued, the vestiges they have left on successive times and nations. A religion **that** declines **to** be united with the past will hardly avail **to** combine men in the present; in ceasing to be historical, it loses its best hope of becoming social. So long as its life is continuous, it will bear large reformations, **to** clear it from perishable elements; and the sacred **truth** which emerges as the pure residue will concentrate its attraction, and forbid dispersion of the old affections. But to break with the past, and try a new creation, **whether** by philosophical building up from the foundation, or by eclectic appropriations from the remains of other faiths, is to substitute a school **for a Church**, and expect, from agreement in individual opinion, the effects of a consensus of human generations; and the very belief which may be thus gained, however right, will have to grow **old** and win a history, ere it can become a blending spiritual power. The relative persuasiveness of Natural Theology and of a living embodiment of **pure Religion** is strikingly seen in Mr. J. S. Mill's posthumous essays. In speculation he reaches only so dismal a world **and so mere a dream of faith**, as to depress and even irritate his temper. His eye, changing its direction, falls upon the figure of **Christ**; and its uncertain look appears to vanish, and words of reverence succeed, as if some mysterious power passed upon the troubled waters, and left a sudden calm.

It is the distinctive glory of the Christian Religion that it is a tissue of *Personal Affections*, sweetening, expanding, exalting human life, by ties of relation with all known ranks of being; fraternal service to equal men, filial trust towards the "Father in heaven," reverent allegiance to the "Son of Man" who has brought them into open communion. Other systems have had their sublimity of conception, kosmical, metaphysical, poetical; but here alone have we an organisation of the universe by an omnipresent network of moral sympathies. Unless **this glory is to fade**, no living object in the associated family of minds must be removed,—either dropped from the series as a superfluous link, or construed from a reality into a dream, reduced **from One who thinks** and loves to That which blindly necessitates. Religion, it has been said, is "Morality coloured with **Emotion**;" yes, but the emotion of a dependent mind looking up to a Mind all-righteous and **supreme**. Again it has been said, Religion

d

is "Moral Idealism;" yes, but with eye upon an ideal which has been humanly realised on earth, and for ever constitutes a Divine Perfection in heaven. Take away all objective seat for your inward vision, turn it from a perception into a phantom, let it hang in the air and never have been; and, though it may raise a sigh, and pour a plaintive music over life, it can inspire no worship and nerve no will. There is a wave of heathen Pantheism sweeping over our time which threatens to obliterate the consciousness of this truth, and to leave us only the phrases of ancient piety with the life washed out, the empty ghosts of the saints' prayer and the martyr's cry. Trust, love, reverence, between person and person, speaking in living communion, and quickening all faithful action, are the central essence of pure Religion, and the special gift of Christianity. This gift it is the highest function of spiritual philosophy in our age to protect and hand down with unabated power.

PREFACE TO FIRST EDITION.

THE idea which possessed my mind, when I first sketched out the plan of this volume, was the desirableness of embracing in a common point of view, the phenomena of the different religious parties, whose unintermitted strife and sharp contrast of manners and opinions have given such a deep and varied interest to the spiritual history of England, during the three centuries which have elapsed since the Reformation. In pursuing this idea, I have tried to discover the governing principle and understand the characteristic working of each party; to apprehend their mutual relation; to show how they have occasionally passed off into each other; and out of their joint operation, to trace the evolution of a more comprehensive principle which looks above the narrowness of their respective views, and, allying itself with the essential elements of the Christian faith, may in time perhaps devise some method of reconciling an unlimited freedom and variety of the religious life with the friendliness and mutual recognition of universal brotherhood. Such an idea it is more easy to conceive than to execute. The more I have read, the more I have felt the inadequacy of my materials for fully developing it; and though every fresh inquiry has confirmed me in my general view, I am conscious, that, with ampler opportunities of research and more leisure for concentrated thought, I could have produced a more useful and satisfactory book. My hope is, that with all its deficiencies, it may still be of some service to that portion of society for which it was immediately designed.

What I here offer, is little more than a sketch—exhibiting the general outline and prominent features of the historical development of the religious life of England. I make no pretension to deep and original research. The facts recited or alluded to, are such as are familiar to every student of our national history. All that I present of my own, is simply the conception of those facts; the relation that I have ventured to establish between them; the principles to which I have thought they might be referred; and the inferences which they have seemed to me to yield. I have wished to find out, if I could, the *meaning* of our religious history. Whether I have in any degree succeeded, the reader will judge. I may, however, state, that I have endeavoured to take my facts from the most authentic sources accessible to me; and that the authorities immediately quoted, are those which I have either read or consulted myself.

Our practical English mind—so different from that of our French and German neighbours—concentrates its interest on the present. It will very probably be asked, "Why lead back our thoughts to the disputes and struggles of our forefathers? We live in an age of light, and may be pardoned, if we wish to forget the history of their prejudice and absurdity." But is it all prejudice and absurdity, which the religious history of the past reveals to us? There is a wisdom and a virtue, which comes and goes with the fleeting generations of men, and which in its everchanging manifestations, shaped though it be by the influences of the age, it is always instructive and delightful to contemplate. We may be—I trust we are—in a course of progressive advancement; but the present is the daughter of the past—

"Matre pulchra filia pulchrior"—

and only as the present comprehends and wisely reverences that filial relationship, will she become the mother of a still more beauteous future.

The fanaticism which disowns the past, is not less ridiculous than the superstition of the antiquary which blindly worships it. The open, thoughtful mind, desirous to apprehend the great idea of providence, takes a wide retrospect of the past, that it may embrace the connection of ages, and discern their subordination to a common plan. Nothing has more contributed to keep up a narrow party feeling, than the limited field of vision on which the mental gaze has been usually fixed. The relations of different religious bodies to each other—the controversies between them—the peculiarities of doctrine and practice distinguishing them—acquire an undue and absorbing importance that excludes the light of true wisdom, from their being looked upon as distinctions founded in the unchangeable nature of things, rather than as historical results, not without a relative value for the individual, and fit subjects for conscientious reflection and comparison, but of which the real nature and significance are only to be understood by reference to the circumstances in which they originated. The revival of a more historical view of the mutual relationship of different churches, seasoned with a spirit of philosophical generalization—offers the fairest prospect of extricating our national mind from that abyss of hopeless sectarianism, in which our religion and our literature seem at times to be in danger of being for ever engulfed.

No history has yet appeared, so far as I know, of the general progress and development of our religious life up to the present day. To accomplish such a work adequately, would demand far higher qualifications than I can bring to it. This little volume must be accepted rather as an expression of my wish to see it competently undertaken, than as indicating the unpardonable presumption of attempting it myself. But an imperfect work, if it does not wholly miss its object, may sometimes help to put the general mind in action, and prove the incentive to works greatly surpassing itself. Should any such result hereafter ensue, I shall be perfectly satisfied with the effect of this publication.

PREFACE TO SECOND EDITION.

The first impression of this work being disposed of, the publisher has undertaken to issue a new edition of more convenient size and at a reduced price; and the opportunity has been seized to subject the whole to a careful revision. All the more important statements have again been verified; errors pointed out or discovered in the first edition, wherever known, have been corrected: but it is probable, that in a work embracing so wide a range of historical particulars, not a few inaccuracies may have escaped the author's vigilance, for which he craves the indulgence of the critical reader. He has not intentionally let them pass unnoticed. Several passages have been re-written; and some amount of fresh matter has been introduced into the notes, which, for convenience of reference, have been removed from the end of the volume, and placed under the text to which they belong. An index of principal matters is now for the first time added.

The imperfection of form, as well as of execution, with which this volume is justly chargeable, has arisen in some degree from the occasional nature of its origin. To remedy effectually this inherent deficiency, would have involved a re-casting of all the materials, and required an entirely new work; and for this I have at present neither time nor inclination. I may, however, be permitted to remark, in reply to some friendly criticism on the first edition, that this small volume was never intended to embrace a complete ecclesiastical history of England from the Reformation, but only to develope three great tendencies that were the immediate result of that event. Hence the condition of the Roman Catholic Church, which subsisted through the whole of this period, as a latent residuum from a former state of things, has been wholly passed over. And for the same reason, the efforts and influences of the Moravians and Swedenborgians, as a religious element imported from abroad, and having no original connection with the great English controversy, were not supposed to come within the proper scope of the present inquiry. This limitation should be kept in view, to pronounce a fair judgment on the book.

J. J. T.

August 24, 1853.

CONTENTS.

CHAPTER I.

INTRODUCTORY. pp. 1-28.

Sect. i. p. 1—Relation of the religious history of England to the general history of the Church. Sect. ii. p. 7—Sketch of the external history of religious parties in England.

CHAPTER II.

THE CHURCH. pp. 29-87.

Sect. i. p. 29—Difficulty of defining a Church. Sect. ii. p. 31—Preparatory changes under Henry VIII. Sect. iii. p. 39—The Reformation of Edward VI. Sect. iv. p. 48—Fixation of the constituent elements of the Anglican Church, after the accession of Elizabeth. Sect. v. p. 58—General characteristics of the Anglican Church. Sect. vi. p. 61—Erastian and Calvinistic Period. Sect. vii. p. 65—High Sacerdotal and Regal Doctrines, and prevalence of Arminianism, under the Stuarts. Sect. viii. p. 74—Influence of Low Church principles after the Revolution. Sect. ix. p. 82—Modern Period.

CHAPTER III.

PURITANISM. pp. 88-170.

Sect. i. p. 88—Predominant Idea of Puritanism. Sect. ii. p. 90—Spirit and Affinities of Lollardism. Sect. iii. p. 93—Incipient Puritanic Movements. Sect. iv. p. 99—High Presbyterianism under Elizabeth. Sect. v. p. 109—Qualified Presbyterianism at the close of the sixteenth, and in the first half of the seventeenth, century. Sect. vi.

p. 118—Independency, and **the more** extreme forms **of** Puritanism. Sect. vii. p. 128—Results of **Puritanism** under the Commonwealth. Sect. viii. p. 145—Influence of distinguished Teachers on the historical development of Puritanism: Baxter and **Owen**. Sect. ix. p. **158**—Anabaptists **and Quakers: Rise of** permanent Nonconformist Societies.

CHAPTER IV.

THE CHURCH AND PURITANISM CONTRASTED. pp. 171–192.

CHAPTER V.

FREE INQUIRY. pp. 193–315.

Sect. i. p. 193—Distinction between the independence **of Religious So**cieties and the freedom of the Individual Mind. **Sect. ii. p. 196**—Evolution of the different elements **of** Religious **Freedom, in the** course **of the seventeenth century.** Sect. iii. p. **200**—Reaction against the doctrines of the first Reformers. Sect. iv. p. 203—Rise of Latitudinarian principles. Sect. v. p. 210—Effect **of philosophical theories and scientific discoveries.** Sect. vi. p. 218—**First School of English Unitarianism. Sect. vii.** p. 230—Influence **of the writings of Locke. Sect. viii. p. 244**—Christian Rationalism after **the Revolution**: Dissenting Academies: Character **and** position **of Doddridge.** Sect. ix. p. 267—**Character** and tendencies of English **Deism, or** Freethinking. **Sect. x. p. 286**—Influence **of** Hartley's **philosophy**: Revival **of** the Unitarian **controversy by Dr. Priestley.** Sect. xi. p. 300—Orthodox Dissent: **Popularity of Channing: Influence of Germany**: Powerful organization **of Independency.**

CONCLUSION. pp. 316–324.

A RETROSPECT OF THE RELIGIOUS LIFE OF ENGLAND.

CHAPTER I.

INTRODUCTORY.

SECTION I.

RELATION OF THE RELIGIOUS HISTORY OF ENGLAND TO THE GENERAL HISTORY OF THE CHURCH.

CONFLICT under some form or other seems an indispensable condition of social progress. The repose and uniformity so ardently desired by some theorists, are the unequivocal signs, wherever they occur, of a stationary or a declining civilization. Exemption from opposition and questioning relaxes the motives to exertion and brings a torpor over all the faculties. This is especially true of the intellectual and spiritual life of man. Without antagonism—mental health, practical wisdom and the constant development of fresh truth are impossible. We have a proof this, if we compare the condition and influence of communities, like England, Holland, North America, and the Protestant States of Germany—where mental freedom has been largely enjoyed—with such countries as Austria and Spain, where the priest and the sovereign have combined to crush in its germ every rising of independent thought. Civil and religious freedom are essential to each other's existence. Where one is stifled, the other languishes; and apart from their blended influence, neither commerce nor art nor genuine science nor a noble literature nor high national character can long endure. Whenever we are inclined to deplore the strife and the turbulence which mark the former periods of our history, and the divided state in which, after the contests of centuries, they have left our people at the present day—we should remember, that these things are the indications of an energy and a self-reliance, without which England could never have been what she is, nor occupied the same high place among the nations of the earth.

A right appreciation of the antagonistic tendencies, in whose balanced working a nation's vitality resides—supplies a key to the true reading of its internal history. And if our literature, the joint produce of Norman and Saxon influences, is rich, varied and original beyond any other in Europe—if our political experience abounds with ampler instruction, finer examples, and more fortunate results, than that of any society which has grown out of the feudal constitution of the Middle Ages;—our religious life, which stands in a still closer relation to our national character, and, welling up from the deep fountains of the soul, has watered the roots both of our liberties and our literature—possesses features peculiarly its own; exhibits struggles not exactly paralleled in any of the countries where the great battle of religious freedom has been fought; and has terminated in a state of things, at once different from the limited, but, so far as it extends, impartial, toleration of some continental states, and the complete religious freedom and equality of North America.

The principles which distinguish Christianity from all previous religions, are—spirituality and mental freedom. In its original records no provision exists for the appointment of a priesthood, the determination of a metaphysical creed, or even the regulation of a form of social worship. The refinement and elevation of the human soul, through the power of faith and love borne into it by the doctrine and the life of Christ—constitute the specific work of the Gospel. Everything beyond this, is extraneous, conventional, disciplinary—to be settled by considerations of time and place and practical expediency. In a few words, Paul has described its true character—" where the Spirit of the Lord is, there is liberty." On the other hand, Heathenism in all its forms, and not less Levitical Judaism, identified religion with national laws and institutions, to which the worship and outward reverence of individuals were expected to conform. Beyond the recognition of these national religions, the boasted toleration of the Romans never extended. The rights of the individual conscience were overlooked, and seem hardly to have been suspected. In this reverence or disregard for personal convictions of religious truth, and in a practice corresponding to it, we discover an essential distinction between the spirit of Christianity and the spirit of Heathenism.

But the vast machinery of the ancient superstition remained, when the superstition itself was professedly renounced; and Christianity, already imbued with sacerdotal tendencies, slid into its abandoned forms and usurped its abdicated functions, and from them contracted not a little of the spirit by which they were infected. It cannot perhaps be denied, that in the confusion which attended the destruction of the old civilization, the restoration of priestly authority was unavoidable, and might be even necessary to reorganize the scattered elements of society. For ages the forms of Heathenism lay heavy on the mind of Europe, and only here and there the faint pulsations of a true Christian life were perceptible.

This subjugation of the independence of conscience was not however effected without a struggle, which never entirely ceased. The last vestiges of the Donatist schism in North Africa, which was in principle a resistance to the advancing encroachments of episcopal domination[1], were hardly swept away in the tide of Saracenic conquest, when fresh elements of religious excitement and ecclesiastical reform, which had long been silently fermenting, began to circulate actively in Europe soon after the age of Charlemagne.—Cherished by sectaries of various name but kindred principle—Waldenses, Cathari, Albigenses—amid the valleys of Piedmont, along the shores of the Mediterranean, and in the rising cities of the Rhine—they rapidly drew within their influence the young life and blossoming poetry of an awakening civilization, and prepared the mind of Europe for more extensive change. All these sects were distinguished by a spiritual and enthusiastic conception of Christianity, an aversion to the hierarchy, and

---

[1] The protracted conflict of the Donatists with the African hierarchy, bears considerable resemblance to the Puritan struggle in England—the parallelism extending even to the names which they delighted to give themselves, Deodatus, Deogratias, Quidvultdeus, Habetdeum, like the appellations Praisegod, Accepted, Godbehere, etc., assumed by English sectaries in the seventeenth century. See Gibbon, Decline and Fall, ch. xxxvii., note 95, with Milman's remarks.

a denial of the claims of the priesthood—but above all by a profound reverence for the Scriptures, of which several versions were already current among them, and which they appealed to, as a standing witness against the corruptions of the Church, and a faithful record of the spirit and principles of the primitive Gospel[1]. This struggle between sacerdotal usurpation and the unextinguished sense of spiritual rights, runs through the whole of Christian history from the first establishment of episcopal jurisdiction in the third and fourth centuries, down to the time of Wycliffe, Huss, and Luther. It is, in truth, the prolongation of the original conflict between the principle of Heathenism and the principle of Christianity; nor has it yet reached its termination.

The religious history of England exhibits only another form of this vital struggle, modified by our insular position and by our national character and institutions. The struggle with us differs from that on the continent, in being mainly a domestic and national struggle—not directed, as in Germany and France, (except for a short time and to a limited extent,) against a foreign power seated beyond the Alps, but involving a conflict of elements within the limits of our own nationality. In Germany and in France a similar contest did indeed spring up: but in the former country, it was practically settled by the Treaty of Westphalia[2]; in the latter, violently crushed by the despotic bigotry of Louis XIV. In England the dispute has been prolonged, with little change in the aims and principles of the parties, to the present day. This circumstance constitutes, I apprehend, the peculiarity of our religious history.

---

[1] On the free sentiments of the Troubadours and their brethren the Minnesingers on the other side of the Rhine respecting religion, their aversion to the Catholic clergy, and their friendly relations with the sectaries of the time, compare Sismondi, De la Littérature du Midi, tom. i. ch. 5 & 6, with 'Lays of the Minnesingers' by the late Edgar Taylor, pp. 99-101 & 210, and Raynouard, 'Choix des Poésies Originales des Troubadours,' tom. ii. pp. lxi.-lxiv., and in the same volume p. 73 *et seq.*, specimens of the ' Poésies des Vaudois.'—Frederic Barbarossa and his grandson Frederic II., distinguished patrons of these poets, have both been charged with encouraging the famous book 'De tribus Impostoribus;' if indeed any such work then existed. See Bayle, art. Aretin, and Grotius, Oper. iv. p. 502.—Claude of Turin, whose principles are supposed to have found a shelter in the recesses of the Alps, where they were afterwards taken up by the Waldenses, died in 840, and thus forms a link between the age of Charlemagne and these later sectaries.

[2] See the late Professor Smyth's wise and noble reflections on the Treaty of Westphalia, as terminating the grand religious warfare of Germany. Lectures on Modern History, vol. i. pp. 336-43.

For two centuries after the Conquest, our domestic history is distinguished rather by the strife of races than by a contention of principles and classes. By some Becket has been extolled as a protector of the people against Norman oppression; but in heart he was a thorough churchman. It is difficult to believe in the pure humanity of his intentions. If he put himself at the head of the suffering Saxon population, and so acquired the reputation of a martyr in their cause—it was in the spirit of a priestly demagogue, to sustain more effectually the pretensions of the Church against the Crown. Towards the close of the Plantagenet line, in the course of the fourteenth century, under the advancing civilization of the long and brilliant reign of Edward III., the discussion of the rights of classes, and of the various social and religious questions connected with them, began to supersede the blind and passionate animosity which had once separated the Norman and Saxon races. It was now first, that the spirit of ecclesiastical reform, in unison with kindred movements on the continent, assumed an earnest and practical character. It is probable indeed, that the pride of Norman descent still predominated in the minds of the great feudal lords and of the higher clergy—prelates and mitred abbots—who sat with them in Parliament; while a Saxon love of freedom and a yearning after independence harboured in the bosoms of the commonalty. But these opposite feelings were becoming the characteristic of classes—the expression of conflicting principles rather than of national antipathies. In the insurrectionary movements under Richard II., we find priests among the leaders of the populace, and reverenced as their ministers;—a proof of the readiness of the people to blend the expression of their wrongs with the sentiments of religion, and of their susceptibility of better influences, had such been offered them. These movements were almost wholly political, produced by intolerable oppression—and terminated in no important result. The reformation attempted by Wycliffe originated in purer and more elevated motives; and with him the history of English Puritanism properly begins.

Some one word is wanted to express, through its entire course of continuous development, that principle of resistance to the hierarchy which pervades our religious history from the middle of the fourteenth century to the present time. To avoid periphrasis, the term Puritanism, though strictly applicable to only one period, may be adopted, as conveniently embracing the religious movements which preceded and prepared the revolutions of that period, and the modified but analogous effects which have followed them. The history of religious parties in England falls, in fact, of itself into three great and plainly distinguished periods:—1st, that of Lollardism—the name given in the fifteenth century to the principles of Wycliffe[1]—extending from the reign of Edward III. to that of Henry VIII.; 2ndly, that of proper Puritanism, from the Reformation to the extinction of the Commonwealth on the restoration of Charles II.; 3rdly, that of Protestant Dissent, from the Restoration to the present day.

If we compare these periods with each other, we shall find in them only different manifestations of a common principle, tempered by the condition of society and the vigour of opposing tendencies. In the first—we witness resistance to an authority which no government had yet ventured to disown, and which seemed fast cemented in the general fabric of European civilization;—a struggle, which had nothing but individual conviction and some popular sympathy to uphold it, which the Crown, the Church, and for the most part the Parliament, combined to crush. In the second—resistance found a sanction and a precedent in the conduct of the Crown and the Parliament. The question no longer respected the principle of resistance, but only the mode and extent of it. Encouraged by such high authority and instinct with all the energy of a new freedom, Puritanism, in the issue of the struggle, obtained a temporary ascendency over the hierarchy. In the third—we see Protestant Dissent advancing by painful steps and through many persecutions towards a legal toleration—

---

[1] The name Lollard or Lollhard (from the German lollen or lullen, to sing or hum in a low, plaintive tone) was first given to a sect, which arose about the beginning of the fourteenth century in Cologne and other cities on the Rhine and in the north of Germany—in consequence, it is said, of the mournful strains with which it was their practice to accompany the interment of the dead. In the fifteenth century, the name passed over into England, and was applied by the Catholics to the followers of Wycliffe. Gieseler, Kirchengesch. B. II. 3. §§ 113 & 124. Guerike, Kirchengesch. §§ 158 & 162.

The French prophets who came over to England at the beginning of the last century, in their ecstasies or fits of religious excitement, made a strange humming noise. See Calamy's account of a Mr. Lacy, one of his flock, who had joined them; Calamy's Life and Times, vol. ii. p. 97. Fuller (IV. ii. 18) derives the name from Walter Lollardus, "a German, many years before Wycliffe, quasi lolia in ará domini."

with efforts from time to time renewed to gain more freedom and rise to a complete religious equality.—In the ensuing pages an attempt has been made to discover the distinctive principles, and contrast the effects on our national mind and character, of the Anglican hierarchy and of Puritanism—to exhibit their mutual relation—and to trace out of their joint influence the evolution of a third principle, distinct from each —that of free religious inquiry. For the sake of the general reader, and to render future statements more intelligible—I shall occupy the next section of this chapter with a brief survey of the most important events in the external history of our religious progress during the three periods just enumerated.

SECTION II.

SKETCH OF THE EXTERNAL HISTORY OF RELIGIOUS PARTIES IN ENGLAND.

I. Wycliffe was a native of the north of England, where the old Saxon character endured in its greatest strength and purity, and whence most of those men came who were distinguished at this period by the boldness of their attacks on ecclesiastical abuses and by their zeal for reformation[1]. He would have been a remarkable man in any age: but two influences appear early to have imbued his mind with a severe and earnest spirit;—a close study of the doctrinal system of Augustine, which resulted in an anticipated Calvinism; and the desolation of the great European pestilence, which visited England when he was entering life, and produced a most disastrous and demoralizing effect on society. Drinking deeply into the spirit of his master, who also wrote under the wide-

[1] The spirit of reform and freedom in the University of Oxford, during the fourteenth century, was most active among the "Northern men." Huber's 'English Universities,' vol. i. §§ 41, 44, 45 (Newman's Transl.) The satirical poems of Longland and his imitators, reflecting on the monks and the clergy, which appeared about the same period, are written in the dialect and versification peculiar to the North. In the civil wars of the seventeenth century, Lancashire was the only district in England, except the neighbourhood of London, in which the Puritans succeeded in procuring for their Presbyterian discipline a complete establishment. Bolton was called by the Cavaliers, the Geneva of Lancashire. Hunter's 'Life of Oliver Heywood,' p. 35. Lancashire and the West Riding of Yorkshire are still the strongholds of Protestant Dissent.

spread shadow of impending calamity, just before the overthrow of the Western Empire, he saw in the ravages of disease and the moral disorders accompanying them, clear indications of approaching judgment and the end of the world. His first publication was entitled, "The last Age of the Church." In these gloomy forebodings, and the earnest purposes of reformation which grew out of them, he was confirmed by strong sympathy with the mystics and prophets of the continent. For the work of a controversialist he was admirably prepared by the severe discipline to which he had subjected his understanding, and by his skill in the scholastic exercises of the period. The court of Rome, with characteristic policy—to counteract the popular movements of the time, and allay the rising storm against the monks and clergy—had sent out among the lower classes vast swarms of itinerant preachers under the name of mendicant friars. The two orders of Franciscans and Dominicans, which made their appearance at the beginning of the thirteenth century, were rival candidates for the popular favour. It was against the ignorance and baseness of these preaching friars, that the earliest zeal of Wycliffe was directed.

So long as he confined his attacks to foreign ecclesiastics who monopolized the best English benefices, to the grosser corruptions of the clergy, and to the exactions of the Papal ministers—he carried along with him the sympathy of the court and of not a few among the aristocracy. He found a zealous patron in John of Gaunt; and by Edward III., who subsequently beneficed him, he was sent on a deputation to confer with the papal commissioners at Bruges. He also acquired great celebrity as a teacher at Oxford. His doctrines spread into Bohemia[1]; and the Queen of Richard II., who came from that country, brought with her a disposition to respect his character and principles. Such influences threw a protection round the person of Wycliffe; and a man more selfish and ambitious might have turned them to his advantage, without wholly forfeiting his reputation for consistency as a reformer. But his honest, straightforward mind penetrated deeper into the evils of society, and was bent on their eradication. Much of the prevalent wickedness and irreligion he traced to the hierarchy itself, the very principle of which his reasonings led him to condemn. He preached vehemently

[1] Collier, I. 586.

against the riches and corruption of the clergy, and affirmed the complete right of the state to resume and re-appropriate their property. He contended, that the influence of the clergy should be derived, not from their sacerdotal functions, but from their personal qualities; and that only those priests whose lives were holy and laborious, were entitled to pecuniary support. In some points he anticipated the principles of the Quakers. Like them, he asserted the unlawfulness of all war; denied the divine institution of tithes, which he would have left to be paid as a voluntary contribution; and for the splendour and ceremony of the Catholic service, would have substituted an extreme simplicity of worship.

Among his contemporaries his chief distinction arose from his zeal to spread the knowledge of the Scriptures, which he translated into English, and widely circulated among the people[1]. In the pulpit his favourite mode of instruction was scriptural exposition, or, as it was then called, *postillating*. From this circumstance he acquired at Oxford the title of the Gospel Doctor. His tendencies as a preacher were in direct antagonism to those of the friars, who set the Church above the Gospel, and whose principles were anti-scriptural. To disseminate his doctrines, he associated with himself, in his sphere of pastoral labour at Lutterworth, a number of village missionaries, under the name of "Poor Priests," who had no benefices, and whose life and preaching, he thought, would furnish the example of a true Gospel ministry. Some have supposed Chaucer, in his well-known description of the "Poor Parson," to have had these preachers of Wycliffe in his eye. It is so far an evidence of general sympathy in that age with the most prominent of Wycliffe's principles, that there is not a line throughout that beautiful portraiture, which speaks of devotedness to the Church; while it is set forth as the peculiar praise of the good man, that

"Criste's lore and his apostles twelve
He taught, but first he folwed it himselve[2]."

[1] Dr. Lingard quotes Sir Thomas More (Dial. iii. 14) in proof of the existence of English translations of the Scriptures before the time of Wycliffe. (Hist. of England, 8vo edit. vol. iv. p. 267, note 64.) Dr. Vaughan (Life and Opinions of Wycliffe, vol. ii. p. 42) says, that these earlier versions were usually guarded by a comment, and that the novelty in Wycliffe's case was the translation of the *whole* of the Scriptures, and putting them by numerous transcripts, through the agency of his Poor Priests, into the hands of the laity at large.

[2] Canterbury Tales, Prologue, 529-30.

Chaucer's tastes and associations, however, connected him rather with the Norman, than with the Saxon, element of the English nation: nor can any inference be drawn as to his participation, in an earnest and positive sense, with the religious movement of Wycliffe, from the sly and pungent sarcasms against churchmen with which his pages are everywhere interspersed; since the same free tone had for more than two centuries distinguished the lighter French literature from which he drew so large a proportion of his materials[1].

The writings and labours of Wycliffe indicated a purpose of thorough reformation which could not expect much countenance from a proud and warlike nobility, and was sure to provoke the bitterest hostility of the clergy. He was removed from the chair of divinity at Oxford, and forsaken by his early patron, the Duke of Lancaster. But such was the consideration he enjoyed[2], that he was allowed to pass the remnant of his days unmolested at Lutterworth: although, thirty years after his death, the feeling respecting him had so much changed, that his remains were disinterred and burnt to ashes, and thrown into the river which flows past the town that had been the scene of his labours[3].

[1] See Le Grand's Collection of Fabliaux of the 12th and 13th centuries, translated by Way, and Bouterwek's Geschichte der Englischen Poesie und Beredsamkeit, I. 67. Wycliffe and Chaucer had a common patron in John of Gaunt, and some historians have affirmed that an actual friendship subsisted between the reformer and the poet. (Godwin's Life of Chaucer, III. 55.) But there could have been no deep sympathy between minds cast in so different a mould. The *vis comica* and lighthearted gaiety of the French character are conspicuous in Chaucer. A Saxon earnestness distinguishes Wycliffe. Chaucer's predilections were for the court and nobility. Wycliffe's sympathies were with the people.

[2] Lingard, vol. ii. 8vo, ch. ii.

[3] Wycliffe's opinions have been transmitted to us through so prejudiced a medium, that there is reason to believe many of them have been perverted and exaggerated. It is not difficult, however, from comparing the statements of different witnesses, to obtain a tolerably clear notion of the general spirit and distinguishing features of his system. In essential points, it was an anticipation of the extreme form of the later Puritanism. See 'Life and Opinions of John de Wycliffe,' by Robert Vaughan, D.D. Fuller (Church History of Britain, IV. i. 6) gives a list of dangerous and heretical opinions alleged against Wycliffe by one of his principal adversaries, Thomas Waldensis. Among these are the following, reported also by other authorities, which may serve to convey some idea of his peculiar tenets:—"That Christ is the sole Head of the Church; That the Pope is Anti-Christ; That in the time of the Apostles, there were only two orders of priests, priest and bishop being the same; That the Church consists of predestinated persons; That all beautiful building of churches is blame-worthy and hypocritical; That tithes are pure alms, not due to priests of dissolute life; That what is not plainly expressed in Scripture, is neglected

Various circumstances indicate how widely the principles of Wycliffe had spread. Nor was their influence confined to the lower orders. Many persons of wealth and consideration had embraced them. Collier[1], following the statements of a contemporary writer, mentions the names of several knights who were zealously attached to Wycliffe's party; and tells us, that when a Lollard preacher came into the neighbourhood of any of these gentlemen, they immediately sent out a summons into the surrounding district, and compelled the inhabitants to come and hear; and then assembling at the appointed hour and place with their armed retainers, planted themselves round the pulpit of the preacher, that he might inveigh without fear of interruption or attack, against the superstitions and corruptions of the Church. Many of these preachers were mean persons, of little or no education, who nevertheless well understood their audience, and knew how to work on their feelings. They were aware of the effect that might be produced by the mere change of a word; and in preaching against images, to which they had a strong aversion,—"they called," says Knyghton, "our Lady of Lincoln, and our Lady of Walsingham, the witch of Lincoln, and the witch of Walsingham." In Leicestershire, the scene of Wycliffe's own ministry, the new opinions had made such progress, that, according to the same authority, a man could scarce meet two people on the road, but one of them was a Wycliffite[2]. In the reign of Richard II. the Lollards submitted to Parliament a remonstrance against clerical abuses, in twelve articles; in which, among other things, they protested against war and capital punishments, as absolutely unlawful. In this attack on the Church, the Lollards had miscalculated their strength.

as impertinent by wise men; That general councils are of no authority; That all writers since the thousandth year of Christ, are heretics; That to bind men to set and prescribed forms of prayer, derogates from the liberty God has given them; That purchased prayers are of no efficacy, but men must hope and trust in their own righteousness; That infants unbaptized do not perish, since baptism does not confer, but merely signifies, grace given before; That confession to the truly contrite is superfluous, and only a device to get at secrets, and gain wealth; That the prayers of saints are only effectual for the good; That in causes ecclesiastical and matters of faith, the bishop's sentence may be appealed from to the secular prince; That dominion over the creature is founded in grace; That God loved David and Peter as much when they sinned, as now in their glory; That all things come to pass by necessity—God not being able to make the world otherwise than it is made, or to do anything which he doth not do."

[1] Eccles. Hist. I. 579.   [2] Collier, I. 580.

The fears of the prelates were aroused; and it was probably on this occasion, that a form of abjuration was tendered by Arundel, archbishop of York, to four Lollards of Nottingham, which they bound themselves to observe, under pain of forfeiting all their property[1].

The accession of the House of Lancaster had an unfavourable effect on the condition of the Lollards. Henry IV. found it expedient to sustain a doubtful title by courting the favour of the clergy; and the price of their support was the discouragement and persecution of the reformers. His son, Henry V., whom tradition affirms to have been intimate in his youth with Lollards, on ascending the throne, pursued the same policy, and abandoned them to their remorseless enemies. Yet many facts prove, that under both these sovereigns their numbers and influence must still have been considerable. In Lent, 1409, the Commons presented a bill to Henry IV., for secularizing the temporalities of the clergy; and when he rejected their proposal with high displeasure, they then pressed for a repeal, or relaxation, of the statute recently enacted against the Lollards; on which the king replied, that he would rather increase than abate its rigour[2]. Under these reigns, the prisons were filled with Lollards. For a time, the University of Oxford, the original seat of their doctrines, (which, in consequence of various papal bulls, claimed an exemption from the jurisdiction of the primate) afforded them an asylum: —but, at the instance of the archbishop, these rival claims were brought before Henry IV.; and he decided against the University. How far, in the complication of social interests, their principles were directly involved in the political movements of the age, it is difficult to ascertain. Some of Wycliffe's views, it must be confessed, were easily susceptible of democratic perversion; and the clergy would studiously exhibit them in the most odious light. It was at the instigation of the clergy, that in the reign of Henry IV. the atrocious act was passed, "*De Hæretico Comburendo*[3]," which continued

---

[1] This was in 1395. The form of abjuration is given in Fuller, IV. i. 40, and Collier, I. 596.

[2] Collier, I. 629.

[3] According to Fitz-herbert, an ancient lawgiver quoted by Collier (Eccles. Hist. II. Preface, vii.), burning was the punishment for heresy at common law before this time, though it had never been inflicted till enforced by statute. Upon this Sir James Mackintosh observes (Hist. of England, I. 356), that such "an assertion is easily made, and with difficulty brought to the test of evidence,

to deform our statute book till the reign of Charles II. In 1412 we find the Upper House, with Prince Henry at its head, concurring in a petition to the king against the Lollards[1]. Under the new act, Sautre, a clergyman, sometimes called the first martyr of English Protestantism,—the lord Cobham, an early associate of Prince Henry, and charged with participating in an insurrection of the time,—and some other persons of inferior rank,—were put to death. The most rigorous measures were adopted to check the diffusion of their principles. In the reigns of Henry V. and VI. it was made penal for parents to send their children to any private teacher, lest Lollard principles should be instilled into them[2]. Yet all these severities could not annihilate the party:—they still maintained their "schools," as they called their places of secret meeting, and their "prophesyings," in spite of the laws; and looking back with regret on the comparative tranquillity which they had enjoyed under the Plantagenets, they cherished the belief that Richard II. was still alive, and would come back to their relief.

During the wars of the Roses, the Lollards escaped persecution amidst the general confusion; "the very storm," in the language of Fuller, proving "their shelter." At this time, the learning and morals of the clergy had shrunk to the lowest ebb. A contemporary declares, that "a right discharge of the functions of a parish priest was almost grown into disuse, and made impracticable." They had become, the prelates especially, marked objects of popular odium. During an insurrection, which broke out in the reign of Henry VI., some bishops were driven from their sees and murdered, and their palaces destroyed; several officers of the spiritual courts plundered and killed; and in Kent and Wiltshire the inferior clergy cruelly harassed. In the midst of these disorders, Reginald Pecock, bishop of Chichester, a man of enlightened views but of an infirm and irresolute spirit, attempted a moderate and conciliatory course, and tried to wean the Bible-men, as the Lollards were then called, from their extreme proceedings. He appears to have agreed with them in denying the infallibility of the Church, and maintain-

and, in the lax language of a rude jurisprudence, imported, perhaps, nothing more than that, before the statute, heresy would not, or did not, pass with impunity."
[1] The petition is given in Fuller, IV. ii. 14.   [2] Fuller, IV. ii. 61.

ing the sufficiency of Scripture. But he was overpowered by his ecclesiastical adversaries, and compelled to recant under circumstances of great humiliation[1].

With the return of peace, the trials and sufferings of the Lollards began anew. Henry VII., like his predecessors, allied himself with the clergy, and secured their attachment by gratifying their bigotry. The fires of persecution were rekindled. Those who abjured their principles to escape burning, wore the mark of a faggot on the left sleeve, as a badge of penance for life. A particular part of Smithfield was called the Lollards' Pit, as having been the frequent scene of their executions; and in the old palace of Lambeth, the Lollards' Tower took its name from the prison where these unhappy men were confined. Fuller, who lived in the first half of the seventeenth century, observes, that "the word Lollard had been retained in the statutes since the Reformation, as a generical name, to signify such who, in their opinions, oppose the settled religion of the land." "In which sense," he says, "the modern sheriffs were bound by their oath to suppress them[2]." But "the blood of the martyrs is the seed of the Church:" the sect survived the dungeon and the stake; and the principles which it had diffused, prepared a ready sympathy with doctrines which began to be preached under Henry VIII. Lollardism was absorbed in the new life of Protestantism; and the flames which consumed the last of its martyrs, might have lighted the faggots amidst which an incipient Puritanism gave public witness of having inherited its spirit[3].

II. The decisive act which marked the commencement of the Reformation in England, was the transference of the headship of the Church from the Pope to Henry VIII. This was an act which satisfied nobody but the king himself and a few of his courtiers. The mass of the nation, including a majority of the nobility, was still Catholic; and those who had imbibed

---

[1] Collier, I. 676. Pecock's opinions are variously represented; but the verses which Collier says he was accustomed to repeat to those who visited him in his confinement, indicate doubt respecting some fundamental points of the orthodox system.

"Wit hath wonder that Reason cannot skan,
How a Moder is Mayd, and God is Man."

To which a contemporary made this reply:
"Leve Reason, Beleve the Wonder,
Belef hath Mastry, and Reason is under."

[2] Church History, IV. ii. 18.
[3] Burnet's Hist. of the Reformation, I. pp. 27–33, fol.

Protestant principles, could not desire that the will of the sovereign should fix the standard of faith and worship. Nevertheless, as Henry was popular with his subjects, and the temper of Parliament was subservient, there was a general disposition to conform to circumstances, and acquiesce in the king's ecclesiastical supremacy. The Catholic and Protestant elements of the population were never, therefore, distinctly separated from each other. Few were prepared, like Bishop Fisher and Sir Thomas More, to sacrifice their lives to their principles; and of the clergy an immense majority, with a Catholic faith and Catholic predilections in their hearts, were incorporated at once into the new constitution of the English Church[1]. The more ardent Protestants withdrew to the Continent, or paid the penalty of imprisonment and death at home. Cranmer, more decidedly Protestant in principle than he ventured to avow, retained by seasonable compliances his influence over the king, and promoted further reformation whenever the opportunity occurred. He represented the *new* learning, as Protestantism was then called, and Gardiner, bishop of Winchester, the *old* or Catholicism[2]; and to the effort to combine these opposite tendencies in one system, which was among the results of Cranmer's deference to his master's will—the Church of England owes that mixed character by which it is peculiarly distinguished. Fuller remarks, that Cranmer and they who "weathered out" with him "the tempest of king Henry's tyranny," were the first conformists, and the more zealous reformers who fled beyond the seas, the founders of nonconformity[3]; thus tracing back the great national schism to the very commencement of the Reformation in England.

Cranmer agreed with Cromwell, whom Henry constituted his vicar-general as head of the church, in deriving all ecclesiastical power from the will of the sovereign. Upon this principle they acted together in carrying out their plans of reform, and in their attempt to fix and settle a national system of religion. Henry's own creed was essentially Catholic; but he was sensitively jealous of his supremacy; and the limits of his doctrinal system were marked by so fine and impalpable a line, that the most circumspect could not always discern them, though fearful penalties attended their trans-

[1] Hallam, Constitutional Hist. ch. ii.
[2] Lingard, vol. vi.   [3] Church Hist. VII. i. 24.

gression on either side. He gave a striking proof of the impartiality of his ferocious intolerance, when in 1540 he ordered three Lutherans and four Catholics to be dragged to the stake on the same hurdle for denying his supremacy—with this nice distinction in their fate, that the Protestants were to be burnt, and the Catholics hanged[1].

The principles of the Reformation made great progress in the short reign of Edward VI.; and had his life been spared, the character of our Church and our Universities would have been very different from what they now are. Articles of faith were drawn up; the entire liturgy, out of which, during the preceding reign, only the Lord's Prayer, the Creed, and the Ten Commandments had been recited in English, was translated from the Latin; and the service generally was simplified and adapted more to a Protestant taste. Already there were those who, like the earlier Lollards, did not approve of set forms of prayer though sanctioned by Calvin[2], but preferred the mode of public devotion observed in the Protestant churches of the Continent. The interval of Mary's reign rendered good service to Protestantism by putting to a severe test the strength of its principles, and calling forth many illustrious examples of heroic martyrdom.

It was not till the reign of Elizabeth that the Church of England was settled on its present foundations, and the opposing tendencies of Puritanism came out in full operation against it. Elizabeth inherited the religious principles of her father. She was attached to the forms of the hierarchy: and her faith had more affinity with the Catholic than with the Protestant system. Of all the foreign churches she sympathized most with the Lutheran, because it receded less than the Calvinistic and the Zwinglian from the ancient religion[3]: whereas those of her subjects who returned from exile on the death of Mary, and who had met with a more cordial reception abroad among the Calvinists than among the Lutherans,

---

[1] Neal's History of the Puritans, 4to, I. 22.

[2] Fuller, VII. ii. 18. "Publicam formulam precum et rituum Ecclesiasticorum valde probo, ut certa illa extet, à quâ ne pastoribus discedere in functione suâ liceat." Lib. Epistol. 69, quoted by Fuller. In the appendix to the 'Catechismus Genevensis,' which was put forth by Calvin in 1545, is a complete Form of Common Prayer (Precum Ecclesiasticarum Formula), with offices for the administration of the Sacraments, the celebration of Matrimony, and the Visitation of the Sick. Niemeyer, Collectio Confess. Reformat. pp. 170-190.

[3] Hallam, Constit. Hist. ch. iv.

brought back with them a spirit of fervid Protestantism, and an eager desire to carry reformation in England beyond the point to which it had been advanced by Edward VI. Thus the seeds of discord were germinating from the very commencement of Elizabeth's reign, and the fruit soon became visible. The bishops of Elizabeth were content, like Cranmer, to derive their authority from the Crown, the supremacy of which in religious matters was the fundamental article of the new ecclesiastical constitution. The divine right of Episcopacy was a doctrine not put forth till a later period. It was too perilous a question to agitate at a time of recent change, when men's minds were hardly yet familiarized with the great revolution which had occurred. Cast down from its ancient foundation, Episcopacy, exposed and attacked, clung with the instinct of self-preservation to the royal prerogative; and fortunately for itself, this was an alliance which the crown was very willing to accept.

In the first year of her reign, Elizabeth, at the suggestion of the primate, Parker, instituted the Court of High Commission; by which she united the sovereign power of the State with the Church[1], and through which she exercised her supremacy, as her father, under different circumstances, through the single person of Cromwell. The Queen and her primates, Parker and Whitgift, guided by the same despotic principles, were resolved to enforce uniformity; the Queen expressing more apprehension of the Puritans than of the Catholics. She disliked the interference of Parliament, where Puritan doctrines sometimes found a voice, in matters relating to the Church; and it was the advice of Whitgift, that, in all ecclesiastical regulations, she should proceed by canons framed in Convocation rather than by parliamentary statute[2]. With the increasing stringency of the measures of the High Commission, the force of resistance became more intense and unmanageable. The earliest Puritans—among whom were Fox the martyrologist, and Myles Coverdale who had been bishop of Exeter in Edward's time and declined resuming his see on his return from exile—did not wish to consider themselves as separatists, but merely craved exemption from certain forms and ceremonies to which they had a conscientious objection. With the progress of time, however, men's passions became excited on both sides, and the breach grew wider and more

[1] Hallam, ibid.   [2] Neal, I. 306.

irreparable as the discussion was prolonged.—In the second stage of the dispute, the relation of the two parties to each other was more distinctly marked. The supporters of the hierarchy contended, that the Roman Catholic was a true church, though corrupted; and that, while Scripture was a final standard in points of doctrine, it prescribed no absolute form for discipline and government. On the other hand the Puritans affirmed, that the Pope was Antichrist; that no communion should be maintained with churches acknowledging his authority; and that Scripture exhibited not only a perfect rule of faith, but a complete model of ecclesiastical polity.— In the third stage of the movement under Elizabeth, the more extreme Puritans proceeded to the length of asserting the divine right of the Presbyterian form of church government— its independency of all civil control—and the duty of Christians to set it up, and conform to it, in defiance of the existing establishment. Some of Elizabeth's courtiers who had at first looked on the Puritans with a favourable eye, abandoned them on their beginning to proclaim such doctrines.

It is remarkable, that these high notions of ecclesiastical government, as founded on a divine right, should have been advanced by Presbyterians before they were ventured on by the bishops. The bishops were kept in awe by the Queen, who would not allow her supremacy to be questioned. They possessed substantial power and great worldly distinction; and these they were not inclined to put in jeopardy for a theory. Parker, perhaps Grindal, certainly Whitgift—the three first primates of Elizabeth—were Erastians[1] in their views of church government.—Towards the close of her reign when the hierarchy felt itself secure, the divine right of Episcopacy began to be asserted by the zealous adherents of the Church, provoked to it in part by the high ground already taken by their adversaries[2]. In the meanwhile the conflict

---

[1] The term Erastian is derived from Erastus, a German physician in the sixteenth century. The fundamental principle of the system seems to have been this—that the Church should exercise no coercive and punitive power, except through the arm of the civil magistrate—and especially should be restrained from inflicting, by its own authority, the penalty of excommunication, to which, in that age, such a fearful importance was attached. This system, which took the Jewish polity as its model, recognized the Church as only a member of the general body of the State. See the 'Thesis of Erastus, touching Excommunication,' translated from the Latin, by the Rev. Robert Lee, D.D., Edinburgh: 1844. Also Hallam, Constit. Hist. II. p. 272, note.

[2] Hallam, Constit. Hist. I. 293, note.

between Prelacy and Puritanism was maintained in a fierce warfare of pamphlets and graver productions. The tracts of Martin Marprelate, which produced such a sensation at the time, were showered forth all over the country from an ambulatory printing-press, which ended its migrations, and was at last discovered and broken up, in the then remote but strongly puritanical town of Manchester[1]. Learning and eloquence were also engaged in the contest. Whitgift and Hooker on one side, Cartwright and Travers on the other, brought the aid of great abilities, extensive acquirements, and undoubted zeal and sincerity, to the support of their respective systems.—A temporary cessation of controversy—a sort of theological truce—marked the closing years of the Queen's reign. Both parties looked with some anxiety to the influence on their respective interests, of the arrival of a new sovereign from the north.—But in the heat of the preceding disputes more extreme opinions had been elicited, which denied the divine right and scriptural precedent alike of Episcopacy and of Presbyterianism, and, regarding every association of Christians for worship and edification as a complete church, vested in their separate and independent assemblies all authority for spiritual purposes. Men of these principles, called from their leaders Brownists and Barrowists, were the founders of the system of Independency. Several members of this sect were put to death for their opinions in the reign of Elizabeth. Numbers fled over into Holland, where they met with a kind reception, cultivated learning, and sometimes taught in the Universities, or became pastors to congregations of emigrants. It was not till a later period that this party acquired a powerful influence in the ecclesiastical affairs of England[2].

The expectations of the Presbyterians from the accession of James to the English throne, were speedily destroyed by the result of the conference, held in his presence at Hampton Court, between some of their principal divines and the bishops. James soon renounced the Calvinism in which he had been bred and of which he had once stood forth as the defender[3], for Arminianism, which was now becoming the badge of the prelatical party: and the system of Episcopacy agreed so well with his arbitrary principles of civil government, that he could not long hesitate in preferring it to the democratic platform of Presbyterianism. The reign of James is distinguished by

[1] Neal, 4to, I. 337. [2] Neal, I. 436. [3] Neal, I. 348, 350.

the growth of high episcopal doctrines, very different from the principles which had been maintained by Cranmer and the bishops of Elizabeth. The Church courted a close alliance with the Crown; while Puritanism found many advocates in Parliament. It has been noticed, however[1], that for twenty years before the breaking out of the civil wars, the zeal for Presbyterianism had declined; and that if a moderate Episcopacy, under the control of Parliament, and with a restriction of the power of the ecclesiastical courts, could have been then established, the great body of the nation would have been satisfied. But the high churchmen hated Parliament and the common lawyers; and it has been thought, that the enigmatical word *thorough*, so frequently occurring in the correspondence of Laud and Strafford, refers to some deep-laid design of overturning their authority, and substituting a more despotic tribunal in its stead[2]. "But this arrogant contempt of the lawyers manifested by Laud and his faction of priests, led," as Mr. Hallam has remarked, "to the ruin of the great churchmen and of the Church itself."

The cause of Presbyterianism was revived by the alliance of Parliament with the Scots, who made the establishment of that form of church government a condition of their support. The Westminster Assembly of divines became in the main, under these influences, a Presbyterian body, though it numbered among its members moderate Episcopalians, Independents, and some lawyers who were Erastians. It had been convened by Parliament to settle the religious affairs of the nation, during the progress of the war, and aspired to the exercise of a co-ordinate authority: but Parliament kept a strict watch over all its proceedings; confirmed its enactments before they could have force; and never parted with the power of the Keys, as the right of inflicting ecclesiastical censures and penalties was called in the peculiar phraseology of those times. Its intolerance was thus fortunately held in check. Nevertheless, it abolished Episcopacy; prohibited the use of the liturgy; and opposed the concession of a toleration to the Independents. For some years Presbyterianism struggled for ascendency as the established religion of the nation; but owing to the strong resistance which it encountered, and the disordered state of the country, its system of church govern-

---

[1] Neal, I. p. 715.
[2] Hallam, Constit. Hist. ch. viii. p. 65. So interpreted, we may consider this phrase as the counterpart of *root and branch* among the Puritans.

ment was nowhere carried fully into effect except in Lancashire, and less perfectly in London and its vicinity.

The principles of the Independents were widely spread in the parliamentary army, and acquired political ascendency chiefly through the energy and enterprise of Cromwell. But they had much to recommend them to generous and thoughtful minds; and not a few of the aristocracy and learned class embraced them.—Among the most eminent of these were the Lord Brook, Sir Harry Vane the younger, Mr. Francis Pierrepont, Milton, and probably Sir Thomas Fairfax[1]. They were also diffused among the yeomanry of the rural districts, and found numerous supporters in the wealthy and substantial citizens of London and other trading towns. In his appreciation of the claims of religious liberty Cromwell was far before his age, and much in advance of the clergy even of his own denomination. His mind, indeed, seems to have been deeply imbued with the spirit of toleration. His own religious earnestness, though closely bordering on enthusiasm, did not hinder him from looking at this question with the clear and open eye of an unprejudiced statesman. He connived at the use of the liturgy by the deprived Episcopalians; and when he adopted harsh measures respecting them, it was not on religious but on political grounds[2]. His severities towards the Papists must be ascribed partly to the same principle, and partly to the general prejudice entertained by all Protestants in that age against the adherents of the old religion. His own feelings would have led him to allow the Jews the free exercise of their religion in London[3]. He protected the person of the

---

[1] See Mrs. Hutchinson's evidence of Fairfax's Independency, in her Memoirs of her husband, p. 268, 4to edit.

[2] "To give the devil his due," says Dr. George Bates, an impartial witness, who in the midst of these concessions, does not spare the bitterest charges against Cromwell, "he restored Justice as well distributive as commutative almost to its ancient dignity and splendour;—though the public use of the Service-book was denied to the Episcopal party, yet in private houses he allowed them the use of their rites;—and though the state of the Church seemed now sad and deplorable, yet it is not to be denied, but that milder courses were used than under the rigid tyranny of others (the Presbyterians) that went before." Rise and Progress of the late Troubles in England. London: 1685, 2nd part, pp. 192–93. Bates was in succession physician to Charles I., Cromwell, and Charles II. His work was originally written in Latin, and entitled, 'Elenchus Motuum Nuperorum in Anglia.' Baxter, also no friend to Cromwell, adds a similar testimony. "I perceived that it was his design to do good in the main, and to promote the gospel and the interest of godliness, more than any had done before him; except in those particulars which his own interest was against." Narrative of his Life and Times. London: 1696, P. I. p. 71.

[3] Bates, Rise and Progress, etc. II. p. 211.

Unitarian Biddle from the bigotry of the Council, and allowed him a maintenance of a hundred crowns a-year during his exile[1]. Had Cromwell ruled longer, and been able to found a dynasty, it is possible that his masculine sense and tolerant principles might have practically solved not a few difficulties growing out of the actual constitution of our Church and Universities, and that many occasions of strife and uneasiness, not yet disposed of, might have been spared to posterity.

III. The ascendency of Puritanism terminated with the death of the Protector. The Presbyterians, attached on principle to monarchy and never cordially acquiescing in the Cromwellian rule, united with the Episcopalians to restore the royal family. They hoped now to attain their favourite object of a purification of the national church, and abandoning the high Presbyterian ground, would have been satisfied with the establishment of a moderate Episcopacy. Influenced by these feelings they placed too implicit a reliance on Charles's Declaration from Breda, which promised liberty to tender consciences and led them to hope for a national settlement of religion. But the exasperation of the Episcopal clergy, who felt they had been excluded by the Puritan ministers from their lawful honours and emoluments, was extreme, and only checked by prudential considerations till they could find an opportunity of giving it full effect. Hyde, afterwards Lord Clarendon, was their chief adviser, and a devoted adherent of the hierarchy, the interests of which, in the true spirit of Toryism, he preferred even to those of the Crown[2]. Under such circumstances all attempts at comprehension were fruitless. The conference at the Savoy had no other effect than an increased alienation between the parties whom it was professedly convened to unite. All the influences most active at Court and in Parliament tended to reinstate the Church in its ancient power and dignities, and to depress those who had been the cause of its humiliation. A part of the Act which in the preceding period had abolished the court of High Commission, was now repealed, though the court itself was not restored[3]. The Corporation Act, passed in the first year of the King's reign, by imposing the sacrament of the Lord's Supper as a qualification for municipal office, effectually excluded all conscientious Nonconformists from corporations. Besides

---

[1] Neal, II. ch. iii. p. 471.
[2] Hallam, Constit. Hist. II. p. 467.
[3] Mackintosh, Hist. of the Revolution, p. 66.

this, all the penal statutes of Elizabeth were confirmed by Parliament.

But the most decisive measure of vengeance, and that from which this third period of our religious history derives its peculiar character, was the Act of Uniformity in 1662, carried through Parliament by the influence of the bishops, and zealously promoted by Lord Clarendon. The Upper House would have tempered the severity of some of its provisions, but was overborne by the High Church spirit which predominated in the Commons. By this Act, which required an "unfeigned assent and consent to all and everything contained and prescribed in and by the Book of Common Prayer," and which in other respects was purposely framed in direct opposition to the known conscientious scruples of the Puritan clergy[1], nearly two thousand ministers[2] were all at once cast out of their benefices, prohibited from preaching, and thrown for support on their own resources and the charity of their friends. When the Episcopalians had been deprived by the Long Parliament, for refusing to take the Covenant, a fifth part of the profits of their livings had been reserved for their maintenance; but no such consideration was now shown for the ejected Presbyterians.

The effect of this Act was to constitute Protestant Dissent a distinct and powerful element in the composition of English society. Hitherto the great mass of the Puritans had cherished strong feelings of attachment to the national church, and had only sought its further reformation: they were now forcibly excluded from it—never, as a party, to be incorporated with it again. During the quarter of a century which elapsed from the day of St. Bartholomew, August 24, 1662—the date of the ejectment—to the passing of the Toleration Act in 1689 after the accession of William III.—the Nonconformists were exposed to every species of persecution and annoyance. In the reign of Charles II., no less than six acts—including the Act of Uniformity and that relating to Corporations—were passed, subjecting them to various restraints and penalties[3]. They were put without the pale of the constitution; they were

---

[1] See the abstract of it in Neal, II. p. 625.

[2] This is about the mean of the extreme calculations on the opposite sides. Baxter states the number of the deprived at 1800. See Hallam, II. 462, note. Hunter's Life of Oliver Heywood, p. 137.

[3] These were the two Conventicle Acts, the Five Mile Act, and the Test Act. Neal, II. p. 695.

doomed to struggle for the mere recognition of their political existence: and their religious assemblies to which they attached a conscientious importance and which yielded their highest consolations, were held in stealth and jeopardy, by the connivance of magistrates, and now and then more openly through the questionable indulgences of the Crown. Yet it was during this period of suffering and humiliation, that they learned their most valuable lessons, and developed those genuine principles of religious liberty which have imparted a real dignity and deep significance to their cause. Smarting under the rod of tyranny, they looked beyond the arm immediately wielding it, to the hidden principle which put it in motion; and they found the root of all persecution in that assumption of infallibility and of right to domineer over conscience, which is not peculiar to any one church, but has uniformly been displayed by all, when placed in circumstances to exercise it. Had Presbyterianism succeeded in obtaining an exclusive establishment, there is every indication that her rule would have proved as oppressive as that of her rival. Nothing indeed can exhibit a more striking contrast than the spirit of Presbyterianism in the ascendant, and the spirit of Presbyterianism excluded, humbled, and tolerated: and these two periods in its history should be carefully distinguished, when we are speaking of that large and important section of the old Puritan party. Baxter's autobiography furnishes a beautiful illustration of the effect of this mellowing discipline on an earnest and noble mind[1].

At the time of the Restoration, a great majority of the church livings were held by those who ranked as Presbyterians but had no objection to a moderate Episcopacy; some, with stations of dignity in the Universities, by Independents; and a few by Anabaptists and other sectaries. Out of this number those who could not comply with the terms of the Act of Uniformity, were deprived of their legal maintenance; and in many instances, carrying with them a large part of their congregations, became the founders of new religious societies, most of which have subsisted to the present time.

---

[1] Baxter's Life and Times, Part I. § 213. Here occurs that beautiful and truly catholic sentiment "I can never believe that a man may not be saved by that religion, which doth but bring him to the true love of God, and to a heavenly mind and life; nor that God will ever cast a soul into hell that truly loveth him."—p. 131.

These different parties, thrown by a common misfortune into one class, and comprehended under the general title of Nonconformists, were still divided among themselves. The Presbyterians, seeking immediately only the free exercise of their worship, did not give up the hope, that through some combination of events, the Church might yet be so enlarged and reformed as to re-admit them to a participation in the national ministry: while the Independents, the Baptists, and still more the Quakers, desired no comprehension, but merely asked for an impartial toleration. These different views had a corresponding influence on their conduct in the confused state of public affairs, and in the anomalous position which all parties political and religious now sustained towards each other. The Church of England had fenced herself round with penal statutes, for the oppression of the Roman Catholics on one side and of the Protestant Dissenters on the other, and was sustained in her high pretensions by a powerful party, of which at the beginning of Charles's reign Lord Clarendon was the acknowledged head. The principles of this party were identical with those of Laud. The Church was their idol and bond of union; and they strove to secure her in a position unparalleled among the Protestant communities of Christendom. Meanwhile the king and his brother were Catholics, anxious to seize every opportunity of befriending the religion to which they were attached:—but this was impracticable, except by measures which brought relief to the Nonconformists, who in their turn were often restrained by conscientious scruples from accepting benefits, which they thought would give encouragement to Popery.

From this strange mixture of bigotry, prejudice, and craft, resulted a division of interests and a complication of policy, which threw parties into unprecedented relations towards each other. James, on acceding to the throne, pursued his designs with more openness and decision than the late king, and thus accelerated the Revolution. To allure the Dissenters into concurrence with his views, he issued successive Declarations for liberty of conscience, in virtue of the dispensing power which he affirmed, against express resolutions of Parliament, to be inherent in his crown. All who valued the constitution, and understood the necessary contrariety of religious freedom and civil despotism, perceived the tendency of these measures and were afraid of the ensnaring boon. Some of the court bishops,

c

in their slavish adherence to the maxims of passive obedience and non-resistance, surrendered the Church to the royal will. A few of the Presbyterians, more of the Independents and Baptists, with the Quakers under the guidance of Penn[1]—caught by the promises of universal toleration, and led by their peculiar principles to separate the idea of religion from all considerations of civil government—fell into the snare, and publicly thanked his majesty for this exercise of the dispensing power. But the better part of the clergy, and the more eminent of the Presbyterians with Howe and Baxter at their head, discerned the danger and stood coldly aloof. "Thus," says Sir James Mackintosh, "the sects who maintained the purest principles of religious liberty, and supported the most popular systems of government, were more disposed than others to favour a measure which would have finally buried toleration under the ruins of political freedom[2]." The acquittal however of the seven bishops, put on trial for their refusal to order the reading of the royal Declaration in the Churches, gave very general satisfaction, and indicated a strong determination among men of different parties to uphold the established Protestantism.

But this coalition of the Church with the Dissenters, as it originated in fear, so it was but of temporary duration, and gradually ceased, as the apprehensions which had occasioned it, lost their force. In 1689, after the settlement of the crown on William and Mary, the Toleration Act was passed, which first secured a legal existence, with the free exercise of their religion, to the Protestant Dissenters. It embraced the

---

[1] Sir J. Mackintosh expresses a very high opinion of Penn's character, and ascribes his acceptance of this measure to his simplicity. "Compassion, friendship, liberality and toleration led him to support a system of which the success would have undone his country, and afforded a remarkable proof, that in the complicated combinations of political morality, a virtue misplaced may produce as much immediate mischief as a vice." Hist. of the Revolution, p. 171. Perhaps Penn might be unconsciously flattered by his supposed influence over the mind of James. Bishop Burnet, who was acquainted with him in Holland, where he had been negotiating with the Prince of Orange on behalf of the king's views, and who, it must be owned, was prejudiced against his mission—speaks of him in different terms. "He was a talking, vain man, who had been long in the king's favour, and had such an opinion of his own faculty of persuading, that he thought none could stand before it; though he was singular in that opinion, for he had a tedious, luscious way, that was not apt to overcome a man's reason, though it might tire his patience." Hist. of his own Times, I. p. 693, fol. edit.

[2] Hist. of the Revolution, p. 167. Compare Neal, vol. ii. ch. xi.

Presbyterians, the Independents, and the Baptists—thenceforth known as the Three Denominations—as well as the Quakers; but it exempted from its benefits those who impugned the doctrine of the Trinity. It would have been more complete, but for the strong prejudices which it had to encounter. The same bigoted influence defeated all designs of comprehension, which William and the liberal Churchmen would have gladly entertained. Some clergymen of high principles, refusing to take the oaths to the new government, seceded from the Establishment under the name of Nonjurors. These were the most respectable men of their party. Others holding the same views but less conscientious, remained behind, and were mischievously active in the Lower House of Convocation, during the reign of Anne. Through their influence, the Acts against Schism and Occasional Conformity were passed for the annoyance of Dissenters[1]. Had such principles long continued predominant, the Toleration Act would have been reduced by successive limitations to a dead letter. The Dissenters did not enter on the tranquil enjoyment of all the benefits secured to them by this Act, till the accession of the House of Brunswick. The reigns of the two first Georges were distinguished by a general prevalence of religious peace[2]. Amid the quiet cultivation of learning and rational piety, the exercise of public spirit, and a reciprocation of friendly feeling with many liberal divines who then filled stations of eminence in the Church—Protestant Dissent attained its highest state of social influence and worldly consideration. But it was not an age of strong conviction or enthusiastic enterprise. Doddridge and Lardner represent its spirit among the Dissenters; Jortin and Herring in the Establishment.—The rapid progress of Methodism among the lower classes, the nearly contemporaneous rise of the evangelical party in the Church, the petition of a considerable body of clergymen for relief from subscription to the Thirty-

---

[1] Hallam, III. p. 332.
[2] In 1721, Lord Willoughby de Broke, Dean of Windsor, brought in a Bill for the more effectual suppression of blasphemy and profaneness, by which it was proposed to give additional force to the Act passed in the 9th and 10th of William III. commonly called the Blasphemy Act, which affected all impugners of the Trinity. Though several bishops, including Wake the primate, were in favour of the measure, it was lost by a majority of sixty against thirty-one. Calamy's Life and Times, vol. ii. p. 450. Rutt's note. Compare the Book of Rights by Edgar Taylor, p. 252.

nine Articles, and the open preaching of Unitarianism by Dr. Priestley and his followers,—are indications in the latter part of the eighteenth century, of the approach of a more exciting period, when opinions must again become more widely divergent, and the conflict of minds be kindled anew. The American and French revolutions infused fresh activity into these elements of change, and broke up many relations that seemed firmly knit by the usage of near a century; inspiring strong conservatism and a sensitive apprehension in the Church, and an ardent spirit of liberty among the Nonconformists.

The protracted war with France so fruitful of anxieties and fears, and the important events which crowded in quick succession upon each other in the ensuing years of peace, have calmed down many of these earlier and more speculative excitements, and brought graver and more practical questions into view. But the repeal of the disabilities affecting the Catholics and the Dissenters, the new composition of the House of Commons, the proposed reforms of the Church and the Universities, and the rapid increase of the democratic element in society,—are not events that have been calculated to allay either the hopes or the fears of the two great religious parties which divide the nation; and the Church and the Dissenters stand now at as great a distance from each other as ever. The old Puritan contest with the hierarchy is still undecided. In the middle of the nineteenth century we find ourselves yet implicated in some of the deepest questions of the cause for which our forefathers made such noble sacrifices and heroic efforts. Change in the outward show of things, should not blind us to the identity of principles continually re-appearing in new forms. We owe, indeed, much to the progress of civilization. It has converted the weapons of annoyance wielded by the hierarchy, from the badge, the dungeon and the stake, into the compulsory demand of a church-rate and the claim of exclusive education. But in its assumption of superiority, its disdain of equal intercourse, its virtual denial of Christian brotherhood, the spirit of the hierarchy has undergone no change. It cannot be uninteresting to investigate the principle, the effects and the apparent tendency of this grand English controversy. Fully to comprehend the present, we must survey its relations with the past. To attempt this, will be the object of the following chapters.

CHAPTER II.

THE CHURCH.

SECTION I.

DIFFICULTY OF DEFINING A CHURCH.

Few things are more difficult to define than a church. What constitutes a church? In the heterogeneous mass of human beings who continue through changing generations to bear its name and observe its usages, how shall we discover the common property which makes it a moral unity and invests it with a distinctive character? Where shall we look for the genius of a church?—In the opinions and feelings that may for the time be predominant in it?—or in its recognized creed, ritual and discipline?—in its invisible soul?—or in its material organization?—These difficulties are increased in the case of a church established by law; because every establishment possesses a vast power as such, to attract to itself out of other communions, men of the most opposite views, each of whom finds something in it, to justify his attachment to the religion of the State. Still, every religion that is taken into alliance with the government, must possess certain principles of its own, which belong to it independently of that connection, and which modify its operation as an establishment. Very different forms of Christianity have been established in England, in Scotland, and in Prussia, though they all partake more or less of the common spirit of establishments. Some persons conform on principle to the established Christianity, whatever it may be; and would be Episcopalians in England, Presbyterians in Scotland, and members of the Evangelical Church in Prussia. Others, again, have so decided a predilection for Episcopacy, that they adhere to it in Scotland where it is simply tolerated, and in America where it stands on the broad footing of religious equality with other sects.

Two things must, therefore, be considered, in examining the character and operation of the Church of England:—first, what it is in itself, regarded as a particular religious community, held together by certain Articles and Canons, and by the use of a common Liturgy and Discipline; and secondly, how these its constituent principles are qualified by its civil establishment. The Church of England is kept under great control by the State; and this external constraint unavoidably impedes the free and natural development of its inherent tendencies. We see it working in the fetters of its political subordination. To detect its genuine character, we must watch its operation in those periods of its history, where it has been left most to itself and enjoyed the greatest freedom of action, or where its latent principles have been most strongly called out in the conflict with hostile agencies.

And here a question meets us on the threshold of our inquiry:—what are we to assume as the primary element, the determining principle, of the English hierarchy? Its Articles and Homilies, or its Liturgy, Canons and Government? For it will not be denied, that a diffcrent spirit pervades these two parts of its constitution.—Writers on comparative grammar assert, that the characteristic features of a language are more discernible in its structure than in its vocabulary;—that the genius of the informing mind is more clearly shown in the organism which acts, than in the subject-matter which is acted upon: for the former endures, while the latter is exposed to constant change. We may apply the analogy to the constitution of the Church of England. Its structural arrangements—its organism—must be sought in its Prayer-book, Canons and episcopal discipline:—whereas its Articles and Homilies partake more of the nature of a foreign substance, grafted as it were on the original stock, which has done its best to assimilate them to its own constitution, and has caused them very generally to be received in a spirit widely different from that in which they were at first introduced. The liturgy and government of the Church and certain deep feelings of reverence and attachment cherished by them, have subsisted with little or no alteration for three centuries: but, though the spirit of the Articles and Homilies is Calvinistic, there have been long periods in which the predominant belief of those who subscribed to them, was notoriously Arminian; and the sense in which they should be interpreted, is still a matter of eager controversy betwen the two great parties of the Church.

SECTION II.

PREPARATORY CHANGES UNDER HENRY VIII.

In the reign of Henry VIII. little change was made in the constitution of the Church, but what resulted necessarily from dissolving the connection with Rome, and transferring the ecclesiastical supremacy to the Crown. Cranmer, though decidedly Protestant in heart[1], pursued his ends cautiously and indirectly, by always avoiding extreme measures and keeping on terms with his royal master;—a subserviency which procured him from his enemies the opprobrious title of a *Henrician*[2]. In 1533, on the death of Warham, he accepted the primacy, with a reservation that was discreditable to him. He was promoted by the authority of a papal mandate, though an act had already passed, which forbade the procuring of bulls and dispensations from Rome. Its execution was suspended at the royal pleasure for the occasion. But he quieted his scruples against taking the oath required by the Pontifical, with a previous protest recommended to him by the canonists, that he took it in no sense hostile to his duty to the King, the Church, and his country[3]. With this act of duplicity, Cranmer entered on his public career. The statutes which took away the supremacy of the pope and substituted that of the Crown, were enacted in 1534. Many elements however of the German Reformation had already found their way into England; and these, combining with the unextinguished tendencies of the native Lollardism, threatened to carry the movement begun, far beyond the point where the king wished it to cease. Bilney, Byfield, Frith, Lambert and other zealous spirits, paid the penalty of their lives for their intrepid exposure of popish errors and corruptions, and their assertion of the new doctrines. To the death of Lambert, Cranmer himself was a consenting party[4]. Henry resisted strenuously all popular innovations, and early took measures for fixing the national standard of faith and worship. He

---

[1] The advice which first procured Cranmer the favour of Henry, was founded on a Protestant principle; viz. to consult the Universities whether the marriage with Catharine were conformable to Scripture,—as, if it were not, no dispensation of the pope could make it valid.

[2] Strype's Life of Cranmer, p. 67.

[3] Burnet, History of the Reformation, II. p. 128. Collier, Eccles. Hist. II. p. 74. Both agree in condemning his conduct.

[4] Strype's Cranmer, p. 65.

constituted Cromwell his ecclesiastical vicegerent; gave him rank above the primate himself; and invested him with functions never before exercised by a layman: so that he assumed in fact a sacerdotal character, and was addressed by the pompous title of "Most Reverend Lord in God." When Cromwell fell, it was one of the charges against him, that he had invaded the prerogatives of the Christian priesthood[1].

It is important to notice the prominent activity of a layman in the earliest proceedings of the Reformation. By Cromwell some of the most important changes in the religious condition of England, more particularly the visitation and subsequent dissolution of the monasteries, were accomplished. He even took a part more decidedly theological. The Articles of 1536—the earliest public confession of the English Church—after approval and correction by the king, were first signed in Convocation by Cromwell, as his vicegerent, and then by the two archbishops and the other prelates and inferior clergy, in succession: and somewhat later in the same year, the Injunctions relating to religion were issued in the king's name by Cromwell alone, without consulting the clergy. "This," says Burnet, "was the first act of pure supremacy done by the king. For in all that went before, he had the concurrence of the two Convocations[2]."

A small practical work, answering the purpose of an elementary catechism, had been issued by royal authority, under

---

[1] Strype's Eccles. Mem. I. ch. 34, 35.—A letter addressed to Cromwell by a monk, during the visitation of the monasteries, begins in the following strain: —"Most reverend Lord in God, second person in this land of England, endowed with all grace and goodness," etc., p. 411.

[2] Burnet, Hist. Reform. Book III. p. 225. The Articles insisted on the following points, as necessary to salvation:—"The acceptance of the whole Bible and the three Creeds; the Sacrament of Baptism, essential for washing away original sin; the Sacrament of Penance, not excluding the use of auricular Confession; the Sacrament of the Altar verily, substantially, and really containing, under the form of bread and wine, the very body and blood of Christ, who was born of the Virgin and suffered on the Cross; Justification, a perfect renovation in Christ, but contrition, faith and charity to be included in it." As conducing to order and decency, though not expressly commanded by God—"the use of images and invocation of the saints were not to be forbidden, if rightly understood; rites and ceremonies might be retained as possessing a spiritual significance; praying for the dead in masses and exequies on their behalf, was declared a practice good and charitable in itself—if the abuses of the popish doctrine of purgatory should be clearly put away."—In these Articles, four out of the seven Sacraments of the Catholic Church were passed over in silence. The Injunctions were intended to enforce the articles and good discipline among the clergy, who were required by them to set forth periodically to the

the title of the King's Primer, during the preceding year [1]. In 1537, the Articles were explained and illustrated in a work entitled, 'The Institution of a Christian Man,' **which was** drawn up in Convocation, and published by the joint authority of the bishops. It was called, in consequence, the Bishops' Book. It betrays a strong attachment to the old faith, though written with an obvious design of reconciling the Reformers and the doctrinal Romanists or those who differed from the Papists only in the question of the supremacy. It recognizes the seven sacraments, **but** places those of Baptism, Penance **and the Altar, in the first** rank. It affirms that all particular churches are parts of **the** Church Universal, denying the superiority of any one of them **over the rest**; and maintains that all bishops are equal **in jurisdiction and** authority—their powers having been communicated to them by Christ, and continued amongst them in due succession from the Apostles. This claim of a divine right for the episcopal **order, independent** of the civil magistrate, indicates the **influences under** which the work had been prepared. A strong tide of reaction had set in against the measures of Cromwell and Cranmer, which overpowered all resistance. Henry was disturbed and alarmed by the rumours of spreading heresies. The domestic influences which, **in** the days of Anne Boleyn and **Jane** Seymour, inclined him to favour the Reformers, had ceased; and his fickle temper was left exposed to the full force of **the** representations of the Catholic party. Swayed by them, he gave his consent to the introduction of an Act "for abolishing diversity of opinions in **certain** articles concerning Christian Religion." The tendency of this celebrated statute, usually called "The Six Articles," is sufficiently marked by the fact, that Cranmer, in spite of his caution, and though the king had requested him to go out of the House, since he could not vote for the Act, was compelled to protest against it; while Shaxton and Latimer, to escape the necessity of reading it from their pulpits, threw up their **bishoprics**. It was, in fact, a re-enactment of the old religion, **hailed** with joy by all who **were averse to** the progress of reformation. In the Six

people the King's **supremacy** and the usurpation of the Pope. The most important feature in them, was the direction to teach children the Lord's Prayer, the Creed, and the Ten Commandments, in English. Burnet, Book III., Collection of Records and Addenda.

[1] Strype's Eccles. Mem. I. ch. **31**.

Articles, the doctrines of transubstantiation, of communion in one kind, of the celibacy of the clergy, of the divine obligation of vows of chastity, of private masses, and of auricular confession—were distinctly asserted; the denial of the first, made a capital offence without the power of abjuration; and any speaking or writing against the five last, judged felony[1]. Only one mitigation of this terrible Act was conceded: parties accused under it, were not brought before the ecclesiastical courts, but were entitled to a trial by jury. Cromwell's fall soon after followed. With him the office of ecclesiastical vicegerent ceased, and the triumph of his enemies, the doctrinal Romanists, was complete. But in both the parties by which the king's council was now divided, the acknowledgment of the royal supremacy was equally decisive and explicit; they even vied with each other in professions of subserviency to his will. Gardiner and Bonner, as well as Cranmer, had taken out commissions, to hold their bishoprics from the Crown, and only during the royal pleasure. It was probably the firmness with which Cranmer adhered to this first principle of the English Reformation, combined with his consummate tact and policy, that enabled him to maintain to the last his place in his master's favour, amidst the perilous machinations which constantly beset him[2].

The last formulary of belief set forth in the reign of Henry, was digested out of the answers to certain questions propounded to two committees of bishops and theologians, that had been appointed by the king, and confirmed by Parliament in 1540. It was entitled, "The Necessary Doctrine and Erudition of a Christian Man;" and has been sometimes called from the way in which it had been prepared, "The King's Book," to distinguish it from the earlier work "The Institution, or Bishops' Book," which it was intended to supersede[3]. In the deliberations which preceded its appearance, Cranmer stood almost alone in his clear Protestant view of the various points that came under consideration, and in his strong assertion of the regal supremacy as the only legitimate source of ecclesiastical power. On the subject of apostolical authority, he decided against most of his colleagues, that the Apostles had no command or supremacy over a Christian people, but merely acted as counsellors in

---

[1] Burnet, Hist. Reform. I. p. 259. [2] Collier, II. p. 170.
[3] Carwithen's Hist. of the Church of England, vol. i.

the absence of a Christian prince; **maintaining that all Christian princes have the care of their subjects' souls immediately committed to them by God.** In the same spirit he argued, that in a land of infidels, a Christian prince may preach the **word of** God, and also constitute priests; that the power **of** excommunication is founded entirely on the positive law of a country,—that *without* that law priests may not, and that *with* it laymen may, excommunicate[1]. But he was unable to overcome the strong Romanist feeling of his associates. **Denying the supremacy of the bishop of Rome, maintaining the competency of every national church to govern and reform itself,** and in the definition **of** faith as well as on some other topics, pursuing **a sort** of middle **way between** the Romish and the Protestant view—this **work still** retained the seven sacraments, (though Cranmer **had contended** for only two,) together with the tenet of **the corporal presence** in the Eucharist; and, on the whole, was more positively **Catholic** in its tone than the preceding formularies. The "Necessary Doctrine and Erudition" was drawn up with great care and deliberation, and did not make its appearance till 1543. Before the close of Henry's reign, the rigour of the Six Articles **was** abated, though the execution of them was still left dependent on the **royal** will; and some further **measures were** taken for the **abolition** of superstitious practices[2].

The public **service** of the Church—with the exception of the Creed, **the Ten** Commandments, some prayers that **were** taught in the Primer or Catechism, and the litanies used in processions on festival days—was still conducted **in** Latin. Before the Reformation a different ritual called the Use, was observed in different parts of the kingdom. Thus the Use of Sarum prevailed in the south of England; the Use of York in the north; and the Use of Lincoln in the midland counties; while South and North Wales followed respectively the

---

[1] The discussions preparatory to the publication of the "Necessary Doctrine and Erudition," are given in the Appendix to Burnet, Book III. No. xxi. Burnet, vol. i. p. 289, notices the singularity of Cranmer's opinions about ecclesiastical offices, and says—though without stating his grounds for the assertion—that he afterwards changed them. Cranmer's language on the subject of ecclesiastical authority, seems to have varied at different periods of his life. See Collier, II. p. 198. It should, however, be observed, that, on this occasion, as Burnet has himself remarked, the answers to the questions were framed with great care, and must be regarded as a deliberate expression of opinion.

[2] Collier, II. pp. 188-204. Burnet, I. pp. 286-322. Carwithen, I. ch. vii.

customs of St. David's and of Hereford and Bangor. Of these Uses, that of Sarum was the most widely diffused. It has been asserted, that it was adopted in some part of France and even in Portugal[1]. To establish uniformity, sometime before the publication of the "Necessary Doctrine and Erudition," the rites and ceremonies of the Church appear to have been brought under review; and a new impression of the liturgy, according to the Use of Sarum, with corrections and omissions, was issued under royal authority, accompanied by a Rationale to explain the meaning and justify the usage of different parts of the service[2]. But this liturgy does not seem to have been everywhere introduced; in many churches, the breviaries and missals already in use were retained[3].

The most important event of this reign in its influence on the Reformation, was the sanction given by the king to the translation of the whole Bible into English. Before this occurred, some intrepid scholars, Tyndale, Myles Coverdale and Rogers, thwarted in their plans of serving divine truth by the jealousy of the hierarchy at home, had withdrawn to the Continent, and at different places, under great disadvantages, and amidst frequent perils, had made a version first of the New and then of the Old Testament. Copies of these versions crossed the sea into England; and though prohibited by the interference of the bishops and ordered to be burnt, still found extensive circulation among the people. At length through the influence of Cromwell and Cranmer with the king, orders were given for the publication of the entire Scriptures in the vulgar tongue. A Bible called Matthew's, published abroad and founded on the previous labours of Tyndale and Coverdale, was assumed as the basis of the new work; which was issued in 1539 under Cranmer's name and authority, and is known as "Cranmer's Bible" or the "Great Bible." This continued the authorized English version, till the appearance of the "Bishops' Bible" in 1568. Henry fixed its price by proclamation,

---

[1] Palmer's *Origines Liturgicæ*. Dissertation on Primitive Liturgies, Sect. xi. The Use of Sarum was of English origin, having been introduced by Osmund, bishop of that see, in 1078.

[2] Collier has transcribed the Rationale from the Cotton Library. The title of the authorized liturgy was as follows: "Portiforium secundum Usum Sarum, noviter impressum, et a plurimis purgatum mendis. In quo nomen Romano Pontifici falso ascriptum omittitur, una cum aliis quæ Christianissimi nostri regis statuto repugnant. Excusum Londini per Edvardum Whytchurch, 1541. Cum privilegio ad imprimendum solum." Collier, II. p. 191.

[3] Carwithen, vol. i.

and ordered a copy to be procured for every parish church before an appointed day. Bonner who was then bishop of London and distinguished by an officious obsequiousness to the royal pleasure, set up six copies fastened with chains to pillars in St. Paul's[1]. But the privilege apparently conferred by this ordinance, was soon restrained within very narrow limits. By an Act passed in 1542—chiefly, it is said, at the instance of Gardiner—the reading of the Bible was prohibited to all under the degrees of gentlemen and gentlewomen; and the king himself in the preface to the "Necessary Erudition," had declared that the reading of the Old and New Testament was not necessary for the laity, but that liberty or restraint in this matter must be referred to the laws and government[2].

[1] Strype's Cranmer, B. I. ch. xxi. Lewis's History of English Translations of the Bible, p. 187, 2nd edit.

[2] Collier, II. 188, 189.—The following may be taken as a brief account of the principal versions of the Scriptures into English.—Wycliffe's is usually considered the first translation of the whole Bible. It was made, not from the Greek, but from the Vulgate, and appeared some time subsequent to 1380. What versions existed in English before his time, is not very clearly ascertained. Sir Thomas More speaks of "translations done of old by virtuous and well-learned men, that before Wycliffe's days had been known and seen by the bishop of the diocese, and were used with devotion and soberness by good and Catholic folk:" but his expressions have been charged with vagueness and a confusion of dates. The dissemination of Lollardism in the fifteenth century, created an earnest desire to have access to the Scriptures in English. This is evident from the decree of a Convocation held under archbishop Arundel in 1408, which enacted that no unauthorized person should translate any portion of the Bible; and that no one, without the sanction of the bishop of the diocese or a provincial council, should read either in whole or in part any version made in Wycliffe's time or since. The versions made before Wycliffe's were sometimes in verse, and seem to have been chiefly of those parts of the Scripture that were read in the public service of the church, such as the Psalter and the Gospels. * Nearly contemporary with Wycliffe's, two other translations are said to have appeared;—one, it is supposed, by a follower of his, named Purvy or Purnay, preceded by a prologue, and distinguished from Wycliffe's in being less literal, and aiming only to give the sense; the other, by John de Trevisa, a Cornish gentleman and vicar of Berkeley, whom Bale and Fuller represent as joining with Wycliffe in strong opposition to the monastic orders. Fuller's Church History, Book IV. Sect. i.; Lewis's Complete History of Translations of the Bible into English, 2nd edit.; and the Historical Account of English Versions prefixed to Bagster's Hexapla.

Many of these earlier versions, or parts of them, were circulated in manuscript among the Lollards and first Protestants, before Tyndale and his coadjutors undertook the task described in the text. Tyndale's was the first translation of the New Testament into English direct from the Greek. He commenced soon after a translation of the Old Testament from the Hebrew, and executed the Pentateuch and the book of Jonah. In 1535, Myles Coverdale published the whole Bible in English, the translation of the Old Testament being his own or adopted by him, that of the New taking Tyndale's version as

In the statute declaring the royal supremacy, provision had been made for a reform of the canon or ecclesiastical law, which being of papal origin was unsuited to the present circumstances of the country; and a commission was appointed with that view. The work, however, was not prosecuted after its basis. In 1537 Tyndale's translations completed from the version of Coverdale, the whole revised by Rogers, were published under the title of Matthew's Bible. This appears to have been the groundwork of the edition which appeared in 1539, and is usually called Cranmer's Bible—either from having Cranmer's preface prefixed, or because it adopted his recension of the New Testament. The psalter of this version (probably by Rogers) is still retained in the English Liturgy. In the same year, another revision of the same text was issued by Richard Taverner, a layman, who devoted himself to theology, and after the fashion of those times, in the lack of good ministers, had a license from the king to preach. (See Fuller's account of his sermon at St. Mary's in Oxford, Church Hist. B. IX. Sect. i. 35.) In 1541, it was brought out by authority, under the title of the "Great Bible," or "Bible of the largest and greatest Volume," "overseen and perused" by Tonstal, bishop of Durham, and Heath, bishop of Rochester. The versions of Tyndale, Coverdale and Matthews were all first printed abroad. Meanwhile the English exiles at Geneva had been employed on another translation of the Scriptures; and among them were Myles Coverdale and John Knox. This version was first published complete in 1560. A new impression, revised and corrected, was prepared in 1565; but its immediate issue was checked, from the bishops demanding too direct a control over it. It was nevertheless reprinted in 1576, and again in 1579. It had no public authority, but was much used in private, especially among those who were Puritanically inclined. Archbishop Parker, dissatisfied with the version commonly in use, designed a new translation; and under his auspices, what is called the "Bishops' Bible" appeared in 1568. It was only, however, a revision and correction, not a fresh translation. The whole Bible was distributed into parcels, and assigned to different hands. Sandys, bishop of Worcester, had a chief share in the work, and the primate himself superintended the whole. The Rhemish version was made from the Vulgate by Catholic exiles, and chiefly promoted by Cardinal Allen. Its publication began in 1582 with the New Testament, at Rheims; but it was not completed till 1610, at Douay.

In the reign of James, of the two versions in use, the Bishops' Bible being disliked by the Puritans, and the Genevan with its notes, being objected to by the king and the bishops, steps were taken for bringing out a new translation that might satisfy both parties. Some of the leading bishops were at first opposed to the scheme, but at length, in deference to the king's wishes, the task was commenced. It was a result of the conference at Hampton Court. The "Bishops' Bible" was assumed as the basis of the work. Forty-seven translators were appointed by the two Universities and the king; and very full instructions were delivered to them. The version was reviewed by twelve scholars, selected out of the whole number of translators. Three years were employed on the undertaking; and the Bible, in its new form, appeared in 1611. Strype's Lives of Cranmer (B. I. ch. xxi.), Parker (B. III. ch. vi. and xxi.), and Whitgift (fol. p. 500). Lewis's History of Translations. Newcome's Historical View of English Biblical Translations. Fuller's Church Hist. B. X. Sect. iii. Account prefixed to Bagster's 'Hexapla,' which is very minute and full.

In 1657, a committee of Parliament was appointed to procure a new trans-

the enactment of the **Six** Articles; **though Cranmer** repeatedly tried to convince the **king, that the** pontifical **code was no** longer applicable to the ecclesiastical **condition of** England[1].

At the close, then, of Henry's reign—notwithstanding the **separation** from Rome, and notwithstanding the strong Protestant tendencies of Cranmer—the Mass was still celebrated in Latin; the authorized confession of faith differed in no essential particular from the ancient creed; and the papal canons were still in force:—in other words, the Church, though it **had changed** its head, **was in** doctrine, ritual and discipline as **Romanist** as ever and much less free.

SECTION III.

THE REFORMATION OF EDWARD VI.

Events took a different turn on the accession of Edward VI. Indeed, the Reformation can hardly be said to have begun before **his** reign. He had been educated by Coxe, a decided Reformer; and **the** protector Somerset warmly espoused the Protestant cause. Cranmer immediately adopted measures for prosecuting **his** own views. He took out his episcopal commission anew from **the** young king; and in his speech at the coronation, reminded his sovereign, that his right to the crown was derived **immediately** from God, and wholly independent of all sacerdotal sanction and **ceremony**. In conjunction with Ridley, he appointed **visitors, accompanied** by zealous preachers of the new faith, to perform a progress through the kingdom, and inspect the different dioceses, and make gradual preparation for more extensive change. This visitation appears to have been regulated **by the** Articles and Injunctions that had been drawn **up for a** similar purpose by

lation of the Bible. Whitlocke had the chief care of this business, and often consulted with Cudworth respecting it. But the design never came to effect. Lewis's History of Transl. p. 355. Biographia Britannica, Cudworth [E]. It thus appears, that the early labours of Tyndale, Coverdale and Rogers furnished the basis on which our present authorized version rests. Dr. Geddes (quoted by Newcome, p. 181) asserts from habitual comparison, that James's translators have made large use of the Geneva version.

[1] Carwithen, I. ch. x.

Cromwell in the preceding reign.—Still there were many circumstances to check the impulse with which the Reformation had proceeded in other countries. Two elements of opinion were in latent conflict throughout the land; and restrictions were laid on preaching, to prevent the universal dissensions that must else have broken out. The majority of the nation and the great body of the clergy were attached to the ancient faith; and though pretty well reconciled to the changes of the late reign, were not very willing to proceed further. At the coronation, mass was celebrated with the elevation of the host after the old usage[1]. Cranmer was timid and cautious, always disposed to yield to public opinion. Ridley was averse from the extreme views of the more ardent Reformers, and a firm supporter of the episcopal discipline; so that he has been called the pillar of Protestant Episcopacy[2]. The two grand points on which he dissented from the Church of Rome, were, —its idolatrous abuse of the Lord's Supper, and the usurpation of the pope.

To promote their object of gradually inuring the people to a reformation of religion, Cranmer and Ridley published twelve Homilies on Christian faith and duty, to be read by the curates on Sundays—composed with the special view of reconciling the moderate Romanists and Reformers, but still insisting on faith as the root of all moral goodness, and on the necessity of Christ's satisfaction to the divine justice to procure the salvation of men. The Romanist party resisted the introduction of these Homilies; and Gardiner objected in particular to the Homily "On the Salvation of mankind by Christ only," which was said to be composed by Cranmer. To the Homilies they soon after added a Catechism which contained, not in the usual form of question and answer, an exposition of the Creed, the Ten Commandments, and the Lord's Prayer, the doctrine of the three sacraments of Baptism, the Eucharist, and Penance, and strong warnings against the sin of idolatry. This Catechism, though published with Cranmer's name in the title-page, asserted more strongly the divine institution of Episcopacy, and the necessity of reviving the primitive discipline, than was in unison with his language on other occasions[3]. It

---

[1] Strype's Cranmer, p. 143.   [2] Carwithen, I. p. 269.

[3] The matter of this Catechism is said by Strype (Life of Cranmer, B. II. ch. v.) to be taken from a German work, that had been previously turned into Latin. It was different from the Catechism inserted in the First Service Book

bears traces, therefore, of the influence that was still ascendant. They then proceeded to the preparation of the Communion service, as a substitute for the ancient Mass.

In all these works, their principle was avowedly conciliatory and conservative. They wished to retain of the ancient doctrines and formularies whatever was not inconsistent with indispensable reform, and to shun the extremes both of the bigoted Papists and of the ultra Protestants. The weight and numbers of the Romanist party rendered it necessary to make some compromise with them. The most gratifying evidence of the progress of the Protestant cause was the repeal of the statute of the Six Articles and of the Acts against the Lollards[1], with the renewal of the injunction to set up in every parish church a copy of the Bible, accompanied now by a translation of Erasmus's paraphrase of the New Testament. In the same year it was enacted, that in place of the ancient *congé d'élire*, the bishops should be appointed at once by letters patent from the Crown, and that they should henceforth exercise no jurisdiction but in the king's name[2].

Their next object was to draw up a book of Common Prayer and other devotional offices. That the establishment of a form of public service should have preceded the publication of articles of faith—so contrary to the practice of the continental Reformers—is a significant fact in the history of the English Church. It was owing to the caution of Cranmer and the judgment of Ridley, who thought it desirable to reconcile the bulk of the nation to the changes that were proceeding in religion, by the use of a liturgy not too widely divergent from the forms they were accustomed to, before they set forth a public declaration of belief. It is said, that Cranmer had prepared a service of a more decidedly Protestant tone, but that

of 1549, which, so far as it goes, is substantially the same with that in the present Prayer Book, containing only the Creed, Ten Commandments, and Lord's Prayer, with the questions and answers pertaining to them—the part relative to the sacraments being added for the first time by bishop Overall, to satisfy the objections of the Puritans, after the conference at Hampton Court in 1604. Both the Catechisms now mentioned, were again different from a third, which appears to have been sometimes confounded with them—a Latin Catechism entitled, " Catechismus Christianæ Disciplinæ summam continens," which was issued by royal authority in the last year of king Edward's reign, and after its revisal by Nowell, Dean of St. Paul's, acquired high repute as a manual of the Protestant faith established in England, during the reign of Elizabeth. Shepherd on the Common Prayer, II. p. 269, note.

[1] Taylor's Book of Rights, p. 143.   [2] Burnet, II. p. 43.

the Romanist influence was too powerful in the committee charged with the business, to admit of his procuring its adoption. Many of the more zealous Protestants and the Calvinistic Reformers generally (though there were exceptions) disliked a liturgy; and the course taken by the divines of Edward's time, while it conciliated numbers who were attached to the old religion, distinguished the Church of England by a broad external sign from the Reformed Churches of the continent, and has had a lasting influence on its constitution and character. In the composition of the Prayer Book, a respect for antiquity and established usage—characteristic from the first of the measures of the Anglican reformation—largely predominated. A great part of it was translated from the Latin of the previous Catholic service, enriched by selections from the ancient Gallican, Spanish, Alexandrine and Oriental liturgies.

The English ritual, exclusive of the occasional offices, consists of three principal parts—the Common Prayer for morning and evening (the ancient Matins and Even-Song), the Litany, and the Communion. In the old Catholic ritual, there were appropriate offices for the different canonical hours during the day. Out of these offices the substance of the Common Prayer was composed and abridged—the morning prayer being taken from the Matins, Lauds and Prime—and the evening, from the Vespers and Compline. Parts of both these services are said by Palmer to be found in rituals that were in use before and immediately after the Conquest.—Litanies are characteristic of the Eastern Church, out of which they have been imported into the West, where they were anciently called Rogations or Supplications. They were at first employed in processions on festival days. We are told by Palmer, that an ancient litany of the English Church, referred by him to the eighth century, contains much the same matter, and in the same form of petition and response, as that which has been incorporated into the present Service Book. When it was adopted by the Reformers, the invocations to the saints were omitted, and it was enriched and embellished by sentiments suited to the altered circumstances of the times.—The eucharistic service constitutes the proper liturgy, though the name has been extended to every prescribed form of Common Prayer. This was adopted from the Catholic office of the Mass, which was thus converted into a general Communion in both kinds. It had been drawn up, as already stated, after much deliberation, before the other parts of the public service[1], and was now incorporated with the rest.

The first Service Book of Edward VI. was issued in 1549, and is distinguished from the several revisions which succeeded it, by a closer approximation to the forms and language of the old Catholic Missal. It chiefly followed the Use of Sarum, though the customs of York and Hereford were not overlooked[2]. It commenced the morning service, like the ancient office for Matins, with the Lord's Prayer. The Communion was described as, "The Supper of the Lord, commonly called the Mass;" and various directions were given about the vestments of the priest and his attendants, which were omitted in the subsequent revisions. In the rubric of this part of the service, many Catholic terms remained—*corporas* (corporale, the linen cloth of the altar, whereon the elements were placed), *patin* and *chalice*; and there was an instruction to put "a little pure and clean water" to the wine. During the prayer—"with thy holy spirit and word vouchsafe to bl+ess and sanct+ify these thy gifts and creatures of bread and wine, that they may be unto us the body and blood of thy beloved Son Jesus Christ"—the priest was to cross the elements. At the same time the rubric added, "these words to be said without any elevation or showing the Sacrament to the people." In the prayer for the church militant, there was a thanksgiving "for the wonderful grace and virtue in all the saints," and "chiefly in the glorious and most blessed virgin Mary, mother of Jesus Christ, our Lord and God." The flesh and blood of Jesus Christ were spoken of, as "holy mysteries,"—terms omitted in the later revisions. In the act of communion, these words were used—"The body (blood) of our Lord Jesus Christ which was given (shed) for thee, preserve thy body and soul unto everlasting life."

Nevertheless, strong anti-papal expressions occur in the course of the service. In the litany is a prayer for deliverance "from the bishop of Rome and all his detestable enormities;"

---

[1] See Collier's account of the preliminary discussions respecting it, II. p. 243 et seq.

[2] Hermann's Consultation is also said to have been used.—Riddle's Ecclesiastical Chronology, p. 358. Hermann was archbishop of Cologne, in the middle of the sixteenth century, and submitted to the subjects of his electorate a scheme of reformation drawn up by Bucer and Melanchthon. Schröckh, Kirchengesch. seit der Reformation, I. p. 627.

and in the exhortations to frequent communion and due preparation for it, which are said to have been adapted from the missals of York and Hereford and Salisbury, and other ancient liturgies—it is strongly urged, that without repentance, and reconciliation to God through the virtue of Christ's passion, the absolution of the priest is unavailing, and that spiritual communion of the body and blood of Christ is dependent on penitence and faith. The divided state of public opinion is indicated by its being left to people's own judgment, to use auricular or general confession, as they deem best, without judging other men, and in following the rule of charity[1].

Such were some of the peculiarities of Edward VI.'s first Service Book. After its completion by the committee, it was revised and approved by a majority of the two Convocations of York and Canterbury. It passed the Commons; but it did not get through the Lords without a protest from several lay peers, and some bishops, three of whom had been members of the committee[2].

In the meantime, with the progress of the Reformation at home and abroad, the influence of foreign Protestants began to be more sensibly felt in England. On all sides there was a tendency towards union, to make head more effectually against the awakened strength of the papal cause, now in process of active organization during the protracted sittings of the Council of Trent. Cranmer and Melanchthon wished to have convened a meeting of the heads of the Reformed Churches in England. It is said, that neither Calvin nor Bullinger had any invincible objection to episcopacy in itself, and would have gladly entered into closer alliance with the English Church, if they could have obtained the benefit without submitting to a papal imposition of hands[3]. England at this time, as Holland in a later age, seems to have been a general asylum for the persecuted. During the reign of Edward, there were Dutch, Walloon, French, Italian, Polish and even Spanish congregations of Protestants in London[4]. Bucer, Fagius and Peter Martyr, friends of Calvin, came over

---

[1] Keeling's *Liturgiæ Britannicæ*. The form of communion in Edward VI.'s First Book is given by Shepherd, On the Common Prayer, II. p. 236–255, from Whitchurch's edition.—Compare Hippolytus and his Age, by the Chevalier Bunsen, III. pp. 296–303.

[2] Carwithen, I. ch. viii.

[3] Strype's Life of Parker, p. 140, Oxford edit. 1821. Strype's Cranmer, pp. 234–246.

from the continent, and lectured on divinity—the two former at Cambridge, and the latter at Oxford; and it is undeniable, that they introduced a different spirit from that which had hitherto swayed the councils of the English Reformers. The first Service Book was submitted to their criticism; and in 1551 Bucer published his animadversions upon it, with those of Calvin and other foreign Protestants, in a long treatise, wherein he strongly urged a further simplification of the English service, and the removal of many forms and expressions which in their judgment still left it too nearly approximated to the old Popish ritual[1].

Under these influences the second Service Book of king Edward was put forth, in which the English ritual was reduced nearly to the form in which it now exists. The expressions most offensive to the Reformers were taken away or qualified, though many things were still left, which they rather tolerated than approved. The Exhortation, Confession and Absolution were now first added, as the commencement of the Morning Prayer. According to the earlier ritual, the whole service was performed in the choir, and during prayer the priest, whether standing or kneeling, had his face turned towards the altar. This practice was objected to by Bucer and Calvin; and it was reformed according to the usage which now prevails. Bucer in the same spirit wished to unite the choir with the body of the church, as the separation between them seemed to imply a peculiar sanctity in the clergy and an undue reverence for them—and to convert the altar into a simple table standing east and west[2]. But this change he could not completely effect. In consequence of similar suggestions, the habits of the clergy, which many Reformers objected to as having a superstitious significance—though not abolished, were simplified[3].

The character of a church may be considered as fairly indicated by the light in which it exhibits the Sacraments, and the efficacy which it attaches to their due administration. Edward VI.'s second Service Book demands in this respect a brief notice.——Mr. Hallam has remarked, with the masculine sense which distinguishes his judgments[4], that there cannot at bottom be more than two opinions respecting the elements

[1] Collier gives the substance of Bucer's objections, II. p. 296 et seq.
[2] Which would reverse the preceding position of the altar.
[3] Carwithen, I. p. 339.   [4] Constit. Hist. I. p. 124.

in the Lord's Supper; that of Zwingli, which regarded them simply as commemorative symbols; and that of the Papists, which supposed them converted in the sacrifice of the Mass by a standing miracle into the actual body and blood of Jesus Christ; and that the intermediate theories of Luther and Calvin derive an appearance of support only from the use of vague and obscure terms. The policy of the English Reformers, whose object was to reconcile the bulk of the nation, still essentially Catholic, to as much of the Protestant doctrine as they could bear—led them naturally to express themselves on this subject with a studied indeterminateness of phrase, so as to embrace in one form of Communion very opposite views without mutual repulsion. Bucer who exercised much influence on their deliberations respecting the Sacrament, and sided with Calvin in this controversy, possessed just that kind of metaphysical subtlety which fitted him for the task of tracing out shadowy distinctions and combining inconsistencies[1]. Bucer contended, that the words of Scripture must be adhered to, but their meaning not too closely pressed; since being significant of spiritual mysteries, they are to be understood in faith. He affirmed, that Christ is present with us in the Sacrament, not *really* and *substantially*[2], (since his body is in Heaven,) but as the bread and wine, exhibitive of his body and blood, are received in faith[3]. The influence of these views may be traced in the looseness and generality of the language employed in the English Communion Service. The bread and wine are called simply the body and blood of Christ, and represented as the vehicles of a divine life, when they are spiritually received in penitence and faith; but the rubric distinctly repudiates the doctrine of any corporal presence of Christ. The language of the Catechism respecting the elements, which was added in 1604, is equally vague and general. —To the words of the first Service Book used in the act of communicating, expressions were added in the second, signifying that the act was commemorative—"Take and eat this in remembrance that Christ died for thee." The object of the commemoration is declared to be—"Christ's one oblation of himself once offered, as a full, perfect and sufficient

---

[1] See the discussions between him and Peter Martyr, Collier, II. p. 273.
[2] *Realiter et substantialiter.*
[3] Sententious Sayings of Master Martin Bucer upon the Lord's Supper.— Strype's Cranmer, Append. No. xlvi.

sacrifice, oblation and satisfaction for the sins of the whole world."

Intimately connected with the Common Prayer and the Communion, are the offices for Catechizing, Baptism and Confirmation. These appear to have formed originally parts of the same office, as the acts themselves immediately followed each other in the ancient church. They were exhibited in this order in the first Service Book, (the materials[1] of the two last offices being taken from the Uses of Salisbury and York,) where the rite of Baptism was preceded by an act of exorcism, and the ceremonies of anointing and investiture called the chrism. These relics of Catholic superstition were removed from the subsequent revision, though the prayers still retain some traces of the original character of the service. The fundamental idea of the office, **as it now stands, is that** of man's being born in sin, and regenerated and united with Christ's mystical body in Baptism.

Among other reforms, a committee was appointed to prepare a new service for ordaining ministers of the Church. The old usages were laid aside, and imposition of hands with prayer was now adopted as the Scriptural mode. Only three ecclesiastical orders—bishops, priests, and deacons—were recognized; but they were required to derive their functions from episcopal authority[2].

By these labours, including the preparation of forty-two Articles of Faith[3], the external framework of the Church of England was completed in the year 1552, when the second Service Book superseded the first by Act of Parliament, though several members of the Upper House temporal and spiritual recorded their dissent. Uniformity was now enforced with a terrible rigour. No diversity of public worship, or in the administration of the sacraments, or in the appointment of ministers, was tolerated. For the first transgression the offender was to be imprisoned six months without bail; for the second, one year; and for the third, during his whole life.

---

[1] Palmer, II. p. 174, 202.
[2] Carwithen, I.
[3] Not published till May, 1553, just before the king's death. Lamb's Hist. Account of the Thirty-nine Articles, p. 3.

SECTION IV.

FIXATION OF THE CONSTITUENT ELEMENTS OF THE ANGLICAN CHURCH, AFTER THE ACCESSION OF ELIZABETH.

On the accession of Elizabeth, the second Service Book was restored, though there were many dissentients in the Lords; and the Queen herself who had embraced the Protestant cause more from policy than affection, did not give it her cordial approval. Some passages were therefore omitted, out of deference to these feelings, as the petition in the litany for deliverance from the tyranny of the pope, while others were remodelled according to the form of the first Book. But the substance of the service continued the same. The new rubric directed in general terms, that the chancels of the churches, which the Reformers of Edward's reign had wished to deprive of all resemblance to an altar, should remain as they had been in all times past; and the ecclesiastical habits, enjoined in the first Service Book and prohibited in the second, were ordered to be resumed. On the whole, the alterations introduced at the revision in the first year of Elizabeth's reign, softened down the harsher expressions of Protestant feeling, and tended to bring back the service a step nearer to the Catholic standard.

The practice which commenced at the Reformation, of reading a portion of the Communion office with the Common Prayer and the Litany, when there is no actual Communion, affords another trace of the derivation of the Morning Service of the Church from the ancient Mass. The eucharistic sacrifice with the elevation and adoration of the elements, constituted the most important part of the old service. By way of distinction it was called the *Canon*[1]. This it was found impracticable to replace every Sunday by an actual distribution of the bread and wine to communicants; for which however the solitary communion of the priest was no longer admitted as a substitute. The result was the retention of only the introductory and concluding portions of the Communion office: the place once occupied by the sacrificial act, was on ordinary occasions left a blank, after a precedent of the Middle Ages, where the Mass with a similar omission was called *Missa Sicca* or *Missa Nautica*[2]. Bishop Hall has very fairly stated the fact as to the composition of the Liturgy, in his observation,

---

[1] *Canon Missæ.*—Du Cange, Glossar. in voc.   [2] Palmer, II. p. 164.

that "the English Prayer-book was not taken out of the Mass, but that the Mass was thrust out of the Prayer-book." James I. in his coarse way, while he was yet a zealous Presbyterian, expressed nearly the same idea when he said, that "the Liturgy was an evil-said Mass in English without the liftings." The last alterations in the Book of Common Prayer, reducing it to its present form, were made after the Restoration, as the result of the conference which Charles II. had appointed between a select number of Episcopalian and Presbyterian divines. Little was to be expected from the temper in which the parties met. The proposals of the Presbyterians were abruptly rejected; and the changes introduced, mostly at the suggestion of High Churchmen, seemed purposely framed, as bishop Burnet agrees with Baxter in declaring—rather to prevent than facilitate any union of the two bodies[1]. The peculiar character which the Liturgy took in the first age of the Reformation, has therefore subsisted unaltered to the present day[2].

[1] Neal, II. p. 613.
[2] The English Prayer Book has passed through the following revisions. Its basis, as stated in the text, was the use of Sarum,—the most widely diffused formulary of the old English Catholic Ritual. From this was taken in 1549, with various omissions and additions, the First Service Book of Edward VI. This was followed in 1552, by the Second. The revision under Elizabeth occurred in 1559, when the prayers for the sovereign and the clergy—taken, it is said, from the Sacramentary of Gregory the Great (Carwithen, II.), were inserted. Some slight alterations were introduced by order of James I. in 1604, as one of the results of the conference at Hampton Court. In 1662, according to archbishop Tenison, about six hundred small alterations and additions were made, but not of a kind to remove the scruples of the Presbyterians. At the same time some fresh prayers were added, as those for the 30th of January and the 29th of May, forms to be used at sea, and a new office for the administration of baptism to adults. (Neal, II. ch. vi.)

A high-churchman, well qualified to give an opinion—the late Alexander Knox—has observed, that these changes, minute and unimportant as they appear, sometimes only affecting the rubrics, have silently, and as it were by stealth, imparted to the Liturgy, and especially to the Communion Service, a more Catholic tone than they possessed previous to this revision; and that the effect is in a great measure due to the closer study of the Prayer Book by the Episcopalian clergy during their depression, their deeper insight into its peculiar character, and their familiar acquaintance with the early fathers of the Church, from whom so large a portion of its materials has been derived. (Remains, vol. i. pp. 59, 66.)

When the question of a Comprehension was under consideration in the reign of William III., some further amendments of the Liturgy were proposed, which fell to the ground with the Comprehension itself.

In 1637 a revision of the Liturgy was prepared by Laud, at the command of Charles I., for the use of the Scottish Church. This Liturgy, the basis of that

Whatever objections may be taken to the Liturgy as a whole, the excellence of particular parts cannot be disputed. Many of its prayers and collects are surpassingly beautiful, models of devotional composition, embodying some grand and holy thought, in diction venerable from its antique simplicity, and steeped in the richest spiritual unction. The deep religious convictions of the early Reformers had a marked effect on their language. It has nothing hollow and artificial. It lies close, as it were, to the thoughts which it utters, and seems the natural overflow of a full soul. All that has come to us from them, bears this character. Even when they took the material from another language, it underwent a change, and appeared to imbibe an element of new life in passing through their minds[1]; as every one must feel who has compared the richness and deep-toned pathos of many passages in the

---

still in use among the Scottish Episcopalians, is said to bear more resemblance, especially in the office of the Eucharist, to the First, than to the Second, Service Book of Edward VI. It is deserving of notice, that the revisions of 1604 and of 1637 were put forth by royal proclamation, without any reference to the resolutions of Parliament. The temper of the two first Stuarts is conspicuous in the imperious style of both these proclamations. "We will not give way," says James, "to any to presume, that our own judgment, having determined in a matter of this weight, shall be swayed to alteration by the frivolous suggestions of any light spirit." His son adopts a still more insolent tone to the Scottish authorities, who were ordered to announce the new Liturgy at the market-crosses and other public places throughout the realm:—"Our will is, and we charge you straitly and command,"—"that our subjects conform themselves to the said public form of worship, which is the only form which we (having taken the counsel of our clergy) think fit to be used in God's public worship in this our kingdom."—These several revisions of the Liturgy have been recently collected and published together, in a work by the Rev. William Keeling, entitled, 'Liturgiæ Britannicæ' (2nd edition, 1851), where for the sake of readier comparison, they are arranged in parallel columns. The two Service Books and other documents relating to the Reformation of Edward VI., form one of the volumes issued by the Parker Society, which has been edited by the Rev. J. Ketley, 1844. Compare the 'Reliquiæ Liturgicæ,' and the 'Fragmenta Liturgica,' collected by the Rev. Peter Hall of Bath; also Bunsen's Hippolytus, III. pp. 310–330, with Appendix, note D. During the conference at the Savoy in 1662, Baxter offered for consideration a reformed Liturgy, which he had drawn up for the use of those who objected to the old one. It is given at the end of the first volume of Calamy's Abridgment. It is richly scriptural in its phraseology, and breathes a deep and fervent devotion; but its long unbroken addresses, so different from the short prayers, the varied forms, and frequently interposed responses, of the Anglican Service Book, have so marked a Puritan character, that it is not surprising, it found little favour with those who had formed their taste on the received model, and were resolved on Uniformity.

[1] No one can be insensible to a certain quaint beauty in the ecclesiastical Latinity. Yet the language of the Romans, so practical and business-like, so

Common Prayer with the cold, hard meagreness of the original Latin.

An important element in the constitution of a Church, is its government and discipline. In England, the ancient framework of the Catholic hierarchy was not broken up at the Reformation. The bishops still exercised jurisdiction in their respective dioceses, and retained their seats in the House of Lords; and the Convocation which represented in its two Houses the whole body of the clergy, was regularly summoned with every session of Parliament. But the laws by which the Church had been governed, required essential modifications, after it had ceased to be connected with Rome, and become an independent national communion. In the reign of Edward VI. under an Act of Parliament passed in 1549[1], a commission was appointed, consisting of divines, canonists and common lawyers, to draw up a body of ecclesiastical laws, in prosecution of a design which had already been conceived under Henry VIII. Cranmer was very active in this undertaking; but the king died before the work could receive his confirmation, and the project was never revived. This compilation, which is still extant, was framed after the model of the Pandects of Justinian. They who have examined it, affirm, that it discovers more of a sacerdotal tendency than

admirably fashioned to the purposes of war, and politics, and jurisprudence, never seems an adequate vehicle of those vast and deep ideas of the spiritual, which enter into the very essence of Christianity. It is one proof of the wonderful power of this religion, that it should have succeeded to such a degree in subduing so refractory an instrument to its own ends, and adapting to the passionate strains of self-reproach and intense devotion, the abrupt and imperious speech of a nation of soldiers. It is impossible to read a page of the Confessions of Augustine, whose earnest spirit has left such deep traces on the language of the whole Western Church, without feeling how great was the change which had taken place since the time of Tacitus and Seneca; and that, while the mass of individual words continues nearly the same, their collocation and use imply the presence of a new organic agency which had revolutionized the old world of thought, and created a moral scenery altogether different from that with which those great writers were familiar. Still, even in the Latin of Augustine, the genius of Christianity seems to live a sort of exile and captive; whereas in the German languages, it meets the element designed for it by providence, and finds a congenial resting-place and home. When the old Mass-book was transformed into the English Liturgy, the spiritual element was liberated, and assumed its natural utterance.—On the capacity of Latin for theological and ecclesiastical purposes, see the preface to Woodham's edition of the Apologeticus of Tertullian, xxii. xxiii.

[1] The Commission was not actually nominated till 1551. A preceding Act under Henry VIII. had been passed in 1543. Lamb's Historical Account of the Thirty-nine Articles, p. 2.

might have been expected from the known principles of Cranmer, and that it retains much of the substance, and more of the spirit, of the pontifical law[1]. In 1565, archbishop Parker issued under the Queen's sanction a body of Articles and Ordinances for regulating the discipline of the clergy, many of whom had scruples about the ceremonies and habits of the Church.—In 1604, a book of Canons which had been collected by Bancroft, bishop of London, out of the Articles, Injunctions, and Synodical Acts of the reigns of Edward and Elizabeth, was passed by both Houses of Convocation and afterwards ratified by the King's letters patent. The last attempt to compile a body of laws for the government of the Church, was in 1640, on the very eve of the civil war, when Laud produced in Convocation a commission under the Great Seal for altering the old canons and framing new. These canons were of a very arbitrary character, and became exceedingly obnoxious, especially from the oath enjoined in them against all innovations in the doctrine and discipline of the Church, which, from the looseness of its wording, has acquired the name of the *et cætera* oath[2].

It is remarkable, that none of these canons were ever confirmed by Parliament; so that, although they have still a kind of authority founded on usage, and regulate the practice of the ecclesiastical courts, they have no force in opposition to statute and common law[3]. The Long Parliament denied the power of Convocation to frame laws even in matters of doctrine and discipline, without the consent of the civil legislature. Originally the two Houses of Convocation formed a sort of distinct estate in the realm, sitting side by side with Parliament, granting subsidies to the Crown, and enacting laws for the government of the Church. These high prerogatives were gradually restrained by the royal supremacy, by acts of Parliament, and by doctrines established in the courts of common law. It was ruled at last, that the clergy could not even tax themselves without parliamentary sanction; and in the reign of Charles II. the practice of ecclesiastical taxa-

---

[1] Carwithen, I. x. It was entitled "Reformatio Legum Ecclesiasticarum," and put into very correct and elegant Latin by Dr. Haddon, University orator of Cambridge, assisted by Sir John Cheke. Burnet (II. p. 196–202) and Collier (II. p. 326–333) have given an abstract of its contents.

[2] Collier, II. p. 793.

[3] See Sir Michael Foster's Examination of the Scheme of Church Power laid down in bishop Gidson's Codex Juris Ecclesiastici Anglicani, etc.

tion silently expired. Since that time, though Convocation has frequently assembled, its functions have been few and unimportant. Its last meeting for business was in 1717. During the reign of Anne, urged on by the high Tory and Jacobite party, it was mischievously active in attempts to revoke the scanty measure of Toleration conceded at the Revolution, and to crush every manifestation of the spirit of religious freedom[1].

The extravagant pretensions advanced by Convocation in the reigns of the first James and Charles, and the efforts of the clergy to acquire an independent jurisdiction, have justly awakened the jealousy, and called forth the resistance, of Parliament and the common lawyers. One effect of this conflict has been, to prevent the Church from establishing such a code of discipline, in harmony with the principles of our mixed constitution, as might have conduced to internal order and spiritual efficiency. Considering its wealth, its influence, and its manifold relations to society, the Church of England is confessedly deficient in a well-balanced power of self-government. Since the Revolution, its ancient discipline has gone into disuse; and the canons could not be generally put in force, without coming into collision with the now universally admitted principles of civil and religious liberty. How far such incompetency to the ends of a spiritual institution, does not necessarily result from the conditions of its existing relations to the State, especially when combined with a toleration of Dissenters, is a question worthy of consideration. Happily for the peace and freedom of society, the Church cannot act in its corporate capacity without the sanction of Parliament. Parliament has a control over all its movements. It is the subject of the State, made over and bound to it, and holding all its endowments on condition of this subjection. It is disabled for much spiritual good by the very riches and dignities of its secular connection. Some of its best and wisest prelates have deplored this result. Still further to limit its usefulness, what is just and salutary in episcopal control, is impaired by the effects of state and private patronage[2].

[1] Hallam, Constit. Hist. I. 413, 439; III. 324–331. Within the last year or two Convocation has ominously resumed its pretensions; but it cannot be supposed, that in the middle of the nineteenth century, the laity of the Church of England will submit, even in ecclesiastical matters, to the exclusive legislation of the clergy.

[2] See bishop Burnet's Reflections at the close of the History of his own Times.

The theology of the Church, as expressed in its Articles and Homilies, has yet to be noticed. From the commencement of the Reformation, England showed a fixed purpose to maintain the independence of her national position. In this spirit she declined adopting any of the foreign confessions. By an order of Edward VI. and his council, Cranmer and Ridley, assisted by Bucer, Peter Martyr and Cox, drew up forty-two articles declaratory of the faith of the Reformed Church of England. These articles were submitted to the revision of Grindal and Knox, two of the most popular preachers and most zealous Protestants of the time, and were put forth by royal authority a few weeks only before the king died.—These forty-two articles were the basis of the thirty-nine promulgated in the reign of Elizabeth[1]. The plain language of the articles themselves, no less than the known principles of the parties engaged in framing them, are conclusive evidence of the Calvinistic spirit in which they were conceived. In the Convocation of 1562, the thirty-nine Articles were finally settled. Parker and Jewel had the chief hand in preparing them. They differ from the forty-two, principally in the use of more temperate language in the denial of the corporal presence, with a view to conciliate the Romanists and please the Queen; and in the omission of some particulars respecting heresies which had ceased to excite apprehension. In 1571, the doctrinal Articles were confirmed, and subscription to them made imperative on all ecclesiastical persons, by parliamentary statute. There is no increase of Protestant feeling in these thirty-nine Articles; that had attained its maximum in the symbol of Edward VI.; and what remains, is rather softened down from the more decided expression of it in the forty-two. Still these Articles, notwithstanding some modifying phrases, are in their spirit and intention essentially Calvinistic, and utter the sentiments which were almost universal among the prominent Reformers of the age. The chief points of Calvinism are set forth very plainly in the ninth, tenth, thirteenth, seventeenth and eighteenth articles. The two articles on the Sacraments agree in the main with the doc-

---

[1] The forty-two articles, compared with the thirty-nine, are printed by Burnet, Hist. Reform. Collection of Records, P. II. B. I. No. 55. They were printed for the first time in Latin and English in the Appendix to a Catechism, 1553. This Catechism is exceedingly rare. Lamb, on the Thirty-nine Articles, p. 7.

trine of the Book of Common Prayer, though conceived in cautious and general terms. The first clause of the twentieth article respecting the Church's power to decree rites and ceremonies, and its authority in controversies of faith, was exceedingly offensive to the Puritans, as contradicting their fundamental principle of the absolute sufficiency of Scripture. In the reign of Charles I., Burton, a clergyman of that party, declared the clause was not to be found in the original draught of the Articles, and charged Laud and the other prelates, his contemporaries, with having surreptitiously inserted it. Laud retaliated on his accusers, that they had dishonestly omitted it, affirming that it was as great a crime to leave out, as to put in. The question was left in a very dubious and unsatisfactory state, assertion and denial being dictated on both sides more by party feeling than by consideration of evidence. Selden, no favourer of the Church, declared in his Table Talk, that it was most certain, the disputed words were in the Book of Articles that was confirmed, though in some editions they had been left out. On the other hand, Mocket, chaplain to archbishop Abbot, who was Puritanically inclined, omitted them in the Latin translation of the Articles which was published in 1617. What is certain is, that from the time of Laud, they were introduced into all the authorized copies of the Thirty-nine Articles[1].

[1] Fuller (B. IX. S. i. 56–59) speaks doubtfully about this clause, 'leaving it to more cunning state-arithmeticians to decide, whether the Bishops were faulty in their *addition* or their opposites in *subtraction*.' Collier (II. p. 486–90) who goes into the question with his customary clearness and precision, decides unhesitatingly in favour of the authenticity of the disputed words. The real facts of the case have been brought to light by Dr. Lamb, late Master of Corpus Christi College, Cambridge, in his 'Historical Account of the Thirty-nine Articles.' On the accession of Elizabeth, Parker revised the forty-two Articles of Edward VI., and added to the thirty-fourth a clause affirming the power of a particular or national church to make alterations in rites and ceremonies, which had been established by human authority, provided such changes conduced to edification. This revision he submitted to the Convocation of 1562, when the Articles were reduced to thirty-nine. In the following year they were printed by the Queen's authority, in Latin by Reginald Wolfe, and in English by Jugg and Cawood. When the articles came under discussion of Parliament in 1571, the English copy printed in 1563, was adopted; and in that same year, they were printed in Latin by Day, and a second time in English by Jugg and Cawood. In the articles passed in the Convocation of 1562, Parker's clause about rites and ceremonies is retained, but not the words which now stand at the head of the twentieth article. These first appear in Wolfe's Latin edition of 1563. The explanation is probably this. When the articles had been adopted in the Convocation of 1562, a fair copy was made of them and transmitted to the Queen, who kept them by her a twelvemonth;

Two works appeared at the same time with the Articles, designed as a recommendation and exposition of them; Jewel's Apology for the Church of England[1], which was undertaken at the suggestion of archbishop Parker, and published at the Queen's command and expense; and the second Book of Homilies, which has been ascribed, though its authorship is not certain[2], to the joint pens of Cranmer, Ridley, and Latimer. The tone of both these productions is very similar, and plainly shows, they were written under the same influence and for a common object. The Calvinism of their theology is subdued, and chiefly brought out in contrast with the errors of the Papal system. Their controversy is with Roman Catholics, not with Puritans, who do not seem to have been objects of any solicitude to the writers. Both are designed to vindicate the position of the Church of England as a purified and independent national communion, and to justify its secession from idolatrous Rome; the Book of Homilies exhibiting the practical, and the Apology the argumentative,

and it must have been at her suggestion, that the words in question were inserted in the Latin edition. It is here expressly stated, that the articles had been carefully read and examined by the Queen herself, a statement which occurs in no other edition. Under similar influence, the twenty-ninth article is omitted both in the English and the Latin copies printed before 1571. Dr. Lamb thus sums up the evidence about the introductory clause of the twentieth Article. It is *not* found: (1) in the Latin MS. signed in the Convocation of 1562; (2) in the English editions of Jugg and Cawood, 1563; (3) in the English MS. signed in the Convocation of 1571; (4) in the Latin edition of Day, and the English editions of Jugg and Cawood, both published under the direction of Jewel in 1571. It *is* found (1) in the Latin edition of Wolfe, 1563; (2) in later English editions occasionally from 1571 till the time of Laud. Laud finding it in Wolfe's edition, inserted it in the authorized copies, and hindered the publication of the Articles without it. Bishop Burnet (Exposition of the Articles, Introd. p. 16) expresses his full belief, that the Latin and English MSS. deposited by archbishop Parker in Corpus Christi Coll. (the same that have now been printed by Dr. Lamb) were authentic Acts of the Convocations of 1562 and 1571. The authenticity of this twentieth article was attacked at the beginning of the last century, by the celebrated Freethinker, Anthony Collins, first in a couple of pamphlets entitled 'Priestcraft in Perfection,' and afterwards in his 'Historical and Critical Essay on the Thirty-nine Articles.' Biographia Britannica, Collins [E] and [K].

[1] Jewel's doctrine respecting the Sacraments, is that of the Articles and the Liturgy, which in this point closely sympathize. We are not to regard them as mere ceremonies; Christ is really present in them; "in baptismo, ut cum induamus; in cœnâ, ut cum fide et spiritu comedamus, et de ejus carne et sanguine habeamus vitam æternam."—p. 9. The distinctive element of Protestantism is indicated in the following proposition: "fides nostra mortem et crucem Christi nobis applicat, non actio sacrificuli."—p. 10. Jewelli Oper. Genevæ, 1585. fol. Apologia Ecclesiæ Anglicanæ.

[2] Fuller, Book IX. 63. Carwithen's Hist. of the Church of England, vol. ii.

side of the question. Both are written with caution and moderation, rather than with enthusiasm; but the racy, vigorous English of the one, and the clear and elegant Latinity of the other, leave a favourable impression of the literary accomplishments of the first race of English Reformers. The Homilies and Apology were published together during the last session of the Council of Trent[1].

[1] Previous to the settlement of the Thirty-nine Articles, a provisional form of belief was set forth by the bishops in eleven articles, at the beginning of the Queen's reign, which the clergy were required to read from their pulpits, on taking possession of their cures, and afterwards twice every year. Collier, II. p. 463. By the statute of 1571, it is observable, that the clergy "are required to declare their assent to all the Articles which *only* contain the confession of the true Christian faith, and the doctrine of the Holy Sacraments," the word *only* seeming to exclude from this obligation, the Articles relating to the Homilies and Ordinal, and the Church's power to decree rites and ceremonies, and to decide in controversies of faith;—although in the canons passed by Convocation in the same year, the clergy are bound absolutely to subscribe all the Articles as a condition of retaining their preferments and cures. These facts indicate a disagreement between the views of Parliament and of Convocation, and betray the influence of a strong Puritanical feeling in the former assembly Collier, II. 529, 30. Indeed, it is well known, that the terms of the statute were the occasion of a sharp altercation between archbishop Parker and Sir Peter Wentworth, who conferred with his Grace during the progress of the bill, and who told him plainly, the House would not allow the bishops to decide for them what was agreeable to the Word of God; "for that," said he, "were to make you popes: make you popes who list, for we will make you none." In the Commons, the bill ran originally thus: "*All* the Articles which contain," it being supposed that the limitation would in this form be sufficiently distinct and express; but the Lords, in their amendments, introduced the word *only*, to remove all doubt, though this addition combines awkwardly with the preceding *all*. It is certain, therefore, that the Parliamentary confirmation was limited to the doctrinal articles. Nevertheless, in the Canons of 1604, the 36th requires all ecclesiastical persons to subscribe Three Articles, of which one contains a declaration, that the whole of the Thirty-nine Articles are agreeable to the Word of God. So that Parliament ratified the Articles *with a restriction*, while the Canons enforced the subscription of "all and every the Articles, being in number Nine-and-Thirty," *absolutely*. Thus we see, singularly enough, the *bellum intestinum* between Parliament and the Canonists penetrating to the very foundations of our ecclesiastical establishment. As might be expected, parties according to their principles, varied in their interpretation of the extent of the subscription demanded: the Puritans taking it in the parliamentary sense, and at a later period Hoadly and archdeacon Blackburne (in his Confessional) contending for the same liberal construction; the High-churchmen, on the contrary, admitting no distinction between the doctrinal and other articles, and insisting on an unqualified assent to all. In practice, subscription has always been understood to embrace, in whatever sense, the whole of the Articles. Sir Edward Coke argued, that even the parliamentary statute must be so interpreted. Selden, in his Table Talk (Articles), after observing, that by the original Act of Parliament, ministers were bound only to subscribe those Articles which contain matter of faith etc., adds—"but latterly, all were subscribed." Chillingworth on his final acceptance of preferment, signed the

SECTION V.

GENERAL CHARACTERISTICS OF THE ANGLICAN CHURCH.

Such are the elements which enter into the composition of the Church of England, as exhibited separately in its Prayer Book, its Discipline, and its Articles. It remains to inquire, what has been their operation, combined as an organic whole, and viewed in the course of their historical development. How shall we express the individuality which has marked the Anglican hierarchy, since it acquired a fixed character and subsistence, and which still distinguishes it from other religious societies?—If I mistake not, we find its distinctive attributes in a certain assumption of national independence and ascendency, kept in check by the power of the State and often greatly neutralized by the influence of enlightened and moderate men within its pale, but always perceptibly manifesting itself when circumstances throw it back on its inherent tendencies and allow it free scope for action; in a spirit of domination and exclusiveness; in a haughty and aristocratical bearing, fitly represented by its episcopal constitution, and betraying equal impatience of the foreign jurisdiction of the Pope and of democratic pretensions at home. Herein we discover the reason of its reluctance to acknowledge the Protestant Churches of the Continent, and of its instinctive aversion from the popular elements which entered so largely into the original constitution of those Churches. These tendencies may be ascribed in part to the circumstances of a wealthy and powerful establishment; but they have a deeper source in the spirit of the Prayer Book itself, and in the very nature of episcopal government; for they do not entirely cease among the Episcopalians of Scotland and the United States, where the peculiar influences of an establishment are wanting. The Church of England displays the pride of an ancient lineage, and has many sympathies with the recollections of feudalism. She claims a high descent and the prescription of a long-established title. Exulting, in the spirit of the old baronial independence,

---

Three Articles required by the 36th Canon of 1604: and in the book which contains his subscription, his name appears at the foot of these and the accompanying words—"Omnibus hisce articulis et singulis in iisdem contentis volens et ex animo subscribo," etc. It is important to notice this, as Hoadly had denied the fact. Collier, II. 530; Confessional, 2nd edit., preface, pp. x. xi. xii., with note; Des Maizeaux, Historical and Critical Account of the Life and Writings of Chillingworth, p. 64, note Q. and p. 265, note PP.

at the thought of having cast off a foreign yoke and purged herself free from the corruptions of Popery, she still holds herself aloof with an air of conscious superiority, from the sects of more recent origin which have rapidly shot up into consequence at her side. She takes her stand on the principle of authority. Although appealing to Scripture in her fundamental charter, for her right to exist, she nevertheless authoritatively defines the sense of Scripture, and in her practice forbids any one to dispute it.

These feelings, so characteristic of Anglicanism, (a term which conveniently expresses the predominant spirit or genius of the English Church,) did not originate with the Reformation. The idea of a national hierarchy, one and independent, early took a strong hold of the English mind. Before the popular outbreak of Luther, the bishops of western Christendom betrayed a decided purpose to resist the usurpations of their brother of Rome and render him amenable to a general council: and in this conflict of the aristocratical with the monarchical principle, which Mr. Hallam has aptly designated the Whiggism of the Catholic Church, the English hierarchy was not backward to participate. At the Council of Constance in the beginning of the fifteenth century, we find its representatives contending zealously for their national rights[1]. The regularity with which Convocation held its sessions along with Parliament, and the right of the bishops and mitred abbots to sit in the upper House with the lay peers, tended silently to strengthen the feeling, that the Church was an essential part of the hereditary nationalty, interwoven inseparably with the other branches of the constitution. In the beginning of Henry VIIIth's reign, before Cranmer and Cromwell came on the scene, Wolsey designed a general reformation of the monks and clergy in both provinces, and was strenuously supported in this purpose by Fox, bishop of Winchester[2]. Archbishop Warham, the patron of Erasmus, though never suspected of a leaning to Protestantism, but charged, on the contrary, with undue severity to the Lollards, was himself not indisposed to acknowledge the king's supremacy and abate the pretensions of the bishop of Rome[3].

---

[1] Hallam's Middle Ages, ch. vii.
[2] "Cleri, et præcipuè Monachiæ." Fox's Letter to Wolsey. **Strype's Memorials**, vol. v. Records and Originals, No. X.
[3] Strype's Cranmer, fol. p. 15.

These circumstances show, that from the beginning of the sixteenth century and previously, there was a feeling in England not adverse to a renunciation of papal authority, and friendly to a reform of religious institutions at home. This feeling must not be confounded with the native Lollardism, or with the Protestantism imported from Germany; although the three currents might flow for a time in one channel, while the direct struggle with popery was in progress. But it was no doubt one cause, aided by less worthy motives[1], which induced the nobility and gentry to acquiesce so patiently in the changes introduced by Henry VIII., and at the same time made it so difficult for Cranmer and Ridley to carry them beyond it: and its deep, latent influence must always be considered, in accounting for the peculiar character of the English Reformation[2]. Had Mary's reign, with a restoration of the old religion, not intervened, it seems probable, there might have been a less decided assertion of Protestantism on the accession of Elizabeth. Those who might have accommodated themselves to the unbroken ascendency of a Protestant government, which would have found its interest in conciliating them, having accepted preferment under a catholic Sovereign, could not for shame, in the sight of the whole world, again renounce their profession. The refusal of all Mary's bishops, with one exception, to take the oaths of Supremacy and Uniformity, and their consequent ejectment from the establishment, called at once into action a strong antagonistic power, against which the friends of the Church thought it wise to provide, by surrounding her with legal defences and infusing a strong anti-papal element into her articles and constitution. But the mass of the people were not sufficiently awakened and instructed, to feel any deep interest in the question. Out of

---

[1] The growth of luxury and increased expense of living whetted the appetite for ecclesiastical spoliation. A change was taking place in the tastes and habits of the aristocracy, which shows itself in a general raising of rents, an inclosure of common lands, and a proportionate depression of the ancient yeomanry. See an interesting chapter in Strype's Memorials, vol. iii. pp. 306–333.

[2] Fuller, a moderate Churchman (Church Hist. Book V. Sect. iii. 25–32), assigns the three following justifications of the English Reformation: (1.) the gross corruptions and abuses of Popery; (2.) the due exercise of the rights of a national Church by the King, with the advice and assistance of Convocation and Parliament, a free and general council being under the circumstances impossible; (3.) the moderation of receding from Rome only in things corrupt and false. Jewel has taken the same ground. Apolog. Eccles. Anglican. edit. Genev. fol. pp. 35–37.

9400 of the inferior clergy, only 177 are said to have thrown up their livings; and except in the secluded districts of the kingdom, especially Lancashire, the **Catholic laity at the commencement of Elizabeth's reign, very generally conformed to** the established worship[1].

Composed of divers elements, and passing through **many revolutions of political affairs, the English Church does not present the** same external phasis at every period of its history; **but on** closer inspection, we may always discover, sometimes **more** latent, sometimes more fully developed, the unchanged operation of its inherent principles. Modifications of its outward character, **resulting** from causes which I shall briefly notice, may be **traced in each of** the four following periods: (1) from the **elevation of Cranmer to the** primacy, till the close of Elizabeth's reign; (2) **during the** entire dynasty of the Stuarts; (3) **from** the **Revolution till the latter** end of the last century; (4) **from the decline of the old Low** Church doctrines, to the present time.

SECTION VI.

ERASTIAN AND CALVINISTIC PERIOD.

The spirit of a religious institution may be inferred **from** two circumstances; the theology actually taught by it, **and** its conception of **its relation** to the State. The first age **of the** English Reformed **Church** was Calvinistic in its theology, and Erastian **in its** principles of ecclesiastical government. If the precise doctrinal **views** of Cranmer and Ridley may be open to question, there **can be** no doubt, that the exiles **who** returned home on the death **of** Mary, and possessed the ascendant influence at the beginning of Elizabeth's **reign, and** furnished her earliest bishops, brought back with **them a** strong attachment to the Genevan theology[2]. **In accordance** with this system the Articles had **been framed; and the** Anglican doctrine of the Lord's Supper, though **designed** to embrace in

---

[1] Strype's Annals, I. p. 106; II. p. 253. Oxford edit. 1824. The visitors appointed at this time, reported on their return that two hundred **and forty-three** clergymen had quitted their livings, mostly of superior station in **the Church.** Lamb's Hist. Account of the Thirty-nine Articles, p. 12.

[2] Hallam, Constit. Hist. I. p. 549.

the generality of its language a wide range of opinion, bears a close affinity to that of Calvin. In fact, the stern and despotic system of Calvinism, tenacious of principles and intrepidly consequential in applying them, was not ill-suited either to the temper or to the circumstances of the first race of English Reformers; and though associated by an accident in the country of its birth, with the democratic platform of a republican Church, had no invincible antipathy to the episcopal discipline, which Calvin, it is said, theoretically preferred[1].

Erastianism, as the theory is called, which derives all ecclesiastical power from the State, and resolves the Church into a branch of the executive, was the resource on which the Church of England was necessarily thrown, in the first struggles of its separation from Popery. The arm of the Sovereign had dissolved the ties of its ancient dependence; and now, conscious of weakness, torn from the hand that had once upheld it, it cast itself with abject servility at the feet of the State, for without the State it was helpless. These Erastian principles maintained their ascendency till the close of the Tudor dynasty. Elizabeth was not a princess to allow them to be forgotten; and they were in harmony with the views of her chief counsellors. Parker, her first primate, the college friend of Bacon and Cecil, strenuously asserted them. He was at once anti-papal and anti-puritan, and enforced uniformity with an inflexible severity. His Erastianism was the result of necessity; for he had a strong leaven of High Church principles. His pursuits and his tastes were antiquarian[2]. He regarded Popery as an encroachment on ancient doctrines and usages; and maintaining the identity of the Reformed Church of England with that which had been at first established in the island, he was solicitous on that account to uphold its national character and independence. His successor, Grindal, had more sympathy with the Puritans, and incurred the Queen's lasting displeasure and his own sequestration, by venturing to oppose the authority of Scripture to her prerogative[3].—The principles of Parker were revived, and carried out with even greater rigour, by Whitgift. Puritanism in his time, exasperated by harshness and oppres-

[1] Hooker's Ecclesiastical Polity, preface.
[2] He was a great promoter of Anglo-Saxon learning and antiquities. Strype's Parker, p. 455.
[3] See his Letter to the Queen. Strype's Grindal, B. II. Appendix No. ix.

sion, assumed its fiercest and most rancorous tone : and the better to restrain its vehemence, he procured enactments in the Star Chamber for subjecting the press to a rigid censorship. The Court of High Commission, armed with the power of administering the oath *ex officio*[1], was in that day the great instrument of ecclesiastical tyranny. Yet Whitgift had not always resorted to such means for silencing his adversaries. Before his elevation to the primacy, he had engaged at the instance of Parker, in controversy with Cartwright, one of the most learned and zealous advocates of the Presbyterian discipline. The Erastianism and Calvinism of this primate are undoubted. He published anonymously in London a work of Erastus, on Excommunication[2]. When Arminian views began to excite controversy at Cambridge, to counteract them, he put forth a declaration of doctrine in the Lambeth Articles which exhibited Calvinism in its harshest features. The Queen was greatly displeased, and the Articles were suppressed[3].

The principles of this earliest school of Anglicanism have been developed, and vindicated against the Puritans, with a calm philosophical breadth of view, and a most majestic eloquence, in the celebrated work of Hooker on Ecclesiastical Polity. Setting out from the fundamental position of Erastus, that in a Christian country no distinction should be admitted between Church and State, which are only different names for the same society surveyed from opposite

---

[1] The oath *ex officio* compelled an individual, brought into court, to answer every question that should be put to him, though tending directly to criminate or endanger himself; a practice wholly at variance with the principles of English law. "This oath," says Blackstone, (Commentaries, Coleridge's edit. Book III. Ch. xxvii. [447]) "was made use of in the spiritual courts ;" "whereof the High Commission Court in particular made a most extravagant and illegal use; forming a court of inquisition, in which all persons were obliged to answer in cases of bare suspicion, if the Commissioners thought proper to proceed against them *ex officio* for any supposed ecclesiastical enormities. When the High Commission Court was abolished by statute, 16 Car. I. c. 11, this oath *ex officio* was abolished with it." This statute of Charles I. was confirmed by 13 Car. II. Fuller, in his usual quaint way, (Church Hist. Book IX. Sect. vi. 51,) has given in parallel columns the arguments for and against the oath *ex officio*, which were put forth respectively in those days by the High Churchmen and the Puritans.

[2] On the authority of Selden, cited by Warburton in his notes on Neal.

[3] Strype's Whitgift. Collier II. p. 644. Fuller IX. sect. viii., who says, these Articles may be received as an infallible evidence, "what was the general and received doctrine of England in that age."

points of view[1], he argues, that ecclesiastical and civil polity should always be in the closest harmony with each other; and, as Scripture has laid down no absolute rule respecting them, must be regulated by the exigencies of a particular age and country, in accordance with the general principles of Christianity. In unfolding the great idea of his work, Hooker takes a magnificent range of vision. From the widest laws which embrace the whole universe of being, he descends with an easy and graceful sweep to the derived and successive adjustments of the subordinate divisions of creation, bringing them all within the limits of one connected and harmonious legislation, and thus impressing on every arrangement that enters into the permanent constitution of society, a divine sanction and authority. At the very time therefore that Hooker is defending the principles of Erastus, and anticipating Mr. Locke's theory of the derivation of all government from an implied consent of the people, he has the appearance, owing to the vast extent of his generalizations, and his constant reference of all things to a primal law of God, of conceding a divine origin to regal and sacerdotal power; and thus he announces a transition to the less noble and philosophical doctrines which distinguished the leading churchmen of the next period. He died in the last year of the sixteenth century[2].

[1] B. VIII. p. 440, fol. 1676.
[2] B. VIII. pp. 442, 444, 468. From the peculiar train of his reasoning, some have erroneously inferred, that Hooker was an advocate of the *jus divinum* of Episcopacy. James II. ascribed his re-adoption of Roman Catholicism to the impression left on his mind by the preface to the Ecclesiastical Polity. The three last books of Hooker's work were not published till after his death; and a suspicion was expressed, that they had been tampered with by the Puritans. Mr. Hallam, a very competent judge, declares his belief in their authenticity from internal evidence. (Constit. Hist. I. p. 299, note.) There seems as much ground for imputing interpolations to the Church party, as omissions from the original MS., to the Puritans. See Strype's Life of Whitgift, fol. p. 544; and the preface to Hanbury's edition of Hooker's works.—Hooker's anticipation of Locke may be seen, Eccles. Pol. B. I. 10, where, among other passages, occurs the following: "Laws they are not, therefore, which public approbation hath not made so; but approbation not only they give, who personally declare their assent, by voice, sign, or act; but also when others do it in their names, by right originally, at the least, derived from them. As in Parliaments, Councils, and the like assemblies, although we be not personally ourselves present, notwithstanding our assent is, by reason of other agents there in our behalf."

SECTION VII.

HIGH SACERDOTAL AND REGAL DOCTRINES AND PREVALENCE OF ARMINIANISM UNDER THE STUARTS.

A new view of the source of ecclesiastical power, and of its relation to the State, came into vogue under the Stuarts, and was accompanied by a corresponding modification of theological opinion. Indications of such a change had occurred before the Queen's decease. Some have found traces of it in Bancroft's Sermon preached against the Puritans at Paul's Cross in 1588. There cannot be a doubt, that the tendencies which a protracted struggle with the Puritans, and a deep-felt necessity of repelling one assertion of divine right by another, had been strengthening in the Church, clearly pointed to such a result, and only waited for an opportunity to manifest themselves without disguise. Dr. Benjamin Charior or Carier, who had been Whitgift's chaplain, and wrote the inscription on his monument, withdrew to the Continent on the death of that primate, and was suspected of having changed his religion. He declared however in a letter to archbishop Abbot, that he was no papist, but merely anxious to heal the breach between the Anglican, and the ancient European, Church, by the establishment of the religion which he called Catholic. He distinguished between the Protestants and the Puritans of the English Church; disliked Calvin and Calvinism; and disowned all communion with the Reformed Churches of France and the Netherlands, whose members he contemptuously designated Huguenots and Gueux[1]. His views were evidently an anticipation of the system, soon after maintained by Laud, and in the present day revived by the authors of the Tracts for the Times. For Erastianism this system substituted the divine right of Episcopacy; and for the doctrines of the Geneva school those which had a nearer affinity to Arminianism. Yet it did not enter into any contest with the sovereign, or slide into Popery. On the contrary, it was as much opposed to Popery as to Puritanism. It professed to be at once Catholic and national; Catholic in its relation to the one universal Church; national in its close alliance with the Crown. It exalted the regal and the sacerdotal powers in an equal degree; traced them back to a patriarchal origin; and claimed for both a co-ordinate authority.

[1] Strype's Whitgift, p. 533, fol.

Instead of recognizing with Hooker, the free choice and judgment of man as links in the vast chain of supreme legislation, which carry with them, in their enduring results, the clear evidence of a divine sanction to the thoughtful mind; it assumed, in the outset, a positive institution of authority direct from God, descending unbroken from age to age, independent of human approval and beyond human control. The power actually constituted might, on either theory, be regarded as, in one sense, divine; but the argumentative process through which that view of it was attained, made a wide difference in its practical bearing on the freedom and progress of mankind.

From the system which now became ascendant, two inferences were naturally deducible; the doctrine of indefeasible legitimacy in regard to the crown; and the assertion of an indelible consecration, derived from the apostles, in the priesthood. These despotic principles met with a cordial reception in the arbitrary temper of the Stuarts, expressed in their favourite adage, "no bishop, no king:" and, combining with the worst elements of our constitution, which had been infused into it from the old Roman law, attracted to themselves a host of zealous defenders in churchmen and civilians[1]. Bancroft who had succeeded Whitgift as primate, petitioned against the infringements on the jurisdiction of the ecclesiastical courts, as closely affecting popular rights[2]: and in the true spirit of a priestly demagogue, availed himself of some recent unpopular enactments, to excite among the people a feeling of dissatisfaction with their parliamentary representatives and the judges of the common-law courts.[3] These high doctrines were put forth systematically in a series of canons passed by Convocation in 1606[4]; and their appearance may be taken as an indirect evidence of the growth of popular

[1] See Allen, on the Rise and Growth of the Prerogative. A great jealousy had sprung up at this time between the common lawyers and the practisers of the canon and civil law. The former were attached to the old traditional liberties of the subject; the latter were the supporters of the prerogative. When James I. visited Cambridge in 1615, he was entertained by the scholars with a play called Ignoramus, the object of which was to exhibit the common lawyers in a ridiculous light. Fuller, B. X. Sect. iv. 39.

[2] In what were called, from a precedent of Edward II.'s time, the "Articuli Cleri."

[3] Strype's Whitgift, B. IV. Append. No. 41.

[4] These canons, though circulated among the clergy, were not published till the close of the century. Hallam, Const. Hist. I. p. 439.

principles in Parliament and the bulk of the nation. Laud's Conference with the Jesuit Fisher exhibits the views of this rising party, respecting Scripture and the Church. "According to Christ's institution," he says, "the Scripture, where 'tis plain, should guide the Church; and the Church, when there's doubt or difficulty, should expound the Scripture; yet so, as neither the Scripture should be forced, nor the Church so bound up, as that upon just and further evidence she may not revise that which in any case hath slipt by her[1]." Yet he denies that "any private man whatever can be judge of controversies, which must be referred to the decision of Scripture, interpreted by the primitive Church, and a lawful and free general council determining according to these[2]." Here we have ambiguities that might breed endless controversy; Protestantism in semblance, Catholicism in reality; each to be drawn out and employed in argument, according as the adversary was a Romanist or a Puritan.

It is remarkable, that the Synod of Dort, to which the Anglican Church had sent representatives in the interest of Calvinism, and which finally condemned the Arminian party, was soon followed by the rapid spread of Arminian principles in England[3]. Possibly this change was promoted by the revived study of the old Greek theology. Greek learning had made great progress in England during the sixteenth century. The Queen herself had cultivated it with ardour. Bishop Cox who was a strict Calvinist, expressed his high displeasure, when he found her deeply intent on some fathers of the Eastern Church. The theology of Western Europe had been deeply impregnated for a thousand years with the spirit of Augustine's writings; from them, Wycliffe and Luther had imbibed their earliest and strongest religious convictions; and this circumstance must be allowed its weight, in accounting for the readiness of the popular mind, after the Reformation, to embrace the doctrines of predestination and grace. But the Church of England had put herself in a singular position, midway, as it were, between the old and the new religion of Europe[4]. Her attention and interest were thus diverted to a remoter branch of the universal Church, which possessed the essential characters of Catholicity, and afforded her a ground

---

[1] Dedication to King Charles I.   [2] Conference, etc., p. 386.
[3] See a long note of Mr. Hallam's, Const. Hist. I. p. 551.
[4] Tracts for the Times, No. 38.

to rest upon, disentangled from modern controversies. In writers of the Anglican communion, especially in their disputes with the Romanists, we may often notice a marked sympathy with the Greek Church[1]. In regard to the doctrinal points most strongly insisted on by the Puritans, the general sense of the Eastern Fathers was against them. The new learning found a zealous patron in Dr. Lancelot Andrews, bishop of Winchester, a man of profound acquirements in the Oriental languages, but of a cold and ascetic spirit, whose principles had great influence on Laud. These anti-Calvinistic tenets were so generally entertained by the supporters of the arbitrary measures of the Star-chamber and the Court of High Commission, that any manifestation of them was supposed to indicate a feeling unfriendly to civil and religious liberty, and was often brought as a charge against individuals, by zealous members of the House of Commons. Arminianism and tyranny were believed to have some secret affinity with each other. Erastianism and Calvinism, which had been the distinguishing marks of the Anglican Church in the last age, now took refuge in Parliament; and those who associated them with the retention of a predilection for the Episcopal discipline, acquired the name of doctrinal Puritans[2].

The change of opinion that was taking place in the Anglican party, respected chiefly their conception of the Church, and of its ordinances and ministers. The Greek theology which obtained in that party almost exclusively the name of learning, took away men's thoughts from the *facts* of human nature, to occupy them with mere abstractions, coined in the wanton idleness of a speculative brain. It was the learning of an enfeebled race and a declining civilization. With the never-failing resource of those who prefer dreaming to active inquiry and free thought, it converted ideas, its own arbitrary conceptions of spiritual relations, into objective realities, and fixed them as articles of implicit belief, to the suppression or exclu-

---

[1] Jewel, Apolog. Eccles. Anglican. p. 29.
[2] This name was first given to them by the celebrated Antonio de Dominis, who had been archbishop of Spalato under the Venetian republic, but, quitting the Church of Rome, came over to England, where he was handsomely beneficed by James I. Afterwards retracting, he died miserably at Rome. See Fuller's interesting account of him, B. X. Sect. vi. Other learned foreigners, such as Saravia, Casaubon and Isaac Vossius at this time and later obtained preferment in the English Church. Casaubon united with Andrews in reviving a reverence for Christian antiquity.

sion of every independent conviction at variance with them. It was one branch of that baseless philosophy, which the inductive logic has swept away from the entire field of natural, and from a large and increasing part of the field of moral, science; and the retention of it in theology, by those who embrace the doctrine of Andrews and Laud and their modern followers, sufficiently accounts for their antipathy to a method of investigating truth, which must effectually destroy its pretensions. According to this system, nothing is left to the suggestions of the inward man; all is outward and prescribed. Nothing may be determined by a fresh inquiry; everything is authoritatively settled *à priori*. The present and the future have no value and significance; progress is forbidden as impiety; all things have been already accomplished in antiquity[1]. The Church is not a free and spontaneous association of sympathizing minds, but a great indivisible unity, a vast impersonation, endowed with immutable attributes, and preserving a sort of mysterious existence through ages, independent of the actual conduct and opinions of the aggregation of individuals which visibly represents her. She is the hind of the poet, "immortal and unchanged,"

> "Without unspotted, innocent within,
> She fears no danger, for she knows no sin."

Derived from this divine entity, of which they are parts or functions, the priesthood and offices of the Church possess the same indelible character and unfailing efficacy, of which nothing human can deprive them. The Sacraments are conduits of life and immortality to the soul, independent of any appropriation of them by the personal convictions of the recipient[2], or of any moral fitness in the administrator, if only communicated by those to whose words and acts a peculiar virtue has been imparted by some secret, inexplicable influence, transmitted in regular descent from the Apostles. Apostolical succession, Baptism, the Eucharist, Good Works, Divine Acceptance—all form mutually related parts of one compact and self-consistent scheme. Through such channels alone the personal influence and authority of Christ himself pass into his Church; which thus provides in her ritual one great external process of salvation for all men, conveying to

---

[1] Tracts for the Times. Rationalism and Catholicism. No. 73.
[2] Pusey's Scriptural Views of Holy Baptism. Tracts for the Times. No. 67.

them the elements of a divine life, bringing them into a direct communion with God, declaring the absolution of their sins, and opening to them the gates of the invisible world. In accordance with such views, the doctrine of the Eucharist was modified by the divines of this school. The first Reformers, though the language of the Communion Service was purposely left vague, evidently conceived it in the Calvinistic spirit, and supposed the participation of the Lord's body to depend on the faith of the partaker; but the notions which now became prevalent, chiefly through the influence of Andrews and Casaubon, differed by a scarcely perceptible shade from the Romanist theory. Denying a corporeal, they acknowledged a real presence; they admitted the fact, but would enter into no discussion of the mode[1].

A theology of this description, by requiring the prostration of the intellect, was favourable to the designs of tyranny, and entered into ready alliance with the doctrines of passive obedience and non-resistance. It combined also more easily with the Arminian, than with the Calvinistic, view of man's relation to God. It offered salvation to all who would submissively accept it on the Church's terms; whereas Calvinism demanded a change within, which no external ordinances could reach, and which left the human soul more directly in the hands of God. Such tendencies might seem calculated to lead back the mind to Popery; and many of the nobility and the gentry, and some even of the clergy, it is now well known, were reconverted to the faith of their fathers, if indeed they had ever really renounced it. But there is no proof, that either Charles I., or Laud, or any of the leading Churchmen, ever seriously entertained the thought of a submission to Rome[2]. The adop-

---

[1] Hallam Const. Hist. ch. viii. — It is significant, that the authors of the Tracts for the Times decline appealing to the Reformers of the sixteenth century. They affirm, that in the effort of reform, the first race of Protestant divines lost sight of great truths, which were recovered and reinstated in their just influence, by the Churchmen of the seventeenth century, in whose writings must be sought the true exposition of Anglican theology, developing itself in reaction against Puritan principles. Tracts, No. 81. Mr. Hallam takes the opposite view. Const. Hist. II. p. 86, note.

[2] When Laud was raised to the See of Canterbury, on the death of Abbot, he was twice offered a Cardinal's hat by an emissary of Rome; to whom he replied, "That somewhat dwelt within him, which would not suffer him to accept the offer, till Rome were otherwise than it was." Heylin's Life of Laud, Book IV. p. 253. The context shows, what hopes the Jesuits then entertained of the re-conversion of England.

tion of so much that was Catholic in doctrine and ceremony, was rather intended, like the efforts of modern Puseyism, to retain those who from disgust at the opposite extreme, were strongly tempted to throw themselves into the arms of the ancient church of Christendom.

The overthrow of the Church strengthened the attachment of its adherents to the principles which distinguished them from the Puritans. In Hall, bishop of Norwich[1], in Jeremy Taylor[2], and even in Barrow[3], we may trace the same general features of theology, refined indeed and subdued, which assume a more exaggerated form in the views of Andrews and Laud. It is still the idea of the Church, of its unity and supremacy, and of its title to obedience, which is prominent in their writings; although the equality and independence of each of its national sections, are strenuously maintained against the Papists. The doctrinal Puritans ceased at length to exist as a party; and many who, like Usher and Sanderson, had once been Calvinists, abandoned their earlier tenets for a milder system.

After the Restoration, the union of high regal and sacerdotal doctrines, was more firmly cemented than ever. Lord Clarendon was the great supporter of these principles. In his hatred of Presbyterianism, he would almost have placed the Church above the Throne. The views of this High Church party have been expounded by archbishop Bramhall in his "Vindication of the Church of England," which he wrote during exile. In it he argues, that no spiritual jurisdiction is derived from the Crown, but only liberty and power to exercise actually and lawfully, on the subjects of the Crown, the habitual jurisdiction received by the priesthood at ordination. "We hold our benefices," says he, "from the king, but our offices from Christ[4]." Slavish doctrines were never carried to a more shameless height than under the two last Stuarts. Papists and High Churchmen were rival candidates

---

[1] Episcopacy by Divine Right.
[2] Of the Sacred Order and Offices of Episcopacy by Divine Institution.
[3] On the Pope's Supremacy, and on the Unity of the Church.
[4] Bramhall admitted three conditions as the possible basis of an union among all Christians: (1.) an abatement of the Pope's pretensions to a mere *principium unitatis*; (2.) a reduction of the essentials of faith to what they were at the time of the four first General Councils; (3.) an exclusion of some things which give offence, from the Divine offices, for the sake of peace. Works, fol. Dublin, 1677, pp. 136-7.

for the royal favour; and if the more conscientious Churchmen unduly exalted the priesthood, the sycophants of the court fell into the grossest Erastianism. Burnet declares, that Parker, bishop of Oxford, a renegade from Independency, went so far as to assert, that "to say the king was under God and Christ, was a crude and profane expression; for though the king was indeed under God, yet he was not under Christ, but above him[1]."

Stillingfleet's progress illustrates the spirit of the times. Having passed his youth amidst the excitements of the Commonwealth, he opened his theological career with a production distinguished for its moderate and conciliatory tone[2]. Following the track of Hooker, Hales, and Chillingworth, he denied the divine right of episcopacy; and contended for an ecclesiastical settlement, in which, by mutual concessions, the points most eagerly contended for by Independents, Presbyterians and Episcopalians, might be combined, and to which, when it had once been decided by competent authority, every man should hold himself bound in conscience to conform. Stillingfleet disowned Erastianism, as the result of a reaction against the inordinate elevation of Church power, and maintained that the right of excommunication was inherent in the very nature of a religious society[3]. His tolerant principles could not stand the test of altered circumstances. When the Church was firmly established in its ancient seat, and there was no prospect of any further changes for the relief of Nonconformists, Stillingfleet denounced Separation in the worst spirit of the persecuting edicts of Charles II.'s reign; and objected to concession except on terms so hard and offensive as effectually to prevent compliance. He took the high ground of a national establishment, and would admit of no parallel between the two cases of separation from the Church of Rome and separation from the Church of England. The defective

---

[1] History of his own Times, I. p. 696, fol. 1724. Parker was capable of a good deal, and the expression, if correctly reported, was offensively strong; but Burnet may have misunderstood him. He may have only meant to assert, that the Church should be subject to the State, in opposition to the fanatical doctrine, that the saints must rule the earth. Disappointed of preferment, Parker afterwards veered round to the opposite view, and maintained doctrines that made the Church independent of the civil power. Sancroft the primate would fain have declined consecrating him, but was afraid of a *præmunire*.

[2] Irenicum, or Weapon-Salve for the Church's Wounds.

[3] Discourse concerning the Power of Excommunication. Works, fol. II. pp. 419–38.

and inconsequential reasonings of the Dissenters themselves, furnished him with the most specious arguments against them[1]. Stillingfleet's case was not singular. Even Jeremy Taylor who under oppression had so eloquently vindicated in his Liberty of Prophesying, the rights of conscience, did not, when times changed, commit himself unconditionally to those broad principles, but deemed it necessary to explain in what sense he had once asserted them[2].

The fear of Popery on one hand, increased by the known predilections of the Sovereign, and a perpetual strife with the Protestant Dissenters on the other, gave a peculiar bitterness and activity to the exclusive tendencies of the Church of England, during the two last reigns of the Stuart dynasty. In this state of things, a new school of Anglican divines presents itself to our view. Disgusted with the extremes of wild fanaticism and priestly arrogance, a set of men had arisen, mild, peaceable, and unambitious, who sought for truth with an open and candid spirit, and studied religion in the blended lights of reason and learning. Not limiting themselves to the textual controversies of Scripture, or weighing with superstitious reverence the conflicting judgments of Fathers and Councils, they traced out the broad coincidence of Christian truth with the eternal laws of nature and providence, and brought to bear on its illustration and enforcement, all the treasures of heathen poetry and philosophy. Such men were Cudworth, Whichcot, Wilkins and More, who adopted in their studies and practice, the maxims of toleration and free inquiry already enunciated by Chillingworth and Hales. They had no sympathy with the Calvinistic sectaries, but were attached to the Liturgy and Episcopal government. The breadth of their principles, taking in fundamental truths, but neglecting

---

[1] On the Unreasonableness of Separation. Works, vol. ii.—Stillingfleet was very anxious (differing in this respect widely from Laud) that the Reformed Churches of the Continent should approve of his conduct to the Dissenters. Appended to his Discourse on Separation, are three letters from Protestant clergymen in Holland and France, which are remarkable for the cautious and almost reverential phraseology in which they are couched. They recommend peace and union, and intercede gently for their Presbyterian brethren in England. Claude, one of their number, says, that the French Reformed Church acknowledged episcopal ordination, and that some of their ministers had been ordained by English bishops.

[2] Dedication to Christopher, Lord Hatton, prefixed to his work on Episcopacy. He compares his former conduct to pulling down outhouses, to save the family from the flames.

the vexed points of popular debate, and the comprehensiveness of their charity, embracing good men of all religions, procured them from persons of narrower minds, the name of Latitudinarians. Some of the most celebrated preachers in the latter part of the seventeenth century, Tillotson, Patrick and Lloyd, had been formed in the school of these eminent men. With these last bishop Burnet had been on terms of the closest intimacy; and in his History of his own Times, speaks with affectionate warmth of their spirit and character, and his personal obligations to them. They reformed the style of preaching which had been previously in vogue; and by their pastoral diligence not less than by their acceptableness in the pulpit, recovered great numbers of the citizens of London to the Church. Their extensive popularity enabled them to disseminate among the middle classes, that respect for reason and moderation, which had been conceived in the studious retreats of their teachers, and which contributed to prepare the public mind for the Revolution.

Their rise and influence announce the approach of a new period[1].

SECTION VIII.

INFLUENCE OF LOW CHURCH PRINCIPLES AFTER THE REVOLUTION.

In spite of the corrupting influences of the Court, society had made great progress in the reigns of the second Charles and James. The public mind was aroused to reflection and inquiry by the speculations of Hobbes and Locke, which grew naturally out of foregoing controversies, and by the surprising discoveries of Boyle and Newton in the yet almost untrodden fields of physical science. The Latitudinarians constituted that party in the Church, which felt most strongly the in-

---

[1] Vol i. fol. pp. 186–91. Compare Butler's account of this school, in his Memoirs of British Catholics, and Wordsworth's beautiful sonnet on Latitudinarianism. Burnet's notice of the Latitudinarians is one of the most interesting passages of his very interesting book. He classes Stillingfleet among their pupils; but adds, that the publication of his Irenicum proved a great snare to him; "for, to avoid the imputations which that brought upon him, he not only retracted the book, but he went into the humours of that high sort of people beyond what became him, perhaps beyond his own sense of things."

fluence of this new direction of thought, and showed most eagerness to bring their principles and practice into harmony with it. Their generous aspirations and their frequent obliquities and inconsistencies equally resulted from this unavailing endeavour; but the circumstances of the Revolution gave a prominence and an authority to their principles, which had a visible influence on the character of the Church during the greater part of the ensuing century.

One of the first effects of the intimate connection of this party with the new government, was the appointment of an ecclesiastical commission, to prepare such alterations in the liturgy and rubrics as, approved by Convocation and ratified by the Legislature, might lead to a very general comprehension of the Protestant Dissenters. Even before the Revolution, the dread of Popery had compelled the primate Sancroft to entertain the design of some accommodation with the Nonconformists. The constant state of apprehension and excitement in which the Church had been kept, for more than a quarter of a century by its enemies on both sides, made all prudent men, while events of great moment and uncertain issue were impending over them, desirous of a more satisfactory arrangement with their Protestant brethren, than had resulted from the conferences at the Savoy in 1661. The ecclesiastical commission under William was in truth, therefore, only the carrying out of a measure which had been already meditated by the High Churchmen themselves; and the persons who were most active in it, Patrick, Tillotson, Burnet and Tenison, gave sure promise of a disposition to concede all unessential points of difference, for the sake of conciliation. They proposed a new selection of lessons, taken wholly from the canonical Scriptures; they left it to the minister's option to substitute the Apostles' for the Athanasian Creed; new collects were drawn up, in the first instance by Patrick who excelled in devotional composition, but revised and perfected by his associates; a fresh version of the Psalms was made, more conformable to the original; words and phrases that had been objected to, were collected out of the Liturgy, and others clearer and plainer and less exceptionable, proposed in their room. Suggestions were offered for meeting other scruples of the Dissenters, especially in regard to Baptism and Ordination. Had these proposals been adopted, it is probable that the largest portion of the Presbyterians would have been absorbed into the Church, and Nonconformity shorn at once of half its glory and its strength[1]. But the known principles of the men who were most prominent on the Commission, raised a host of prejudices against them. The hostility of the lower House of Convocation was invincible; and these projected reforms, with the comprehension that was to be founded on them, never came to effect[2].

Notwithstanding the failure of this design, men of liberal views and friendly to Toleration, were selected for preferment by William and the two first Georges. Tillotson, Tenison, Burnet, Hoadly, and Herring, were prelates of this stamp; nor were there wanting many clergymen in the inferior stations of the Church, of whom the accomplished Dr. Samuel Clarke, the friend and interpreter of Newton, and the learned and candid Jortin, may be selected as different specimens, to partake of their spirit and approve their policy. Never perhaps was moderation of spirit more conspicuous in the Church of England. Never was a larger share of practical piety combined with learning and good sense. Never were the peculiar features of episcopal arrogance and exclusiveness more generally kept out of view. Yet they were amiable, intelligent and enlightened, rather than great and high-souled men. We miss the unequivocal expression of genuine elevation of character. Their whole policy was founded on compromise. Tillotson whose many estimable qualities cannot shelter him from the imputation of weakness and timidity, was always intent on what he called healing measures and middle ways[3]. These men, with the best intentions, were entangled in the sophistry and inconsequence, inseparable from their efforts to reconcile what Locke calls just and true liberty, with the preservation of the actual establishment. They had accepted preferment with the implied understanding of being friendly to the rights of conscience, and they had to justify their position; nor did they always conceal their dislike of those, who could not bring

---

[1] Calamy says distinctly "two-thirds of the Dissenters."
[2] Calamy's Abridgment, vol. i. pp. 447–465. Birch's Life of Tillotson, pp. 174–184.
[3] Calamy's Life and Times, vol. i. p. 3; Tillotson's Letter to Lord William Russell just before his execution (Birch's Life of Tillotson, p. 102); in which he plainly inculcates the doctrine of non-resistance. Burnet took the same view. Another instance of Tillotson's weakness is mentioned by Calamy in his Life of Howe, fol. p. 25.

themselves to take the same accommodating view. By a strange inconsistency they approved of Toleration, while they condemned Dissent.

Hoadly was the most conspicuous man of the party, and vindicated its principles with the greatest intrepidity. His Sermon on the Nature of the Kingdom of Christ, preached before George I. in 1717, which gave occasion to the celebrated Bangorian controversy respecting the limits of free inquiry, asserted religious liberty in the broadest sense, and contained positions which, carried out to their legitimate consequences, would not only have required his secession from the Church, but destroyed the foundations of the Establishment itself. His own conduct was strangely inconsistent with his principles. In his anomalous position, he had to make good his ground against both the Protestant Dissenters and the Non-jurors. His 'Reasonableness of Conformity,' in answer to the statements contained in the 10th chapter of Calamy's Abridgment of Baxter's History, is a reiteration, in milder and more courteous terms, of the arguments which had been already advanced on the same topics by Stillingfleet; the necessity of supporting one undivided Church, the actual settlement the best attainable, and the duty of acquiescing in it: and it exhibits such specimens of nice casuistry and refined ingenuity as are unworthy of a noble and honest spirit. He is strong only where his adversaries are weak; in the *argumentum ad hominem* addressed to those who themselves stopped short of the just demands of reason and conscience[1]. In the course of the Bangorian controversy the views of Hoadly were attacked by the Non-juror, William Law, on narrow grounds indeed, but with straightforwardness and simplicity, and the genuine heartiness of tone peculiar to one, who is faithful to his own convictions, and has attested his value for them by making the sacrifices which they have asked[2]. Burnet was a man of more earnest character than Hoadly; but his principles and his position were not less at variance. Early in life, when he was visiting the foreign Protestants, he had induced the Church of Geneva to release its

[1] Reasonableness, etc., Lond. 1703. Defence, etc., Lond. 1705.
[2] See his Letters in the 5th vol. of the Tracts respecting the Hoadlyan Controversy. If Hoadly may be taken as a fair sample of the principles that were brought into fashion by the Revolution, he is not fitted to inspire us with any deep veneration for them.—With a vigorous and manly intellect, a generous and courteous temper, and a sort of constitutional sympathy with the cause of

clergy from the *Consensus Doctrinæ*[1]. It was therefore with some reluctance and embarrassment, that he afterwards undertook, at the request of archbishop Tillotson and queen Mary, an Exposition of the Articles of the Church of England[2].

But all this trimming and accommodation led to no result: the High Church party was not conciliated; nor were the Dissenters reclaimed. What were the prospects in this age of any man who resolved fearlessly to investigate Scriptural truth, are unfolded with admirable clearness and bitter irony in bishop Hare's celebrated Letter to a young clergyman on the difficulties and discouragements attending the study of the Scriptures. His subsequent practice leaves us almost in doubt, whether the advice did not after all express in sober earnestness, his own view of the question, and indicate the spirit that was too widely diffused among the Low Churchmen of the day. Whiston stands forth an almost solitary example of single-minded devotion to the cause of Christian truth, and of heroic willingness to endure all the consequences which its service entailed[3].

But there was another party in the Church, active, implacable, and disaffected to the government, all whose prejudices

liberty, he was nevertheless deficient in that moral earnestness and magnanimous fidelity to conscience, which must enter into all our conceptions of a great man. His principles at least cost him nothing. Preferments were showered on him in profusion after the accession of the House of Hanover. He was rapidly advanced in succession to the sees of Bangor, Hereford, Salisbury and Winchester; and Whiston (Memoirs, P. I. p. 244) charges him with having drawn the revenues of the see of Bangor for six entire years, without ever once seeing that diocese in his life. Notwithstanding the principles so broadly set forth in his Sermon on the Kingdom of God, he made no scruple of regularly reading the Athanasian Creed; and in 1724, he refused a prebend in Salisbury Cathedral to a liberal-minded clergyman, without enforcing a fresh subscription to the Articles. Nichols's Literary Anecdotes, vol. ii. p. 524, and vol. iii. Addit. and Correct. p. 748. It may be said, that in all this he was simply obeying the rubric of the Church in which he held office. But the very defence makes the falseness of his position more conspicuous. He used to justify his conformity by saying: "I see that I can still promote the Christian religion in general, though cramped in some points which I judge not to be very essential to it. This is the rule by which I conduct myself in these matters." MS. of Jones of Welwyn, 1761.

[1] Life, appended to the History of his own Times, vol. ii. fol. p. 693.
[2] Confessional, p. 81.
[3] In the years 1715, 16, and 17, Whiston formed a society for the promotion of primitive Christianity, which met weekly at his house, and to which persons of all Christian persuasions were equally admitted. Sir Peter King, Dr. Hare, Dr. Hoadly and Dr. Clarke were particularly invited, but never came. Nichols's

were wrought up to madness by seeing the individuals whom they hated, elevated to posts of the highest dignity and influence. Such were the men who entertained the high notions of kingly and priestly power, that had been ascendant under the Stuarts, and who associated with them the doctrines of passive obedience and non-resistance. They were sadly perplexed by the events which prepared and accompanied the Revolution. Their attachment to the Establishment forbade their supporting James II., when he attacked the independence of the Church by attempting to restore Popery; yet the principles which placed the Prince of Orange on the throne, were at variance with their whole theory of submission to legitimate rule. The conscientious men of the party, with Sancroft the primate and four bishops, Ken, Turner, Lake and White at their head, refused the oaths of allegiance to the new government, and forfeited their preferments. These were the Non-jurors; and however false and mischievous we may deem their principles, their conduct is entitled to our respect and sympathy. They suffered for conscience' sake. Many of them were men of sincere piety and unblemished purity of life, who adorned their retirement with a meek and patient virtue[1]. It is remarkable, that the two writers who protested most energetically against the immoralities which defiled the stage at this period, belong to the Non-jurors; Collier, the ecclesiastical historian, and William Law. In an age of compromise, this party had at least the merit of earnestness and consistency. Law was a writer of great power and extensive influence. Dr. Johnson has acknowledged the deep impression made on his mind by his principal work, the Serious Call; and Gibbon, with no fondness for his principles, has rendered an honourable tribute to his character and genius[2]. The exemplary bishop Wilson, who with so much wisdom and practical benevolence, in the earlier part of the last century, reduced his scheme of primitive Christian discipline to practice, in the secluded diocese of Sodor and Man, without conforming to the political conduct of the Non-

---

Lit. Anecdotes, vol. i. p. 500. Whiston's character and situation are delineated with a pathetic truthfulness in Hare's Letter, referred to in the text, pp. 17, 18. There is an admirable passage on the inefficacy of "trimming methods in matters of religion," in the Confessional, p. 87.

[1] For a favourable view of the spirit and temper of the Non-jurors, see the Memoirs of the Rev. John Kettlewell.

[2] Gibbon's Memoirs of his own Life and Writings, 4to, vol. i. p. 15.

jurors, had imbibed the spirit of the best men of their party. He has been honoured with a place in the *Catena Patrum* of the Oxford Tractarians, and is numbered amongst their Confessors. If we may reason from the obvious tendency of some passages in his works, the benevolent and simple-minded bishop Berkeley must be considered as belonging to the same religious and political school[1].

But the great majority of the High Church men accommodated themselves to the new state of things. At the same time they cherished a secret attachment to the exiled family, and harassed the government; and by their activity in the lower House of Convocation, thwarted all measures for the relief and conciliation of the Dissenters. Sacheverell was the demagogue of this party; Atterbury, its representative among the bishops; and its high sacerdotal doctrines and mystical theology were set forth with a great, but misapplied, apparatus of learning in the writings of Brett, and Hickes, and Dodwell[2]. Some men of a milder temper, who were advanced to eminent stations after the Revolution, continued to assert

---

[1] See his Discourse of Passive Obedience. His language here is most decided and unqualified: "The least degree of rebellion is, with the utmost strictness and propriety, a *sin*; not only in Christians, but also in those who have the light of reason alone for their guide." Works, II. p. 15. Berkeley's attachment to religion as the sole basis of civil government, and his abhorrence of the modern free-thinking, are very conspicuous in his Essay towards preventing the Ruin of Great Britain, and his Discourse addressed to Magistrates and Men in Authority. Works, vol. ii. He was too enlightened and philosophical to be a slavish worshipper of sacerdotal tradition, and he adhered to the Hanoverian government as established *de facto*; but, had he lived earlier, his principles must have made him a Non-juror.—Hoadly and Berkeley were men who had no sympathy with each other. Hoadly's mind was marked by strong, worldly sense, exactly fitted to adopt and justify the consequences of a practical measure like the Revolution. Berkeley's was distinguished by a refined delicacy of sentiment, and a romantic enthusiasm for the beautiful and good. At queen Caroline's literary parties, where Clarke and Berkeley were constantly opposed to each other in metaphysical gladiatorship, Hoadly always supported the former, and treated Berkeley's philosophy and philanthropy (such as his scheme for the conversion of the Americans by the establishment of a college in the Bermudas) as the reveries of a visionary. Berkeley's Life, prefixed to his Works, 4to, p. xviii.

[2] Burnet's Own Times, II. p. 603–4. All the notions of Andrews, and Laud, and Bramhall, were maintained by these writers. They affirmed, that there was a proper sacrifice in the Eucharist; they condemned the Royal Supremacy and the Reformation; they asserted, that priestly absolution was necessary to give effect to repentance; and that the Sacraments, administered by persons episcopally ordained in the true apostolic succession, were indispensable to salvation; all who were shut out from them, being left to the uncovenanted mercies of God; and that consequently all Dissenters, to be admitted into the

High Church principles. Among these were Bull, profoundly versed in patristical learning and a celebrated defender of the Nicene Creed, whom Bossuet regarded as half a Catholic[1]; Wake, who succeeded Tenison at Canterbury, and engaged in a correspondence with some doctors of the Sorbonne, on the possibility of an union between the English and Gallican churches[2]; and Gibson, bishop of London, whose exalted ideas of Church power were effectually confuted by an eminent constitutional lawyer, Sir Michael Foster.

Soon after the middle of the eighteenth century, these earlier excitements died away. The Church and the Dissenters, recovering from the disturbing forces of the Revolution, had settled themselves each on their respective foundations, and pursued their separate course. Some highly respectable men, brought up among the Dissenters, conformed at the opening of George II.'s reign. They complained of the spirit of imposition that was working in the Nonconformist body[3]. The most eminent of these were, Secker, afterwards primate of all England, and Butler, far less illustrious for his elevation to the see of Durham, than for his profound and original writings. No measures, however, for widening the terms of communion and reconciling Dissenters to the Church, were proposed by either of these prelates[4]. The old idea, once so fondly cherished, of a comprehension, seemed to have vanished among the idle dreams of the past. No attempts were ever made again to unite the two great religious bodies of the nation; which assumed thenceforward

---

Church, must be re-baptized. Dodwell, though sceptical about the canon of Scripture, went so far as to contend, that the principle of immortality was infused into the soul by baptism duly administered. These doctrines were condemned in the Upper House of Convocation by a vote of the bishops; which the Lower House, thinking it struck at the dignity of the priesthood, refused to take even into consideration. Burnet, II. p. 604–5. More than a century after this time, we have seen the same doctrines revived by the Puseyites.

[1] Nelson's Life of Bull.
[2] There is an account of this correspondence by Dr. Maclaine, in the appendix to the 4th Volume of Murdock's translation of Mosheim's Institutes, in which he qualifies the unfavourable inferences of the author of the Confessional (preface, pp. lxxiv.–lxxxiii. and p. 88, note, 2nd edit.).
[3] Calamy's Life and Times, II. p. 506.
[4] Secker was very reserved in the expression of his opinions; a strict disciplinarian in his own Church, and shy towards Dissenters. When Doddridge congratulated him on his elevation to the bench, and hoped that it might lead to a closer union between the Church and the Dissenters, Secker at once discouraged the idea. Nichols's Lit. Anecd. III. 748, on the authority of Jones of Welwyn.

that fixed attitude of mutual alienation, which they have ever since retained.

The great bulk of the inferior clergy, weaned at length from the hopeless cause of the Stuarts, and anxious for preferment, resumed once more their natural habits of deference to the established government, and attached themselves to the aristocracy,—which had become since the Revolution, and was every day becoming more, the predominant element in the constitution. **The** great champion of the Church of England at this period of its history, was Warburton, whose celebrated work on the alliance of Church and State, is **an** ingenious defence of the actual position of the hierarchy in relation both **to the** Dissenters and to the government. It endeavours to combine the assertion of principles which could no longer be contested, with the retention of privileges which it was not agreeable to relinquish. It recognizes Toleration; but it **up**holds all the legal defences and ancient prerogatives of **the** Church[1].

SECTION IX.

MODERN PERIOD.

The eighteenth century was distinguished by a widely-diffused culture and superficial elegance of mind, the result of general tranquillity and a high material civilization, **in which** those **prominent** expressions **of strong conviction** and **deep**

---

[1] Warburton's **theory of the** Alliance **of Church** and State, may be thus stated. The Church and **the State are** originally and *per se* two distinct and independent societies, but essential nevertheless **to** each other's security and efficiency; on which account, they voluntarily, and, in the nature of things necessarily, enter into **a** compact with each other, whereby the Church parts with **its** supremacy, and submits to the supremacy **of** the Civil Magistrate; the State bestowing maintenance, dignity and power on the Church; the Church ennobling and sanctifying the State. His theory, therefore, differs from that of Hooker, who considered Church and State as only different names for the same **society,** and supposed, that, had they been originally distinct, they must always have continued **so;** whereas the Church was, as it ought to be, incorporated with the general frame-work of the Commonwealth. It differs also from that of the Puritans, who maintained the original, and necessary, and constant, distinctness, of the two societies (so Calvin argued at Geneva, and Cartwright in England); and who founded on that principle their doctrine of the independence and supremacy of the Church, involving all the inconvenience and absurdity of **an** *imperium in imperio.* Warburton affirmed, that Hooker was wrong in his

feeling, called out by the conflicts of the preceding century, gradually disappeared. The Church of England partook of the general quietude and the absence of all high enthusiasm which characterized the period. Without formally renouncing its ancient standards of faith and worship, it softened down its distinctive features and suppressed the manifestation of its inherent tendencies. Rather avoiding than seeking any collision with controverted points, it studied ease and repose; dealt in truisms and generalities; and subsided into a calm ethical view of Christianity. The old High Church principles of the seventeenth century were fast disappearing with the Jacobites and the Non-jurors; and the Evangelical spirit was yet in its infancy. Such was the state of things at the commencement of the reign of George III. But change was already in preparation. **This negation of all** individuality was intolerable to **sincere and earnest men. Two tendencies,** originating in an opposite view of Christianity, and leading **to** very different results, the Calvinistic and the Latitudinarian—had begun to display themselves.

Methodism exhibits the most remarkable phenomenon in the religious history of England, during the eighteenth century. It had its source and impelling principle in strong reaction against the cold, negative and powerless character of the prevailing religion, blended with a benevolent compassion **for** the neglected condition of the humblest classes. While Hoadly and a host of speculative theologians were beating the air with abstract discussions on the rights of the inquiring **mind,** the sad and solemn facts of living and suffering humanity were overlooked by them; and myriads of their fellow-creatures were sunk in an abyss of heathenish ignorance and brutality. It is a singular fact, which marks the secret link of spiritual connection between one manifestation of earnest Christianity and another, that the writings which made the first serious impression on Wesley's mind, and first awakened its devotional fervour, were those of the Non-juror Law; and they produced the same effect on Mr. Venn, though he afterwards embraced **a** very different theological system[1], as one of

premises, **but** right in his conclusion; that the Puritans were right in their **premises,** but wrong in their conclusion. He insisted on the secular ascendency of the Church, and the necessity of a Test-law for its protection; but asserted with equal vehemence what he called the "divine doctrine" of Toleration. He **took** for the basis of his system, the ideas of Mr. Locke, and adroitly applied **them** to the support of an existing institution.

[1] Venn's Life by his Son.

the earliest Evangelical preachers in the Church of England. The eagerness with which persons of all classes, even the very highest[1], flocked to hear the Methodist preachers, and gave themselves up to the stirring or insinuating appeals that were made to their hearts and consciences by the stern impassioned Calvinism of Whitfield or the more persuasive Arminianism of Wesley, affords the strongest proof of the inefficiency of the Establishment for its high function: whilst the absurd and improvident bigotry with which it disowned the ministrations of pious and devoted men, sincerely attached to its formularies and discipline, gave birth to a vast and compact hierarchy, distinct at once from the Dissenters and the Church, whose manifold relation to the old religious divisions of the country might well deserve a chapter to itself. The disinclination of the higher orders permanently to separate themselves from the national religion, and the exertions of such men as Mr. Wilberforce and Mr. Thornton to place zealous preachers of the doctrines called Evangelical, in the pulpits of the Establishment, prevented a more extensive secession; and though accompanied at times with some extravagance and uncharitableness, brought back into the Church a religious life which had almost disappeared. It cannot be denied that the Evangelical party has wrought much good in the revival of personal religion, and meritoriously co-operated with the Methodists and some classes of Dissenters, in labours of piety and benevolence. No religious body is competent in itself to the entire work of religious renovation. Great earnestness in what is essentially holy and good, is often shaded with attendant infirmities. It is sufficient for one who wishes to survey the wide and variegated field of human action and opinion with an open eye and a brotherly spirit, to discover, if he can, the specific task of service, which God has assigned to different classes and sects, and to acknowledge with respect and thankfulness its faithful and energetic performance.

Intellect is less contagious than sentiment and feeling. The men who think freely and act independently, will always form a small minority. Far less striking and palpable were the results of the effort made by another section of the Church, to promote freedom of Scriptural inquiry, and to obtain a release from subscription to the Thirty-nine Articles. With this view an association was formed of clergy and laity, who in

---

[1] See the curious and instructive Memoirs of the Life and Times of the Countess of Huntingdon.

1772 petitioned Parliament for relief; but their application was rejected. The Evangelical party, with Mr. Venn and Lady Huntingdon at their head, opposed the measure with all their influence; and Mr. Burke, though in general friendly to the extension of religious freedom, resisted the concession, and with great force pointed out its incompatibility with the principles of the Establishment[1]. The principles entertained by the promoters of this scheme and made the ground of their petition to Parliament, had been exhibited in a work called the Confessional, published anonymously, but known to be the production of archdeacon Blackburne[2]. This work assumed the preservation of the Establishment; but, as the condition of admission to its offices, proposed to substitute for subscription to the Articles a simple declaration of belief in the Scriptures, and a promise to make them the rule and standard of public teaching. This was coming as near to the attainment of religious freedom as the retention of the Establishment would permit. But the plan, though specious in theory, is burdened with great practical difficulties. The terms suggested are themselves so vague, that they must have led in usage to an arbitrary limitation, which would have excluded some parties. Viewed abstractedly they do not satisfy the full demands of the rights of conscience. Any one who had studied the history and genius of the English Church, and watched the feelings that were deeply cherished by its most devoted adherents, might have foreseen the reception which the proposal of so sweeping a change would be certain to encounter; and however groundless these feelings may to some appear, it is still a question, whether it would have been prudent and right, harshly to violate them. In consequence of the frustration of this measure, a few clergymen who were dissatisfied with subscription, and among them, that meek confessor, the Rev. Theophilus Lindsey, seceded from the national Church. The mental tendencies of which the petition to Parliament was an expression, no longer finding a vent in the Establishment, henceforth took refuge, where they have been expressed at all, in the Presbyterian and Anti-trinitarian section of the Dissenters.

[1] Venn's Life, with Lady Huntingdon's Memoirs, II. 286-7. Burke's Speeches, Vol. I. p. 94. Feb. 6, 1772.
[2] Its title ran thus: 'The Confessional: or a full and free Inquiry into the Right, Utility, Edification, and Success of establishing Systematical Confessions of Faith and Doctrine in Protestant Churches.' The second edition, enlarged, was published in 1767.

Since the peace in 1815,—called forth by alarm at the strong measures of civil and ecclesiastical reform, introduced in rapid succession by a liberal government, an intense revival has taken place of the old High Church principles. In 1833, a few individuals holding these sentiments met at Oxford, to agree upon a course of joint action to resist the democratic tendencies of the age. Hence the publication of the Tracts for the Times. The deep feeling at the heart of this party, is distrust of popular progress, and aversion to the shallow, vulgar Protestantism which courts popular sympathies. But this system, though it has acquired a modern name, is no novelty in the history of the English Church. It is only an exaggerated expression of its inherent principles, called out by vehement reaction. It is the system of Dodwell and Leslie, and the Non-jurors at the time of the Revolution; of Bramhall, Laud, Andrews, and Bancroft under the Stuarts. It is not Popish; though some minds have been driven by it into Popery. It loves the old English ritual, and the high sacerdotal doctrines which have been associated with it; and avails itself of every grammatical license, to extract from the Articles a sense that is **Anti-calvinistic**[1]. This party finds itself in a position unparalleled by any former period of its history. Popular principles have made an immense advance. Moored to the precedents of the past, it sees the strong tide of public opinion flow past it, and is afraid of being swept away in the stream. Its old trust in the Crown is gone; Parliament is against it; the aristocracy is divided; and there is now no exiled Royalty on which it can bestow its sympathies. Forsaken by its ancient supports, it has only the Church to lean upon; and this may account for the display of a stronger feeling towards Romanism.

A retrospect of the history of the Anglican Church demonstrates the utter inefficiency of Creeds, Articles, and a settled form of Prayer, to preserve agreement in belief, or even harmony of feeling, among its members. Three parties exist, and long have existed, within it, devoid of all sympathy with each other, but each sustaining a most intimate relation to certain bodies that are external to it. It is encircled by Catholics, by Evangelical, and by what are called Rational, Dissenters. Within it, we recognize the same three elements, the Catholic, the Evangelical, and the Liberal. We have traced the filiation of the Catholic element from Andrews

[1] See Tract 90.

and Laud through the Non-jurors to the Oxford Tractarians. The Evangelicals find their counterpart in the doctrinal Puritans of the seventeenth century. Hales, Whichcot, Wilkins and Tillotson are the predecessors and spiritual progenitors of a most respectable, but now, it is to be feared, the smallest and feeblest, party in the Church; the moderate and rational party; attached to truth and science and social progress; friendly to Dissenters; not confounding an Establishment with the vital principles of Christianity, but regarding it as a human instrument for their support. With differences resulting from the complexion of their minds or the state of the times, we may assign to this class, in the last and preceding generation, Jortin, Law, Newcome, Shipley, Paley, and Parr, and in the present, Maltby, Whately, and Arnold[1]. Such men would liberalize the Church, if it were possible. They have no superstitious reverence for episcopacy as such; they regard it simply as a discipline and an instrumentality for the accomplishment of a great social object. They would gladly make the Establishment express and cherish the religion of the nation, and cease to be an instrument of insult and annoyance in the hands of selfish and ambitious men. But what can we think of the unity of a Church, in which men, so opposite in their views, as Dr. Pusey, archdeacon Hare, and the present most respectable primate of all England, Dr. Sumner, are equally recognized as ministers, and required to use the same formularies and to sign the same articles? After the debates of centuries, it is yet a matter of dispute, which of the three is the truest son of the Church of England. It is strange that the controversies of the first Reformers should still be left unsolved; and that one half of the Church should deem the other heretical, for preferring the Catholic or the Calvinistic elements, which may be found in its Prayer-book, its Articles, and its Homilies.

[1] These distinguished men have differed in their conception of an Establishment. Paley adopted substantially, with increased liberality to Dissenters, the views of Warburton. Dr. Whately, as appears from his work on the Kingdom of Christ, regards all Churches as voluntary associations of such individuals as agree in their ideas of faith and worship, and treats the establishment of any one of the number, as a mere social accident. Dr. Arnold, who has expressed his opinions very plainly in the preface to his Roman History (p. ix.), in various passages of his published Correspondence, and more recently in his posthumous Fragment on the Church (appendix, ii. and iii.) is an Erastian, admitting no distinction between a Christian Church and a Christian Commonwealth.

CHAPTER III.

PURITANISM.

SECTION I.

PREDOMINANT IDEA OF PURITANISM.

HAVING attempted in the preceding chapter to describe the constitution and historical development of the Anglican hierarchy, I proceed now to contrast with it the nature and operation of the antagonistic principle of Puritanism. It is from the conflict of these opposing tendencies, that the peculiar character of our religious life results. The spirit of Puritanism must not, however, be confounded with the principles of free inquiry and mental independence, which ultimately grew out of it, and by those who were capable of reasoning it into its consequences, might have been seen to be involved in it. The fundamental idea of Puritanism, in all its forms and ramifications, is the supreme authority of Scripture, acting directly on the individual conscience, as opposed to a reliance on the priesthood and the outward ordinances of the Church. To realize the standard of faith, worship and conduct, recorded in Scripture, has ever been the object of Puritanism; and to attain that object, in defiance of a hierarchy, requires no small degree of self-reliance and decision of purpose. But with Puritanism the range of inquiry is shut up within the limits of the written Word. It does not venture to sally forth beyond them, to survey the Scripture under a broader aspect, from some point of view external to it. Where, as with Baxter and others of a later period, the principle of rigid Scripturalism was less firmly grasped, they approached the confines of the Latitudinarian system, and ceased, to that extent, to be proper Puritans.

In truth, absolute freedom of inquiry in the present condition of society can be exercised, if at all, by only a few minds. It may belong to individuals; it cannot belong to the multitude. It is one of the latest results of advanced intellectual culture. The mass of men will long, perhaps must for ever, continue to recognize a practical rule of faith and conduct somewhere or other out of themselves. Puritanism which from its origin was rather a product and expression of popular feeling, than the impulse of a speculative intellect, casting off by a spasmodic effort the constraint and oppression of the old sacerdotal yoke, threw itself with implicit trust on Scripture, as a substituted authority; and opposed the claims of God and Christ to those of uninspired and erring men. The idea was grand and animating. Though it involved assumptions, and drew after it difficulties, not very distinctly apprehended in the first outbreak of reforming zeal, it contained enough of undoubted and most valuable truth, to apply a powerful lever to the public mind in its resistance to the domination of the hierarchy.

Thus the sufficiency of Scripture is the fundamental postulate of Puritanism; the authority of the Church, the ground practically taken by the Anglican hierarchy: and these incompatible assumptions have been the cause of the unintermitted strife between them, through the last four or five centuries of our history. Scripture, the record and depository of the free and popular spirit of the primitive Gospel, the Magna Charta of religious liberty, is a standing witness and protest against the pretensions of spiritual despotism. In the spirit which it breathes, we find a reason of the profound reverence for it ever manifested by those, who at different periods have struggled against episcopal tyranny and called aloud for ecclesiastical reform, from the African sectaries who resisted Cyprian and were persecuted by Augustine, down to the Waldenses, the Hussites and the Lollards of the Middle Ages; and in the same spirit we detect a motive for the efforts of the priesthood to keep the dispensation of the Word of life in their own hands, and to prevent its free circulation among the laity. The conflict pervades the whole of Christian history, and goes back to the first ages of the Church. If mere antiquity could decide the question at issue, Puritanism through its authentic representatives from the earliest times, might at least make out as venerable a pedigree, and establish as clear a line of apostolical descent, as Episcopacy. Taking the word Puritanism in the large sense which has been explained in a former chapter, we may trace the identity of the principle, in all its most striking manifestations, through every period of its history, whether oppressed by a Catholic, or in collision with a Protestant, hierarchy. Under all outward changes, we shall find, that Scripturalism, a severe morality, popular sympathies, and ardent attachment to civil freedom, have constituted the sign and peculiar distinction of Puritanism.

SECTION II.

SPIRIT AND AFFINITIES OF LOLLARDISM.

Many points of coincidence at once present themselves between Lollardism and the later Puritanism, especially in its more extreme forms of Independency, Anabaptism, and Quakerism. In the antagonism of minds, as in the collision of bodies, action and reaction are equal. Intolerable tyranny or shameless corruption call forth in resistance to themselves, an overstrained spirituality of devotion and extravagant asceticism. Where the pressure is relaxed, the opposition becomes less intense. It was under an establishment itself reformed, still working with the leaven of recent change, and believed by numbers to be destined to further purification, that Puritanism, in the days of Edward VI. and the first years of Elizabeth's reign, put on a respectful and conciliatory demeanour towards the hierarchy, and aimed at renewal and perfection, rather than destruction. On the other hand, it was in open defiance of the unbroken strength of the Romish priesthood, and in full view of its undisguised avarice and immoralities, that the followers of Wycliffe took their stern measure of ecclesiastical reform. Pursued with implacable malignity by the clergy through the whole course of the fifteenth century, imprisoned, fagoted, and burnt, they planted deep those principles of religious democracy, which were never afterwards eradicated from the mind of the English commonalty, but, after the lapse of a century, shot up again with new vigour, when the power of the bishops once more became oppressive. The Independents, and not the Presbyterians, derive their origin from the Lollards.

In perfect consistency with their fundamental principle, the Lollards admitted nothing into their faith, worship, or practice, which had not the sanction of Scripture. They did not acknowledge the authority of general councils; and Wycliffe treated all ecclesiastical writers, since the thousandth year of Christ, as heretics. Their doctrinal system was nearly identical with Calvinism, a form of belief which has always prevailed among the Puritans. They held, that the true Church of Christ consists of predestinated persons, and of none else. With this notion they combined the allied doctrines of election by grace, remission of sins through the satisfaction of the cross, justification by faith, sanctification by the Spirit, and, in a modified sense, without distinctly acknowledging its application to the present relations of society, the obscure and suspicious tenet of "dominion founded on grace[1]." It was probably only another mode of stating the doctrine, that spiritual must finally prevail over temporal interests in the affairs of men; and that no power can permanently endure, which is opposed to the will of God. It is a literal adoption of Paul's words, that "the saints shall judge the world." The rigorous and consequential intellect of Wycliffe had firmly grasped the doctrine of philosophical necessity, and saw all things under the control of the irresistible decrees of God.

All these views were closely connected with each other, as parts of a common system; and had their source in the reaction of intense personal religion against the externality and spiritual deadness of the hierarchy; in a deep feeling, that nothing but the immediate operation of God upon the soul, could extricate men from the foul sink of an abounding wickedness and infidelity. Scripture therefore in its literal simplicity, was eagerly embraced, as a medium of direct intercourse with God and Christ; from whom alone, in entire independence of all human aids, a new and higher life was sought, and all blessings temporal and eternal were implored: while the whole apparatus of priestly mediation and church ceremonies was cast aside, as thrusting a heathenish barrier between Christ and the individual soul, and obstructing the sole fountain of its salvation.

Doctrines akin to these, have usually been taken up in the first strong, convulsive wrestlings of the human spirit with

[1] Vaughan's Life of Wycliffe. Lingard's Hist. of England, vol. iv. 8vo. This last historian has remarked (ch. ii.) that in the doctrine of dominion founded on grace, there is a mixture of feudal and theological ideas: all property, being held of God, is forfeited by sin, which is treason against God.

inveterate corruption and deep-seated unbelief; and Scriptural authority has been claimed for them, in the burning and impassioned words of Paul, whose warfare was with the gigantic iniquity of the ancient world. When the faith and morals of mankind have undergone a long and deep decay, nothing but an intense concentration of the soul on God, as the only and immediate source of all spiritual power, with the consciousness which is its result, of an intimate, indissoluble, personal relation to Him—can furnish motives sufficiently powerful, to break the chains of previous habit and association, and throw men at once on a totally new course of life. If every popular belief of wide and enduring diffusion must have some particle of truth for its nucleus, it is perhaps this law of our spiritual being which is expressed, only too absolutely and universally, in the doctrine of "election by grace." The individual must first be purified and renovated, before he can beneficially entertain an indiscriminate sympathy with the whole human race. While his process of self-renewal is still in progress; while he feels how difficult and critical it is; how easily it may be stayed, and frustrated; how awful is the alternative which it involves; he must keep aloof from the world, as set apart for an object beyond the world, and cannot as yet, with safety to himself, look on the great mass of his fellow-creatures as otherwise than reprobate. Whatever abuses this exclusiveness may ultimately have led to, it is certainly the fact, that in our own country, the spirit of moral and religious reform began in rigid Calvinism, and gradually softened down into the milder character of Arminianism.

As with the later Puritans, so with the Lollards, resistance to ecclesiastical tyranny aroused a kindred love of political freedom. If they contended for the liberty of prophesying, in spite of prelatical restrictions; they also asserted, that just government in the magistrate, is the condition of obedience in the people, and that the abuse of power deprives it of its right. The democratic outbreaks in Richard II.'s time had affinities more or less direct with the Lollard doctrines. Though an obscurity invests the charges against Lord Cobham, the most eminent of the party in the reign of Henry V., yet the very nature of them, however vague, implies a supposed connection between the principles which he was known to profess, and those of civil liberty.

The spirit of Wycliffe himself was tinged with the gloom of

a deep and thoughtful earnestness. His biographer observes, that he has not remarked a single passage in his writings which indicates a sprightly and mirthful state of mind. The work which occupied him was too grand and solemn, to allow him to relax for a moment the rigid bent of his faculties. His followers inherited the same stern and enthusiastic temperament, worked up into fanaticism by unceasing persecution. How completely all these things were the foreshadowings and prolusions of a bolder and more triumphant exhibition of the same principle, which came forth in the seventeenth century; how entirely Lollardism and the extremer forms of Puritanism are identical; we shall perceive with abundant evidence as we proceed.

SECTION III.

INCIPIENT PURITANIC MOVEMENTS.

The revolution occasioned by Henry VIII.'s rupture with Rome, affected chiefly the outward relations of the Church, which internally experienced little essential alteration, till the accession of more powerful reforming influences under Edward VI. The act of Henry was only a link in a chain of causes already in active operation. Of the three religious parties which had existed in England from the time of Wycliffe, we find the exact counterpart—merely substituting the Church of which the king had become the head, for the old Catholic hierarchy —after the Reformation. There were those who adhered to the actual constitution of things, and opposed all further change—the selfish or timid and peace-loving conservatives; there were others, attached to the forms and discipline of a national Church, but desirous of proceeding further in reformation; and lastly, those who wished to destroy every vestige of a hierarchy. Some minds are constitutionally averse from change. They resist innovation as long as they can; but when it has once taken place, and something is fixed, they make the best of it, and stand as firmly by the new establishment, as they did by the old. Men of this disposition temporized under Henry, and acquiesced in the settlements made by Edward and Elizabeth. Abhorring democratic movements and deeply

Catholic in all their feelings, they widely spread through the English Church that reverence for tradition and authority which is peculiar to it, and of which we have traced the effects in the preceding chapter.

Of the two other parties alluded to, loosely comprehended under the name Puritan, and exhibiting in fact only different stages of the same general tendency, the character and operations are yet sufficiently distinct, to justify us in considering their history separately. The terms Presbyterian and Independent express a difference of principle respecting the constitution of a Church, which makes its appearance soon after the Reformation; and running through the entire history of Nonconformity, has not yet ceased to produce its effects. Those who scrupled to comply in all things with the ritual and canons of the Church, acquired early in Elizabeth's reign, by way of reproach, the name of Puritans or Precisians. It was often given, says Fuller, by the profane to such as manifested any deep sense of religion, although they were strict Conformists[1]. The objections of such persons at first related chiefly to certain parts of the clerical dress, and some ceremonies retained from the Catholic service, that were disliked as the outward marks of a superstition which they tended to keep up in the popular mind. Such was the ground taken by the more moderate Nonconformists, who did not go the length of objecting absolutely to episcopal government. In the progress of the controversy, exasperated by the harsh measures of Parker and Whitgift, a bolder tone was assumed; the episcopal hierarchy was denounced as infected with the dregs of Rome; and it was broadly affirmed, that the presbyterian platform had a warrant from Scripture and a divine right, to take its place, as the form of the national church. The Nonconformists of this class, whether extreme or moderate in their views, were for the most part men of learning, who had enjoyed an university education. Many of them had been in exile in Mary's days, and still maintained a close correspondence with the foreign reformers. In Frankfort, in Zurich, and above all in Geneva, they had imbibed principles which powerfully influenced their conduct on their return home. In the churches which acknowledged the authority of Calvin, they experienced a most cordial reception, and with these they entered into the closest intimacy. A division of opinion, however, respecting liturgies

[1] Church History, Book IX. sect. i. 67.

and episcopal government, took place even among the exiles; and the "Troubles of Frankfort¹" were but a prelude to the strife between Conformists and Nonconformists, which was destined to agitate England for more than a century to come. Many circumstances strengthened the influence of the early Puritans. They saw their cause triumphant in Scotland, and Presbyterianism established by the invincible zeal of Knox who had been their companion in exile. The first generation of Elizabeth's bishops treated them for the most part with respect and tenderness, and some had even a lurking sympathy with their scruples. Grindal who was primate after Parker, incurred the lasting displeasure of the Queen for the countenance he afforded them, and his resistance to her despotic proceedings[2]. The course of events had placed Elizabeth at the head of the Protestant interest in Europe; and her counsellors were not sorry to strengthen their hands with the influence of a powerful body of men who regarded Catholicism with abhorrence.

Leicester, Knollys, and Walsingham, were puritanically inclined; Raleigh pleaded their cause in Parliament; and Burleigh sometimes interposed to shield them from the severities of the Court of High Commission[3]. Jealousy of episcopal pretensions far more than religious zeal, inspired statesmen

---

[1] A work under this title, "The History of the Troubles of Frankfort," was published in 1575. The substance of it may be seen in Fuller, Book VIII. sect. iii. 1-29, and Neal, vol. i. pp. 72-78. The exiles at Zurich were attached to the Service Book established under Edward VI. Those of Frankfort, guided by Knox and others, wished to come nearer to the Genevan model; but in this they were vehemently opposed by Cox, afterwards bishop of Ely, who was zealous for the English Liturgy.

[2] Those who took Grindal's view of the case of the Puritans, were called by the high Episcopalians, Grindalizers. Spenser in his Shepherd's Calendar, inverting the syllables of the name, celebrates Grindal as "old Algrind," and describes his suspension in the following lines; July, vv. 215-20.

"Hee is a shepheard great in gree,
 But hath bene long ypent:
One day hee sat upon a hill,
 As now thou wouldest mee;
But I am taught, by Algrind's ill,
 To love the lowe degree."

In the fifth, seventh, and ninth eclogues, Spenser betrays symptoms of Puritanical feeling, particularly in his preference of Grindal to Aylmer, bishop of London. See Todd's Life of Spenser, prefixed to his edition of the poet's works, p. xiv.

[3] Strype's Lives of Parker and Whitgift. Burleigh's Letter to Whitgift in Neal, I. p. 285.

and courtiers with these sentiments; but the result was, that Puritanism acquired the weight and consideration which attach to a political body. In doctrine, its adherents agreed entirely with the Establishment: but they desired a simpler ritual and a stricter discipline; and their reverence for the supreme authority of Scripture, made them object to the Erastian principle of its subordination to the State. Such was the commencement of the great Presbyterian party. It was powerful from its numbers, its learning, its foreign connections, and the high station of many of its supporters; it was aristocratical rather than popular in its tendencies; and through all its gradations of opinion it clung to the wish for a reformed national church in place of the actual hierarchy.

While these movements were agitating the upper regions of society, at a lower depth a strong popular fermentation was going on, which had originated long anterior to the Reformation, and was pregnant with effects far more extensive than any as yet distinctly contemplated by the learned. The Gospellers who abounded at the commencement of Henry's reign, were the same people with the Lollards; and this name sufficiently indicates their distinguishing principle. They were devoted to the study of the Scriptures, and would sit up all night to read and hear the word. No expense was spared by them to obtain books, and some were known to give a load of hay for a few chapters of St. James or St. Paul in English. "But the Word of Truth," says Fox, writing in the days of Elizabeth, "did, notwithstanding, multiply among them exceedingly. Wherein is to be seen no doubt the marvellous working of God's mighty power. For so I find and observe in considering the Registers[1], how one neighbour resorting and conferring with another, eftsoons with a few words of their first or second talk, did win and turn their minds to that wherein they desired to persuade them, touching the truth of God's Word and his Sacraments. To see their travels, their earnest seeking, their burning zeals, their readings, their watchings, their sweet assemblies, their love and concord, their godly living, their faithful marrying with the faithful, may make us now in these our days of free profession, to blush for shame[2]." They were very numerous in the midland and eastern counties, where they were often severely perse-

[1] Of the diocese of Lincoln.
[2] Book of Martyrs, II. fol. p. 23.

cuted by the bishops. Among other names, they had that of *known men* and *known women*, or *just fast men;* and were mostly persons of humble origin[1].

During the reign of Mary, when the more learned Protestants suffered martyrdom or fled beyond seas, these humble Gospellers, sheltered by their obscurity, still kept up their secret meetings for worship; and, in the absence of regularly educated ministers, were preached to by laymen of mean condition, such as weavers and wheelwrights[2]. In the city of London they assembled privily, sometimes in one place and sometimes in another, to escape the pursuit of the officers of justice; and having many adherents among the mercantile and seafaring class, they held their service occasionally, for the sake of greater security, on board the vessels in the river. This London congregation varied in numbers from forty to one or two hundred, and towards the end of Mary's reign greatly increased. It had several ministers; one of them, Mr. Bentham, who was a learned man and a scholar of Oxford, was made bishop of Lichfield and Coventry on the accession of Elizabeth[3]. The principles of these people, maintained in the face of danger, were thorough and uncompromising; their devotion to the Scriptures most ardent; their dislike of the hierarchy and of every approach to it, intense. In the present condition of society, we can hardly estimate the strength of these feelings. What has been withheld or forbidden by an arbitrary and tyrannical power, excites an interest and curiosity, with a dislike of the restraining hand, beyond all bounds. When the Scriptures began to be circulated in English under Henry VIII., the Lollard tendencies came out in all their force. Old people learned to read, that they might study the Bible; and young people and children flocked to the churches to hear it. Strype tells an anecdote of a young man, who exposed himself to the deadliest rage of his father, who was a papist, for joining with a fellow-apprentice to purchase a Bible[4]. Penry, an ardent Brownist, who was executed for his principles under Elizabeth, in a paper addressed to the Queen from Edinburgh, 1593, comparing the mitigated Protestantism then established in England with the martyr-like zeal of a

---

[1] Strype, Ecclesiast. Mem. I. ch. vii. viii.
[2] See an account of two such in Strype, Eccl. Mem., vol. v. ch. xlvii.
[3] Fox, vol. iii. p. 774.   [4] Life of Cranmer, p. 64.

former period, expresses a sentiment similar to that already quoted from Fox, and declares his belief, that in all likelihood, if the days of queen Mary and her persecution had continued unto that day, the Church of God in England would have been far more flourishing than it then was, and have far surpassed all the Reformed Churches in the world[1]. It was this deep popular feeling, working in the heart of society, and owning no distinct impulse but unmeasured hatred of prelacy and enthusiastic reverence for the Word of God, which found a wild and turbulent utterance in the tracts of Martin Marprelate. Many natives of the Low Countries, exiled by religious persecution, had settled in Norfolk and Suffolk as early as 1560; and meeting with congenial elements in the native population, excited a spirit of religious enthusiasm, which spread over that part of England, and has left traces of its influence there to the present day. Early in Elizabeth's reign, a sect appeared in the diocese of Ely, many of whose tenets were irreconcilable with any form of church government, and resembled those of the Anabaptists and Quakers[2].

By Puritanism, as already explained, I designate the general tendency which moved onward, after the settlement of the Church by Elizabeth, in the direction of further reform. Under that title are comprehended very different manifestations of the religious life, all springing originally from a common impulse. The movement was arrested at different stages of its progress, in only a few cases proceeding to its utmost length; and it thus gave birth to successive waves, as it were, of assault on the hierarchy, each advancing beyond its predecessor, till at length the fabric fell under the joint influence of their repeated attacks. It will conduce to the clearer understanding of this part of our religious history, briefly to exhibit in

---

[1] Neal, vol. i. p. 376.
[2] Strype's Parker, p. 287. Hanbury's Historical Memorials of the Independents. Religious peculiarities adhere to certain localities. Edwards in his Gangræna describes the sectaries as very numerous in the eastern counties, and mentions the Isle of Ely as a notorious resort of them. Calamy, at a later period, speaks of Bedfordshire and Essex, as abounding with Dissenters of an enthusiastic character, regardless of ordination and a learned education. (Defence of Moderate Nonconformity, etc., 1703.) Norwich, and Braintree in Essex have been the seats in the present day of the most vigorous resistance to church-rates. The Baptists were till lately very numerous among the yeomanry of the Weald of Kent. Cheshire, Lancashire, and Yorkshire, were anciently the strongholds of Presbyterianism.

succession the principles and operations of the several parties that were involved in the great Puritanic movement. Of these the Presbyterians or proper Puritans, from their numbers and social influence, claim our attention first.

SECTION IV.

HIGH PRESBYTERIANISM UNDER ELIZABETH.

Two circumstances distinguished the Presbyterian party at its origin: an attachment to the doctrines and usages of the Calvinistic churches of the Continent; and a persuasion, that the model of a national Church polity was authoritatively laid down in Scripture. Valuing exceedingly the learning of schools and universities, especially when devoted to the service of divine truth, they nevertheless agreed with the more extreme Puritans and the old Lollards, in a strong dislike of the coldness and formalism of the Establishment. Like them they wished to introduce a stricter religious discipline, and a more primitive fervour and earnestness, guided by Scriptural rule, into the Church. But their scruples met with no toleration from the Queen and her most favoured bishops: and thus, while a moderate concession in matters indifferent would have satisfied and reconciled the most eminent among them, they were driven by conscience on the separation they dreaded and abhorred; and being once released from control, they reasoned out their fundamental ideas consequentially, and set up in opposition to the prelates, the divine right of Presbyterianism. For refusing to perform a few insignificant ceremonies and wear certain garments, the most pious and acceptable ministers were deprived of their licenses and suspended from preaching. Even the years and virtues and useful labours of Miles Coverdale did not exempt him from this ecclesiastical persecution. The consequence was, that, from the want of *conformable* ministers, as they were then called, many parishes were left wholly unprovided; and the Church, defeating the express object of its own institution, was the immediate cause of spiritual destitution throughout the land. In London and many other parts of the country, a large proportion of the laity were puritanical, and shunned the services of a compliant minister who was willing to do the bishops' bidding, with almost as much horror as those of a Papist.

Among other methods of aiding the cause of evangelical reform and spreading a knowledge of the Scriptures, must be mentioned the *prophesyings*, a kind of religious exercises, which prevailed chiefly in the counties of Norfolk, Essex, and Northampton, and which afforded, it might have been supposed, a harmless and salutary vent for the religious enthusiasm of the day. In these prophesyings the ministers of a district met at some central place to exercise themselves in the exposition of Scripture. The Scriptural precedent for such meetings was founded on that text of the Apostle (1 Cor. xiv. 31), "Ye may all prophesy one by one, that all may learn, and all be comforted;" and being much resorted to by the neighbouring gentry, they proved a great means of diffusing puritanical sentiments. Fuller has described their mode of proceeding[1]. The junior divine went first into the pulpit, and for about half an hour, treated of some portion of Scripture which had been previously agreed on; and after him, four or five others in the order of seniority dilated on the same passage. At last a divine of more years and experience, appointed on purpose, reviewed in a somewhat longer discourse the preceding exercises, and made his comments on them, solemn prayer terminating, as it had opened, the whole service. A public refection then followed, at which the time of the next meeting was fixed; the text assigned; the preachers appointed; and the moderator elected. Fuller, with the feelings of a Churchman, but not unkindly, has noticed some of the abuses to which these prophesyings led. Modest ministers were loth to put themselves forward; while young men of more boldness than learning, forgetting their text and launching out into vehement invectives against the discipline and government of the Church, excited great applause and carried off all the credit of the meeting. Thus parties arose among the auditory, some extolling one minister and some another; and heat of temper with sharp personal recrimination, accompanied the difference of opinion inevitable among disputatious theologians. But allowing the utmost force to these imputed evils, the prophesyings were a natural expression of the spirit of the time. Their very existence proclaimed the inadequacy of the established system to the religious

---

[1] Church Hist. Book IX. Sect. iv. 2, 3.

wants of the community. Under proper guidance they might have become nurseries of a learned and pious clergy. Such was the judgment of no less a person than Lord Bacon. Some of Elizabeth's bishops regarded them with indulgence; but the Queen herself was resolved on their abolition. Parkhurst, who would fain have tolerated them in the diocese of Norwich, was obliged to suppress them; and Grindal's honest and courageous refusal to put them down altogether, cost him his Sovereign's favour, and sequestered him from the functions of the primacy, for the remainder of his life[1].

Thus the spirit of Puritanism was restricted at every point in its free and natural expression; both within the limits of the ordinary services of the Church, and in the occasional exercises which were designed as supplementary to them: and the necessary consequence was, a proportionate development of resisting force. The Puritans themselves were perplexed and distracted by opposing tendencies; by their reverence for a national Church and their dread of schism; and by their persuasion of the Scriptural authority of Presbyterianism. According as the one or the other tendency predominated in their minds, they submitted to the Establishment with all its evils in hope of future reform, or they resolved on separation. This gave occasion to the distinction between *conformable* and *nonconforming* Puritans. The former avoided as many of the objectionable ceremonies as they could, by accepting the office of lecturers and of chaplains in private families, which did not involve parochial duty or the necessity of reading every part of the liturgy. The latter adopted the Geneva service-book; justified their conduct by that of their predecessors, who had set up separate congregations during exile and in Queen Mary's days; and held their meetings for worship in woods and solitary fields, and wherever else they could hope to escape the vigilance of government. The era of this separation is placed by Strype and Neal about the year 1566[2]. In the following year, about a hundred persons were surprised by the sheriffs in Plumbers' Hall, which they had hired, under pretext of a wedding, to hear a sermon and join in the communion. Most of them were taken into custody; and the leaders brought up for examination before the chief authorities

[1] His long letter to the Queen, remarkable for its plain speaking, is given by Fuller, IX. iv. 3.
[2] Neal's Hist. of the Puritans, I. p. 154.

of the city and diocese of London. We cannot be surprised, that an earnest religious spirit thus pent up and irritated by ecclesiastical tyranny, should have become harsh and vehement, and have sometimes vented itself in sallies of coarse invective. But there were men of learning and piety in the movement, who attempted to regulate and organize it. In 1572, the very year after Parliament had confirmed the doctrinal articles by statute[1], the first English presbytery was set up at Wandsworth in Surrey, where elders were chosen and a system of rules agreed upon. We find the same efforts gradually spreading into other parts of the country. Under Whitgift's primacy in 1586, presbyterian classes were established in Warwick and Northampton; where the Geneva Book of Discipline was subscribed, and a mutual engagement entered into to observe its articles. Cartwright, of whom we shall speak presently, was the first subscriber in the Warwick Classis[2]. It seems probable, that similar associations were very early introduced into Cheshire and the adjoining county of Lancaster[3].

In 1574, a Directory of Church Government for English Nonconformists was drawn up in Latin by Travers, and printed at Geneva. Ten years afterwards, this first draft was translated into English by Cartwright, revised, corrected, and improved, by himself and other divines; and with a preface from his own hand, was intended to be published for more general use. The work was seized, as it was going through the press at Cambridge; and Whitgift ordered all the copies of it to be burnt. Our knowledge of it is derived from a copy which was found in Cartwright's study after his decease[4]. A brief account of its most important articles may serve to convey an idea of the presbyterian system, as it was conceived by

---

[1] See note [1], p. 57, Ch. II. Sect. iv. [2] Strype's Whitgift, B. III. ch. xvii.
[3] See the Advertisement prefixed to Paget's Defence of Presbyterian Church Government. London, 1641. We learn from this, that the Presbyterian interest had once been very strong in Cheshire; there having been monthly exercises at Northwich, Namptwich, Knutsford, Macclesfield, Bowden, Frodsham, Tarporley, and other places, which were "frequented by divers of the renowned gentry." When the Advertisement appeared in 1641, there was already a reaction among the gentry and freeholders, in favour of prelatical government. On the early prevalence of Presbyterianism in Lancashire, see Hunter's Life of Oliver Heywood, and Dr. Hibbert Ware's Hist. of the Collegiate Church of Manchester, vol. i. pp. 231–373.
[4] It is given at length in the second Appendix to Neal's first volume.

its first assertors in England, and, so far as the times would admit, attempted to be carried into practice[1].

It lays down, as a fundamental position, that, as the presbyterian discipline is necessary for all times and authoritatively prescribed in Scripture, every other form of Church Government is unlawful.

It recognizes the equality in right, order, and form, of all particular churches; no one having any authority over the rest; and the presbytery or consistory of each church being composed of the teachers and elders belonging to it, with the minister as president. A distinction is made between *pastors* and *teachers*: pastors administer the word and sacraments; teachers are occupied with doctrine. *Elders* superintend the morals of the church; and *deacons* have charge of the poor. In these presbyteries is vested the entire government of each particular church; but in more important matters, the consent of the Church at large is required to confirm their acts. Discipline proceeds according to the following scale or measure of penalties: first, reproof, private or public; then, suspension from the Lord's table; lastly, deposition or excommunication.

There must be assemblies of different churches, with power to decide on ecclesiastical matters affecting the churches within their resort; assemblies of greater number and higher authority, being empowered to reverse the decisions of the inferior. Such assemblies are distinguished as *Conferences* or *Synods*. Conferences consist of representatives from different churches, both ministers and elders, to be held once in six weeks. Synods are provincial, national, ecumenical. All that relates to the discipline of particular churches must be determined by the express word of God. All that is synodical, rests indeed on the analogies and general rules of Scripture; but, as it is not positively enjoined, may be modified and changed according to circumstances. It is observable, that the system fails here to carry the Scriptural principle throughout.

Ministers, having first subscribed the confession of doctrine and discipline, must be lawfully called, and proved competent

[1] In the Warwickshire Classis to which Cartwright belonged, the book subscribed was entitled, 'The Holy Discipline of the Churches described in the Word of God.' From Neal's account of it, I. p. 323, it differed somewhat from that contained in his Appendix.

by trial of their gifts; and after election they must be ordained by the prayers of the church to which they are called. They can only be ordained (a point on which the Puritans laid great stress) to a *particular* charge.

The liturgy or order of public service is as follows: a *psalm* sung by the whole Church; a short admonition of *preparation* for prayer; a *prayer*, including confession, acknowledgment of Gospel promises, supplication of pardon, petition for grace both in regard to the general duties of life and a due improvement of the present administration of the Word, concluding with the Lord's prayer; the *sermon; prayer* for grace to profit by the word delivered, with a recapitulation of its chief heads, an intercession for the Universal Church, and all sorts and conditions of men, and the Lord's prayer; *psalm* by the whole church; *benediction* and *dismissal* in some Scriptural form.

Catechising in a shorter and ampler form, is specially provided for in this directory; and care is enjoined to prepare poor scholars by suitable training in every congregation for future preachers and expounders of the Word.

Such is an outline of the system which the ancient Presbyterians under Elizabeth, would have substituted for Episcopacy.

This system did not want learned and eloquent advocates to defend it. Of these the most eminent both in themselves and for the distinguished men to whom they were opposed, were Cartwright and Travers. Cartwright was Lady Margaret's professor of divinity at Cambridge, and in the judgment of Beza, one of the most learned men of his day. In his lectures at St. Mary's, he boldly maintained the chief positions of Puritanism, and drew such crowds that the windows were taken out to admit the auditors. This was a defiance of authority, which the ruling powers in Church and State could not pass over with impunity. He was denied his doctor's degree; prohibited from lecturing; deprived of his fellowship; and expelled the University. He then spent some time among the Reformed Churches abroad; and at length returned home, confirmed in his principles, and prepared to render fresh service to the cause for which he had suffered. In 1572 the Puritans, finding remonstrance with the Queen and the bishops fruitless, addressed an Admonition, setting forth their demands, to the Parliament. For this the authors of the

Admonition were committed to prison; and Whitgift, then Master of Trinity and Vice-Chancellor of the University of Cambridge, was directed by Parker to answer it. Cartwright now stepped forward to defend his imprisoned brethren in a second Admonition, which was replied to by Whitgift; and thus arose a controversy, in which the arguments for Presbyterianism and Prelacy were arrayed in their utmost strength against each other, by disputants well matched for learning and abilities[1]. Starting from different premises, it was impossible they should agree in their conclusions; and they separated therefore where they began. Cartwright appealed to Scripture alone; Whitgift included with it as authoritative, the practice of the four first centuries.

Cartwright's work indicates great vigour of mind, and is written in clear and forcible English which at this day may be read with pleasure. Without wholly discarding as unimportant, the question about the garments, he took higher ground than the first race of Puritans, and contended for a purer discipline and more scriptural form of Church government. He advanced some doctrines which were quite at variance with the Erastian system of the Court, and might well awaken the jealousy of a sovereign so tenacious of her prerogative as Elizabeth. "We ought," says he, "to be obedient unto the civil magistrate which governeth the Church of God, in that office which is committed unto him, and according to that calling. But it must be remembered, that civil magistrates must govern it according to the rules prescribed in his Word, and that as they are nurses, so they be servants, unto the Church; and as they rule in the Church, so they must remember to subject themselves unto the Church; to submit their sceptres, to throw down their Crowns, before the Church; yea, as the prophet speaketh, to lick the dust of the feet of the Church. Wherein I mean not, that the Church doth either wring the sceptre out of princes' hands, or taketh their crowns from their heads, or that it requireth princes to lick the dust of her feet (as the Pope under this pretence has done); but I mean, as the prophet meaneth, that whatsoever magnificence, or excellency, or pomp, is either in them or in their estates and commonwealths, which doth not agree with the simplicity and

---

[1] For the details, see Neal, vol. i. ch. v., and Strype's Whitgift, B. I. ch. ix. and x.

(in the judgment of the world) poor and contemptible estate of the Church, that they will be content to lay down."—" For as the house is before the hangings, and therefore the hangings, which come after, must be framed to the house, which was before; so the Church being before there was any commonwealth, and the commonwealth coming after, must be fashioned and made suitable unto the Church[1]."

The contrasted features of the Puritanical and Prelatical parties, are well brought out in the controversy between Travers and Hooker. Travers was lecturer at the Temple, and a very acceptable preacher; for the Inns of Court where new ideas rapidly germinated among the free spirits of the time, were the natural seats of Puritanism. Travers having many friends, and some interest at Court (for he was domestic chaplain to Lord Burleigh), an effort was made to promote him to the Mastership. But as he had entered into orders abroad, Whitgift refused to confirm the appointment, unless he would consent to be re-ordained; and when he objected to this, Hooker obtained the preferment. Some disappointment may have given additional sharpness to the controversial spirit, with which Travers now put forth his own views. It was observed, that the forenoon's sermon spoke Canterbury, and the afternoon's Geneva. The dispute proceeding, Travers was suspended from his office. He addressed a supplication to the Council against his suspension, which was replied to by Hooker[2]. Travers and Hooker were relatives, and in spite of controversy respected each other[3]. There is no trace of malignity in the dispute between them; only the earnestness of strong conviction on both sides; and in Travers, an overweening persuasion of the certainty of his own principles, and of the duty of others to submit to them.

The points on which they held opposite opinions, were chiefly three; predestination, justification by faith alone, and the claim of the Church of Rome to be considered a true and saving Church. On all these points Hooker leaned to the milder and Arminian view; while Travers adhered to high Calvinism. The latter seems never to have suspected, that he

---

[1] A Reply to an Answer made of Mr. Doctor Whitgift against the Admonition to the Parliament. By T. C. 1573. p. 144.

[2] See the Supplication and Answer in the Appendix to Hooker's Ecclesiastical Polity, fol. London. 1676.

[3] Fuller, Book IX. Sect. vii. 59.

could himself be in error, while he censured Hooker **for persisting in it**; and thought he had for ever damaged his cause, by declaring there were passages in his sermons on Justification, "**that** had **not** been heard in public places within this land since Queen Mary's days." He discovered the same intolerant and impracticable spirit in **other matters. He wished** for example, to institute a particular mode of administering the Sacrament, at once different from the usage of the Church, which was to receive it kneeling, and from that practised in **the** Temple (which enjoyed some special ecclesiastical privileges), where it was taken sitting, and handed round; and be**cause his** own views were not complied with, he refused to join with other clergymen in the celebration of the rite. From a similar perversity **of conscientiousness,** when Hooker was presented to the Mastership, he fancied it **his duty to attempt** the introduction **of** something **like a Church call; and the** evening before Hooker's first sermon, called upon him with some friends, to induce him to postpone it, **that time might** be given for this partial adoption of the presbyterian system. Hooker's very natural refusal was regarded as a sin against the truth; and for his adherence to his convictions on this **and** other points, Travers, never suspecting for **a** moment his own infallibility, made it a point of conscience to admonish him in private, and publicly to preach against him. Travers's style, as **it** appears in his Supplication, is obscure and involved, a **great contrast** to that **of** Cartwright; and these imperfections of form are not redeemed by close reasoning or felicity of illustration. His **success as** a preacher, must have arisen from the vehemence **of his** manner and the popularity of his topics. On reviewing the controversies of this time, one cannot help wishing, that Hooker and Cartwright, representing the full strength of their respective causes, had been confronted with each other. The intolerance of Travers would have been **well** matched with the arrogant acerbity of Whitgift[1].

---

[1] Nothing can convey a clearer idea of the difference in the style of preaching, between a Puritan minister and a regular conformable clergyman, or set before us a more distinct image **of the** time, than Fuller's graphic description of Hooker and Travers. Book IX. sect. vii.

"Mr. Hooker his voice was low, **stature** little, gesture none **at all, standing stone-still in the** pulpit, as if the posture of his body were the emblem of **his minde, unmovable in** his opinions. Where his eye was left fixed at **the beginning, it was found** fixed at the end of his sermon : in a word, **the doctrine he delivered had nothing but** itself to **garnish** it. His stile was long and pithy,

Contemporary with these controversies were decisive indications of a strong fermentation of Puritanical feeling throughout the nation; and the popular sentiment found a voice in Parliament. In 1584, bills were introduced into the Commons for abating the power of the bishops and the spiritual courts, and subordinating the canon or ecclesiastical, to the common, law; for admitting the people to a share in the trial and election of their ministers; and for associating a presbytery or eldership with the minister, to manage the spiritual affairs of every parish, subject to an appeal to higher judicatories. These proposals were followed next year by a bill for the more reverent observance of the Sabbath. Such measures were distinctly expressive of Puritanism. The Queen quashed them by her prerogative. It was on this occasion, that Whitgift advised Elizabeth to proceed not by statute, but by canon, in her government of the Church[1]; and the fact is to be noticed, as already indicating the divergent tendencies which

---

driving on a whole flock of several clauses before he came to the close of a sentence. So that when the copiousness of his stile met not with proportionable capacity in his auditors, it was unjustly censured, for perplext, tedious and obscure. His sermons followed the inclination of his studies, and were for the most part on controversies, and deep points of school divinity.

"Mr. Travers his utterance was gracefull, gesture plausible, matter profitable, method plain, and his stile carried in it *indolem pietatis—a genius of grace* flowing from his sanctified heart. Some say, that the congregation in the Temple *ebb'd in the forenoon, and flowed in the afternoon*, and that the auditory of Mr. Travers was far the more numerous, the first occasion of emulation betwixt them. But such as knew Mr. Hooker, knew him to be too wise, to take exception at such trifles, the rather because the most judicious is always the least part in all auditories.

"Here might one on Sundays have seen almost as many writers as hearers. Not only young students, but even the gravest Benchers (such as Sir Edward Cook and Sir James Altham then were) were not more exact in taking instructions from their clients, than in writing notes from the mouths of their ministers. The worst was, these two preachers, though joined in affinity (their nearest kindred being married together), acted with different principles, and clashed one against another. So that what Mr. Hooker delivered in the forenoon, Mr. Travers confuted in the afternoon."

After the lapse of more than a century, the same distinction was noticed between the preaching of the Established clergy and that of the Dissenting ministers. James Peirce, in his Vindication of the Dissenters against Nichols (London, 1718), evidently alludes to it in these words: "If there are any, who use an indecent gesture (as a man may err on that hand), I will not undertake to defend them. But they are in a worse mistake, who would have all action laid aside in preaching, and that ministers should read their sermons with their eyes fixed upon their notes, without so much as looking, it may be, on the people."—Part III. ch. xiv. p. 551.

[1] See his Letter in Neal, I. p. 306.

became so marked under the Stuarts, of Episcopacy to ally itself with the Crown, and of Puritanism to seek the aid of Parliament. From this time, after the close of the controversies which I have been describing, Puritanism gradually became less of a purely ecclesiastical, and more of a parliamentary, movement. That efforts in the way of Church reform were not uncalled for, is evident from the survey of the spiritual condition of England, contained in a petition addressed by the Puritans to the House of Commons in 1586; from which it appeared, that owing to the number of suspensions, after the Church of England had been established twenty-eight years, there were only 2,000 preachers to serve 10,000 parish churches[1]. The Universities, the proper sources of a nation's spiritual life, shared in the general disorganization. Oxford under the corrupt chancellorship of the Earl of Leicester, had sunk to so low a state of learning and morals, that Whitgift thought it necessary to devise measures for its renovation. Cambridge under the purer direction of Burleigh and Essex, still preserved some taste for studies, and was the seat of the rising controversy between the new Arminian doctrines and Calvinism[2].

SECTION V.

QUALIFIED PRESBYTERIANISM AT THE CLOSE OF THE SIXTEENTH, AND IN THE FIRST HALF OF THE SEVENTEENTH, CENTURY.

The closing years of the Queen's reign were marked by a decline of zeal for the proper presbyterian discipline[3]. Cartwright himself who since his controversy with Whitgift, had been thrown into the Fleet, for refusing to take the oath *ex officio*, became more moderate with advancing years, and died peaceably in the hospital at Warwick, of which Leicester had appointed him master. To this change of public feeling various causes may have contributed: experience of utter inability to overturn or materially change the existing establish-

[1] Neal, I. p. 320.
[2] Strype's Whitgift, p. 318. Huber's English Universities, by Newman, I. p. 364.
[3] Strype's Whitgift.

ment; a more learned and candid appreciation of the scriptural evidence on which either Presbyterianism or Episcopacy was alleged to stand; the rapid spread of principles which took a bolder view, and had as little respect for Presbyterianism, as a national system, upheld by the state, as for Episcopacy; and the tranquillizing expectation of ecclesiastical reform, from the accession of a Presbyterian sovereign to the throne. It must also be observed, that Presbyterianism, in its strictest sense, has never been a product of genuine English growth, but whenever it has gained a temporary ascendency, has been imported from abroad. The principles of the Lollards led to Independency. Under Elizabeth Presbyterianism was brought in by men who had studied abroad, from Geneva, and supported by the high influence of Calvin and Beza. Afterwards, during the war, it was forced on the Parliament who watched its pretensions with the greatest jealousy, by the necessities of their alliance with the Scots. From the beginning of the seventeenth, to the middle of the last, century, the section of the Puritans which is historically known under that designation, has been distinguished, from the Independents and other Nonconformists, through all its doctrinal and social changes, less by an absolute preference for Presbyterianism as such, than by a general attachment to a national establishment of religion, and the wish for such reforms in the discipline, ritual and doctrine of the Church of England, as would admit of a conscientious conformity to it. Individuals may have been rigid Presbyterians; but that this was the spirit and governing principle of the party, its history fully proves.

It was the lax discipline of the Church that peculiarly scandalized the Puritans. With them a pure and godly ministry, the personal sanctity of their pastors, was everything. And these notions, the persuasion, that by their strictness in the trial and election of their ministers, they secured a large portion of the divine spirit in their churches, led to very extraordinary pretensions, which their enemies made use of to disgrace and humble them. Taking Scripture to the strict letter, and believing that presbyterian ordination conferred a divine right and apostolical authority, some of the Puritan ministers affected to cast out devils. In 1597, Darrel, a Puritan minister of Nottingham, was brought before the High Commission, and committed to close confinement, for pretending to exercise gifts of this description. Bishop Bancroft's chaplain published an exposure of what he called his fraudulent practices; but Darrel, who was weak rather than dishonest, wrote in prison a vindication of himself, and ascribed the power he possessed, to the virtue of the new discipline[1].

The seventeenth century opened with an eager rivalry between the two great religious parties, to secure the favour of the new King. As soon as the Queen was dead, special messengers were despatched by the Puritans and the Episcopalians to inform James of the event[2]. On his progress to London, the former presented to him the celebrated millenary petition[3], in which, it is to be noticed, they disclaimed "affecting a popular parity in the Church," and prayed, not for a dissolution, but a reform, of the state ecclesiastical. The result, however, of the Conference between the divines of the two persuasions, which was shortly summoned by James at Hampton Court, put an end at once to the hopes of the Puritans, though they asked only for a redress of particular

---

[1] See the particulars in Strype's Whitgift, p. 495. In the investigations of that age respecting witchcraft, the Anglican clergy appear to have been much less infected with the popular superstition, than the Puritan ministers. One reason might be, that their position made them more independent; they stood more aloof from popular sympathies. They were, moreover, less wedded to a belief in the strict letter of Scripture. Baxter, in his Certainty of the World of Spirits, affirms the existence of witches, alleging, as proof, the case of great numbers that were executed in Suffolk and Essex in 1645 and 1646; on which occasion, Mr. Calamy a celebrated Presbyterian divine, went along with the Judges on circuit, to hear their confessions, and see there was no fraud or wrong done to them. Several cases of imputed witchcraft occurred in Lancashire, in some of which the Puritan ministers incurred ridicule, by their fruitless endeavours to exorcise those who were said to be possessed. See an account of the Surey Demoniac, in Hunter's Life of Oliver Heywood, p. 363. Artful men made a profit of the reigning superstition. One Hopkins, about the year 1646 or 7, who is said to have been too much countenanced by the Committees of the Long Parliament, went on a mission of inquiry through the eastern counties, and took to himself the title of Witchfinder General. See a collection of curious narratives, and an exposure of the popular belief, in an Historical Essay concerning Witchcraft, by Francis Hutchinson, D.D., Chaplain in ordinary to his Majesty, London, 2nd edit. 1720. On the other hand, this was not wholly a question between the Puritan and the Anglican parties. Sir Thomas Brown, Glanvil, and Henry More, who were Churchmen, believed in communications with the world of spirits; while Owen, Gataker, and Nye, who were Puritans, were very active in opposing the pretensions of Lily, the astrologer.

[2] Fuller, X. i. 13.

[3] It was not actually signed by more than 750 preachers, out of five and twenty counties. Fuller, ibid.

grievances, and desired rather a mitigation, than an abolition, of Episcopacy[1]. This harsh and unqualified rejection of its claims, only gave new vigour to the spirit of Puritanism. Some of the more ardent men of the party, as we shall presently see, embraced the principles of Independency; and not a few sought refuge from ecclesiastial oppression in foreign lands. A much larger number, though non-conforming in many points, were averse from a total separation. These were the source and strength of the great parliamentary action which now commenced against the hierarchy, and are usually described under the general name of Presbyterians.

The controversy between the Puritans and the Church turned from this time more on doctrine and manners, than on forms of ecclesiastical polity. Calvinism and Arminianism became the distinguishing tenets of the two parties. Calvinism prevailed among the popular leaders of the Commons, who insisted on interpreting the Articles of the Church of England in that sense; while the bishops brought the aid of their Greek patristical learning to the support of Arminianism. Calvinism was viewed by the people as the sign of an earnest personal religion, and of attachment to the cause of freedom and reform. Arminianism was regarded with suspicion, as clinging to outward observances, tinged with a spirit of servility, and secretly sympathizing with Rome. Some circumstances appeared for a time to favour the cause of Puritanism. Prince Henry was suspected of a leaning towards it. The primate Abbot, another Grindal, was well affected to it. The king sent deputies to the synod of Dort, which was a Presbyterian assembly; and his divines supported, on doctrinal questions, the Calvinists, who overpowered the Arminians. On their return, however, James, with his usual inconsistency, took the Arminian clergy into his especial favour, and discountenanced the Calvinian. As if to make the breach between them irreconcilable, he wounded the Puritan conscience in its tenderest point, and offended its deepest feelings of religious propriety, by issuing the Book of Sports, which, in the same declaration, required every one to attend the whole divine service at his own parish church, and authorized

[1] An account of the Conference is given by Fuller (X. i. 20), and by Collier (Part II. Book viii.) from the report of Barlow, dean of Chester, who was present. Collier gives his reasons for regarding this report as trustworthy.

the usual popular games and recreations in the latter part of the Lord's day[1].

The State or doctrinal Puritans, as those were called, who united Calvinistic sentiments with a preference or toleration for episcopal government, devised methods for the satisfaction of their religious wants, bearing considerable resemblance to the expedients which have since been resorted to by their representatives, the modern Evangelicals. With a retention of the forms of the Establishment, they combined some of the practices of Nonconformists, particularly the free choice of their minister, and his voluntary maintenance. With this view the Puritans in the larger towns founded lectureships, which might be filled by men who had scruples about the ceremonies and objected to many parts of the Common Prayer. In extension of the same design a society was formed about 1627 for the purchase of lay-impropriations, which were to be vested in feoffees, and applied to furnish salaries of moderate amount for an active and preaching ministry. The project illustrates the spirit of the time. "It is incredible," says Fuller, "what large sums were advanced in a short time towards so laudable an employment. Had the design not been obstructed, it was verily believed, within fifty years, rather purchases than money would have been wanting[2]." Similar efforts were made by religious laymen at the beginning of the present century, to buy up church livings, and bestow them on evangelical clergymen. The design of the Puritans was defeated by Laud, who dreaded the popularity of the lecturers, and urged the attorney-general to proceed against the feoffees as an illegal society. Full of fire and energy, awake to all the greatness of the questions that were engaging the national mind, and finding an unfailing spring of courage in the sympathy and enthusiasm from which they derived their support, and which had placed them in their stations of eminence—the influence of these lecturers from the strong impulse which it gave to the public sentiment, might be compared to that of the modern press; did not the simplicity and directness of their

---

[1] The avowed object of the Book of Sports, was to reconcile the Papists, who were disgusted at the severity of the prevailing Puritanism. In Lancashire, the population of which was almost equally divided between Puritans and Papists, it was ordered to be read in every parish church. Archbishop Abbot, from his Puritanical feelings, forbade its being read at Croydon, which was his own residence. Neal, I. p. 486.

[2] Church Hist., Book XI. Sect. ii. 6.

earnest appeals to moral and religious feeling, suggest rather a resemblance to the prophets of the Hebrew commonwealth. With much extravagance and fanaticism, they worked substantially for good, as a counteraction to the hierarchy and the court. Their influence was exercised chiefly in the towns, where the topics of the day were keenly discussed, and where they contributed with other causes to maintain that high temperature of religious fervour which warmed and strengthened the inner heart of Parliament, and made it capable of an unyielding conflict with tyranny and wrong[1]. Writers and speakers on behalf of Puritanism found shelter also in the chaplainships of private families; in situations at the Universities; and in livings scattered over the country, where personal consideration, or family connections, or the connivance of the ordinary, permitted them to indulge their scruples without molestation. Combined, they formed a large and powerful body, and sustained by the co-operation of the most thoughtful and virtuous of the gentry and nobility, exerted an immense effect on the moral condition of the country.

The feelings of the aristocracy towards the Church, were very different in those days from what they are at present. The deep and serious impressions produced by the Reformation had not yet lost their force. Men of lofty and earnest minds with whom the assertion of religious truth was a duty of the highest moment, refused to comply with the terms of the actual establishment, and employed all their zeal in promoting reform. There was consequently a great deficiency of competent men to fill the offices of the Church, and their place was often supplied by individuals of mean extraction and imperfect education, without high learning, or high cha-

---

[1] The Lecturers were exceedingly obnoxious to the High Church party. Heylyn, in his Life and Death of Laud, speaks of them in the bitterest terms. He says that they were neither lay nor clergy, having no place at all in the prayers of the Church, and compares them to bats and rere-mice, "being neither birds nor beasts, and yet both together," London, fol. 1668, pp. 9, 10. Selden who looked on these matters with a calmer spirit, bears witness to the great influence and popularity of the Lecturers. "Lecturers," says he, "do in a parish church, what the friars did heretofore, get away not only the affections, but the bounty that should be bestowed on the minister. Lecturers get a great deal of money, because they preach the people tame, as a man watches a hawk; and then they do what they list with them. The lectures in Blackfriars, performed by officers of the army, tradesmen and ministers, is as if a great lord should make a feast, and he would have his cook dress one dish, and his coachman another, his porter a third, etc." Table Talk, p. 95. Edinburgh edit. 1819.

racter, who took up the ministry for the sake of the subsistence which it brought. A strong prejudice was thus created against the conforming clergy, in the minds of many persons of station and breeding. They were looked down upon as ignoble time-servers, the mere creatures of the State. Selden who speaks with the knowledge of a contemporary, tells us, that, in his days, they were less respected than either the Roman Catholic priests or the Puritan ministers, both of whom claimed an authority from Christ; and that for this reason, " the nobility and gentry would not suffer their sons or kindred to meddle with the Church[1]." Among the Puritan writers of the day we may sometimes notice a certain tone of aristocratical contempt freely mingled with the language employed towards the prelates. Lord Brook who was an Independent, taunted Laud with his low origin. Milton himself discovers traces of this feeling in some of his bitter invectives against prelaty[2]: and when he expresses a wish, in a passage full of the noblest eloquence, that the rich would devote their children to the service of the Gospel, and nobles make their sons God's ministers, that so the necessity for a hireling ministry might be removed, he is only uttering the same sentiment in another form[3]. Among the Puritans generally there was a deep and reverential feeling about religion, which made them shrink from the thought of prostituting it to worldly or selfish ends. The facts just mentioned, show how widely Puritanical feeling was diffused among the English aristocracy in the earlier part of the seventeenth century; nor was it till a later period, when this feeling had nearly died out, that church livings came to be regarded as a provision for the younger sons of good families.

Had Charles I. not been swayed by the violent counsels of such men as Laud and Strafford, the state of parties at this time renders it probable, that changes might have been introduced into the discipline and government of the Church, which would have permanently reconciled to it a vast majority of the nation. How far this result might have been more favourable to truth and liberty than the actual course of

[1] Table Talk, p. 104, Ibid. [2] As in his Apology for Smectymnuus.
[3] Animadversions upon the Remonstrants' Defence against Smectymnuus. Mr. Macaulay substantially confirms this view of the social position of the Anglican clergy in the seventeenth century. History of England, vol. i. ch. iii. p. 324. 4th edit.

things, is a point on which it is more difficult to decide. The aims and principles of the party called Presbyterian, have been already described. With them the large body of the doctrinal Puritans would have gladly entered into negotiations, to promote a reform that would have been satisfactory to both. The great patriots of the Commons, Pym, Hampden, Sir John Eliot and others shared in this spirit; they were opposed to the lofty claims of high churchmen, but were not averse to a mitigated Episcopacy[1]. Lord Falkland and Hyde himself (afterwards Lord Clarendon) were quite prepared, at the commencement of the dispute with the Crown, to restrain the power of the bishops and the ecclesiastical courts, and thus render the Church more acceptable to the popular feeling. Hall bishop of Norwich and archbishop Usher defended Episcopacy in a very moderate and conciliatory spirit, and would have met the Presbyterians half way. Indeed, Usher's scheme of Synodical Episcopacy, approved by Baxter, was only a modified form of Presbyterianism. The spirit of Fuller to whose Church History reference has so often been made, pursuing a mean between the extremes of both parties and acutely observant of the follies of each, represents, there is little doubt, the feelings of a large and respectable body of his contemporaries.

Parliament from the first assumed the ground, that the power of reforming the Church rested with them; and they would have mediated between the contending parties. "It belongs to Parliaments," said Mr. Pym in 1628, "to establish true religion, and to punish false. We must know what Parliaments have done formerly in religion. Our Parliaments have confirmed general councils[2]." In the exercise of this function it was the object of Parliament, sustained by the great Puritan movement without, to settle a reformed national church, sometimes by methods not very consonant to our ideas of the rights of conscience. But when the movement once began, it is wonderful to observe, with what rapidity men's ideas grew larger on this subject. Of this I shall speak hereafter.

In 1640 an order passed, that none should sit in Parliament but such as would take the sacrament according to the Church of England. In the grand Remonstrance which the Commons put forth the next year, they declared, it was not their intention to leave private persons or particular con-

---

[1] Such is Lord Clarendon's judgment of Hampden.   [2] Neal, I. p. 531.

gregations to adopt what form of divine service they pleased, but that there should be throughout the whole realm, a conformity to that order which the law enjoined according to the Word of God[1]. The Smectymnuan divines who replied to Hall's Defence of Episcopacy, though pleading in the main for Presbyterian government, still kept to the ground of a national religion, and contended not for the overthrow, but for the purification, of the Church[2]. In the sub-committee appointed by the Lords in 1641, to assist them in considering of ecclesiastical innovations and reforms, we find Twisse, Marshall and Calamy, who were Presbyterians, associated with Usher, Williams and Hall, who were bishops; Williams, bishop of Lincoln, acting as its chairman. Even Milton, in his earlier pieces written at the commencement of the war, in his second book of Reformation in England, in his Reason of Church Government, and in his Apology for Smectymnuus, though vehemently opposed to Prelacy, and handling neither Hall nor Usher with much courtesy, had not yet entirely shaken off the idea of a national church, and of a state maintenance for its ministers, but with Parliament and the great body of the nation was still friendly both to the presbyterian discipline and to monarchy. The folly of the King and the interference of the Scots dissipated this spirit of mutual conciliation; brought in again a bigoted and exclusive Presbyterianism; and drove parties once more asunder into violent extremes. Yet it has been remarked, that the claim of a *jus divinum* had been abandoned by the English Presbyterian divines who took their seats in the Westminster Assembly. Nor should the significant circumstance be overlooked, indicating a relaxation from the rigid principles of Cartwright and Travers, that the vow or promise required of members of the Assembly on taking their seats, pledged them to maintain in *doctrine* what they believed agreeable to the Word of God; but in point of *discipline*, contrary to the ancient principle, left them at liberty to establish whatever might make most for God's glory and the peace and good of his Church[3].—But

---

[1] Neal, I. p. 642.

[2] Smectymnuus was an assumed title, made up of the initial letters of the names of its authors—Stephen Marshall, Edmund Calamy, Thomas Young, Matthew Newcomen, William Spurstow.

[3] The form of this promise and vow is prefixed to most editions of the Westminster Confession of Faith.

it is time to look back, and trace the rise and progress of new tendencies.

SECTION VI.

INDEPENDENCY, AND THE MORE EXTREME FORMS OF PURITANISM.

To the first wave of ecclesiastical reform, another had succeeded issuing from a lower depth, which went beyond it. The stern unbending policy of Whitgift, which had broken the strength and diverted the purposes of Presbyterianism, produced a very different effect on those minds, in which the principles of the old Lollardism, a native growth, had taken root. It called them out in fresh vigour. The origin of Brownism is contemporaneous with the severities of the court of High Commission, directed by Whitgift. Browne, the most conspicuous instigator of this new movement, was a gentleman of good family, educated at Cambridge, and a relative of Lord Burleigh, to whom he was occasionally indebted for protection. He agreed with the later Independents, in regarding every association of Christians for worship and edification, as a church complete in itself, competent to the exercise of every ecclesiastical function. But his principles were violent and exclusive. He thought a perfect system of discipline and government was prescribed in the New Testament, and refused to hold communion, not only with the Church of England, but with all other Churches that did not adopt his model. In fact, he viewed the Church of England, in the same light as the Puritans generally viewed the Church of Rome—as an institution essentially corrupt, in which salvation was not to be found. After a wandering, unsettled life at home and abroad, he died at an advanced age, not respected by any party, a member and minister of the Church which he had vilified. Many who had embraced his views, withdrew into Holland, where they found shelter under the general toleration. In England they were adopted by another gentleman, named Barrowe, who signalized himself by a very coarse attack on the Liturgy. Lord Bacon says, that Browne and Barrowe, being gentlemen of education and good connections, disseminated their principles by **their free** speaking and writing in the Inns of Court and other places of public resort. Their adherents **began now to be distinguished by the name of** Separatists, **from the regular Puritans, whom** they denounced as time-servers for resting **in a Church which** they judged unscriptural. They were often compared by their contemporaries **with** the ancient sect of the Donatists; and Barrowe's language **is** marked by some peculiarities which afterwards distinguished the Quakers. Barrowe, Greenwood, and Penry, all of this party, suffered death for their principles in 1593[1].

But their doctrine did not perish with them. It was soon taken up by men of calmer mind and graver character. Bradshaw's English Puritanism **which was** published in 1605, exhibits **a singular mixture of Erastianism with** Independency, **in the** great power **which it gives to the** civil magistrate, of redressing **the internal disorders of Churches;** of guarding them **against** ecclesiastical oppression from without; and of punishing ecclesiastical officers, if they **abuse their proper** functions and encroach on the civil authority. This **tract** was produced under the primacy of Bancroft; and it bears clear traces of the conviction which his tyrannical policy was strengthening throughout the nation, that more was to be feared for religious freedom from the ecclesiastical, than from the civil, governors of the realm[2].

While Bancroft and Laud were pursuing their career **of** persecution at home, the flourishing States of Holland **reaping** in peace the fruits of their hard-earned freedom, offered to the fathers of Independency, the authors of the new Reformation, the same asylum which Frankfort, Zurich and Geneva had afforded to the first Reformers in the reign of Mary. Johnson, Ainsworth, Jacob and Robinson, were the earliest professors of these principles in Holland. There they planted congregations; devoted themselves to their studies; and, surveying **the** troubles of their native land from afar, gradually **enlarged** their ideas and became fully aware of the mischiefs of allying religion with the civil power. At first, their views were very crude and narrow. In a Confession published in 1598, **they refuse to** admit members **from** another congregation without a certificate of **soundness** in the faith; and de-

---

[1] Hanbury's Historical Memorials of the Independents, vol. i.

[2] Neal, I. p. 447, who gives an abstract of the Tract. The element of **Independency** is very conspicuous in Ch. II. 1, 2, 3, 4.

fend the startling position, that it is the duty of princes and magistrates to root out all false ministers and counterfeit worship. It was through a painful and trying novitiate, that the Independent Churches in Holland passed on to a juster sense of religious liberty. Many dissensions, fomented by the spread of Anabaptist principles, disturbed their early career[1]. Henry Jacob, on his return from exile, became in 1616 the pastor of the first Congregational or Independent Church in England.

Robinson is usually considered the father of Independency; and any Church may well be proud of such a parentage. He was educated at Cambridge, and commenced his ministry in connection with the National Church in the neighbourhood of Norwich; but being thwarted in his plans of usefulness by the ecclesiastical authorities, became for about a year the pastor of a small Separatist Church in the north of Nottinghamshire, with which he finally emigrated to Holland[2]. When he first went abroad, his views were exceedingly rigid. Intercourse, however, with Dr. William Ames, who was then resident in that country and for some time professor of divinity at Franequer, rendered him more moderate; so that compared with the earlier Brownists, he acquired the character of a semi-separatist; that is, while maintaining the lawfulness of a separate communion, he did not deny that other Reformed Churches, which held the essentials of faith, were true Churches. This was the proper distinction of Independency from Brownism. Robinson was pastor of a church at Leyden during the height of the Arminian controversy, and had an opportunity of thoroughly weighing the arguments on both sides, by attending the lectures of Episcopius who espoused, and of Polyander who attacked, the doctrines of Arminius. Deeply imbued like all the Puritans of that day, with the spirit of Calvinism, he was urged to answer Episcopius, and executed his task to the great satisfaction of

[1] Hanbury, I. p. 98.
[2] This was the church to which Brewster and Bradford belonged, who headed the earliest colony of pilgrim fathers to the New World. Cotton Mather (Magnalia, B. I. ch. ii.) says, that their church was first organized in 1602, in the north of England. Mr. Hunter (Critical and Historical Tracts, No. II.) has discovered in the villages of Austerfield and Scrooby, the former a little to the N.E., the latter to the S., of the town of Bawtry, the birthplaces respectively of Bradford and Brewster, and in the manor of Scrooby occupied by the Brewsters, has probably identified the very house where many of their religious meetings must have been held.

those who embraced his view of the question. **During the sitting of the** Synod of Dort, **which** was **prolonged till 1619,** he published in Latin **an Apology for** the **Independent Churches**[1].

The closing years of his ministry were marked by an event of deep and solemn interest. His flock having been reduced by deaths and by marriages into Dutch families, its younger members seeing no prospect of a happy settlement in England, and disliking the tolerated condition of exiles, determined to seek a new home on the western shores of the Atlantic. In the summer of 1620 they set sail for America. Before they embarked, the venerable **man knelt down** and prayed with them on the beach; **and in view of the great** waters that were to carry them **to their future home, affectionately** commended them to the care **of heaven.** In a previous farewell address he had warned them of the narrow, stationary spirit **which was** already infecting the Reformed Churches of the **Old World,** and expressed his full persuasion, that "the Lord had more truth yet to break forth out of his holy word." Under these hallowing influences the pilgrim band went forth to reclaim and beautify the wilderness; and the spirit thus early infused into **them,** has survived to the present day amidst **great diversities of theological** sentiment, in the **learning and holy enterprise of a Stuart** and a Robinson, as well **as in the refined devotion,** the exalted humanity and **catholic** spirit of a Channing and a Ware[2].

Five Independent **ministers,** who had retired into Holland, Thomas Goodwin, Nye, Simpson, Burroughes and Bridge[3],— have acquired notoriety from the part they played in the Westminster Assembly of Divines, where their resistance to

---

[1] This work, of which a copy exists in the National Library at Paris, bears date 1619. In 1644 it was printed in English.—It is described by an adversary, as 'moderata, docta, brevis.' Memoirs of the Pilgrims at Leyden, by George Sumner, Cambridge (U.S.) 1845. Note E. The collected works of Robinson, with a biographical memoir prefixed, have been published in 3 vols. by Robert Ashton; London: 1851.

[2] This report of Mr. Robinson's farewell address appears to rest on the remembrance of Mr. Edward Winslow, who was present when it was delivered, but did not record it till many years afterwards. It is in itself, however, so characteristic, and must have made so deep an impression at the time, that there is every probability, the substance of it has been faithfully preserved. Mr. Sumner's scepticism leaves thus much at least. Mem. of Pilgrims at Leyden. Note F. Mr. Robinson died at Leyden in 1625.

[3] Goodwin and Nye were at Arnheim in Guelderland; the other three, at Rotterdam. Hanbury's Memorials of the Independents, II. p. 40.

the measures of the Presbyterians, procured them the name of the Dissenting Brethren. The Apological Narration which they submitted to Parliament in 1643, contains a clear statement of their principles; describes what had been their situation abroad; and exhibits with great distinctness the points of difference between themselves and the original Puritans. They had formerly been ministers in the national church; and in quitting it, had considered at first only what they call the *dark* part of the subject—the superstitions and corruptions of the established worship; but during the leisure of their exile, they had proceeded to investigate the *light* part—what was the worship and discipline enjoined by Scripture itself. They found that in the foreign churches, the question of doctrine had engaged more attention than that of discipline; and that the distinction between vital Christians " having the power of godliness and the profession thereof," and formal, carnal Christians, was not so much observed by them, as among the Nonconformists of England. But the errors and excesses of the Brownists at home, were a warning on the other hand. " We resolved, therefore," they say, " not to take up our religion by or from any party, and yet to approve and hold fast whatsoever is good in any, though never so much differing from us, yea, opposite unto us." To guide themselves in this search, they acknowledged three especial principles :—(1) the fulness and sufficiency of Scripture, not daring to eke out defectiveness of light in matters divine, with human prudence ; (2) not to make present judgment and practice, a binding law for the future; (3) to receive as members of the Church, none but such as all the churches in the world by the balance of the sanctuary acknowledge faithful ; the rules of their judgments being of such latitude, as would take in any member of Christ, the meanest, in whom there may be supposed to be the least of Christ; taking measure of no man's holiness by his opinions, whether concurring with them or adverse to them.

While contending for the complete and independent exercise of ecclesiastical government by each society of Christians within itself, they did not exclude the advice and admonition of neighbouring churches, or hold their religious assemblies exempt from the notice and censure of Christian magistrates. The officers chosen by each of their churches for self-government, were—pastors, teachers, ruling elders *i. e.* not lay, but ecclesiastical, persons, separated for that service, and deacons.

As a proof, that they did not partake of the narrowness of Brownism, they mentioned, that they had never broken off communion with godly members and ministers of the Church of England, but had received some such to the Lord's Supper during their exile, and had had their own children baptised in the parish churches. In Holland they had been not merely *tolerated*, but *owned*, by their Protestant brethren; who granted them the use of their churches at certain hours of the day, and permitted them to summon their assemblies by the public bell—a privilege denied to the merely tolerated—and provided " a full and liberal maintenance annually" for some of their ministers, with a constant allowance of wine for their communions. The brethren conclude their Apology with the expression of their belief, that God had left the Church of England more unreformed as to worship and government, than the neighbouring churches; " as having, in his infinite mercy, on purpose reserved and provided some better thing for this nation, when it should come to be reformed, that the other churches might not be made perfect without it[1]."

I have extracted these particulars from the Apologetical Narration, in order to convey a more correct impression of the Independency which confronted Presbyterianism in the Westminster Assembly. The statement breathes throughout a liberal, benignant and conciliatory spirit; and Herle who had

[1] Apologetical Narration, humbly submitted to the Honourable Houses of Parliament etc. London, 1643. The high character of the authors of this Narration makes it impossible to doubt the fact which they so distinctly assert, of their friendly recognition by the foreign Churches. Mr. Sumner in the Memoir already quoted, shows indeed the improbability of Robinson and his followers having ever had the use of a public church at Leyden, and even proves from church records, that at the time of his death, his congregation must have been in very low worldly circumstances. But the earlier Puritans who settled in Holland, enjoyed unquestionably a public recognition and a public maintenance for their ministers (Sumner, Note A). Ames who exercised so powerful an influence over the mind of Robinson, was professor of divinity at Francquer. Now it appears from the work of Bradshaw, previously alluded to in the text, that among the Puritans of this date, there was a great leaning towards Independency. Ames himself is classed with the Independents. Robinson in his parting address to the pilgrims, disclaims the name of Brownist; which he would hardly have done, unless his people in general estimation had lain under the stigma of it. It is obvious therefore, that some distinction was made between his case and that of the earlier English churches in Holland, with which Goodwin and his companions must have chiefly fraternized during their temporary sojourn in the Low Countries. Even with regard to Robinson himself, it appears that ten years before his death, he was admitted a member of the University of Leyden (Sumner, p. 18 and note D.) which entitled him, with other privileges, to receive a certain allowance of beer and wine duty free.

succeeded Twisse as prolocutor of the Assembly, though himself a staunch Presbyterian, introduces it with a very friendly prefatory notice to the reader, and expresses the warmest respect and affection for its authors.

It must be borne in mind, that the questions which most interested the various sections of the Puritan party, related less to doctrine in which they were for the most part agreed, than to the constitution of a true church and the source of ecclesiastical power. With all the zeal against Romanism, some ideas inherited from Catholic times, still harboured in the mind, and exercised an immense influence. Among these was the persuasion, that salvation could only be found within the pale of the true Church; and that consequently exclusion from ecclesiastical communion was the greatest calamity incident to man, since it affected his relation to God and his prospects beyond the grave. This fearful power of excommunicating and absolving, was called in the theological vocabulary of those days, as I have before mentioned, the power of the Keys, in allusion to Christ's language to Peter, Matthew xvi. 19. The question was, where such a power conformably to the directions of Scripture, should be lodged. According to the true theory of Episcopacy, it ought to be placed in the hands of the bishops, or of priests canonically ordained by them: but in the Church of England, it was delegated to laymen representing the bishop in the ecclesiastical courts; and this usurpation of an ecclesiastical office by an unecclesiastical person, was one of the strongest objections urged by the Puritans against her discipline. In Presbyterianism, it was vested in the Church Courts composed of a mixture of laymen and ministers, and belonged in the last instance to the representation of the whole Church convened in General Assembly. The Independents deposited this power with those who were deemed worthy of Church membership and admissible to the Lord's table, in every separate association of Christians; but it was applicable to such association alone, and could not be exercised over any other society. For their system of Church government the Independents, no less than the strict Presbyterians and the high Episcopalians, claimed a divine right, deduced, as they thought, direct from the injunctions of Scripture. This was the weak side of Puritanism; but it is one of the many manifestations of that earnest scripturalism, which was its governing principle.

The Anabaptists, whose tenets had spread into England from Germany at the very beginning of the Reformation (if indeed traces of them might not be found in Lollardism) and who had mingled themselves with the rising Independent Churches in Holland, only carried out still further, and with an unflinching consequentiality, the fundamental doctrine of Puritanism, that every doctrine and practice of the Christian Church must be brought to the literal standard of Scripture. They argued, that if re-ordination be necessary for one who has come out of an impure Church, to constitute a true minister, re-baptism is equally necessary to constitute a true Christian; and that of such alone a pure Church can be composed; that since baptism was instituted by Christ, as the rite of admission into his Church, it can only fulfil his intention, when administered to those who are capable of making an intelligent confession of faith. On other points of Church government, and in the general spirit of their religious life, the Anabaptists nearly agreed with the Independents, and were often confounded with them.

But the restlessness of the public mind was insatiable. Nothing could arrest the movement now begun. A swarm of sects, most of them issuing from some narrow scriptural conceit, and so proclaiming their affinity with Puritanism—came forth under various names and leaders. The Fifth Monarchy men, expecting the immediate reign of Christ on earth, revived the dreams of the ancient Chiliasts. An exclusive reverence for Scripture involving a total renunciation of all traditions and human ordinances, led in its last result to the craving for an authority anterior to Scripture itself. This—the earnest, meditative mind of Fox, retiring in disgust from the hopeless controversies of the rigid Scripturalists, looked for in the revelations of the Spirit within, awakened by Scripture, but derived from direct communion with God. He penetrated through the letter, to the living truth which lay under it, and which he saw mirrored in the quiet depths of his own mind. The principles of the Quakers, originating with him towards the close of the war, and exaggerated in the wild vagaries of Naylor, completed the cycle of Puritanic change.

Tendencies akin to these, have ever manifested themselves in periods of strong religious excitement, when the mind breaks away from the fetters of form and conventionalism.

We trace their influence among the Lollards, the early Anabaptists, and the Brownists. They stripped Christianity, as far as it was possible, of all outward organization, and reduced it to a simple influence—the free working of the Spirit. Owning no other tie than that of spiritual brotherhood, the Friends (for so the new society designated themselves) abandoned the forms retained in other Churches; admitted no separate and paid ministry, no ceremonial observances of any kind, no distinction of times and places as more sacred than others; condemned war; refused to take oaths; shunned human tribunals; and renounced the elegant recreations of society. Surrendering themselves up to the immediate guidance of the Spirit, they endeavoured to bring back and realise in their life and manners, the condition of the first Christians as described in the New Testament.

The whole framework of the Church was now undone; and the religious constitution of society seemed about to be resolved into its first elements. Things were approaching the state in which the Gospel had been originally preached to the world. For the last century there had been a continuous effort to reverse step by step, the process by which the Church had gradually arranged and consolidated its constitution, and grown up into the form and organization of the papal hierarchy. First, the connection with Rome was dissolved; and national independence was acquired under the sovereign and the bishops. This was the work of the Anglican party; and its result was the Church of England as constituted under Elizabeth. The next move was to reduce bishops to the rank of presbyters, and to govern the Church by subordinated assemblies of pastors and elders; the national unity in religion being still preserved. This was the aim of the Presbyterians, who thus got a step further back towards primitive Christianity. Then came the Independents who renounced the idea of a national religion altogether; and while they retained a fixed discipline, a regular ministry, and a due administration of ordinances, approached in their congregational system still nearer to the ancient practice of the Church. Lastly, the Quakers, the Seekers, the Fifth Monarchy men, throwing off the restraint of any definite system, carried away by a wild enthusiasm, and living in the vague expectation of some great approaching change—remind us in the absorbing spiritualism of their views, and in their renunciation of the ordinary concerns of life, of the description given in the Acts, of the infant Church at Jerusalem and terminate this progressive picture of the reversal of the Christian story[1].

This was a strange chaotic scene which different men surveyed with different feelings: Baxter and those who like him cherished the idea of a national religion, with pain and disquietude; Milton, the younger Vane and a few other minds of the same earnest and thoughtful cast, with trust and hopefulness, as the presage of future renovation. Milton's prose works afford a fine illustration of the growth and ripening of his opinions on religious subjects, during the exciting scenes through which he passed. In his earliest pieces extending from his Treatise of Reformation to the Apology for Smectymnuus, we find him entertaining the general views of the great Puritan party in and out of Parliament. In his Iconoclastes, his Treatise of Civil Power in ecclesiastical causes, his Considerations touching the exclusion of hirelings from the Church, and in his two Latin Defences of the People of England—all produced under the Commonwealth—he shows himself a decided republican and Independent, as strongly opposed to Erastianism and Presbyterianism as to Prelaty. In his last piece[2], written only a year before his death, when his spirit was mellowed by years, though unbroken by calamity and disappointment, and he was gathering in neglect and poverty the fruits of his rich experience, we find him calmly pleading for a general toleration of all Christians, and defining with moderation and charity the ideas of schism and heresy. The Papists alone, from their imputed guilt of idolatry and the implication of their cause with political interests, he refused to admit within the wide embrace of his Christian love. Of Anabaptists, Arians, Socinians, Arminians, he speaks respectfully, as of persons who may have some errors, but are no heretics; commending their teachers "as learned, worthy, zealous, and religious men, powerful in the Scriptures, holy and unblamable in their lives;" and advancing a plea for the free circulation of their writings. It would have been well for our country if such had been the conclusion not

[1] The Gangræna of Edwards, a Presbyterian Minister, is a bitter attack upon the Sectaries of this time, of whose errors it enumerates 176 different kinds. Three editions of this book had already appeared in 1646.

[2] Of true Religion, Heresy, Schism, Toleration, and what best means may be used against the growth of Popery. 1673.

of an individual alone, but of the nation, from the strife in which the worthiest spirits had been else fruitlessly involved.

SECTION VII.

RESULTS OF PURITANISM UNDER THE COMMONWEALTH.

This dissolution of all ecclesiastical organization did not take place without strenuous efforts to counteract it. The patriots of the Long Parliament included the Church as well as the State in their measures of reform. Church and State were, indeed, so closely interwoven in the constitution, that they could not be disjoined; and it was in that age an undisputed parliamentary axiom, that the redress of ecclesiastical abuses belonged in the last resort to the highest civil authority in the realm. With the instinctive aversion of politicians to clerical interference, the Parliament had hitherto refrained from calling any ecclesiastical council to their assistance (though they had occasionally taken the advice of a select body of divines[1]), till the necessity of strengthening their alliance with the Scots, compelled them to adopt another course. The Scots were bigotedly attached to their Presbyterian system, and considered its establishment in both kingdoms, as the only certain means of accomplishing the objects for which the war had been undertaken. Of the English Puritans, on the other hand, a large proportion would have been satisfied with a purified and mitigated episcopacy[2]; and numbers, daily increasing, were indifferent to any national establishment whatever. Such different views in two parties who equally felt the necessity of union for their common protection, led to manœuvre and reservation on both sides. Among the commissioners sent down by the Parliament to treat with the Scots, were Sir Harry Vane, the younger, and Philip Nye, two men whose consummate policy and attachment to the principles of Independency, defeated the deep-laid Presbyteri-

---

[1] As in the Committee of Accommodation, 1641. Neal, I. p. 708.

[2] Baillie, with all his predilection for Presbyterianism, admits that "the learnedst and most considerable part" of England "were fullie Episcopall," and that of those "who joyned with the Parliament, the greatest and most countenanced part were much Episcopall." Letters and Journals. Edinburgh: 1841. vol. ii. p. 250.

anism of their northern brethren. By inserting the word League, as of more general import, along with that of Covenant, into the title of the agreement, they kept open a way for a more liberal construction of the treaty between the two nations. The result was, that the solemn League and Covenant was subscribed by the English Parliament in the autumn of 1643, and required to be taken by all persons above the age of eighteen years, throughout the kingdom[1].

In consequence of this treaty with the Scots, a parliamentary ordinance was issued for convening an assembly of divines at Westminster, to regulate the national faith and worship. Throughout these proceedings, Parliament discovered an extreme jealousy of ecclesiastical pretensions. The Assembly was kept in strict subordination, as an instrument in the hands of Parliament for a particular object. Parliament nominated its members, one or two ministers from each county, to the amount of a hundred and twenty-one; with thirty lay assessors, ten peers and twenty commoners (among them men of great eminence and different opinions[2]) who were empowered to take part in the discussions, and vote with the divines: but the acts of the Assembly had no validity without parliamentary sanction, and it was restrained from the exercise

---

[1] The following analysis of the Solemn League and Covenant will exhibit its object and character. The contracting parties declare, they enter into it, to save "themselves and their religion from utter ruin and destruction;" (1) to preserve the reformed religion of Scotland, and to bring about the reformation of religion in England and Ireland, according to the word of God, and the example of the best reformed churches, and so accomplish an uniformity of faith, worship and discipline, in the three kingdoms; (2) to aim at the extirpation of popery, prelacy, superstition, heresy, schism, profaneness, etc.; (3) to preserve the rights and privileges of Parliament, and the liberties of the kingdoms; (4) to defend and preserve the King's person and authority in the preservation and defence of religion and liberty, (5) to discover all malignants and incendiaries, that have promoted factions and separated the King from his people, and to bring them to trial and condign punishment, as the supreme judicatories of both nations shall determine; (6) to promote lasting peace and union between the two kingdoms of England and Scotland; (7) to defend all who enter into the Covenant, and to keep together in upholding it against all temptations to desertion or indifference, to promote personal amendment of heart and life, and so turn away the wrath which the sins of the two nations have brought down upon them; that encouragement may thereby be given to other nations, suffering under, or in danger of, the like anti-christian tyranny, to enter into the same or like association for the enlargement of the kingdom of Jesus Christ. Fuller, B. XI. sect. ix. 13, who takes exception *seriatim* to the several articles of which the Covenant consists. Compare Neal, II. pp. 51-54.

[2] In the number were Selden, Whitlocke, the two Vanes, Pym, Pierpont, and Sir Matthew Hale. Neal, II. p. 37.

of any independent ecclesiastical jurisdiction. In the composition of this Assembly, Parliament seems to have aimed at combining the different elements of opinion which then prevailed, so as to realize, as nearly as might be, the idea of a free and general council of the whole nation. Among those summoned, were Episcopalians; such as were classed under the general name of Presbyterians; Independents; and lastly Erastians, who with two divines, Lightfoot and Colman, both distinguished for their great rabbinical learning, formed a powerful party among the lay-assessors. "Thus was this Assembly," says Fuller, " (as first chosen and intended) a quintessence of four parties[1]." Baillie, who was one of the Scotch commissioners to this synod, has described its proceedings with the graphic vividness of an eye-witness. It first met in Henry the Seventh's Chapel, but owing to the coldness of the weather, (it was in December, 1643) afterwards removed its sittings to the Jerusalem Chamber, which was a spacious room, well hung, and comfortably warmed. On both sides of the chamber were raised seats which would accommodate rather more than a hundred persons. At the upper end was a raised platform, with a chair for the prolocutor; on the floor in front two others for the assessors. A table ran down the length of the room, where the two scribes had their papers and writing materials. To the prolocutor's right, on the lowest bench, sat the five Scotch Commissioners, three divines, and two laymen; and behind them, the members of the House of Commons deputed to the Assembly. The space between the chimney and the door was left vacant, and here the Lords of Parliament sat on chairs round the fire. There were generally about sixty divines present. The business of the Assembly was distributed among three Committees, to one or other of which every member belonged; but no matter could be taken into consideration without a written order from Parliament. These Committees in their afternoon sittings, prepared the business for the following day. The public discussions were from nine in the morning till one or two in the afternoon every day except Saturday. The forms of Parliament were strictly adhered to. Every man rose to speak of his own accord; when two or more rose at once, he had the word for whom there was the loudest call. In the order of debate, the general proposition

[1] Book XI. sect. ix. 2.

was first discussed, and then the texts of Scripture alleged in confirmation of it. After debate the question was put, aye or no; and when the majority was doubtful, the numbers were counted by the scribes. No member was alluded to by name, but was addressed through the prolocutor, as "the reverend brother who last spoke, or on this side, above or below." Baillie was much impressed by the order and decorum of their proceedings, and admired the learning, fluency and clearness of the speakers[1].

Such a spectacle had never before been witnessed in England, neither has there been any repetition of it since[2]. Of all who were interested in the great cause of freedom civil and religious, and who had dared the last extremity in asserting it, the wisest, gravest and best were now convened in solemn amity, to seek by their united counsels and endeavours, in Parliament and the Assembly, the two highest objects embraced in the social well-being of man; just and equal government, and such provision for moral and spiritual culture, as would secure its perpetuity in a race of virtuous and high-principled freemen. They seemed now to be approaching the end, which the truest patriots had sought through the dark and blood-stained contingencies of civil discord; and some perhaps were already anticipating a long era of peace and glory for their country. If in looking back on their undertaking from our more elevated point of view, we discern in the conditions of human society, insuperable obstacles to its successful accomplishment, we ought not to be insensible to the patriotic motive which prompted it; nor while we deplore that perverted earnestness which often took the form of intolerance, to overlook the patient thoughtfulness, the strong religious conviction, and the high moral purpose, which have conferred an immortal reputation on many of the acts of the Long Parliament, and leave no small praise due to the intentions and efforts of the Assembly. The great and good men of this greatest period of our national history, attempted in the largeness of their patriotism, directed by views which were then all but universal, to combine objects hitherto found incompatible; to blend good government and civil freedom in

---

[1] Letter to Spang, London. December 7th, 1643.
[2] "The like of that Assemblie," observes Baillie, "I never did see, and as we hear say, the like was never in England, nor anywhere is shortlie lyke to be." ibid. II. p. 107.

one compact and harmonious fabric with a fixed type of faith and worship for the entire nation. Most of them seem not to have suspected, that a denial of the fundamental principle of the Reformation was involved in their design. For although there must ever be a close sympathy between Church and State, which will then be most complete, when each most perfectly fulfils its specific object, they pursue nevertheless a separate way towards their common end; the State embracing men's external relations and demanding, so far as it extends, an uniform embodiment of the general will; the Church which cherishes and expresses the inward life, requiring as necessarily for its healthful existence, the greatest freedom and variety of action. Any attempt consequently to fix them permanently in a definite outward alliance, retards the progress of both towards that distant unity which in the natural development of society, they may ultimately attain. Devoted to such incompatible objects, it is not wonderful, that the labours of the Assembly, however virtuously intended, should have proved in the main a failure.

When the divines were assembled, being more accustomed to the formalities of scholastic disputation than to the despatch of public business, they were proceeding, after a pedantic fashion, to encounter their task in strictly logical method; setting out with an investigation of the power and offices of Jesus Christ, and so descending in due gradation to define the functions of those who bear office in his name. But Parliament was impatient for practical measures to meet the necessities of the times, and accelerated their prolix deliberations. They first agreed on a Directory of Worship in place of the old Prayer-book, the use of which was prohibited by Parliament; and introduced that form of conducting the public services of religion, which still subsists in the Kirk of Scotland and in most congregations of English Dissenters. The adoption of it was enforced by parliamentary ordinance August 23rd, 1645[1]. The Assembly next produced the Confession of Faith, and the Form of Church Government, with the Shorter and Larger Catechisms. The Confession and the Catechisms were confirmed by authority of Parliament; but it must be noticed, that all the Articles enforcing Presbyterian discipline, were passed over and never acquired validity in England. In Scot-

---

[1] It was countermanded by a royal proclamation from Oxford of November 13. Neal, II. p. 109. Fuller, XI. p. 10.

land, the whole was adopted, and became the **basis of the national Church**[1].

The Westminster Confession is an elaborate exposition **in clear and forcible** language, of the Calvinistic theology which **was** at that time the almost universal **belief of** the Puritan party. Before the arrival of the Scotch Commissioners, the English divines had commenced a revision of the Thirty-nine Articles, with a view to make the sense of them more decidedly Calvinistic[2]. But they afterwards abandoned this **design**, to undertake a new and original work. The scriptural spirit of Puritanism is very conspicuous in the ample references to the Bible, by which every statement in the Confession is sustained. **The Catechisms are** a reduction of the substance of the Confession, **for the purpose of instruction.** In the Larger a complete **system of practical** duty **is ingeniously** evolved by accommodation and expansion out of **the Ten Commandments.** In spite of its stern Calvinism, there **is much** to admire in this Catechism. Its language is plain and impressive. Its careful adaptation to imbue the mind **with the** principles of personal holiness and piety, the fulness and accuracy **with** which it explains doctrines believed to be essential, and its earnest, solemn inculcation of the duties of public **worship, of Scripture reading,** and of private and **domestic prayer, attest** the **conscientious** zeal with which the Westminster divines discharged **their** sacred task, and are in striking **contrast** with the meagre **brevity of the Catechism of the Church of England.**

It would have been well for their reputation, if their labours had terminated here. They had been convened by Parlia-

---

[1] Hetherington's History of the Westminster Assembly. Edinburgh, 1843. Baillie was aware of the influence which predominated in the Assembly, and has remarked in several passages of his Letters, with a singular mixture of shrewdness and simplicity, that it was not expedient to force on the question of Presbyterian government, till the Scots' army had drawn sufficiently near to overawe the discussion. There is a Journal by Lightfoot of the proceedings of the Assembly, published in the last 8vo edition of his works, which I have had no opportunity of consulting. A similar MS. Journal by George Gillespie (one of the Scotch Commissioners) is in existence; and another ascribed to Dr. Thomas Goodwin, is preserved in Dr. Williams's Library, London. Memoir of Baillie, appended to his **Letters and Journals,** p. li. note. If these Journals were published, we should then possess an Episcopalian and Erastian, a Presbyterian, and an Independent, account of the deliberations of the only Protestant Council that ever met in England.

[2] Neal, II. p. 48. In the Appendix No. I. he has compared the articles so altered with the original Articles.

ment to make a national settlement of religion. Such an object, if practicable at all, demanded mutual concession and forbearance on all sides : but it was defeated by the unyielding bigotry of the high Presbyterian party, who had been urged to advance the most extravagant claims by the presence and countenance of the Scots. The sectaries of the army who would have acquiesced in the subsistence of a national religion and a public maintenance, had a general toleration for Christians been coupled with it, were far more enlightened and more moderate in their views. The confidence with which the Presbyterians maintained the divine right of their system, and contended for its exclusive establishment throughout the land, involved them in discord, first with the Parliament who refused to surrender the power of the Keys, and secondly with the Erastians and the Independents who saw that the free exercise of their own principles would be impossible under the ascendancy of Presbyterianism. The Independents were a small body, not more than six or seven avowedly in the whole Assembly; but the consideration with which they were treated even by the Presbyterians, and the zeal manifested on their behalf in the Grand Committee of Accommodation appointed by Parliament in 1644, are proofs of the weight attached to their character and abilities, and of the spreading moral influence of their principles[1].

The Independents too had their notions of a *jus divinum*; in other words, claimed for their theory of Church government, the express sanction of Scripture. As they did not object to a comprehension in the national settlement, and to occasional communion with the Presbyterians (for in doctrine the two parties essentially agreed), provided they could secure the full exercise of Church power to their separate congregations, and be exempted from the control of the Presbyterian courts; they had proposed at the opening of the debate, that before any system of government was exclusively decided upon, the claims of Independency should be discussed step by step with those of Presbyterianism. In this way possibly a friendly accommodation might have been effected. When however this offer was rejected by the Presbyterians who urged on an immediate vote in favour of their own views, the

---

[1] Neal, II. p. 206. Collier, II. p. 838. Baillie attests the "learning, wit and eloquence" of the Independents in the Assembly, II. p. 145; and Fuller though an Episcopalian, speaks of them in a very kindly spirit. B. XI. ix. 35.

Independents changed their course of action; and leaving the invidious distinction of being the dominant Church to their impracticable brethren, contented themselves with suing for a simple toleration. Even this was contested by the ascendant party, who would nevertheless out of personal regard for the Dissenting brethren, have willingly allowed in their case the *fact* of toleration, by any indirect expedient which would not have conceded its *principle*.

These discussions terminated in no practical result, though they must have aided the progress of just ideas on the rights of conscience[1]. The Independents were shut out from the national establishment, and the Presbyterians were exhibited in the odious light of opponents to all toleration. What the latter party aimed at, was the purification of the Church according to a scriptural model. Episcopacy being now to all appearance destroyed[2], they had set their heart on Presbyterianism as its substitute; and since in their view only one form of religion could be established for the whole nation, they looked on toleration as a lax abandonment of the great principle of reform. After they had outvoted the Independents and Erastians on the question of the *jus divinum*, the Presbyterians remained in undisputed possession of the Assembly, which from that time lost all claim to a national representation. Continually reduced in numbers, sharing in the fortunes of the great civil Court with which it had been associated, it became at length a sort of Presbyterian rump, and broke up of itself in April 1653, when the Long Parliament was violently dissolved by Cromwell[3]. The intolerant spirit of the Assembly was only too consistently exhibited by Presbyterians in other parts of the kingdom, who sent up addresses to Parliament against the threatened Toleration,

---

[1] See the details in Neal, II. pp. 205–210; also the Grand Debate concerning Presbytery and Independency, London: 1652; and the papers given in to the Parliamentary Committee for Accommodation, 1644; from which Neal has drawn his materials.

[2] Episcopacy had been finally abolished, and its property confiscated, by the Parliamentary Ordinances of Oct. 9 and Nov. 16, 1646. Neal, II. p. 246.

[3] The remnant of the Assembly had been converted into a Committee for the examination of ministers, soon after the King's death in 1649. Neal, II. p. 333. From the commencement there had been a small Committee in the Assembly to examine candidates for the Ministry. Certificates were given to the Assembly of their qualifications; upon which they were appointed to vacant pulpits, but without ordination, till some form of Church government should be agreed upon. Baillie's Letters and Journals, II. p. 112.

the great Diana, as it was contemptuously called, of the Independents[1].

The critical state of the times, the seizure of the King's person by the army, the renewal of the war for his deliverance, and the growing jealousy between the army which abounded in sectaries, and the Parliament where Presbyterianism still predominated—exasperated and maddened party feeling to a pitch before unknown. Amidst these excitements the Presbyterians brought the foulest blot on their reputation by the Ordinance against Blasphemy and Heresy, which enacted that for certain specified offences under this head, if the party on his trial should not abjure his error, or if having abjured he should relapse, he should suffer death "as in case of felony without benefit of clergy[2]."

---

[1] Mr. Heyrick, a Presbyterian and Warden of the Collegiate Church of Manchester, replying in 1648, to the "Agreement of the People" issued by the Independents, protests against Toleration, as a violation of the Solemn League and Covenant. "We have searched the Scriptures," say the subscribers to this memorial,—"and yet we cannot find, that ever such a thing was practised with approbation from God, from the time that Adam was created upon the earth." "And therefore we cannot see, how such a kind of toleration as is endeavoured after in these times, can anyways consist with a thorough reformation according to the Word of God, there being nothing more contrary to reformation than toleration." History of the Collegiate Church of Manchester, by Dr. Hibbert Ware: vol. i. Appendix to Ch. xix. p. 394. The same spirit is conspicuous in a Tract of 1644, entitled, "Wholesome Severity reconciled with Christian Liberty, or the True Resolution of the present Controversy concerning Liberty of Conscience." The author admits, that good citizens as well as good Christians have strong temptations to embrace the doctrine of Toleration, and then proceeds: "Under these fair colours and handsome pretexts do Sectaries infuse their poison, I mean, their pernicious, God-provoking, truth-defacing, church-ruinating, and state-shaking Toleration. The plain English of the question is this—whether the Christian magistrate be keeper of both tables; whether he ought to suppress his own enemies, but not God's enemies; and preserve his own ordinances, but not Christ's ordinances from violation; whether the troublers of Israel may be troubled," etc. etc. There is no end to Presbyterian invective on the subject of Toleration. Edwards quite surpasses himself on this inspiring theme. "A Toleration," says he, "is the grand design of the Devil, his master-piece, and chief engine he works by at this time, to uphold his tottering kingdom; it is the most compendious, ready and sure way to destroy all religion, lay all waste, and bring in all evil; it is a most transcendant, catholic and fundamental evil for this kingdom of any that can be imagined: as original sin is the most fundamental sin—all sin—having the seed and spawn of all in it; so a Toleration hath all errors in it, and all evils." Gangræna: Letters and Narrations, p. 58. These intolerant doctrines made the Presbyterian discipline, wherever it was established, exceedingly oppressive, and calling forth at length a strong reaction, favoured the spread both of Independent and of Episcopalian principles. This was the case in Lancashire. See the work of Dr. Hibbert Ware, already quoted, vol. i. p. 287. Appendix, p. 398.

[2] This Ordinance is dated May 2, 1648. Neal, II. p. 338. The disgrace of

In virtue of a Parliamentary ordinance which passed the Lords, June 6, 1646, Presbyterianism had now become the national religion[1], although the disordered state of the country prevented the uniform enforcement of its discipline. It was the most completely reduced to practice in Lancashire, where it was virtually established and annually held its provincial Synods at Preston in the centre of the county for fourteen years[2]. The provincial assemblies of London, besides the weekly meetings of clergy at Sion College, continued to be held half-yearly till 1655, when they were dissolved[3]. Presbyterian associations were also formed, though with less order and authority, in other counties. But there was no uniformity. The spirit of the times favoured toleration, and Independent and Baptist churches were set up in many places. The Presbyterians attached great importance to an educated and duly appointed ministry; and during the ascendancy of their discipline, a committee of divines sate weekly in London, to examine such ministers as presented themselves for ordination and induction. Instructions and authority were sent down to the provincial associations for the same purpose, to secure as much regularity as was attainable. The order of proceeding seems in general to have been this: the patron nominated, and the parish or congregation elected, the minister; who then presented himself with this recommendation to the examining board for ordina-

originating it does not rest on the Assembly of Divines. The Presbyterian members of the Commons who had abandoned the House while the army was quartered in its neighbourhood, resumed their sittings on its withdrawal; and availed themselves of their superiority in numbers and influence, to enact this measure against heretics, which they had previously meditated, under the sharp stimulus of hatred to the various sects with which the vicinity of the army had recently annoyed them. "This," says Neal with just indignation, "is one of the most shocking laws I have met with in restraint of religious liberty, and shows that the governing Presbyterians would have made a terrible use of their power, had they been supported by the sword of the civil magistrate."

[1] Neal, II. p. 200.

[2] From 1646 to 1660. The province of Lancashire embraced the following classes:—Manchester, Bolton, Warrington, Blackburne, Leyland, Preston, West Derby, the Fylde, and Lancaster. In the Manchester classis were included the parishes of Manchester, Prestwich, Oldham, Flixton, Eccles, Ashton-under-Line. The classical meetings of this division were held in the refectory of the Manchester (afterwards called Chetham) College. A full account of Presbyterianism at this time in Lancashire, drawn from contemporary documents and tracts, will be found in Dr. Hibbert Ware's Hist. of the Coll. Church of Manchester. A relic of the old Presbyterian organization still subsists in the Provincial Meeting of Presbyterian ministers, annually held in rotation at different places in Lancashire and Cheshire.

[3] Neal, II. p. 260, 1, and p. 337.

tion and induction; after which he was finally confirmed in his benefice by authority of Parliament[1].

The obstinacy of the Presbyterians and the duplicity of the King, preventing any comprehensive settlement of the great questions of Church and State, threw the chief direction of affairs into the hands of the army, and gave fresh stimulus to the doctrines of the Independents. All public measures affecting religion, which ensued from this time till the death of Cromwell, mark an increasing respect for the principle of Toleration. In the Agreement of the People, put forth as a declaration of the public sentiment not long before the trial of the King, and generally attributed to Ireton, the free exercise of their religion by all Christians is particularly insisted on, as an article that should enter into any future constitution of the government. The Engagement which was required to be taken under the Commonwealth in place of the Solemn League and Covenant, and which may be called the Independent, as the latter was the Presbyterian, oath of allegiance, relaxed much of the preceding strictness, and admitted ministers of different persuasions, even some Episcopalians, to church livings. The Presbyterians who were attached to monarchy and zealous sticklers for Church uniformity, very generally refused to take it. But henceforward under all changes of government, so long as the old monarchy continued in abeyance, provision was always made for Toleration, in the sense which the word then bore, as including all who held the fundamentals of Christianity.

For the Presbyterian committees which had been appointed under the Long Parliament, to examine ministers before induction into livings, Cromwell substituted a select body of divines and laymen chosen by himself and his Council or by Parliament, from the Presbyterians and Independents, with a few Baptists intermixed, who were called Tryers. The functions of the Tryers were further extended, in the appointment of a committee for the ejectment of scandalous and insuffi-

---

[1] Neal, II. pp. 69, 105, 139, 201. Comp. p. 460, and Appendix III. p. 860, with Baillie's Letters and Journals, II. p. 139. Calamy (Continuation, I. p. 461-2) gives a copy of the form of inducting his father, Edmund Calamy the younger, into the rectory of Moreton, Essex, under the protectorate of Richard Cromwell, with an engraving of the common seal then used by the Commissioners for the approbation of public preachers. The instrument is dated Whitehall, April 20, 1659.

cient ministers and schoolmasters[1]. The object of Cromwell in these measures was to keep down the ascendancy of any one denomination. The opinions of these Tryers and Commissioners being generally Calvinistic could not fail to have some influence on their approval or rejection of candidates; but there is no evidence, that worthy and pious men of any denomination, where they did not openly oppose the predominant orthodoxy of the time, were ever refused or deprived by them. John Goodwin, the famous Arminian Independent, complained of their power as more arbitrary than that of the bishops; but Owen who was one of their number, secured Pococke, the Orientalist, although an Episcopalian, in the quiet enjoyment of his cure[2]. Fuller, the historian, also an Episcopalian, was allowed to pass, on simply declaring that "he made conscience of his thoughts," without giving any particular account of the work of grace on his heart[3]. Baxter who was strongly opposed to Cromwell's rule and institutions, has borne his testimony to the general impartiality and efficiency of the Tryers[4].

Cromwell himself was deeply imbued with Puritanical feeling. Protestantism which in his view was the same with Puritanism, he had early learned to associate with the cause of truth, freedom and godliness; while he looked on every approximation to Popish doctrines and usages, as the sign and harbinger of corruption and tyranny. By these ideas his conception of Toleration was determined. Under the same influence, he had formed a design of organizing the whole Protestant interest of Europe into a league, to counteract the efforts of the Propagandists at Rome. The mortal strife between the powers of light and darkness so vividly depicted in the solemn story of the Bible, he saw at work before his eyes in the great ecclesiastical struggle of the age; and he longed to put himself at its head. His earnest and energetic character embodied the spirit of Puritanism in its highest aims, its last and

[1] The first of these ordinances bears date March 20, 1654; the second, August 28, of the same year. Neal, II. pp. 446 and 452.
[2] Orme's Life of Owen. [3] Neal II. p. 451.
[3] "To give them their due, they did abundance of good to the Church." "They admitted of any that were able serious preachers, and lived a godly life, of what tolerable opinion soever they were." "So great was the benefit above the hurt which they brought to the Church, that many thousands of souls blest God for the faithful ministers whom they let in, and grieved when the Prelatists afterwards cast them out again." Baxter's Narrative of his Life and Times. London, fol. 1696, p. 72.

grandest development; and having crushed Prelacy at home, he was eager to pursue it to its last retreats abroad, and exterminate it from the earth. But with this enthusiastic temperament, the source of all true heroism, Cromwell united a most vigorous and capacious intellect, which could distinguish the interest of religion from the ascendancy of a sect. His mind had been disciplined by the debates in Parliament, where Pym, Hampden, Selden and Whitlocke had discussed the highest questions of Church and State. Many of their clear and dispassionate views he had imbibed, and wrought with statesmanlike tact into the temper of his own more fervid Independency; and the uniform policy of his own government showed, that he was prepared to put in practice as the basis of a national settlement of religion, those doctrines of general toleration which were dawning on the convictions of the most enlightened of his contemporaries, and which far transcended the aims of divines of any school.

There is no proof, that Cromwell ever intended to break up a public maintenance for religion, and to throw the support of it entirely on the spontaneous enthusiasm of different sects. The appointment of the Tryers was avowedly designed as a restraint on the license and irregularity which already existed. Individuals here and there, like Milton and Vane, may have anticipated what is now called the Voluntary System; but it had not yet become a distinguishing tenet of the general body of the Independents[1]. The Independents believing in the *jus divinum* of their own system, and in the scriptural duty of gathering separate churches, were compelled to plead for toleration, and in consistency with their own principles, to concede it to all who were *tolerable:* and this was the point of view from which some amongst them advanced to wider and juster ideas of religious liberty. Could they at once have established their own principles, the example of their brethren in New England, and Owen's treatment of some female Quakers at Oxford[2], render it only too probable, that they would have

---

[1] See the 14th article of the Supplement to the Savoy Confession of Faith.

[2] Orme's Life, p. 192. Owen's extreme dislike of the Quakers is evident from his " Exercitationes Apologeticæ adversus hujus temporis Fanaticos." Oxon. 1658. Baxter also speaks of them very contemptuously (Life I. § 123, II. § 431.) Sewel (History of the Quakers, p. 90.) has a full account of the proceedings at Oxford: from which it appears, that Owen, then Vice-Chancellor, approved and santioned the extreme severities of the Justices of the Peace, with which the Mayor refused his concurrence. It must be admitted, however, from Sewel's

called in the aid of the magistrate, to uphold the true religion
and to punish sectaries. The wisdom on this subject was all
with the laity. Cromwell was much in advance of his clergy.
He aimed at balancing by a just and equal policy the different
religious parties in the State; healing their mutual antipathies; repressing their exorbitant pretensions: and uniting
them all in a peaceful subjection to the laws. When the Independents desired to hold a Synod, for the drawing up of a
public Declaration of the Faith and Order of their churches,
Cromwell unwillingly yielded to this request, as fearing it
might separate them further from the Presbyterians[1]. Episcopalians and Socinians were equally embraced within his toleration. He rescued Biddle from clerical tyranny, and allowed
him a maintenance. Usher, we are told by Collier, he treated
with particular marks of esteem, and honoured with a public
funeral in Westminster Abbey[2].

The confinement of controversy during the progress of the
Puritanic movement mainly to questions of Church government, and the almost universal recognition of Calvinism as
the true doctrine of the Reformation, prevented the sects
which had made the greatest advance towards religious freedom, from understanding the rights of conscience in their full
extent, and attaining a clear comprehension of the relations
between the Church and the civil power. When a committee
was appointed in 1654, to decide upon the fundamentals of
Christianity mentioned in the Instrument of Government, the
Independent divines, under the guidance of Owen and Thomas
Goodwin, produced a formidable list of articles, which would
have excluded all who were not Trinitarians and Calvinists. Baxter who required no more than the Lord's Prayer,
the Apostles' Creed, and the Ten Commandments, was reproached by them with opening a door for the admission of
Papists and Socinians[3]. Goodwin, on presenting the Savoy
Confession to Richard Cromwell, addressed him in language

---

own showing, that the Quakeresses themselves had given some provocation. The
name Quakers was first attached to this sect, as a nickname, by the Independents. (Ibid. p. 99.)

[1] Neal, II. p. 506.

[2] Collier, II. pp. 868-9, and Neal, II. p. 477 and 471. Neal quotes, p. 472, a
remarkable passage from bishop Kennet in attestation of Cromwell's toleration
of the episcopal clergy.

[3] Baxter's Account, etc., Part II. p. 198. Dr. Owen, 'the great doer of all
that worded the articles,' was Baxter's principal opponent.

which savoured of the Erastianism of the Long Parliament, as the keeper of both Tables of the Law, the head at once of Church and of State[1]. Owen on conversing with Lord Clarendon after the Restoration, on Toleration, was asked by him what he would require; when he replied, "liberty to those who agreed in doctrine with the Church of England[2]." It is evident, that the greatest men of this period with a few exceptions, though in the way to a just conception of religious liberty, had not yet reached it.

The Savoy Confession acquaints us with the principles of the Independents, now a numerous and powerful body, under the Protectorate[3]. It was drawn up in a Synod, composed of representatives of their Churches, laymen and ministers, which held its meetings at the old palace of the Savoy in the Strand. Its labours were not completed till after the death of Cromwell. The Savoy Confession stands in the same relation to the Independents, as the Westminster to the Presbyterians. The chief hand in preparing it, is ascribed to Dr. Owen[4]. The preface is eloquently written, alluding to the disordered times through which the truth had been preserved, and the surprising readiness and unanimity with which in a very short space of time, not more than eleven days, the members of the Synod had agreed upon their declarations. How little the true principle of the rights of conscience and the spirit of free inquiry were understood by them, is evident from the following passage:—"The authors of this Confession have all along contended for the exercise, among all Christian states and churches, of forbearance and mutual indulgence to saints of all persuasions that hold fast the necessary foundations of faith and holiness, though not requiring such latitude of concession on behalf of their own faith, which they conceive to have in all things a Scripture warrant in support of it." What is said on the subject of Church government is very significant. They apprehend their system is conformable to the Scripture rule. "Varieties of opinion," it is added, "on this subject, have led to the conclusion, that no rule is laid down in Scripture, and that it must be left to the civil magis-

---

[1] Price's Hist. of Nonconformity.   [2] Orme's Life, p. 300.
[3] Declaration of the Faith and Order owned and practised in the Congregational Churches of England, agreed upon and consented to by their Elders and Messengers at the Savoy, Oct. 12, 1658. London, 1659.
[4] See Bright's Apostolical Independency.

trate to adopt such a form as is most suitable and consistent with civil government. When this persuasion is entertained by civil governors, churches asserting their power and order to be *jure divino*, can look for nothing better or more honourable than *toleration* or *permission*. The result of this will be, that all who differ from the magistrate and among themselves, standing in equal and a like difference from the principle of such a magistrate, he is equally free to give a like liberty to them, one as well as the other." If I understand this statement aright, it accepts simple toleration as the unavoidable consequence of disagreement between the Church and the civil magistrate respecting the *jus divinum*, but does not disown the principle of establishment in cases where their views coalesce. In the chapter on the Civil Magistrate it is declared, that "he is bound to encourage, promote, and protect the professors and profession of the Gospel, to manage civil administrations in the interest of Christ, and to hinder the publication and divulging of errors and blasphemies; but in such differences about doctrine and worship as befal men of good conscience, who hold fast the foundation, and do not disturb those differing from them, there is no warrant for the magistrate under the Gospel for abridging them of their liberty." In the Declaration of Faith the Westminster Confession is closely followed. To the chapter on the Law, another is added on the Gospel, being a collection of various statements and indications, scattered up and down the Assembly's Catechism, which is deeply Calvinistic. The part which treats of the Institution and Order of Churches, is separated from the Declaration of Faith, as involving points still controverted among the orthodox. The preface to this Independent Confession breathes a brotherly and conciliatory spirit towards the Presbyterians[1].

[1] The preface to the Savoy Confession contains the following description of the state of things which had preceded its appearance:—"We have sailed through an æstuation, fluxes and refluxes of great varieties of spirits, doctrines, opinions, and occurrences, and especially in the matter of opinions, which have been accompanied in their several seasons with powerful persuasions and temptations to seduce those of our way. It is known, men have taken the freedom (notwithstanding what authority hath interposed to the contrary) to vent and vend their own vain and accursed imaginations, contrary to the great and fixed truths of the Gospel, insomuch, as, take the whole round and circle of delusions the Devil hath in this small time run—it will be found, that every truth of greater or lesser weight, hath by one or other hand, at one time or another, been questioned and called to the bar amongst us, yea, and impleaded, under

Notwithstanding the unquestionable services of Cromwell to religious freedom, he does not appear to have secured the confidence and attachment of the Sectaries. Owen was alienated from him by his suspected design of assuming the crown. Baxter and the bulk of the Presbyterians were attached to royalty; and most of them had taken the Covenant. He did not act enough in the spirit and interest of any one party, to bind it to himself. Yet had his life been prolonged, he might have overmastered all these difficulties. Considering the state of parties and the ends for which the war with the Church and the Crown had been undertaken, his death must be regarded as an irreparable misfortune to the cause of religious liberty. With him perished every hope of settling the religion of the nation on a liberal and comprehensive basis. Only an energy and a vigilance like his, could have subdued and controlled the manifold elements of discord that were at work. When he was removed, these immediately broke out, and there was no one to direct the storm. The republicans wanted unity of purpose and did not carry with

the pretext (which hath some degree of justice in it) that all should not be bound up to the traditions of former times, nor take religion upon trust." It is evident from this, that among those who were classed under the general name of Independents during the Commonwealth, great diversity and great freedom of opinion prevailed, and that one object in putting forth the Confession, was to give some check to this license. The observation is of some importance in its bearing on the future history of Independency. It is further argued in this preface, that Independency is a more ancient way in England than Presbytery, having been adopted in the first breaking off from Episcopacy, and that the old Puritan Nonconformists, Whitehead, Gilby, Fox and others, were inclined to its principles. The following fact in the history of the Westminster Confession, mentioned in this preface, is worthy of notice. When the Articles were presented by the Assembly to Parliament for confirmation,—Ch. 30, on Church Censures, Ch. 31, of Synods, 4th paragraph of Ch. 20, on the Power of the Magistrate to punish offenders against the peace of the Church, and part of Ch. 24, on Marriage and Divorce—were put aside by Parliament, as unsuitable to a confession of faith and involving points on which differences of opinion existed. But the copy, as it came from the Assembly, containing all these articles, being transmitted into Scotland and approved by the General Assembly there, was printed and given to the world in 1647, before the Parliament had declared their resolutions about it, which was not till 1648; and yet this copy, it is observed, though it had never received the sanction of the English Parliament, "hath been, and continueth to be, the copy ordinarily only sold, printed and reprinted for these eleven years." This was written in 1659. The circumstance shows, how different were the feelings of the English Parliament from those of the zealous Presbyterians both in England and in Scotland. The Parliamentary copy, the preface says, was in few hands. The full copy accepted in Scotland, was ratified by the Parliament of that country in 1649.

them the **sympathies** of the people. Richard Cromwell was deficient in energy and misled by his advisers. The Presbyterians were divided, some adhering to the young Protector, some speculating on the return of the king.

Among all these parties, who was equal to the emergency of the occasion? Charles and the exiled royalists remained. The course of events accelerated by the treachery of Monk and the credulity of the Presbyterians, showed but too clearly, that the destinies of this great nation, weak in the very redundancy of its strength, without a head to guide it, must inevitably pass into their hands. With what result to the most precious interests of humanity, for which the best and bravest had toiled and bled—let the sad and disastrous sequel declare. We approach with pain the era of the Restoration; and turn mournfully from an age filled with high thoughts and noble aims, and bright glimpses of a time of equal justice and religious peace, to a period so darkened with dishonour and shame, so stained with persecution and licentiousness, as the reign of Charles. But it must not be supposed, that the struggle of the Puritans was made in vain. Some enterprises are to be estimated from the great idea which they express and strive to realize. Their example, their moral influence, is of infinitely more value than their immediate result. It is by such efforts incessantly renewed, actuated by the same indomitable sense of right, profiting by all past failures, and at each repetition drawing nearer to the desired end—that society advances step by step towards that happier condition, which its very power of conceiving is an assurance that it must ultimately attain:—

> "For freedom's battle once begun,
> Bequeath'd by bleeding sire to son,
> Though baffled oft, is ever won."

SECTION VIII.

INFLUENCE OF DISTINGUISHED TEACHERS ON THE HISTORICAL DEVELOPMENT OF PURITANISM: BAXTER AND OWEN.

The character of the Puritanic movement underwent a change in the interval between the Restoration and the Revolution. The old effervescence subsided, and out of it, amidst new circumstances, distinct historical forms were gradually evolved. Deprived of the support of a reforming and patriotic Parliament, crushed and degraded by the insolent triumph of a crown and hierarchy set up anew, Puritanism lost its political significance, and became every day more exclusively religious. There had been a general disposition on the part even of the more extreme sectaries, to acquiesce in the restoration of the kingly rule, and to recognise in it a providential appointment[1]: and this feeling was strengthened through natural re-action and a desire to give evidence of loyalty, by the outbreak of the Fifth Monarchy men under Venner in London, and the discovery of similar plots in other parts of the country[2].

The circumstances which preceded the Act of Uniformity, and its provisions, have been already described. What we have now to notice, is its influence on the spirit of Puritanism. Up to that event the principal benefices in the Church of England were held by men who would have gladly entered into a friendly compromise with their Episcopalian brethren on principles which Usher and Baxter equally approved[3], and who had promoted the king's return in the hope that it would lead to a national settlement of religion. With such men the Church was an object of deeper interest than the State; and whatever might be their theoretical preferences, they would quietly have reconciled themselves to any government which seemed likely to be stable, and promised religious peace. All these were harshly cast out of the Church by the Act of Uniformity; compelled to be Separatists; and forced against their will into an attitude of apparent disaffection to the Crown. To the last they clung to the hope of comprehension. Three opportunities occurred for effecting it, which issued in no result: at the Restoration in 1660; after the discovery of the Popish plot in 1678; and at the Revolution in 1688[4]. It was not till every prospect was closed against them, that they

[1] See Barclay's Dedication of his Apology to Charles II.
[2] As the Farnley-wood plot, near Leeds, in 1663, and Yarrington's plot. The Rev. Jos. Hunter (Life of Oliver Heywood, p. 155, note) expresses a suspicion that these plots were got up by the government and formed part of the policy of Hyde. For Venner's movement, and the disclaimer of participation in it by the Independents, Baptists and Quakers, see Neal, II. p. 592.
[3] Baxter's Account of his Life and Times, Part II. § 61-64.
[4] Calamy's Continuation, vol. i., Dedication, p. liii.

proceeded very unwillingly to collect and organize **distinct and independent** churches. **Even then** they kept up as close and frequent communion with the national establishment, as their conscientious scruples would allow. Schism **was abhorrent to** their feelings. Many of them, like their ancestors **before the** war, out of deferential feeling to their mother Church, abstained from the exercise of ordination[1].

The men of this period form the transition-class between the old Puritan of the time of the wars, and the Protestant Dissenter recognised by the Toleration Act of the Revolution. With them we are immediately connected through the foundation of our religious societies, and the possession at this day of many principles and tendencies which they have transmitted to us. The **memory of our** great-grandfathers reaches back to the time when their personal influence was strong and active in **the world.** They are our spiritual ancestors—the fathers of English Protestant Dissent. This was the period that witnessed the painful ministry, the prolific tongue and pen, **the severe** and saint-like virtue, sweetened with a holy meekness, of Baxter, Owen, Bates, and Howe in the metropolis; of Hey**wood,** Fairfax, Newcome, Henry, and Flavel in the provinces. **Such** men, like true prophets of God, lived heroically on their convictions; and amidst the disquietudes of a troubled and persecuted life, with the court, the priesthood and the magistracy **leagued** against them, giving themselves up to the single inspiration of faith and duty, strove earnestly to fulfil the solemn **vow they** had laid on their souls, that they would preach at whatever cost the truths of eternal life to sinful and dying men.

The various elements involved in the general principle of Puritanism, which had been mixed up and confounded amidst the fluctuations and uncertainties of the war and the Commonwealth, were more fully drawn out and separated from each other, and impressed with a distinctive character that is **not** yet effaced, by the writings and influence of eminent men **who** prominently expressed and embodied them, during the important interval of which I am now speaking.

Of **the** great Presbyterian party, Baxter stands **forth as the most conspicuous** representative. I have already **explained,**

---

[1] Even **after** the Revolution, **Howe** and Bates declined taking part **in the** ordination **of** Calamy. Howe first consulted Lord Somers. Calamy's Life and Times, vol. i. pp. 545–80.

that the term Presbyterian, as the name of a party, had ceased to denote exclusive attachment to that form of Church government, but embraced all who were not from principle Separatists, and who desired a national settlement of religion on the broad basis of purification and reform. In this aim Baxter heartily concurred. To promote it was the governing principle of his ecclesiastical and doctrinal system. He shunned extremes, and sought a common centre; and in this respect his mind was essentially **eclectic**. His chief ground of difference with **the Independents** was, in his own phrase, "their separating strictness." Under the guidance of this principle Baxter's mind became more tolerant, enlarged and catholic, the longer he lived. Its distinguishing attributes were uncommon vigour and acuteness, delighting to a fault in the exercise of dialectic subtlety, but combined with remarkable fervour of spirit, great simplicity of purpose, and inflexible honesty. Though he had not enjoyed an University education, he was deeply read in the subjects that were then conceived to belong to divinity, and might have had a higher reputation for learning, had he written less. But the pen was scarcely ever out of his hand. Of his innumerable productions, the far greater part were occasional, and thrown off at a heat for some immediate practical object. In the noble earnestness of his character, he thought less of literary fame than the interests of the human soul[1].

He began his career as a strong Calvinist, with much of that exclusiveness and aversion to those who thought differently, which often marks sincere and ardent natures, in the first warmth of young conviction, before they have had extensive intercourse with the world. In the earlier part of his life, during his ministry at Kidderminster, and while he was chaplain in the army, he was continually involved in controversy,

---

[1] Baxter's writings are exceedingly voluminous. The complete list of them occupies nearly twelve octavo pages in Calamy's Abridgment of his Life and Times, pp. 410—422. His practical works were published after his death in four volumes folio. They have been greatly commended by two eminent churchmen. Bishop Wilkins said, that Baxter had cultivated every subject he handled; and Dr Isaac Barrow has remarked—of his practical writings, that "they were never mended," and of his controversial, that "they were seldom confuted."

There is an admirable portrait of Baxter in Dr. Williams's Library, Redcross Street, London. We seem to read his mind in the pale, meditative features, shaded by the long raven hair that escapes with Puritan simplicity beneath his skull-cap, and rising with a soft and earnest expression out of the rich, dark ground of the picture—full of thought and sweetness.

and showed great zeal in putting down the new doctrines of various sectaries. But deeper acquaintance with his own heart, larger dealings with mankind, and frequent observation, during those unsettled times, of the different aspects of religion to different minds, diverted his thoughts more and more from the form to the spirit of Christianity, and fixed his attention chiefly, the older he grew, on inward rectitude of spirit and practical goodness. His later writings, while they still breathe the solemn fervour and strictness of the old Puritan, break forth here and there into beautiful expressions of a sublime and exalted charity, which soars above the narrow divisions of the world, and delights to embrace all good men as the children of God. No stronger proof can be alleged of the strength of this catholic spirit, and of his superiority to the ordinary prejudices of the Puritan, than his belief that there might be a true and availing Christianity even in the Papist. In the same healing temper he endeavoured to show, in his Catholic Theology[1], that the points at issue between the Calvinists and Arminians (the great controversy of the time) did not involve such fundamental truths as were the necessary grounds of separation.

His views of the Trinity (a subject which already excited debate and alienation among Christians) were charged by his distinguished contemporary, Dr. Owen, with deficiency in clearness and precision; and his own later exposition of them took the form of Sabellianism[2]. We have already noticed the liberal and comprehensive spirit which he displayed at the discussion on fundamentals in Cromwell's Instrument of Government. In spite of early Presbyterian bias he was not unfriendly to a moderate episcopacy, in which he hoped good men on both sides might have happily coalesced. He acknowledged an element of truth in the several principles of the Erastians, the Episcopalians, the Presbyterians, and the Independents; nor did he see anything absolutely irreconcileable with unity, in the more peculiar doctrines and practices of the Baptists. He would have brought together and combined what was good in each, and have thus endeavoured to realize his cherished idea of a truly national and Catholic Church[3].

[1] Published in **1675**.
[2] Historical Proofs and Illustrations of the Hewley Case, p. 22.
[3] He has expressed his judgment on the principles of these different parties in his Account of his Life. Part II. § 2-6.

The same spirit he consistently manifested to the close of his life. When he took out a license to preach after the Indulgence of 1672, it was not under the title of Independent, or Presbyterian, or any other party, but **simply as a Nonconformist**; one shut **out** from the Church by conscience, but still hoping **for comprehension**[1]. Yet to this moderate and **conciliatory view of party** differences, which in some men **is only the cover of** a prudent selfishness, he added a scrupulous honesty and sensitive tenderness of conscience. He declined the bishopric that was offered him at the Restoration, till the Church should have been put on such a footing as would accord with his sense of Christian principle. On another occasion, if a story in Burnet is to be credited, he rejected the insidious offers of the government, to which some of his brethren were not equally **proof**[2]. He had never

---

[1] Calamy's Abridgment of Baxter's Life, vol. i. p. **335**.

[2] Burnet's story is as follows. Speaking of the Indulgence in 1672 (Hist. of his own Times, vol. i. p. 308, fol.) he says: "The Duke (of York) was now known to be a Papist; and the Duchess was much suspected. Yet the Presbyterians came in a body: **and Dr.** Manton in their name thanked the **king** for it, which offended many of **their best** friends. There was **also an** order to pay **a** yearly pension of fifty pounds **to most** of them, and **a hundred** pounds a year to the chief of the party. Baxter **sent back his** pension, and would not touch it. But most of them **took it**. All this I say upon Dr. Stillingfleet's word, who assured me he knew the truth of it. And in particular, he told me, that Pool, **who** wrote the Synopsis of the critics, confessed to him, that he had had fifty pounds for two years. Thus the Court hired them to be silent; and **the** greatest part of them were so, and very compliant." This statement comes, **it must be confessed, from** no friendly quarter; but it is distinct, and offered **ready means of** confutation; and the account of Baxter is quite characteristic. Moreover, the fact alleged must in all fairness be distinguished from the construction which Burnet puts upon it. There was nothing in **the principles of the Presbyterians of that age**, which forbade their accepting a maintenance from the State, if disengaged from conditions at war with their **conscientious scruples**. Every thing depends on the understanding with which the Court allowance was taken. They may have been too easy and compliant; but that they took it as a bribe to be silent on the subject of Popery, is only Burnet's interpretation. In the eyes of Burnet, any relaxation of zeal against Popery, would be regarded as a public crime of the deepest dye. Just at that juncture the clergy were maddened by the suspicion of a secret collusion between the Court, the Papists, and the **Dissenters**; all the episcopal pulpits, we are told, being **very** violent **against** Popery, and in favour of upholding the penal statutes. It is in the **highest degree** improbable, and would indicate an amount of profligacy which **neither Burnet** nor Stillingfleet intend to insinuate, that any men of eminence among the Dissenters should **have** acquiesced in any measures tending **to the furtherance of** Popery. With regard **to** Indulgences derived from the dispensing power **of** the Crown, many of them acted on the principle which has been thus expressed by **some** of their modern representatives: "they **wisely** availed **themselves of** their undoubted birthright, without inquiring by

courted the powers that be, and was as little in favour with Cromwell as with the Stuarts. For his **free notions of the use of** the Bible, distinguishing the saving truths of Christianity **from** the Scriptures which **contain** them, the dispensation **itself from its** written documents—he was accused by the Independents of Popery, and of asserting the sufficiency of tradition. Nor can it be denied, that his opinions on this subject differed much from the ordinary Puritanism, and betrayed an affinity both with the views of the Quakers, and with the latitudinarian spirit of some of his contemporaries in the Church. His earnest, practical mind revolted from the idle questions that were raised by extreme parties on all sides; by antinomian Nonconformists on one hand, and **by** high mystical Episcopalians on the other. Sometimes, **in the** silence of his study, yearning after reality and some positive evidence of usefulness, he longed to exchange preaching and controversy for the adventurous life of a missionary; that he might no more be wearied with words but grapple with facts, and go forth **into woods** and wildernesses to preach the gospel to the savage and the heathen[1]. Such was Baxter. The influence of his spirit and example on the next generation of Nonconformists, **can hardly** be too highly estimated.

what authority, or from what motive, it had been bestowed." Bogue and Bennett's History of Dissenters, vol. i. p. 211. Baxter, it is well known, took a different view of this complicated social question. I am not aware, whether any attempt has ever been made to deny the *facts* alleged by Burnet. Calamy speaks of the matter in very brief and general terms, never once alluding to pensions. He says, "the king's suspension of the penal laws was applauded by some of the Nonconformists, while others feared the consequences; that, however, they concluded on a cautious and moderate thanksgiving for the king's clemency and their own liberty, and were introduced by Lord Arlington. Baxter was at first averse to take advantage of this Indulgence, but seeing no hope of better terms, at length procured a license and opened a meeting-house." Abridgment etc. vol. i. p. 335. In a note Calamy observes, that Stillingfleet dated the Presbyterian Separation from this time. Neal (vol. ii. p. 685) mentions the charge of receiving pensions as **a report**, without any formal denial of the facts; and the strong, even vehement, **language** which he quotes from Owen in reply to Stillingfleet, does **not** meet **the** exact point of the case, but simply disclaims, more particularly for Owen himself, the remotest intention of granting indulgence or toleration to Papists.

[1] Life, Part I. § 212, where he **sums** up the results of **his** spiritual experience. Among other things of the same kind, he has the following remarkable words: "I am **not so** much inclined to pass a peremptory sentence of damnation upon **all** that never heard of Christ; having some more reason than I knew of before, to think that God's dealing with such is much unknown to *us*; and that the ungodly here among us Christians are in a far worse case than they."

Agreeing with Baxter in their general view of Church questions, and belonging to the same Puritanical party, but with characters less ardent and earnest, and of manners more gentle, complying and polished—were Bates and Howe. Not hesitating to take the oath required by the Oxford or Five Mile Act, they enjoyed an exemption from many annoyances which visited their more scrupulous brethren; and although they exercised the functions of Nonconformist preachers, lived on terms of friendship with many persons of distinction about Court and in the metropolis, and especially with several divines of the latitudinarian school. Both were men of elegant accomplishments, less exclusively pastors and theologians, than most of the Puritan ministers, and kept pace in their studies with the general progress of polite and philosophical learning. Bates possessed a large and finely-selected library which was purchased at his death by Dr. Daniel Williams, and which now forms a part of the well-known collection deposited in Redcross Street, London[1]. Howe had been educated both at Cambridge and at Oxford. In the former University he was intimate with the Platonic theologians, Cudworth and Henry More; and at the latter, became Fellow of Magdalen when that college was under the presidency of Dr. Thomas Goodwin, the Independent. Though disapproving of the strictness of the Independent discipline, Howe joined Goodwin's church at Oxford; and was afterwards chosen by the Protector under very flattering circumstances for one of his chaplains. In this difficult situation he acquitted himself with great prudence and moderation, showing kindness to men of all persuasions, and at the same time acting with singular integrity[2]. On Cromwell's death, he re-

---

[1] Wilson's Dissenting Churches, vol. ii. Pepys, with no Puritanical predilections, has expressed his admiration of Dr. Bates's preaching. He stood amidst a crowded audience in the gallery to hear his farewell discourse at St. Dunstan's on the Sunday preceding St. Bartholomew's-day, and was struck with the moderation of his spirit and the impressiveness of his devotions. Diary, Aug. 10 and 17, 1662.

[2] While Howe was Cromwell's chaplain, the notion of a *particular faith* in prayer was very prevalent at the Court of Whitehall. Being convinced of the injurious influence of that belief, Howe determined, the next time it came to his turn to preach before the Protector, to beat down the spiritual pride and confidence which such fancied impressions were apt to produce. "He told me," says Calamy, "he observed, that while he was in the pulpit, Cromwell heard him with great attention, but would sometimes knit his brows, and discover great uneasiness. When the sermon was over, a person of distinction came to him, and asked him, if he knew what he had done, and signified it to him

tained the same office under his son, so long as Richard continued in power.

Howe's intimacy with the episcopal clergy and with **persons of rank, engaged him in the various schemes that were** from time to time set on foot for a comprehension; but **his** gentle and courteous temper had no more effect in promoting it, than Baxter's zeal and impetuosity. When this subject was under debate in 1689, Howe published his 'Case of the Protestant Dissenters,' in which he derived a claim for freedom of worship from the universal law of nature; and showed that the Dissenters differed from the Church of England in no substantials of worship and doctrine, not objecting even to its government, if so managed as **to attain** its acknowledged end. It is significant of the principles then prevalent among the leading Presbyterians, that Howe in proof of his position, that the imposers of things indifferent are the true schismatics, appealed to the authority of the celebrated **Latitudinarian,** Hales of Eton. But this mild, conciliatory spirit was blended with firmness and consistency. Notwithstanding his dislike of needless schism, he maintained steadfastly the broad principles of Christian freedom; and when the Bill against Occasional Conformity was introduced, he was roused **by its** injustice to assert the claims of the Dissenters with more than his usual warmth and energy. His principal work, the Living Temple, indicates in its matter and in its style, the change that was taking place in the Nonconformist body. It combines that profound sense and earnest inculcation of personal religion, God living and reigning in the heart, which is so characteristic of Puritanism, with the literary culture and knowledge of recent philosophical systems, which belong to the scholar and the man of the world. Its second part is devoted to a special confutation of the pantheistic theory of Spinoza. Howe made a distinction between Scripture as the sole *mensura mensurans*, and confessions of **faith as** a *mensura mensurata*, useful as a visible bond of actual communion, and thought the latter should be recognised so

---

as his apprehension, that Cromwell would be so incensed upon that **discourse,** that he would find it very difficult ever **to** make his peace with him, or secure his favour for the future. Mr. Howe replied, that he had **but** discharged his conscience, and would leave the event with God. He told me, that he afterwards observed, Cromwell was cooler in **his** carriage to him than before." **Life** of Howe, prefixed to his Works, fol. p. **8.**

far only as they were in the main conformable to Scripture[1]. He and Bates, like Baxter, were zealous for free communion among all visible Christians, of whatsoever persuasion, in things non-essential; understanding by Christianity, whatever is essential to it whether doctrinal or practical, and by visibility, its approvable manifestation in the temper and life. No doubt, the idea of essentials was still left undetermined; but this statement of the case opened the way to a continual enlargement of mind, and marks a healthy direction of religious opinion.

An affecting incident occurred in Howe's last illness. Richard Cromwell now advanced in years, emerged from the rural seclusion in which he had long been forgotten by the world, to visit the friend and counsellor of his youth on his dying bed. The old men exchanged much serious discourse and mingled their tears. We may suppose, that they would revert to past scenes, and dwell on the altered relation in which they were now placed towards each other. The proud and hopeful days of the old Commonwealth came back to their remembrance; the mistakes and the failures attending its dissolution; the treachery of the Restoration; and all the insults and wrongs which had subsequently overwhelmed their broken and discomfited party. Since they stood together on the height from which they had fallen, revolution had twice changed the fortunes of their country; and yet after the lapse of half a century, the old strife continued and the just claims of conscience were still unsatisfied. In the presence of so many affecting remembrances, it was natural their minds should be subdued into religious tenderness, when they rose at that solemn interview from the evanescence and uncertainty of all worldly grandeur, to the unchanging tranquillity and glory of the state which both must shortly enter[2].

There were other distinguished men connected with the Presbyterian party during this period; but I have alluded to the most eminent; and this brief notice will suffice to show what influences were most active amongst them, and at what objects they chiefly aimed.

A man of a different stamp, more profoundly skilled in

[1] Carnality of Christian Contention; Preface: 1693. The form of distinction may have been suggested to him by the celebrated one of Spinoza, *Natura naturans*, and *Natura naturata*. Ethic. P. I. propos. xxix. schol.

[2] Calamy's Life of Howe, prefixed to his Works, p. 74. fol. 1724.

human learning, of an intellect more severely **consequential** and rigidly dogmatic, but less open, genial and **comprehensive**, was Dr. Owen, the celebrated leader of the Independents. The Congregational system had been supported by some **great** names before his time; but his numerous writings, high **reputation** and great personal influence **gave it** form and character, and impressed upon it the peculiar features of his mind, as Baxter transmitted his to Presbyterianism. Owen entered life with the undefined notions respecting Church government, which were common among the Puritans at the commencement of the war, and only gradually embraced the views of the Independents, **which** had the effect of fixing and deepening his early Calvinism. **Cromwell**, with the remarkable sagacity which distinguished **him and** which enabled him to find out the fittest men for all objects, soon discovered the great capacity of Owen and nominated him **one of his chaplains**. From Cromwell he received repeated marks of **favour** and confidence. Having accompanied the army into Ireland and Scotland, he was appointed on his return in 1651, Dean of Christ Church, and next year Vice-Chancellor of the University of Oxford. In this situation he displayed eminent **talents** for business, with great vigour and decision of character. He encouraged studies, and maintained discipline with a firm hand; and **the** fruits of **the** next generation showed, that there had been no decline of learning under his sway. In 1654 he was returned to Parliament as member for the University, but retained his seat only a short time. During the rising under Penruddock in the West, he took very active measures for the defence of the Commonwealth, and himself raised a troop of horse at Oxford. On his protesting against Cromwell's assumption of the title of king, a coolness grew up between them, which was never completely removed; and Richard Cromwell who succeeded his father as Chancellor, removed Owen from the Vice-Chancellorship.

After the Restoration Owen of course shared in the general disgrace and discouragement of the Puritan party; **but** having **a** considerable private estate, he lived in comparative ease and comfort, and enjoyed the protection and **countenance** of **many** persons of **rank** and influence. **Lord Clarendon was among** the number **of** his friends. **His church in** Berry Street was attended **by some** of the **old** Commonwealth officers, Fleetwood and **Colonel** Desborough. Dissatisfied with the state of things in the old country, he was at one time preparing to emigrate to New England, where he had been invited to undertake the presidency of Harvard College. An order from the Council prevented his departure. A similar invitation he had received from some academic bodies in Holland. He died in 1683, on the anniversary of his ejectment under the Act of Uniformity; and though it was still the reign of Charles the Second, such was the respect paid to his memory, that his funeral, we are told, was "attended by sixty-seven carriages belonging to noblemen and gentlemen of his acquaintance, beside many mourning coaches, and gentlemen on horseback[1]."

The character and principles of Owen present in several respects a marked contrast to those of Baxter. Each maintained his own decided view of the great questions of religious truth and liberty, which both had taken up with equal piety and earnestness; and when the grave had closed over Owen's remains, Baxter paid a hearty and generous tribute to the distinguished worth and rare endowments of one who had been so often opposed to him in life. Owen's congregational principles, though involving by necessary consequence a toleration of different forms of worship and church government, at least among Christians, tended rather to encourage narrow and rigid terms of communion within the limits of each particular church. "None," says he, "but those who give evidence of being regenerated or holy persons, ought to be received or counted fit members of visible churches; where this is wanting, the very essence of a church is lost[2]." Baxter, on the contrary, abhorring separation and aiming at nationality, would have taken in all quiet and visible Christians who did not break in on the established church order, from the Papist on one side, to the Socinian on the other. Spiritual purity, freedom from all heretical mixtures, was the essence of a true Church in the view of Owen; comprehensiveness was its outward sign and recommendation, in that of Baxter. Owen disapproved of worshipping in the national churches[3]; Baxter never withdrew from their communion, and only recurred occasionally to the use of separate assemblies, as a

---

[1] Orme's Life of Owen. Wilson's Dissenting Churches, vol. i. p. 278.

[2] Inquiry into the Origin, etc. of Evangelical Churches, 1681, quoted by Orme, p. 427.

[3] Orme, p. 360.

necessity that was forced upon him against his will. Baxter as he advanced in life, approached nearer and nearer to Arminianism; Owen retained his Calvinism to the last. Baxter shrank from a very decided assertion of the Trinity; Owen stood forth in his "Vindiciæ Evangelicæ" to confute the Unitarianism of Biddle[1]. Baxter was for amalgamating all parties; Owen was a chief promoter of the Savoy Confession which had the direct effect of marking off the Independents as a distinct body from the Presbyterians. Baxter interpreted the Bible with a breadth and freedom of view, and a continued reference to the priority and supremacy of the Spirit, which sometimes bordered on the theology of Fox and Barclay. Owen was rigidly Scriptural; he was startled and disquieted at the bold views put forth by Brian Walton in the prolegomena and the appendix to his Polyglott, respecting the sacred text, and vindicated its purity and integrity in a special treatise, "Of the divine original and authority of the Scriptures." Owen was deeply versed in the theology of his age and school, and had communed much with his own heart, and narrowly watched the manifestations of the religious life in close spiritual intercourse with various members of the Church. Baxter had warmer sympathies with general humanity, and read its indications with a more open and excursive eye. Baxter was distinguished by remarkable simplicity of character and directness of purpose; while Owen combined with great spiritual fervour and earnestness, a larger amount of shrewd caution, more knowledge of affairs, more worldly depth and penetration, than usually falls to the share of a student and divine.

On questions of civil government, the views of these eminent men leaned to opposite sides. Baxter was a royalist, and with the intrepid honesty which formed a part of his nature, used his personal influence to prevent people from taking, first the Covenant, and afterwards the Engagement[2]. Owen betrayed on more than one occasion, notwithstanding the studied prudence and reserve of his language, no unequivocal signs of sympathy with the cause of republicanism. The

[1] He was directed by the Council of State to reply to Biddle's Twofold Catechism, 1654.
[2] Calamy's Abridgment, vol. i. p. 104. The second Edmund Calamy, father of the historian, though a Presbyterian, had also never taken the Covenant. Calamy's Life and Times, vol. i.

day after Charles's execution, he preached before Parliament, without any distinct allusion to the event, on "righteous zeal, encouraged by divine protection." In delivering the funeral discourse for Ireton in Westminster Abbey, he pronounced a high eulogium on the republican hero. The same inference may perhaps be drawn from his warlike preparations in defence of the Commonwealth, when he was Vice-Chancellor of Oxford; from his marked disapproval of Cromwell's inclination to assume royal power; and from his active participation in the counsels of the republican officers at Wallingford House, which issued in the deposition of Richard Cromwell[1]. We trace the different principles of the two men, in the divergent tendencies of the Presbyterian and Independent sections of the old Puritan body, of which they were respectively the heads. The Presbyterians were always hoping for comprehension; the Independents were satisfied with a tolerated separation. The former always associated the cause of civil, with that of religious, liberty; the latter were led by their principles to keep the ideas of Church and State more distinct, and sometimes in an aspiration after extreme spirituality, to overlook their reciprocal action and dependence. Among the Presbyterians, the constant movement of opinion was towards Arminianism and its related doctrines; among the Independents we witness an effort in the contrary direction to uphold the primitive Calvinism. We may look on Owen as the founder of rigid, and Baxter of moderate, Dissent.

SECTION IX.

ANABAPTISTS AND QUAKERS: RISE OF PERMANENT NONCONFORMIST SOCIETIES.

The Presbyterians and Independents constituted three-fourths of the Puritan body at the time of the Restoration. In the interval between that event and the Revolution, two other sects, the Baptists and the Quakers, though inferior in numbers and influence, acquired form and consistency, and

---

[1] Baxter was charged with having misrepresented Owen in this matter. But he appears to have spoken on good authority, which was not clearly set aside by Owen's friends. See Calamy's Continuation, vol. ii. pp. 917-22.

present themselves with distinct and prominent features to our view. Under one or other of these four divisions nearly all the elements of Puritanic excitement which had been in high action under the Commonwealth and which are enumerated in the lugubrious pages of Edwards's Gangræna, appear in the course of this period to have gradually settled and adjusted themselves. Other tendencies of opinion which belonged to individuals and were never embodied in a sect, will remain for notice hereafter, as their fruits become more conspicuous towards the close of the century.

The principles of the Baptists come into view at a very early period in the religious history of England. Mixed with some Quaker peculiarities we trace them first among the Lollards, and afterwards among the Brownists and original Independents. Out of the Churches of this latter body the Baptists first emerged as a distinct sect. With the usage that distinguished them from other Christians, they associated various shades of theological opinion, not excluding the reputed heresies of Arius and Socinus[1]. From the first we find among them that division respecting the controverted doctrines of Calvin and Arminius, which has subsisted to the present time, in the distinction between Particular and General Baptists. Finding themselves greatly misrepresented, and charged with holding the wild destructive doctrines of the German Anabaptists, they put forth many confessions of faith and declarations of opinion, in the first half of the seventeenth century; some Arminian, some Calvinistic, but generally expressed in mild, earnest, Scriptural language, and breathing a strong spirit of religious liberty. During the war, they multiplied exceedingly in the army. Many officers in Cromwell's regiment, and in Monk's when he commanded in Scotland, were Baptists. Lord Brook treated the sect with kindness; and Jeremy Taylor pleaded for them in his Liberty of Prophesying. John Fiennes, son of Lord Say, adopted their views as scriptural. Colonel Hutchinson and his accomplished wife, having been induced by the doctrines of some Separatist preachers, to give the subject a close and conscientious examination, came

---

[1] See Crosby's account of the burning of Edward Wightman. Hist. of English Baptists, vol. i. Appendix, No. I. Neal, I. p. 41. Wallace's Antitrinitarian Biography, I. pp. 5-31. He remarks, (p. 43) "Anabaptists and Arianizers were in those days regarded as nearly synonymous terms."

to the same conclusion[1]. The Baptists carried to an extreme the principle of separation between Church and State, and took little part in matters simply political. Upon the whole, they appear to have been royalists. They thought Cromwell had deceived them, and betrayed the cause of public liberty; and it is deserving of notice, that in the remonstrance of a Commonwealth officer with Cromwell on behalf of the Baptists in the army, he specially protests against the Protector's imprisonment of Biddle[2]. The Baptists were among the most determined and consistent advocates of liberty of conscience during this period. Shut out by their peculiar tenets from all chance of comprehension with other religious bodies in a National Church, they had no other resource for the security of their own peaceful existence, than to plead for universal toleration. To this tendency thus forced on them from without, the democratic constitution of their churches, their attaching no essential importance to a regular and separate ministry, and the division of opinion among themselves on some controverted points of theology, only gave additional effect. Burnet's testimony is highly honourable to them: "the Anabaptists," says he, "were generally men of virtue, and of an universal charity[3].

Although in their notion of a ministry they held a sort of middle view between the old regular Nonconformists and the Quakers, not objecting to duly educated and salaried pastors where it was possible to maintain them, without deeming them indispensable to the existence of a true Church; and although on this account, many unlearned persons who followed secular callings, preached in their assemblies; yet their cause did not want expounders and advocates of a different order, in men who had been educated at the Universities, and

---

[1] Memoirs of Col. Hutchinson, II. p. 103–5.

[2] Crosby, vol. iii. p. 231. This remonstrance is the production of a querulous and discontented mind; but some of its queries indicate just sentiments of religious liberty. Art. 22. "Whether you may not as justly suffer all to be put in prison that differ from the Church of England, as suffer Mr. Biddle to be imprisoned?" Art. 24. "Whether your Highness will not appear to be a dreadful apostate and fearful dissembler, if you suffer persecution to fall upon the Anabaptists or the Independents, or them of Mr. Biddle's judgment, seeing you promised equal liberty to all?" Some of the earliest Baptist Confessions of Faith—for instance, that which was published by the followers of Mr. Smith in Holland in 1611, and animadverted upon by Mr. Robinson of Leyden—were decidedly Anti-Calvinistic. Crosby, vol. i. Appendix, No. IV.

[3] History of his own Times, I. p. 702.

who brought to its defence the aids of scholarship. One of the most eminent of these, was John Tombes, B.D., educated at Magdalen Hall, Oxford, a contemporary and opponent of Baxter who has described the controversy between them[1]. But for the single point of baptism, Tombes would have conformed to the National Establishment, to the discipline and liturgy of which he was strongly attached. With him may be mentioned Hanserd Knollys, Henry Jessy, William Dell, and others, who were University men, and had once held situations in the Church of England[2].

The most interesting and characteristic member of the Baptist persuasion at this time, was William Kiffin, a man of humble origin and self-educated, who by native force of intellect and will, impregnated with deep religious feeling, raised himself from a condition of the greatest external depression, to wealth and influence and civic honour in the metropolis. With the energy and earnestness of mind which distinguish the English commonalty and which were so strongly brought out in the contests of the 17th century, he united through a long life under circumstances of no ordinary difficulty, to the successful pursuit of commerce, a diligent cultivation of religious knowledge and the functions of a stated preacher. He was the first pastor of a Baptist congregation which still assembles in London. Though he could not escape the general persecution of the Nonconformists, he rendered on several occasions great service to his denomination, through the influence he possessed with Lord Clarendon, and the two last Stuarts. For the High Church party were disposed to treat some extreme classes of Dissenters with more consideration and tenderness than the Presbyterians, whose numbers rendered them more formidable and threw greater weight into the political scale[3]. To the Baptists of this period belongs the honour of having cherished in their communion, the deep spiritual discernment, the vigorous conception, and powerful imagination of Bunyan.

In 1677, the Calvinistic Baptists published a Confession of Faith, in which they profess to follow the doctrinal statements

---

[1] Life, Part I. § 138.   [2] Crosby, vol. i. and vol. ii. p. 2 et seq.
[3] An interesting biographical notice of Kiffin will be found in Wilson's Dissenting Churches, vol. i. His grand-daughter married the grandson of Cromwell; and from his alliance have sprung the present or recent representatives of the Protector's family.

of the Westminster and Savoy Confessions; but in the appendix they discuss at large the question of infant and adult baptism[1]. The General and Particular Baptists stimulated each other to a declaration of their respective tenets and practices. If one section of the body put forth a confession, the other soon after did the same. We have noticed an affinity between some usages of the early Baptists and the Quakers. These however led to no union and sympathy, as the two sects assumed a more complete development. On the contrary, the remaining points of difference were only the more strongly insisted on; and the year 1674 was marked by vehement and acrimonious disputes, in which the Baptists attacked the opinions of William Penn, and the Quakers sharply retorted, that they had been misrepresented[2].

Of all the forms of Puritanism, that exhibited by the Quakers had arisen under circumstances least calculated to command the respect of ordinary theologians: and, in truth, its first outbreak was accompanied by such wild and extravagant fanaticism, that it is not surprising, those who were accustomed to see Christianity only through the medium of settled ordinances and an elaborate system of metaphysical doctrine, should have looked upon this new sect with mingled contempt and abhorrence. But in its apparent renunciation of all law and reason, it went back to the primitive fountains of religious conviction, and drew from them elements of the deepest spiritual truth, fitted to attract minds of a pure and elevated order. Its extreme simplicity really adapted it to very high mental refinement. Some men of this stamp embraced its tenets in the latter half of the 17th century. The sanguine and benevolent Penn, trained in University learning, with the most alluring prospects of worldly advancement before him, preferred poverty and expulsion from his father's house, to renouncing that life of Christian simplicity, which his conscience told him was the life of heaven and God. In the learned and accomplished Barclay, Quakerism found an advocate whose calm and luminous exposition of its doctrines is in beautiful contrast with the scholastic subtlety and dogmatism which too generally mark confessions of faith.

[1] An earlier Confession had been put forth by divers congregations in London and the country, and signed by their leading members, 1646. Neal, II. p. 111.
[2] Crosby, II., pp. 297–312.

Barclay had compassed a wide circuit of religious belief and sounded various depths of spiritual experience. Nurtured in Calvinism, he conceived a fondness for the Romish doctrines during his education at the Scots' College in Paris; but on his return to his native country of Scotland, he settled down in the principles of the Friends. The style and execution of the "Apology" are, in one sense, at variance with its conclusions. In language exquisitely pure and graceful, the refined utterance of a polished and highly cultivated mind, he condemns the vanities of human rhetoric, and pleads for a simple reliance on the impulse of the Spirit; he employs the treasures of learning to demonstrate its worthlessness; and confutes the scholastic divinity in the syllogistic method.

The outline of his work was first drawn up in Latin, under the title of *Theses Theologicæ*, in fifteen propositions. These were afterwards enlarged with explanations and arguments, and rendered into English. Its theology stands in a sort of middle point between Calvinism, Arminianism, and Socinianism. It acknowledges the fall of all men in Adam, and the necessity of divine grace for their restoration; but sees in Christ the means of universal redemption, the saving spiritual light, "which lighteth every man that cometh into the world," and is at some period or other of their lives, offered to all men, Jews, Heathens, and Christians. It is not, therefore, the outward knowledge of Christ, but the inward reception and formation of him in the heart, which is essential to salvation. This inward light may be resisted or not: where it is not resisted, the subjects of it, being born again and bringing forth the fruits of holiness, righteousness, and purity, are justified, yet not by their own will and their own works, but by the grace of God in Christ. They in whom this spiritual birth has taken place, may attain perfection, in regard to freedom from actual sin, yet not so as to exclude further growth, or the possibility of future sin. Where the grace of God hath only wrought in part, there is a possibility of falling from it; but there may also be such a growth and stability in the truth, as to prevent a total apostacy.

Connected with these fundamental ideas, were others that lay more on the surface of the system, and outwardly distinguished the Friends from the rest of Christendom. They ascribed all true knowledge of God to the testimony of the Spirit alone, Christ formed in the soul; and regarded the

Scriptures as partly historical, partly prophetic, partly an utterance of principles; not, however, the fountain itself of truth, but a declaration of that fountain, a secondary rule subordinate to the Spirit, known only to be Scripture by the inward testimony of the Spirit. For this reason, all true and acceptable worship can only be offered in the inward and immediate moving and drawing of God's own Spirit; no man can be a minister without the grace of God, that inward gift and light which is the only true and indispensable ordination; and the ministry must not be reduced to a trade. Baptism and the Lord's Supper which other Christians observe as outward ordinances, can only be taken inwardly and spiritually.

In insisting on the use of a particular habit and a certain mode of address, and in abstaining from the customary salutations and innocent amusements of the world, the Friends mistook the form for the essence of their system, and rather violated, than consistently unfolded, the simplicity that was inherent in it. Barclay in common with many sectaries of the time, entertained a belief, that the second advent of Christ (by him understood spiritually) was at hand; and he lays great and frequent stress on the fact, that this solemn event was announced, and the true power of the Gospel in preparation for it, brought out, not by the wise and learned, but among poor and illiterate, honest and simple-minded, men.

The Quakers at the commencement of their career, were constantly charged with Popish tendencies. Barclay often alludes to the imputation, and Penn was accused of being a Jesuit in disguise. The idea was mainly the result, no doubt, of that insane suspicion of Popery in every novel appearance, which marked the reigns of Charles and James the Second. But in tracing the circle of opinion, extreme tendencies gradually approximate. The Quaker doctrines of perfection and of the justifying operation of the Spirit, bear more resemblance to Catholic, than to Protestant, theology[1]. Actually the Friends may have stood at the widest distance from Catholicism. Yet it may be questioned, whether their principle of renouncing all external guidance, and of throwing each man on the suggestions of his own spirit, might not issue, if

---

[1] *Justificatio hyperphysica.* In their adhesion to this view the Mennonites of Holland afford another instance of affinity between the Quakers and the early Baptists. Neudecker's Dogmengeschichte, § 41, 42.

it were tried on a large scale, in raising up at last, from the sheer necessity of the case, some great sacerdotal authority, to guide the aimless and fluctuating mass of minds. Such a sense of intellectual helplessness as would probably result, is the very condition which the Catholic priesthood would most desire, for the promotion of its own views. The great desideratum in all religious communities is to secure the means of efficient and progressive culture, without the risk of priestly domination. Perhaps in guarding against the latter mischief, the Friends have not duly provided for the former object, which is its only effectual counteraction[1].

This development and fixation of principles in the four sections of the Puritan body during the latter half of the seventeenth century, took place under outward circumstances of the most vexatious and oppressive description. Continually mocked with hollow promises of relief, now favoured by a temporary indulgence, and then visited anew with redoubled persecution, their whole life hung in suspense on the capricious humour, and on the result of the conflicting purposes, of the Court and the Parliament. Among themselves too the Nonconformists were not agreed in their aims. Some desired comprehension, some, indulgence; some, like Baxter, would have united both. There was but one point in which they all concurred, and that was, a desire to exclude the Papists; although relief to the Papists was the condition on which toleration was offered them by the Court. Hence the complexity and involution of interests which belong to this period. There was a general absence of the working of broad principles. There was bad faith on the part of those in power; and in those who were oppressed, there was a want of unity and consistency of aim. Persecution and indulgence, indulgence and persecution, in ceaseless alternation, make up the

---

[1] Besides Barclay's Apology, which contains the Quaker theology, scientifically expounded, see George Fox's most interesting Journal, which reveals the origin of the sect and throws a very instructive light on the contemporaneous state of manners and religious feeling (edited by Wilson Armistead, 2 vols., with notes. London: Cash etc., 1852); Penn's Brief Account of the Rise and Progress of the People called Quakers, originally prefixed as a preface to Fox's Journal, 4th edition. London: 1708; Penn's Primitive Christianity, revised, etc., 2nd edition. London: 1699; Sewel's History of the Quakers, fol. London: 1722 (originally written in Dutch, and translated by the author); Pennington's Letters, 3rd edition, by John Barclay. York: 1844. For a later phasis of Quakerism, see the Journal etc., of John Woolman, of New Jersey, N.A. Warrington: 1840.

entire history of the time¹. Yet a sense of religious duty withheld the Puritan ministers from laying aside their pastoral functions. The strength of a solemn vow still bound them to

[1] The following is a brief account of the laws affecting **Protestant** Dissenters, with the several Indulgences, during the reigns of Charles and James the Second. After the King's return, a Declaration drawn up by Clarendon, was issued in October 1660, in which among other things, it was conceded for the sake of pacification; "that the Ministers should be freed from the subscription required by the canon, and the oath of canonical obedience, receive ordination, institution, and induction, and exercise their function, and enjoy the profits of their livings, without being obliged to it: and that the use of the ceremonies should be dispensed with, where they were scrupled." Calamy's Abridgment, vol. i. p. 152. This Declaration had no other effect than to postpone for a year the law that was afterwards passed, and to prepare the way for the conference between the Episcopalians and the Presbyterians at the Savoy. The Act of Uniformity took effect on the 24th of August, 1662; and as the tithes fell due on that day, the actual incumbents were cast forth wholly unprovided, and their successors came in for the fruits of the livings. In December the same year, the King issued an Indulgence not excluding Papists, many of whom, he said, had deserved well of him. On this account, it did not take with the Protestant Dissenters; and Parliament remonstrated against it. In 1663, a Comprehension was talked of; and the question was much debated among the Dissenters, whether a Comprehension or an Indulgence would be the more desirable course. The latter must include the Papists; and it was the opinion of some, that the number of ejected Ministers had been purposely made so great, that they might be compelled to ask for Indulgence on these terms, and so incur the odium of favouring the Papists. Baxter was not for Comprehension, without Indulgence for those who could not be embraced in it; nor for Indulgence without an enlargement of the Act of Uniformity, in other words, a wider Comprehension. But instead of either of these measures, in June 1663, the Conventicle Act was passed; which prohibited attendance on any worship but that of the Church of England, under severe penalties; conviction for the third time being visited with transportation. Nevertheless the ejected Ministers continued to exercise their ministry privately, till the breaking out of the plague in 1665, when they preached in the forsaken churches of the metropolis. During the plague, the Oxford Act was passed, which banished five miles from any corporate town, all Ministers who refused to take a certain oath, framed against the known principles of most Nonconformists. After the fire of London, the Dissenters acquired more liberty, and held public meetings. In 1667, Clarendon fell into disgrace; and was succeeded by the duke of Buckingham who professed himself a friend to liberty of conscience. The Dissenters were connived at, and went openly to their meetings. Renewed proposals were then made to them by the Lord Keeper Bridgman, about Comprehension, but without any effect. In 1670, the Act against Conventicles was renewed; and many eminent Ministers were thrown into prison. The persecution continued through 1671. Nevertheless the King made them fair promises, and they were connived at. At the breaking out of the Dutch war in 1672, there was a new Indulgence, including the Papists; for which the Dissenters cautiously expressed their thanks. A certain number of places were allowed to be licensed for the public worship of the Dissenters; while the Papists were to have the privilege of celebrating Mass in their private houses, without any limitation of places and persons. Alderman Love, a Dissenter, was very zealous against it in the Commons; and Parliament voted it illegal. In 1673, various measures for the relief of Dissenters, and accommodation with the Church, were defeated. In 1674, the King's licenses were recalled at the

their flocks. So long as the penal laws were **in force**, they preached to their people in private, and visited them by stealth; while their retreats were hunted out by informers of the most infamous character[1], and their places of **meeting** broken in upon by a licentious soldiery. Learned and **holy** men, dragged to the bar of justice for simply preaching **the** Gospel, were insulted by magistrates, browbeaten by judges, and laid up in fetid and unwholesome gaols, at that time nurseries of pestilence, and destitute of every Christian comfort and decency, among highwaymen and murderers. When the laws were suspended, by a declaration of indulgence, the ministers came forth **more** openly, and gathered round them large audiences of all **ranks**.

suggestion of the bishops, and the persecution was renewed; Baxter and Dr. Manton were among the objects of it. In the course of the year, another effort was made towards accommodation; Tillotson and Stillingfleet acting on one side, Manton, Bates, Pool, and Baxter on the other; but the whole plan was overthrown by the bishops. For an instance of Tillotson's extreme timidity on these occasions, see a letter of his to Baxter, quoted by Calamy, **Abridgm. I.** p. **343.** During the years 1675 and 1676, informers were very active, and the penal laws in full force, against the Nonconformists. In 1678, the nation was distracted by what was called the Popish Plot; and in 1679, the bill for excluding the Duke of York from the succession, having passed the Commons, **was thrown** out in the Lords by a majority of thirty, of which fourteen were bishops. In 1680, bills were introduced into the Commons for Comprehension and **Indulgence.** As it was found these would not pass, another measure was **brought in for** relieving Protestant Dissenters from the penalties imposed on **Papists,** which was carried in **both** Houses; but when the King came down to pass the bills, this was taken from the table and never heard of again. During the **remaining** years of **this** King's reign, from 1681 to 1684, there was an unremitted continuance **of the** severities against Dissenters; in consequence of which many Ministers **died in** prison. The same policy was pursued at the commencement of James the Second's **reign.** In 1685, Baxter was tried before Jeffries for the publication of his Paraphrase on the New Testament, and browbeaten from the bench **with** the greatest insolence. In 1686, the King's dispensing power was affirmed on high grounds by eleven out of the twelve judges. A Dispensation or License Office was set up, where Licenses effectual to stop processes for Nonconformity, might be purchased for fifty shillings. By one of these Licenses through the mediation of Lord Powis, Baxter was released from his fine and discharged from the King's Bench prison. In 1688, James published a Declaration of general Liberty of Conscience for all persuasions, of which some of the Dissenters quietly and cautiously availed themselves, without falling into the measures of the Court. The renewal of this Declaration in 1688, called forth the resistance of the clergy; occasioned the imprisonment of the **seven** bishops; and prepared the way for the Revolution. See Calamy's Abridgment of Baxter's Life and Times, vol. i.

[1] In the Conformists' Four Pleas for the Nonconformists, published between the years 1681 and 1683, we have from an impartial source, an account of the sufferings and annoyances of the Nonconformist Ministers, and of the conduct **and** frequent fate of **the** Informers.

During the ravages of the plague, and after the desolations of the fire of London, the Nonconformists pursued their sacred vocation with a quickened ardour and exemplary humanity; preaching in the forsaken churches, or setting up temporary tabernacles of wood to receive their hearers. And yet it was in the midst of these self-sacrificing exertions, while the plague was still raging, that the Oxford Act was issued, to interrupt their ministrations. When Clarendon was dismissed, and his place taken by the Duke of Buckingham who professed much zeal for liberty of conscience, it was hoped, that the situation of the Nonconformists would be improved; but with the exception of the Indulgence that was granted at the beginning of the Dutch war in 1672, the severities enacted against them went on increasing till the end of Charles the Second's reign.

James's determination to bring back Popery, through the concession of a general toleration to all persuasions, placed the Dissenters in an embarrassing position, in which their principles and their desire of relief drew different ways. I have already described the course which the wiser among them took[1]. They availed themselves of the *fact* of indulgence, without addressing or complimenting the king on its *principle*. Only a few of the more extreme Dissenters lost sight of general considerations, in a one-sided eagerness to secure, as they thought, the freedom of their own worship. Among these the Rev. Mr. Lobb signalized himself, who has acquired the name of the Jacobite Independent[2].

As they felt the increasing improbability of any speedy accommodation with the Church, the Nonconformists adopted by degrees a more independent mode of action, and assumed

---

[1] Ch. I. p. 26.
[2] See an account of Lobb, in Wilson's Dissenting Churches, vol. iii. pp. 436–446. There was a similar approximation of opposite extremes in other instances. Among the cannoneers of Col. Hutchinson at Nottingham Castle during the wars, was Laurence Colin, a sectary, who was protected from the persecution of the dominant Presbyterians by Cromwell. His family afterwards rose to wealth and consideration in the town of Nottingham, and were for some time zealous Nonconformists; but accepting the Indulgences granted by James the Second, they opposed the Revolution, and after that event, became the head of the country or Jacobite party in the town. Life of Col. Hutchinson, vol. i. pp. 202 and 340. An American royalist of the name of Curwen, who came over to England at the breaking out of the revolutionary war, and whose diary was published a few years ago, to his astonishment found a Quaker at whose house he lodged in Manchester, a staunch Jacobite.

the tendencies and habitudes of a permanent, **separate,** body in the State. They maintained a friendly intercourse with the Protestant Churches of the Continent, and sent their young men to be educated in the Universities of Holland. A few Meeting-houses were erected during this period, but mostly as places of temporary occupation[1].

Through all ages we trace a constant, intimate, sympathy between new developments of the religious principle, and the spirit of commerce. Our own history supplies evidence of this general fact. The strength of Puritanism, although it was not without large support from the ancient yeomanry of the country, lay chiefly in the manufacturing and commercial classes of the great towns. The merchants of London were zealously devoted to the cause of Nonconformity. During one of the Indulgences they set up a weekly lecture at Pinners' Hall, in which they invited the most eminent Ministers to take a part. We have another proof of this relationship in the employment of the Halls of different Companies, as meeting-places for the first congregations that were gathered in the metropolis. The earliest assemblage of Puritans that was dispersed by the civil power in the reign of Elizabeth, had met in Plumbers' Hall. Salters' Hall, and the Weigh House which was anciently connected with the Grocers' Company, were Meeting-houses of notoriety in London. Wilson in his History of Dissenting Churches, has mentioned more than twenty of these Halls which were at one time so employed; and of these, some permanently retained the use to which at first they were only intended to be temporarily applied. In Catholic times these Halls had also possessed a religious character, and were often associated with conventual establishments. They would thus, in the course of social revolution, have seemed to revert in the hands of the Puritans, to one of the objects for which they were originally designed. They were fitted up with pews, and galleries, and pulpits, by the zeal of the citizens, who thus signalized their devotion to what they deemed the cause of religious truth and freedom. Their form, dimensions, and general appearance, capacious, massive and plain, and venerable for a sort of gloomy simplicity, have probably furnished the type of the old Dissenting

---

[1] Baxter's wife, who was a lady of property, erected a Meeting-house for him in Oxendon Street, London, near the Haymarket; where however he preached but once. Calamy's Continuation, p. 902. Wilson's Dissenting Churches.

Meeting-house; as the raised tribunal and lateral arcades of the Roman Basilica suggested the choir, nave and side-aisles of the ancient Christian church.

The disputes of the seventeenth century were neutralized, though not settled, in the grand compromise of the Revolution. With that event the age of proper Puritanism expired. Before we proceed to trace the subsequent progress of opinion, it may be advantageous to devote a short chapter to a review of the period now traversed; and to place in a few salient points before the mind, the contrasted features of the two great religious parties, the Church and the Puritans, which we have seen in constant antagonism through the course of it[1].

[1] This seems the fittest place to notice the gradual expansion of the principle of Toleration, of which the rudiments were first recognized after the Revolution. The following Acts of Parliament exhibit the history of Religious Liberty for the last century and a half. The Toleration Act passed in 1689. It was a result of the Revolution. It required those who availed themselves of it, to subscribe the doctrinal articles of the Church of England; it excluded Roman Catholics and those who impugned the Trinity, from its benefits; and it left the Test and Corporation Acts, passed in Charles the Second's reign, which made participation in the Lord's Supper, according to the rites of the Church of England, a legal qualification for civil office—in full force against Nonconformists. Its provisions, scanty as they were, were limited by the Acts against Occasional Conformity and Schism, which were passed in the reign of Anne; the former forbidding habitual Dissenters to attend worship and take the Sacrament occasionally in the Established Church; the latter, making it illegal for any Dissenting Teacher to undertake the education of youth. On the accession of the House of Hanover, these last two Acts were repealed. More than fifty years then elapsed, before any further alteration was proposed in the laws affecting liberty of conscience; though all direct persecution had ceased, and public opinion had become increasingly liberal in the interval. In 1779, profession of a belief in the Scriptures, with a declaration of being a Christian and a Protestant, was substituted for subscription to the doctrinal articles of the Church, as a condition of enjoying the toleration conceded by law. This amendment of the Toleration Act was further enforced in 1812, by some provisions for the due registration of places of worship; but the parties before excluded, were not yet admitted to its benefits, and the clause affecting the Unitarians was still preserved. In the following year, Mr. William Smith, M.P. for Norwich, procured the repeal of this last clause, by which, it was believed, Unitarians would be put on the same footing with other classes of Dissenters. In 1828, the Sacramental Test was repealed; and in 1829 the Catholics were relieved from their disabilities. The Unitarians however remained liable to a danger which was not anticipated, when the Act for admitting them to a full toleration passed. Inheriting in regular transmission from generation to generation, a considerable amount of property which had been left by their Presbyterian ancestors for religious purposes, it was argued, that their claim to it was vacated, because at the time of such endowments and foundations being created, Unitarianism was not yet admitted to a toleration. They were in consequence exposed to attacks, which rendered the tenure of their Chapels and Burial-grounds

CHAPTER IV.

THE CHURCH AND PURITANISM CONTRASTED.

THE primary source of divergency between the Anglican and the Puritan systems, must be sought in their different conception of the standard of final authority in religion. The genuine Puritan acknowledged Scripture only; the Church combined with Scripture, the traditional exposition of its principles preserved in the concurring judgments of Christian antiquity. It was the avowed aim of the Puritans to reduce the Church to the model of primitive usage recorded in the New Testament, without any regard to the changes introduced by time or circumstance. They received the strict letter of Scripture as a final, absolute rule ever applicable; framed for present and constant use; standing in close, immediate contact with the exigencies of man's outward life through the revolutions of centuries. On the other hand, the Anglicans regarded Scripture as indeed the original depository of Christian truth, in which its germs, as it were, and first principles were shut up, but acknowledged ecclesiastical tradition as its legitimate expositor. Scripture and Tradition were viewed by them, as equally under the superintending direction of Providence; alike forming a part of the great dispensation of Christianity; joint witnesses and authorities of Christian doctrine and practice. Of these views, the idea of the Church, as understood by the Anglican party, was a natural result.

It has been shown in the foregoing pages, that the first race of English Reformers made a distinction between doctrine and

insecure. As the trust-deeds of their forefathers rarely specified doctrines, but were usually conceived in such general terms, as left room for a progressive modification of opinion, an Act was introduced by the Government, and passed in 1844, which secured to Unitarians the possession of property for religious purposes, inherited from their ancestors, on the following principle : that, where the trust-deed does not expressly provide to the contrary, the usage of twenty-five years shall be taken as conclusive evidence of the religious doctrine or mode of worship that may be properly taught and observed in any Meeting-house. See Taylor's Book of Rights ; 7 and 8 Vict. ch. 45. Parliamentary Debates on the Dissenters' Chapels Bill. London: 1844.

discipline; deducing the former from Scripture alone; but admitting with regard to the latter, in accordance with the Erastianism then prevalent, that considerations of time and place might justly invest the civil power with some control over the form and administration of the Church. The Puritans argued, that Scripture was the only standard for discipline as well as for doctrine. In the prolonged struggle with them, the Anglican divines gradually abandoned their Erastian principles, and bestowed increased importance on Tradition, as the vehicle of a divine right. They could not assert—for Scripture was at hand to confute them—that the idea of the Church in its full hierarchal development, as constituted under Elizabeth, could be found in the original teachings of Christ and his apostles: but it might perhaps be argued, with some show of probability, that its elements were there; and that these had been wrought out by Providence into the form and organization which had subsisted with no material change from the second and third centuries. The spirit of Christ, it was affirmed, had always been present in his Church. This was the fulfilment of his words; " Lo, I am with you alway, unto the end of the world." The commission entrusted by him to his apostles, had by them been conveyed in an unbroken succession to the bishops through all ensuing ages. In this way, an apostolical authority was claimed for the Church and its episcopal government, in opposition to the divine right urged direct from Scripture on behalf of their own system, by the Puritans: and so Tradition, under the provocations of controversy, again grew up, even among those who had separated from Rome, into the rank of a recognized interpreter of Scripture truth.

This idea of the Church became a very prominent feature in the development of the Anglican or anti-puritan system, during the seventeenth century. The Church from this point of view was an external institution, which had been corrupted by Popery; designed to embrace the whole of Christendom; moulded by the hand of God himself into a permanent shape for the preservation and transmission of Christian truth to the end of time. It was a vast apparatus of means; a visible instrumentality, connecting heaven and earth, and bringing the elements of truth and the influences of divine grace to every soul included within its pale. Of a Church so conceived, it is the essence to be *external;* it applies an outward agency;

it demands submission to **an outward** jurisdiction. Let us clearly apprehend this idea. It suggests the grand distinction of the Anglican Church from Puritanism.

Externality of character is involved, **to some extent,** in the very notion of Catholicity. Catholicity, **as** understood by the Church of England, demands the surrender of individual self-willedness to the expressed consent of ages. Vincentius's cele**brated** definition of Catholic truth, *quod semper, quod ab omnibus, quod ubique,* implies that we are to take it from without, instead of looking for it within. It admits of no appeal to personal experience or intellectual idiosyncrasy, but requires men to acquiesce in the general judgment of antiquity traditionally conveyed.

The doctrine **of** Apostolical **Succession is another** application of the same fundamental conception of **the Church.** The title of ministers to preach the Word and **administer the Sa**craments, is not conferred by their individual **learning, piety** and worth, or acquired through the choice and appointment of those who are already professors of Christianity, but possessed in **virtue** of an external character, transmitted through a long descent from the first depositories of truth. Through such divinely commissioned **men** the spiritual **power of** Christ is perpetuated in his Church. It is they, **and** the faithful, **living** through their ministrations in **communion** with the Church, who constitute **the** mystical **body of Christ; and the Sacra**ments **of** Baptism and the **Eucharist are** the external means through which **the members** of the Church are incorporated with it, and preserved **in** it. According to these views **the** Sacraments are not symbols merely, signs and tokens of **di**vine grace, but its real channels and instruments. By Baptism infants are actually regenerated; brought within the range of God's covenanted mercy; saved from the consequences of Adam's sin; and translated from a state of wrath **to a** state of acceptance and grace. Through this **rite** they are engrafted **into the** body of Christ, and imbued with a principle of divine **life** which they may afterwards by their own efforts unfold and **increase.** But in the first instance, the recipient **is wholly** passive; grace is imparted externally, without any co-operation of faith or **will** or works; the act is God's alone, through **the** hands **of** his accredited **minister.** In like manner, **with** respect to the Eucharist, it must be received indeed in faith, but its efficacy is not wholly due to faith. It really communicates, in some mysterious mode, the body and blood of Christ to the recipient, and thereby actually unites him with Christ. Writers of the high Anglican school look upon it as a commemorative sacrifice, " making that effectual," says Overall, " and in act applied to us, which was once obtained by the sacrifice of Christ upon the cross, and having reference to the daily and perpetual offering of it by Christ now in Heaven in his everlasting priesthood."

Not all indeed who adhered to the Church of England, entertained these views. There was a large body of doctrinal Puritans who never dissolved their communion with it; and these, if they could have had their own way, would have greatly modified its ritual and discipline. Nevertheless, these high doctrines acquired increasing influence and ascendency during the struggle with Puritanism; were drawn out of their latent quiescence in the rubric and liturgy, by strong re-action against it; and expressed most distinctly the tendencies that were opposed to it. We have seen them reproduced at the present day, under a similar stimulus, abhorrence of modern Dissent, in the Tractarian theology of Oxford.

With this conception of the government and ritual of the Anglican Church, its doctrinal system was in unison. Calvinism which lays so much stress on the direct, personal agency of Christ, and discredits in the same degree the efficacy of outward forms and the mediation of a priesthood, which ascribes salvation to a change wrought in the inward man and values any Church service only as a means of inducing or advancing that spiritual work—had no sympathy with the specific tendencies of the English hierarchy. It was brought in, as already explained, by a kind of side force in the vast impulse of the first great Protestant movement; and it has remained as a foreign element, never thoroughly assimilated with the original system. From the time of James I. the character of the English Church may be fairly described in Lord Chatham's celebrated words; that "it has a Calvinistic creed, an Arminian clergy, and a Popish liturgy."

But Catholicity even in its perversion is after all an attractive and beautiful idea. With an undeniable air of haughtiness and of a certain right to command, the Anglican Church still expresses a benignant universalism in the general spirit of her administration. If her language confines all covenanted mercies to those within her pale, she holds out her hand to every one who will acknowledge her. Her instrumentality at least is all-embracing. She does not insist on her laity giving some outward token of their Christianity, before admission to membership, but accepts them as sinners willing to learn and to improve; offers them the outward means of grace; and trusts to time and the continued influence of her services, for forming in them the true life of Christianity. In the Anglican view, the Church is not already a society of saints, but only a provision for forming one; a system of training and discipline for the heavenly world. Some defects and some excellencies equally result from this conception of the nature of her office. We may notice on the one hand, her too great readiness to acquiesce in the mere proffer of external means, without a sufficient intensity of effort to bring out the spiritual result. on the other, we cannot but approve the prominence usually given in her public ministrations, after the example of her Homilies, to plain, wholesome, practical instruction; her approval of moral excellence, as the surest outward sign of inward grace; and the charitable construction put by her most eminent teachers, superior to the creeds, which they nominally accept, on the character and prospects of those who in their deviation from the orthodox standard, give evidence of a pure and honest mind[1].

The principle of the Anglican Church (and it has undergone no material change since the seventeenth century) is conservative, not progressive. She keeps what she took at the time of her separation from Rome, without carefully sifting its quality; and her limits being once fixed, she neither contracts nor enlarges them. Her deference to authority checks the free investigation of truth. She shrinks from the unconditional acknowledgment of the right of private judgment. With her the consent of antiquity must control and subdue the impulses of the individual mind. The high Anglican divines treat the Church, as the majority of Protestants treat Scripture, and the Christianity which they educe from it—as an ultimate fact, the boundary of legitimate inquiry, which must be neither questioned nor overstepped. They admit the right of private judgment, to the extent of examining and determining the claims of the Church, that something more respectful than

[1] Laud's treatment of Hales, described in Clarendon's Autobiography, vol. i. p. 43, contrasts favourably with the behaviour of Cheynel, a Puritan minister, at the interment of Chillingworth. Neal, II. p. 70.

blind, unreasoning obedience may be yielded her; but seem not to think it possible, that an honest inquirer should dispute her authority altogether[1]. There is gross sophistry in this reasoning; but the Church is not more inconsistent than the majority of those who dissent from her. It is flagrantly absurd to invite free inquiry, and yet resolve beforehand, that any conclusion honestly arrived at, must involve criminality. The freest **inquirer may indeed** be willing to allow, that there **are cases, where an external** authority or simple tradition is **the best** guide that he can follow, and a sufficient ground for compliance in matters of form and usage not condemned by **reason** and conscience; but on the nature and claims of that authority or tradition, it must still be his private judgment that can alone decide.

The ascendency of traditional authority over private judgment is very conspicuous in the public services of the Church of England. The forms for every occasion are rigidly prescribed. Nothing is left to **the** feeling, discretion and free judgment of the minister. Every time that her members lift up their voices in common prayer, they **join in the** very words which the pious have uttered on the same occasion, week after **week, for** centuries. There is something, it is true, very solemn **and impressive in this consent** of successive generations to pour out their deepest wants in the same hallowed strain. The words themselves become consecrated by usage and association. But there is a limit to this effect. Experience shows, that it ought to be freely broken with spontaneous utterance. Deadness **and** formalism are the sure result of the present exclusive practice. **The** authoritative element is too largely predominant. The officiating priest is almost reduced to a machine; his individual mind has no space left, within which it can act. The prayer of the preacher before the sermon, has **been** confined by rigid disciplinarians among the bishops, to a prescribed form. Even the substitution of modern hymns for the psalms of David and the ancient chants of the Church, is disliked by the stricter Anglicans as symptomatic of a puritanical spirit. Thus in the doctrine, the government, the ritual, and the general practice of the Anglican hierarchy, as developed by the controversies of the seventeenth century, and still essen-

---

[1] This is the ground taken by Mr Gladstone in his "Church Principles considered in their Results;" and he has urged it with great force against many Dissenters, in their mode of arguing with Deists.

tially unaltered, we observe, to how great an extent tradition embodying the judgment of antiquity, has worked with a reverence for Scripture, in giving to it its peculiar character. It stands before us as an ancient sovereignty, not formally declining an appeal to fundamental charters and the principles of universal reason, but still grounding its most prominent claims on usage and prescription, and demanding from its subjects the deference and submission that are due to the prerogative of years.

To these characteristic features of the Anglican Church, Puritanism in all its more decided and energetic forms, exhibits a striking contrast. It discards tradition altogether, and takes its stand on Scripture alone. In their conception of the constitution of a church, the original **Puritans** or Presbyterians, as acknowledging the necessity of a national religion, and repudiating the principle of toleration, receded least from the idea of the hierarchy. But with them, as with the Independents and the Anabaptists, the alleged practice of Scripture was assumed as the authoritative model or platform. Without the intervention of prescribed forms or ancient rules, and with no respect for the functions of a duly graduated clergy claiming an unbroken transmission of apostolic power, they boldly declared, that they could at once draw nigh to Christ; and by the purity of their doctrine, the strictness of their discipline, and the scriptural simplicity of their worship, preserve his spirit in the midst of them, and prove themselves a true Church resting on a divine foundation. To conform even in the minutest points to the scriptural standard, and so to exclude from their faith and practice all human devices and inventions, of which they pointed with horror to the pernicious consequences in the Church of Rome; this was the great idea of the Puritans: and it was from this idea, that they derived for their system the claim of a divine right, and of exemption from the interference of the civil power. In the assemblies of the faithful, convened and administered according to the scriptural rule, they placed the original source and permanent seat of all Church power. In the exercise of this power they framed a discipline, liable indeed to most dangerous and inquisitorial abuse, by which nevertheless they proposed in all sincerity to christianize the general mass of society: and through the employment of a penal jurisdiction qualified to inflict the final sentence of excommunication, they aimed at keeping the members of the Church sound in the faith and exemplary in life.

This zeal for the conversion and salvation of the individual soul, though sometimes degenerating into harshness and intolerance, was the distinguishing excellence of the Puritan movement. Baxter's parish of Kidderminster which had been previously notorious for its profaneness and profligacy, exhibited a surprising reformation under his faithful and energetic ministry. In his account of his own life, he speaks of the time and pains which he often bestowed in trying to produce an impression on a single obdurate mind; and he thought himself abundantly recompensed, if he could witness at length any spiritual result. The Puritan ministers attached an obligation of peculiar sacredness to their ordination vows; and this feeling was doubtless strengthened by their Calvinistic principles. They believed, that the blood of their perishing fellow-creatures would be required at their hands by the great Judge of all; and that it was the first of all duties, peculiarly incumbent on those who were set apart for the ministry of the Word, to labour unceasingly to call men to God, and save them from everlasting perdition. Hence the pertinacity—to a modern reader seeming almost wrong-headedness and obstinacy—with which they pursued their ministerial functions in defiance of the laws, and amidst the most vexatious obstructions and persecutions. The words of Paul were profoundly engraven on their hearts: " woe is unto me if I preach not the Gospel." The lives of Baxter, Oliver Heywood, and other Nonconformist ministers, in the time of Charles II., abound with instances of this unflinching faithfulness. This deep concern for the spiritual welfare of men irrespective of ceremonies and outward forms, heart acting at once upon heart, continued to the last to distinguish the Puritans, even after they had lost much of their original sternness and fervour. Baxter and the Presbyterians gradually verged towards Arminianism, and would gladly, at the Restoration and afterwards, have entered into accommodation with the Episcopalians But no good could have come out of a forced and hollow compromise. Tendencies strongly felt and springing from the deepest convictions of the inward man, are best left to work themselves out freely and honestly into their natural results.

The essential element of Puritanism was developed more boldly and consequentially by the Independents than by the

Presbyterians. They assimilated their churches to the societies of the first Christians. They were assemblies of saints possessing all Church powers within themselves, and admitting none into communion but those who gave evidence of true conversion. Their conception of a Church was directly opposed to that of the Anglican party. The Church with them was rather a result than a process; not instrumental and preparatory, but a receptacle for those who had been converted from the world, and were already under the regenerating influence of the spirit of God. All Church officers, whether pastors, doctors, or elders, were regarded by them as but the organs and instruments of these societies of the faithful; not exercising any external authority over them; but deriving all their power from their own participation in the spirit which filled the bosom of the Church. The sacraments which they administered among themselves, were considered simply as the signs and tokens of their actual communion with Christ, not as the external channels of divine grace into the heart. Independency did not offer men a Church, as an outward instrumentality for taking them to heaven; but first of all set at work the interior process of regenerating the individual soul by faith, and then collected a Church out of the results. Here alone, within the renovated heart, was the evidence of Christianity to be found. What this extremer form of Puritanism sought to accomplish, was not a vast ecclesiastical unity, embracing the entire national life in its aim, applying its means and its incentives to all alike, according to the Scripture image holding fishes great and small within its capacious net; but the sympathetic approximation and gradual coalescence of earnest, regenerated men, growing up into small religious unions over the face of society, like so many centres of Christian vitality darting out their influence on every side into the surrounding mass of corrupt and torpid humanity.

With the earlier developments of Puritanism, Calvinism was invariably associated. Those who finally lapsed into Arminianism, had either themselves passed through its severe and purifying process, or inherited the tendencies of Calvinistic predecessors. Two valuable results, not wholly free, it must be confessed, from some qualifying evil, may be traced to this fact. The adoption of the Calvinistic faith led to a rejection of the traditional authority of the Church, and demanded a patient and thoughtful exercise of the understanding; first, to ascertain the fundamental truths of Scripture, and then, to reason them out into their consequences. Mrs. Hutchinson has spoken of the unwearied pains of her husband amidst the distractions of a military life, to determine from Scripture and the writings of the most learned commentators, the simple question of baptism[1]. This process of earnest research under a high sense of responsibility, formed habits of mental independence, profound seriousness and manly self-reliance. A more important effect was the intense *personality*, if I may so call it, both of the faith and of the religious life, which the old Calvinistic system exacted and cherished in its adherents. Its convictions were indeed stern and terrific, such as only robust and athletic minds could have endured: but they were real and deep. The forms on which the Church insisted, were despised as vain and unsubstantial shadows. With the ever-burning lights of the Bible in his hand, the searcher descended into the depths of his own spiritual nature, and commenced the work of self-renewal there. He often missed his way, and stumbled on many errors; but he was earnest at his work, and dug up not a little of the rough and unwrought ore of valuable truth. He came at least to one precious conclusion; that all which has enduring worth in man, must proceed from within; that the outward life can have no beauty and nobleness, but as the sign of a spiritual purification which has already taken place in the soul itself.

Some of the best fruits of Puritanism grew out of these principles: its high courage; its stern integrity; its unbending faithfulness; its clear, penetrating, analytic reason; its pure morals. Hence, too, might arise not a few of its follies and extravagancies: its self-willedness and obstinacy; its scrupulousness about trifles; its narrow, intolerant adherence to its own ideas and practices: the unaccommodating strictness of its manners, and its aversion from the innocent recreations of life. But its severe purity was the nurse of the domestic affections. Its homes were blessed with the spirit of conjugal and parental love. Contempt and persecution drew closer the living bonds of the heart. Even the rugged exterior of Cromwell's mind sheltered a spirit of household purity and tenderness. Ludlow, no admirer of Cromwell, attests the effect produced on his mind at the height of his power, by the death of his favourite daughter, Lady Claypole; an effect from which

[1] Memoirs, 4to, pp. 267–71.

he never recovered, and which undoubtedly hastened his own end[1]. This most amiable expression of the old Puritan principle, still subsists in undiminished strength and purity among its worthiest representatives in the Congregationalists of New England.

The rejection of sacerdotal claims, and a close adherence in all things to scriptural precedents, led the Puritans, like their forerunners, the Lollards, to exact very eminent spiritual gifts and a high standard of ministerial faithfulness in their pastors. The minister was greatly magnified and enjoyed vast influence among them. His suitable education and training for his office, followed by satisfactory tests of his proficiency in learning and piety, were points on which they laid the greatest stress. But they honoured him for what he was, and for what he did. It was the man, the earnest, conscientious, well-instructed servant of Christ, that in their view conferred worth and dignity on the office. The office alone, though it might claim a remote derivation from apostolical commission, would never have reconciled them to the services of an ignorant, careless and immoral priest. In the same deep radical appreciation of personal religion, and in the conviction that all acceptable homage should be a direct expression of it, with an invincible prejudice against every relic and every memorial of the Roman Catholic system—originated their general dislike of liturgies and set forms of prayer; the severe plainness of their public worship; and their unsparing removal of all those artistical embellishments, speaking to the imagination through the ear and the eye, with which the ancient Church had conferred an outward and symbolical beauty on the mysteries and traditions of its faith.

The Directory published by the Westminster Assembly, prescribes the form of service still usually observed among Protestant Dissenters. Its chief materials were—prayers, introductory, general and concluding, offered up in the minister's own words (for the gift of prayer was held in great esteem by the Puritans); lessons from the Old and New Testaments, often followed by an exposition; hymns sung by the assembled

---

[1] Ludlow's Memoirs. Vevay: 1699. II. pp. 609 and 607. No one can forget Mr. Carlyle's description of Lady Claypole's death-bed and the Protector's deep affliction, drawn from Thurloe and other contemporaneous authorities. (Letters and Speeches of Cromwell, II. p. 659.) For another instance of the strong domestic affection which distinguished the Cromwell family, see the account of the death of the Protector's mother, in the same work, II. p. 310.

congregation, without any instrumental accompaniment; and a sermon of formidable length, scholastic in its form, sometimes garnished with quotations in the learned languages, and broken up into a great number of divisions and subdivisions, in which the idea of the text was opened out and exhausted. In the interval between the Restoration and the Revolution, the style of preaching lost much of its ancient ruggedness and wild fervour, and became more polished, calm and rational. Oliver Heywood, who retained unabated to the last the character of an old Puritan, complains of the degeneracy which he remarked in the preaching of the younger ministers some years before his death[1]. In the spirit of consistent contradiction, the Puritans substituted for the holydays and festivals of the Church, which they viewed with a sort of horror, frequent fasts, public and private, accompanied by prayers and other religious exercises. The Puritan diaries of the time are full of allusions to these fasts. Calamy has described, on the authority of Howe, the enormous length to which the services accompanying them, were often protracted[2]. The Puritans were all Sabbatarians, and kept the seventh day with a rigid strictness.

[1] Hunter's Life of Oliver Heywood, p. 385.
[2] "He told me," says Calamy (Life of Howe, p. 5), "it was upon those occasions his common way, to begin about nine in the morning, with a prayer for about a quarter of an hour, in which he begged a blessing on the work of the day; and afterwards read and expounded a chapter or psalm, in which he spent about three quarters; then prayed for an hour, preached for another hour, and prayed for about half an hour. After this, he retired, and took some little refreshment for about a quarter of an hour or more (the people singing all the while), and then came again into the pulpit, and prayed for another hour, and gave them another sermon of about an hour's length: and so concluded the service of the day, at about four of the clock in the evening, with about half an hour or more in prayer." Baillie (Letters and Journals, 1644, vol. ii. p. 184) gives a similar description. "This day was the strictest that I have seen in England. Generall Essex sent to the (Westminster) Assemblie, i.e. to entreat that a day of fasting might be kept for him. We spent from nine to five very graciouslie. After Dr. Twisse had begun with a briefe prayer, Mr Marshall prayed large two houres, most divinelie—in a wonderfullie pathetick and prudent way. After Mr. Arrowsmith preached one houre, then a psalme; thereafter, Mr. Vines prayed near two houres, and Mr. Palmer preached one houre, and Mr. Seaman prayed near two houres, then a psalme. After, Mr. Henderson brought them to a short sweet conference of the heart confessed in the Assemblie, and other seen faults to be remedied, and the conveniencie to preach against all sects, especiallie Anabaptists and Antinomians. Dr. Twisse closed with a short prayer and blessing." This is truly graphic! Calamy who only lived in the next generation, calls this "a sort of service that few could have gone through, without inexpressible weariness to themselves and their auditories." In his days the old fervour was already burnt out.

The effect of the two systems, the Anglican and the Puritan, on the moral and religious condition of the people, has been such as might be expected from their respective principles and tendencies. Whatever partisans may urge, unmixed good or unqualified evil can be predicated of neither side. The complex and variegated character of our English population, combining the most diversified elements of social condition, high aristocracy and strong conservatism, extensively interwrought with a vigorous popular life and a restless spirit of innovation and progress—has been one of the results, as it has been in some degree also a condition, of these antagonistic agencies; and it was then most conspicuous, when they were most vehemently in opposition.

The Church with its ample endowments, its titled dignitaries, its territorial influence, has ever inclined to be quiescent and stationary, content with holding out its offices to the world, and preserving its hereditary jurisdiction. Puritanism in the exuberance of strong conviction, has overleapt all forms to carry its aid, wherever wanted, to the penitent, afflicted and craving heart. The former has relied on the sober regularity of its ministrations; the latter, on the prompt energy of its zeal and love. The Church has constantly gravitated towards indifference; Puritanism has as constantly been impelled by its interior restlessness towards fanaticism. If the lax discipline of the Church has sometimes tolerated profaneness and levity, the severity of Puritanism has not unfrequently produced hypocrisy. The Church has enforced attendance on her public services, and inculcated reverence for her authorized formularies and duly ordained clergy. Puritanism has encouraged the free outpouring of every earnest soul in the unpremeditated prayers of the pulpit, and in the spontaneous exercises of domestic and private devotion. In one, we recognize the decorous wisdom of the priest; in the other, the fervour of the prophet. The outward poetry of form, of historical association, of imaginative conception, of sensuous impression—predominates in the Church. Puritanism draws its inspiration from within, yet appeals to the intellect, and delights in abstract and logical expression. The Church's independence of the popular will, has given a certain breadth and freedom to its views—a certain calmness and practical moderation to its spirit. Puritanism has kept close to the suggestions of the popular heart, and with all its earnestness and its honesty, has not seldom been narrow and perverse. We recognize in the Church, the conservator of established order, the champion of law, the patron of the claims of rank and ancestry. Puritanism has allied itself with the cause of liberty and progress; indulged and encouraged popular sympathies; and reserved its highest reverence and admiration for integrity and conscientiousness.

Of course only the prominent points of contrast can be brought out in such a comparison as this. Between the extremes there must naturally have been, as we know there was, a large intermediate class: but the violent and vindictive spirit in which measures were carried against the Puritans on the king's return, almost prevented moderation, and marked off the two great parties in the State by an impassable barrier from each other. Persecution, with a dislike amounting to abhorrence of the free discourse and licentious manners imported from France by the Cavaliers—gave a strong tincture of gloom and severity to the language and demeanour of the Nonconformists in the time of Charles the Second. The healthful development of their distinguishing principles was checked or exaggerated by adverse influences. Yet it is from this period, that the most vivid traditions of Puritanism are derived; with it the names of the great and holy men who were martyrs in its cause, are painfully associated; and it was then that the religious bodies which have inherited its spirit, were in process of formation.

The unkindly atmosphere in which it grew, must be taken into account, in estimating its character. The circumstances of the times influenced the style of preaching, and had a corresponding effect on the studies of the learned. The sermons of the Puritans may be described, generally, as scriptural in their matter, closely spiritual in their application, and in method perfectly exhaustive. They rarely quitted a text till they had resolved it into its elements, and extracted from it every conclusion it could yield. Matthew Henry's Commentary furnishes a good example of their customary method of exposition. To them the Bible was really the book of books; and they sought in it all the wisdom of life. But their preaching, though acute and vigorous, often displaying great knowledge of the heart, and well fitted for strong immediate effect, was too rigidly limited in its object, too little discursive in its view of life's duties and prospects, too bare of illustration and adornment from the fields of philosophy and polite learning —to reach that highest form of Christian eloquence, which takes a permanent place in the classical literature of a nation. In the most eminent Puritan divines, with all their excellencies, we search in vain for passages that will admit of comparison with the rich sentiment and sweet poetic fancy of Taylor and Hall, or with the amplitude of thought and philosophic breadth of vision which we find in Barrow and Cudworth. Direct operation on the outward and inward life, a profound impression of seriousness on the popular mind, was the simple, conscientious aim of the Puritan preacher.

The peculiar learning of the Puritans was determined by the same influences as the strain of their preaching. To be well versed in Scripture, and to be capable of probing the depths, quieting the apprehensions, and solving the perplexities, of conscience—constituted in their estimation the highest accomplishment of a Christian divine. For human philosophy they had little regard, though they employed logical forms to a pedantic excess in their reasonings; and their general contempt of tradition alienated them from minute inquiries into Christian antiquity. This direction of their studies, at first the result of principle and feeling, became afterwards a sort of necessity, when they were excluded from the Universities and the great repositories of literature, and enjoyed diminished opportunities of leisure and research. Scriptural exposition and practical divinity were the pursuits in which they chiefly exercised themselves; and in these they laboured with good effect. The writings of Owen and Baxter have never perhaps been surpassed for the force with which they penetrate to "the hidden man of the heart," and the profound acquaintance they discover with its infirmities and snares[1]. The ex-

---

[1] Arthur Young, a man of science and the world, has shown his value for these two great practical writers, by publishing selections from their works. The preface to his Baxteriana (Hatchard, London: 1815) is affectingly impressive. Owen was perhaps the greatest scholar among the Puritan divines. His Θεολογούμενα παντοδαπά, sive de Naturā, Ortu, Progressu et Studio veræ Theologiæ (Bremæ, 1684) first published after his retirement from all public functions in 1661 (Biograph. Britann.) is a work of immense learning, displaying an intimate familiarity not only with Greek and Latin poetry (*veterum poetarum usum magnum esse fateor.* præfat.) but also with modern literature, in which Dante and Chaucer are not forgotten. Though written, as might be expected, exclusively from the Biblical point of view, the work is not devoid of a critical spirit. See p. 247. Speaking from his own experience, as Vice-Chancellor of Oxford under Cromwell, he complains of the defective constitution of the Academic

pository works of Poole, Goodwin, Caryl, Manton and Owen, evince the unwearied labour and thought bestowed by the Puritans on the Scriptures; but they exhibit only another form of practical divinity. **Spiritual edification is the pre**dominant consideration in them; and they have therefore little in common with the critical and historical spirit of the modern exegesis[1]. In the meantime, the learning of the Church was taking a wider range. At the same time with these Nonconformist productions, or not long after them, the antiquarian labours of Usher, Stillingfleet and Bingham, the Polyglott of Brian Walton, (which disturbed the Scriptural sensitiveness of Owen,) the patristical researches of Bull, and the Platonic speculations of Cudworth and More, were given to the world.

From the phenomena exhibited by Puritanism in its depressed and persecuted condition, which exaggerated its natural tendencies, it is not fair to conclude, what would have been its settled and permanent character, if in the struggle

---

Course, and the too easy admission of youths without ability or aptitude for study. At the close of this very learned book, the Independency of the author appears in all its force. He protests eloquently against national churches (p. 481), and contends that the spirit is a better qualification for preaching than human learning.—The following passage from his 'Grace and Duty of being Spiritually Minded,' ch. ii., furnishes a favourable specimen of his mode of treating spiritual themes :—" Thoughts and meditations, as proceeding from spiritual affections, are the first things wherein this spiritual-mindedness doth consist, and whereby it doth evidence itself. Our thoughts are like the blossoms on a tree in the spring. You may see a tree in the spring so covered with blossoms that nothing else of it appears. Multitudes of them fall off and come to nothing. Ofttimes where there are most blossoms, there is least fruit. But yet there is no fruit, be it of what sort it will, good or bad, but it comes in and from some of those blossoms. The mind of man is covered with thoughts, as a tree with blossoms. Most of them fall off, vanish, and come to nothing, end in vanity; and sometimes where the mind doth most abound with them, there is the least fruit; the sap of the mind is wasted and consumed in them. Howbeit there is no fruit which actually we bring forth, be it good or bad, but it proceeds from some of these thoughts. Wherefore ordinarily these give the best and surest measure of the frame of men's minds." Bradley's Select Works of Owen, vol. ii. p. 163.

[1] The works of the Puritans in this department were immensely voluminous. Those of Thomas Goodwin are contained in five folio volumes. Dr. Manton's 190 Sermons on the 119th Psalm, the hearing of which is said to have given Bolingbroke his first distaste to religion, occupy a folio. Owen's Commentary on the Epistle to the Hebrews, extends through four vols. folio. Caryl's Job fills twelve quartos. These literary phenomena are significant of the body which produced them. They are tokens of that intense *scripturalism*—that reverence approaching to superstition for every word and particle of the Bible —which was the great principle of Puritanism.

with the Stuarts and the Church, it had finally carried the day. Nothing can be farther from historical truth than to represent it, even in what are deemed its extremer forms, as a simple movement of democratic fanaticism. The leaders of the Presbyterian party belonged to the nobility and landed gentry. Of the Independents, whom some writers at once dispose of in the mass as illiterate enthusiasts, it has been observed by Mr. Laing[1], the historian of Scotland, that, "contrary to the progress of other sects, their system was first addressed, and apparently recommended by its tolerating principles, to the higher orders of social life." It is made a serious charge against the Independents, in Edwards's Gangræna, that they were distinguished from the Presbyterians by greater attention to dress and appearance, and a less scrupulous conformity to the manners of the world. "Let a man turn sectary now-a-days," says he, "and within one half year he is so metamorphosed in apparel, hair, etc., as a man hardly knows him[2]." The gentlemen of England would have retained their ancient habitudes and knightly bearing under a Cromwellian dynasty. Hampden followed the chase amidst the beech-woods of his native Buckinghamshire. The Protector himself did not disdain the fashionable pastime of hawking[3]. Milton was skilled in every manly and graceful exercise[4]. In

---

[1] Orme's Life of Owen, p. 75.

[2] At Oxford Owen scandalized the strait-laced by his powdered hair, his elegant band-strings, and the fashionable cut of his Spanish leather boots with wide lawn tops. (Biogr. Brit. Orme, p. 193, who quotes Anthony Wood.) Edwards (Gangræna, p. 63) thought it shocking profanation in John Goodwin, the Arminian Independent, and several of his church, that they should go to bowls and other sports on days of public thanksgiving. "The sectaries," he says, "wear strange long hair, go in fine fashionable apparel beyond their places, feast, ride journeys, and do servile business on fast days." In this same collection of gossip and scandal, curious for the incidental light it throws on the manners of the times, it is stated, that the Independent Ministers were very liberally supported by their hearers, all classes contributing something, and the richer members paying £15, £20, or even £30 yearly towards their Ministers' maintenance. Part II. p. 14. Edwards's chief opponent was John Goodwin under the name of Cretensis. The language on both sides in the controversy is coarse and ungentlemanly. On the pastimes of the Puritans, illustrated from their own writings, see "Letters on Puritanism and Nonconformity," by Sir J. B. Williams, pp. 89-94.

[3] Aubrey's Lives of Eminent Men, vol. ii. p. 433.

[4] How delightfully his earliest poems reflect the healthy enjoyment of his youth!
"Oft listening how the hounds and horn
Cheerly rouse the slumbering morn,
From the side of some hoar hill,
Through the high wood echoing shrill."

the Memoirs of Colonel Hutchinson we have a finished picture of the Puritan gentleman, grave, learned, and accomplished; blending a deep and earnest piety with the courtesies of the world; capable of high service in the senate and the field, and adorning his rural retreat with the elegant entertainments of books, pictures, and gardening[1].

Some of Cromwell's projected reforms anticipated the ideas of a later day, very few of which have been yet realized. He proposed a better distribution and more equal maintenance of the parochial clergy, which would have spread the means of spiritual culture more effectually through the entire mass of the population. Though possessed of little learning himself, he knew how to value it in others, and was surrounded by men, Milton, Howe, and Owen, who would never have suffered him to neglect its interests. He encouraged Brian Walton's great work by allowing the importation of paper for it duty free; enriched the Bodleian library with valuable manuscripts; and granted a charter for the establishment of a college for the North of England at Durham, in which Mr. Frankland, afterwards at the head of a Dissenting Academy, was nominated a tutor[2]. A very remarkable passage in Clarendon distinctly admits, in spite of its obvious malice and perversion of fact, that learning flourished at Oxford under Presbyterian and Independent rule[3]. It is worthy of notice, that in this

---

[1] This age abounded with distinguished excellence in the opposite ranks of the grand controversy. Lady Fanshawe's Memoirs (8vo, 1829) may be placed by the side of Mrs. Hutchinson's delightful work:—a widow in each case recording the virtues and services of a high-minded and patriotic husband.

[2] A draft of this charter was issued by Cromwell in 1657, in accordance with a request which had been addressed to the Privy Council by the gentry and freeholders of the county of Durham in 1650. The College was to consist of a Provost, Fellows, and Scholars; it was to be maintained out of lands and possessions recently belonging to the Dean and Chapter; and to be invested with the same privileges and immunities as the old Universities. The laws for its government were to be framed, and might be modified, by the Sovereign and Council of State, or by Visitors appointed by them. Rutt gives a copy of this charter, taken from the original in the custody of the Dean and Chapter of Durham, in the appendix to vol. ii. of his edition of Burton's Diary, pp. 111–125. When it was proposed to carry this charter into effect in the protectorate of Richard Cromwell, Oxford and Cambridge petitioned against it. The Provost named in this charter, Philip Hunton, M.A., was ejected on St. Bartholomew's day, 1662. Rutt, *ibid.* Calamy's Account, etc., II. p. 754. For Mr. Frankland's connection with this College, see Calamy, II. p. 284, and Hunter's Life of Oliver Heywood, p. 243.

[3] Where he is speaking of the Parliamentary visitation of Oxford in 1647, to enforce the taking of the Covenant, at the time the Earl of Pembroke was made

University, during the same period, the foundations of the Royal Society were laid in the private meetings of a few cultivators of natural science. Had the changes which Puritanism was working in the Church, **the Universities, and the** State, fixed themselves in permanent results, the sternness of its earliest aspect would have worn off with the return of a tranquil civilization. The strong religious impulse, of which it was the expression, and which was needed to countcract an extreme of licentiousness, would have produced its natural effect in giving a more earnest and lofty character to the mind of the upper classes, and by drawing them through education and religion into closer sympathy with the great body of the people, might have obviated **some of** the mischiefs resulting from the intimate alliance between the Church and the Aristocracy, which began with **the Revolution.**

The influence of Puritanism is often represented **as** hostile to elegant literature. Its short-lived ascendency, beset with danger and consumed in strife, had indeed little **leisure for** the soft dalliance of the Muses. But the sublime incarnation of its spirit in the poetry of Milton, must for ever repel **the** imputation of incompatibility with the very highest form of literary excellence. Even its homely, popular expression in the pregnant allegory of Bunyan, yielded nutriment to the na**tional heart fully as wholesome** and generous as the banter of **Hudibras, which was the** delight of the reinstated Royalists.

It is a curious speculation, not so remote from the present subject as **to forbid a** moment's entertainment, what might have been the effect on the subsequent development of our literature, if the triumph of Puritanical principles under Cromwell had been lasting, and prevented the Restoration. Twice in the course of our history has our native literature, the spontaneous growth of the Saxon element which pervades **our** whole population and forms the very heart of our national character, been submerged beneath a foreign influence break-

Chancellor (Hist. of Rebellion, Book X. Oxford edit. 1826, vol. **v.** p. 482–3). "When it pleased God to bring King Charles **the** Second back to his throne, he found that University (not to undervalue the other, which had nobly likewise rejected **the** ill infusions which **had** been industriously poured into it) abounding in **excellent** learning, and devoted to duty and obedience, little inferior to what **it was, before its** desolation." Effects must have some relation to causes. During the interval to which Clarendon here refers, Owen and Goodwin were Heads of Houses, the former of Christchurch, the latter of Magdalen; Cromwell and his son Richard were successively Chancellors; and part of the time, Owen was Vice-Chancellor.

ing in upon it from France. The earliest poetry of our nascent English, if we except a few songs and ballads circulated among the lowest classes, was in its form, its spirit, and for the most part even in its materials, essentially Norman. Chaucer and Gower wrote for the court and the nobles, not for the people. Towards the close **of the fifteenth century,** the genuine English spirit arose, **and** strengthened by a continual accession of popular elements, **in** which religion had perhaps the largest share—**brought forth** in little more than a century and a half, **an exuberance of** literary fruit whose rich juice and racy flavour proclaim it the unforced produce of our native soil. Within this period sprang up our national drama, **that** breathing expression of English life. To this glorious springtime of our country, belong the greatest and most **original** of our authors, uniting a wild fertility of imagination as yet unbroken by criticism, with a masculine strength of thought—the **fathers** of our eloquence and poetry, **Spenser,** Shakspeare, **Milton,** Hooker, Raleigh, and Bacon. **With** whatever **party in Church** and State **they** may outwardly **be classed,** these noble minds are thoroughly English in feeling, **and instinct with** the spirit of progress and mental independence. Their works announce **that** redundancy **of** moral and intellectual energy, which vaguely craving after some higher good, but not at one with **itself** as to the form and measure of **it,** at length broke out **into** action and spent itself on civil discord. The movement in this direction ceased with the dissolution of the Commonwealth. On the return of Charles, a second inundation **of** French **influence** overwhelmed our manners and **our literature.** The poetry **of "the** blind old schoolmaster" **was forgotten.** The drama **of Shakspeare, Massinger,** and **Fletcher,** true to **nature and humanity, whose last echoes died** away in the feebler genius of Otway—was **replaced by the** rhyming tragedies of Dryden; and the soul of native **inspiration** which breathed **in our** ancient song, expired under the fetters of art **imposed** on it by a Parisian criticism.

Such a change could **not** have occurred, had Puritanism maintained its ascendency. Milton would have become the immediate model of **imitation**; and his **influence** must have introduced **a severer taste** and a purer tone of sentiment. At the same time, his scholarlike feelings and healthful mind would have preserved **from** the ignorant contempt and destruction of fanatical **zeal, the** precious remains of our older literature[1]. Even under Puritanical rule, the mind of England would doubtless have been gradually affected by the progress of European ideas; but the very different relation in which we should then have stood towards France, must have prevented our writers from taking her classical productions as a standard of excellence. Dryden and Pope, in the form which their genius actually assumed, and with the influence which they exerted on the literature of the Revolution, could not have existed. Their vigorous and polished couplet embodying sharp epigrammatic contrasts of thought, and their inimitable art of reasoning in verse, so well adapted to a cold and satirical cast of mind, and so natural an effect of reaction against over-strained enthusiasm, were never in perfect harmony with the latent sympathies of the people. They floated over the surface of society, but did not penetrate to its living depths.

Before the middle of the eighteenth century, we perceive already a return, though with a lingering respect for the outward forms of the school of Pope, towards the poetry of feeling and imagination in the lyrics of Collins and Gray and the devotional rhapsodies of Young. Amidst all the inflation of his rhetorical verse,[2] the heart of Thomson was still in living contact with nature, and breathed forth occasionally strains of genuine sympathy. The spirit of the last century was indeed essentially prosaic and artificial; but as it advanced, we can perceive in its best poetry—in the artless sensibility of Goldsmith, in Mrs. Barbauld's chastened religious fervour and deep Puritan love of truth and freedom, in the true English feeling and pensive thoughtfulness of Cowper—a deepening tone of earnestness and simplicity. From that time to the present day, the enthusiasm for our old writers separated from us by the memorable conflicts of the seventeenth century, has been continually on the increase. Imbued with their spirit, the public mind seems now to have fixed its choice on a poetry that springs from a fullness of inward life, that expresses a purpose, and reveals the deep national heart, in preference to the sparkling wit or graceful sentimentality which clothes in elegant verse the conventional taste and transitory opinion of the day.

Had the work of the Puritans endured, the continuous

[1] His lines on Shakspeare, and the genial allusion to the stage in L'Allegro, will recur at once to every reader.

development of a national literature, inspired by reality and uttering the strong emotions and convictions of the popular mind, would never probably have undergone so violent an interruption; and a character, at once more earnest and more refined, more spiritual and more cultivated, would have grown up along with it in the great body of the people.

As it was, the two parties in the State were driven by violent **antagonism** into vicious extremes. Puritanism trampled upon and harassed by persecuting laws, renounced the world, and took refuge in a fervent, and often a narrow, piety. Its representatives in the next generation, gradually forsaken by the higher aristocracy, shut out from the Universities, and for the most part directing all their energies to practical objects—trade, commerce, civil freedom and scriptural divinity—only by degrees came back to the adoption of wider views of life, and began again to take a share and an interest in the general literature of their country. But though the natural influence of **Puritanism was** thus **broken and** perverted by the pressure of outward wrong, it brought many noble and generous principles into circulation, and preserved a sound heart in the **most valuable** portion of the community. Of its **beneficial effects on** the middle **and lower classes,** we become **additionally** sensible, as we trace more carefully the social **progress of** the eighteenth century. It kept alive the spirit of religious earnestness, public liberty, and popular improvement—those vital elements of the social system, the violent expulsion of which cost France her morals and **her faith, and** is now producing among its remoter consequences, a succession of revolutions, whose final issue it is impossible to predict.

CHAPTER V.

FREE INQUIRY.

SECTION I.

DISTINCTION BETWEEN THE INDEPENDENCE OF RELIGIOUS SOCIETIES AND THE FREEDOM OF THE INDIVIDUAL MIND.

In the preceding review of our religious history, we have witnessed a struggle between two different kinds of outward authority for ascendency; that which was urged by the Church in the joint names of Tradition and Scripture; and that which was urged by the Puritans in the name of Scripture alone. In this struggle, the rights and prerogatives of societies founded on these different principles, were more regarded than the claims of the individual conscience. It was, indeed, hardly possible in the first effort to obtain religious independence, that the struggle should take any other course. Men had been nurtured in authority, and could not at once cast it off. The belief was all but universal, that the State must rest on a specific religious basis, must be united with some Church; the only point at issue being, to determine the true Church. It was not at first perceived, how many assumptions, each requiring a separate proof, were involved in this view of the case:—that there must be one true, visible Church, sustained by a *jus divinum*; that the books of Scripture were the sole ultimate criterion of religious doctrine and practice; that the *letter* of these books was inspired, and carried with it a plenary divine authority.

Nevertheless, the broad principle involved in the Reformation, of the right of every man to search the Scriptures for himself, produced as its natural consequence—when the bonds of external discipline in the progress of our civil troubles were dissolved—an immense number of sects putting forth the most discordant views, in some of which we can already trace the

K

germ of more recent theories. Their appearance was a great scandal to the Presbyterians. Edwards, the modern Epiphanius, has enumerated with all the bitterness of his Greek prototype and with perhaps as little discrimination, no fewer than a hundred and eighty flagrant heresies then prevalent in England[1]. This state of things, so destructive of the traditional order and fixedness on which the mind of a lawyer loves to rest, drew from Selden the significant remark; that "the two

[1] In his Gangræna, 3rd edit. 1646. The sectaries, he tells us, however different in their opinions, all agree in Independency, and in forsaking the communion of the Reformed Churches (p. 7). Among the places where Independent principles had taken root, he mentions especially—New England, the Bermudas, Amsterdam, and Rotterdam. (Letters and Narrations, p. 61.)—Of the heresies enumerated by him, the following, as signs of the unsettled state of public opinion, are worth notice (pp. 15–31). (1.) Scripture, not the Word of God; no Word but Christ. (4.) As the patriarchs walked with God by the teaching of God, so should we: half the glory of God is not revealed as yet; we must wait what he will record in our hearts, and in that measure worship him in spirit and truth from the teachings of the Spirit. (5.) All Scripture an allegory, in which its spiritual meaning is contained. (6.) Penmen of Scripture moved by their own spirit. (9.) Right reason the rule of Faith and measure of Scripture. (13.) Free toleration of all consciences, Paganish, Jewish, Turkish, antichristian: "yea, if it be men's consciences, the magistrates may not punish for blasphemies, nor for denying the Scriptures, nor for denying there is a God." Edward adds in the margin—"Last part hath been spoken by some eminent sectaries." (24.) In the unity of God, no trinity of persons; doctrine of the trinity a Popish tradition, and a doctrine of Rome. (28.) Christ's human nature defiled with original sin as well as ours; Christ not of a holier nature than we: "in this appears God's love to us, that he will take one of us in the same condition, to convince us of what he is to us, and hath made us to be in him; the beholding of Christ to be holy in the flesh is a dishonour to God, in that we should conceive holiness out of God, and again a discomfort to the saints, that he should be of a more holy nature than they, as being no ground for them to come near with boldness to God." (40.) Christ came to declare the love of God, not to procure it for us or satisfy God. (45.) Men may be saved without Christ, if they serve God according to the knowledge God has given them. (167.) There shall be a general restoration, wherein all men shall be reconciled to God and saved; only saints shall then be in a higher condition than those who do not believe.

Edwards gives an account of some pantheistic doctrines, which he says were on the increase. (Letters and Narrations, p. 112.) He mentions, that at a meeting of sectaries of different persuasions in London, it was professed by some to be the sin of this kingdom, "that the Jews were not allowed the open profession and exercise of their religion," and that only the Presbyterians dissented and opposed it (p. 12). Edwards, as I have already stated, had a particular spite against John Goodwin, the Arminian Independent. He calls his congregation an unclean conventicle; "Socinian, Arminian, Popish, Anabaptistical, Libertine tenets being held by himself and many of his people." (Gangræna, Part II. p. 13.) Upon the whole we obtain from Edwards's confused medley, a tolerably clear insight into some remarkable tendencies of religious opinion, which had sprung up under the Commonwealth.

words, *scrutamini Scripturas,* had been the undoing of the world[1]." But this fermentation of spirits was necessary to the evolution of the great principles, which were distinctly recognized before the close of the century, and gradually incorporated with public opinion in the course of the next.

Of these principles, the most important was Free Inquiry, Private Judgment, or Rationalism; the right of every man to bring the doctrines and institutions of religion to the test of his individual reason, and to adopt or reject them, as he finds them in accordance with it. I do not assert, that the fullest acknowledgment of this principle is *all* that is needed, to the vital experience of religious influences or even to the right apprehension of religious truths. It will appear, I think, that its undue and exclusive predominance was among the causes of the spiritual weakness of the eighteenth century. But it is certainly an indispensable *adjunct* to the process of religious discipline: in its absence, superstition or fanaticism is inevitable. This principle had established itself in minds of the greatest eminence, the master spirits of the age, at the time of the Revolution; though prejudice and bigotry were still too powerful to allow its public recognition in the Toleration Act. From that time, it gradually increased in strength; and having been adopted by the most distinguished men both in and out of the Establishment, it allayed the old Puritan controversy, and produced a long interval of religious peace. Not that the spirit of Puritanism was wholly extinct; but it worked in a latent and quiet way. With the new rationalistic tendencies it did not very readily combine. And yet even where it retained some portion of its ancient fervour, it was indirectly affected by them; and its future manifestations were so shaped and directed by the intellectual character of the eighteenth century, that what remains to be said of its subsequent history, may not unsuitably be included in the chapter on Free Inquiry.

[1] Table Talk.

SECTION II.

EVOLUTION OF THE DIFFERENT ELEMENTS OF RELIGIOUS FREEDOM, IN THE COURSE OF THE SEVENTEENTH CENTURY.

The elements of this Rationalism which acquired force and consistency after the Revolution, had been in course of preparation during the whole of the preceding century. One or other of them was furnished by every great movement of the time; to say nothing of the minuter contributions of inferior sects and single minds. It will be interesting to trace the various, and apparently opposite, agencies that concurred in the joint result. A singular contrast may be noticed between the progress of free theological opinion on one hand, and the course of civil liberty and ecclesiastical independence on the other. The most strenuous opposers of human authority in matters of faith, those who contended most earnestly for the right of unfettered search into the Scriptures, and who receded farthest from the popular orthodoxy—were supporters of the Monarchy and the Church; while the sign of adherence to the Parliament, was a strong profession of Calvinism. We may find a reason for this distinction in the general principles of human nature. The quiet contemplation of truth in its abstract relations, apart from the passions of the multitude and the practical interests of life, is favourable to comprehensiveness of view and an impartial judgment: but at the same time it renders the mind more aware of limitations and exceptions, of the mischiefs of dogmatism, the risks of sudden change, and the necessity for undisturbed leisure and repose to promote knowledge and disseminate just principles. It inspires, therefore, naturally a cautious and conservative temper. Characters of a very different mould are required for the rough work of social revolution. Intense, exclusive conviction, fastened on a single object, and discerning truth and right in nothing else —is the frame of mind, however unbecoming a philosopher, which fits men for vigorous and decided action and leads to immediate practical results. It was fortunate for our country, that during the momentous contest which has exercised such a lasting influence on its destiny, both these tendencies, the practical and the speculative, had full scope to unfold themselves.

First, there was the great principle of Independency, claiming exemption for Christian societies from the control and interference of the State. It is obvious, however, that the fullest assertion of this principle is compatible with the establishment of a very harsh discipline and complete spiritual despotism within the limits of each separate society. The churches framed under it, may become living centres of the bitterest intolerance and darkest theology; bitter and dark in the same degree that they are responsible to no external jurisdiction, and secluded from extensive communion with other Christians. It secures outward freedom, the rights of the society; but it does not thereby provide necessarily for inward light and progress, or break the fetters of the individual mind. Independency has contributed its element towards the general result of religious liberty; but it has not done everything.

Presbyterianism, as represented by Baxter, did not seek absolute emancipation from the State, but rather invited and cherished the connection, as a means of more easily constituting and keeping together a pure national church. It would have tolerated a wide diversity of opinion and usage, and by its good discipline and the concession of a large Christian liberty, have provided for its own internal growth and development. But though its aims were generous and its spirit catholic, its conceptions were wanting in precision; the line was vaguely drawn between those who should be admitted into communion and those who should be simply tolerated; and still more was its definition of Toleration itself defective. Presbyterianism did much for truth; but it did not work out the whole truth.

Another tendency displayed itself among the Latitudinarians. These acute and learned men clearly discerned the inconsistencies of the vulgar Protestantism, while their conservative spirit and royalist bias held them back from any participation in revolutionary movements. They would have preserved the outward form and discipline of the Church, and upheld its union with the State; but they would also have released the minds of scholars and divines from the ignominy of a disingenuous subscription, and confined the public service to an enforcement of the fundamental truths and practical duties of Christianity and a simple, Scriptural form of devotion.

Setting out from views, and pursuing a course, quite opposite to those of the Latitudinarians, Milton, the younger Vane, and some of the Independents arrived at the same conviction of the rights of the individual conscience and the futility of the disputes of sects. But these men would have dissolved from the first all connection of the Church with the State. They would have allowed each separate society of Christians to work out its way independently to the truth. They sought a unity growing up spontaneously from within, not one that should be imposed artificially from without. Their sympathies were not with monarchy, but with republicanism. They would have had, not a Church embracing all, but a State interfering in the exercise of their religion with none. These tendencies, so distinct, yet leading alike to a common result, indicate the opposition and conflict of the parties with which they respectively originated. One felt the necessity of a well-disciplined learning and intellect to control and direct; the other trusted to the free movements of the harmonizing spirit of God. One dreaded the overthrow of the ancient checks and securities of law; the other entertained a generous trust in the impulses of emancipated and ennobled humanity. Schism and fanaticism might have been prevented by one scheme; more earnestness and zeal would doubtless have been developed by the other.

In the close connection of religious differences with political parties during the century and a half which followed the Reformation, men were visibly classed, whatever might be their private sentiments, either with the Puritans or with the Church Perhaps the more sceptical an individual's cast of mind, the more he would feel disposed to yield an outward respect to doctrines and usages already established. But the age which produced a Bacon, a Raleigh, and a Selden, must have been one of free speculation: and the antipuritanical character of Elizabeth's court would naturally carry this tendency to a licentious excess. As early as 1572 we find the grave and decorous Burleigh complaining of the Queen's own household, as "a coverture for no small number of *Epicures* and *Atheists*, because the Court is not comprehended within a parish, but seemeth to be a lawless place[1]." At the social meetings of wits and scholars in the metropolis, the high questions of Theology and the Church formed a frequent topic of discourse. Selden's Table Talk gives us a good idea of the way in which such matters were discussed. In Sir John

[1] Strype's Parker, p. 207.

Suckling's Session of the Poets, there is an imaginary description of one of these meetings, where we are introduced among others to the great theological scholars of the day, to Chillingworth, Hales, Falkland and Selden, with distinct allusion to their favourite subjects of speculation[1]. Sir Walter Raleigh and Hariot who accompanied him to Virginia, and wrote the account of that country in Purchas's Pilgrims, are put down by Aubrey in his collection of the traditions of those times, among the Deists. Such charges are often vaguely made; but this may be admitted, that Raleigh's writings, though abounding with beautiful expressions of religious sentiment, contain few or no allusions to the positive doctrines of Christianity[2].

Generally speaking, the most eminent men of the sixteenth and seventeenth centuries, whatever exceptions may be taken to their own theories, spoke reverentially of Christianity and the Scriptures. Bacon in various passages of his works, has emphatically declared his belief in revelation, and almost ostentatiously put forth his orthodoxy. Of Selden, Sir Mathew Hale who was one of his executors has declared, that he was a sincere Christian. Harrington and Sydney with all their republican

---

[1] The couplet on Falkland shows how highly his literary and theological accomplishments were estimated by his contemporaries.
"Though, to say the truth, and Apollo did know it,
He might have been both his priest and his poet."

[2] "Hariot," says Aubrey (Lives, vol. ii. p. 369), "made a Philosophicall Theologie, wherein he cast off the Old Testament, and then the New One would (consequently) have no foundation. He was a Deist. His doctrine he taught to Sir Walter Raleigh, Henry Earle of Northumberland, and some others. The divines of those times lookt on his manner of death (he dyed of an ulcer in his lippe) as a judgement upon him for nullifying the Scripture." Retailing the anecdotes of his time, the same author adds (ibid. ii. p. 519): "Raleigh was scandalized with Atheisme; he was a bold man, and would venture at discourse which was unpleasant to the churchmen."—"In his speech on the scaffold," it was said, "he spoke not one work of Christ, but of the great and incomprehensible God, with much zeal and adoration, so that," it was concluded, "he was an A-christ, not an Atheist." In Raleigh's Remains is a little piece called the 'Sceptic.' It has no direct religious bearing, but seems to have been only a sort of philosophical exercitation on man's liability to be deceived by his senses. In his 'Instructions to his Son,' his 'Advice to his Father,' his 'Letter to his Wife' after his condemnation, and throughout his 'History of the World,' there are passages which express strong religious feeling. The lines called the 'Pilgrimage' contain a more distinct reference to the objects of Christian faith; but, generally speaking, Raleigh's allusions to religion, though full of a solemn grandeur and melancholy, turn rather on its general truths than on the doctrines of the Church. Is not this also the case with his greater contemporary, Shakspeare?

enthusiasm express the same reverential spirit. Even Hobbes upheld Christianity as a beneficial institution, and maintained communion with the Church of England, when there could be no interested motive for his conduct[1]. Lord Herbert of Cherbury, a man of far more religious mind, while rejecting the particular revelation of Christianity, affirmed that the principles of a universal religion, including the belief in a moral government and a future life of retribution, were imprinted by God on the minds of all men, and that with these principles the doctrines of Scripture ultimately coincided. Christianity, therefore, was not so much disowned by him, as deprived of its special authority, and embraced in a more general system. It is said, that in his last illness, he wished to receive the sacrament, and applied to archbishop Usher, who refused to administer it. Lord Herbert of Cherbury died before the middle of the seventeenth century. The deistical theory, vanishing for the time in any conspicuous form with him, did not reappear till the close of the century. In the interval the inquiries of earnest and thoughtful minds, assuming Christianity as a divine fact, turned wholly on the mode of conceiving it, and on the interpretation of the books in which it is contained.

SECTION III.

REACTION AGAINST THE DOCTRINES OF THE FIRST REFORMERS.

The externality of the Roman Catholic system, the barrier of sacerdotal and saintly mediation which it interposed between the mind of the believer and Christ, and the stress

[1] See his Life in the Biographia Britannica. Notwithstanding his outward adherence to the Church of England, it appears from a very remarkable passage in the last chapter of the Leviathan, that Hobbes, like many of the most distinguished men of his time, approved of the *theory* of Independency. Speaking of the successive resolution of the old hierarchy into its constituent elements, first of Catholicism into Protestant Episcopacy, then of Episcopacy into Presbyterianism, and lastly of Presbyterianism into the "Independency of the Primitive Christians," he adds; "which, if it be without contention, and without measuring the doctrine of Christ by our affection to the person of his minister, *is perhaps the best*,"—assigning very sound and intelligible reasons for this opinion.

which it laid on the merit of mere works, produced an intense reaction among the Reformers, which determined the governing principle of their theology. The availableness of faith alone to salvation, and the reconciliation of the elect with God, through the atoning efficacy of Christ's blood and the imputation of his righteousness, became the great doctrines of the Reformation, equally recognized, with some modifications of detail, in the Lutheran and the Calvinistic churches. The heart exulted in the privilege of direct access to Christ and of unceasing communion with him. Faith was its joy and its triumph. Those high mysteries of the old theology, which had subsided, in the latter period of papal ascendency, into quiet traditional forms of thought, perhaps of mere expression, were now kindled into living convictions which absorbed the entire energy of the religious sentiment; and every approach to the latent Photinianism and Pelagianism which had once qualified their influence, was shrunk from with horror as the device of Antichrist to bring back the exploded iniquity of Popery. Christ and the Scriptures were the sole foundation of human hopes: it was impious to admit a moment's distrust of them. Of the two elements, the divine and the human, which are so wonderfully combined in the life of Christ, and which account for the different judgments respecting him, the former was elevated into prominence, and the latter kept almost out of view. To exalt faith and give it new merit, precisely those doctrines which are most at variance with the natural reason and moral feeling of mankind—the incarnation of deity, the atonement, election and reprobation, the final perseverance of saints—were most earnestly insisted on as the true orthodoxy. Such was the general character of the Reformed theology: we have an illustration of it in English Puritanism.

But it was soon perceived by reflecting minds, disgusted with the dogmatism and intolerance of the common herd of Protestant divines, that in shunning one extreme, the vehemence of public opinion had only gone into another; and a return towards a more liberal and moderate system was the consequence. Grotius and Leibnitz—the former the greatest jurist, the latter the most universal scholar and philosopher, of the seventeenth century, are known to have cherished the hope, that the differences between the old and the new Christianity might be reconciled, and were even charged by their enemies with being Papists[1]. Similar influences were not unfelt in England. The strength of the popular theology was deposited in two main articles: (1.) satisfaction to divine justice by the death of Christ for the salvation of the elect through faith alone, and the reversion in their case of the consequences of hereditary corruption; and (2.) the proper deity of Christ, qualifying him to make this full and effectual atonement. These dogmas were mutually related parts of a common system, recommended to the religious feeling of the time by the very wonder and mystery in which they were shrouded, and which it was deemed irreverent to attempt to penetrate. But to both of them opposition was now beginning to be made. The first was encountered by the Arminians or Remonstrants in Holland, with the concurrence and under the high authority of Grotius. At a still earlier period both had been rejected by a society of learned men in the north of Italy, which was afterwards dispersed by the Inquisition. Among these were the Socini, uncle and nephew, who afterwards sought refuge in Switzerland and Poland.

The Arminian and Socinian systems were not identical, but they had near affinities and grew out of a common tendency of mind. Both indicated a determination to quit the ground of authority or of mere appeal to enthusiastic feeling, and to bring the doctrines of religion to the test of conscience and the understanding. Arminianism was rather the dictate of moral sentiment; Socinianism, a product of the reason. Of both these systems the knowledge and the influence came into England immediately from Holland. The Socinians had at various times attempted to settle themselves in Holland; and although the Calvinistic synods always protested strongly against their toleration, several of them found shelter without being openly recognized among the Arminians. Even before the close of the sixteenth century, many of their writings had been translated and circulated in that country[2]. There was great religious intercourse and sympathy between Holland and England during the first half of the seventeenth century.

---

[1] Bayle mentions, to refute, the malignant and contradictory imputations to which the moderation of Grotius exposed him. Rivetus was his bitterest enemy. Dict. Hist. et Crit. Grotius.—Gibbon has described with epigrammatic point the comprehensive breadth of the creed of Leibnitz, in his 'Antiquities of the House of Brunswick.' Miscellaneous Works, 4to. vol. ii. p. 368.

[2] Bayle, Dict. Hist. et Crit. Socin, notes K. and L.

Thither the founders of Independency had fled from persecution at home; and there in 1618 the Synod of Dort, though it decided in favour of Calvinism, gave, as already remarked, a strong impulse to English theology in the opposite direction. It was at Dort, influenced by the powerful reasoning of Episcopius on John iii. 16, that Hales, to use his own words, "bid John Calvin good night[1]."

SECTION IV.

RISE OF LATITUDINARIAN PRINCIPLES.

It was in this state of things, while the contest between the Church and the Puritans was every day becoming more violent and implacable, that a small society of learned and intellectual men, keeping far aloof from the public strife, often met, before the breaking out of the war, for free religious discourse, at the seat of Lord Falkland near Oxford: "whose house," says Hyde who was one of the number, "looked like the University itself, by the company that was always found there[2]." Lord Falkland was a most accomplished man. In religion, with that high conscientiousness which was one of the noblest attributes of the period, he was so anxious to satisfy himself, by personal examination, on the great questions which then exercised men's minds, that "he read," we are told by the noble historian, "all the Greek and Latin Fathers, all the most allowed and authentic ecclesiastical writers, and all the Councils, with wonderful care and observation." If Aubrey's account may be trusted, he had passed through somewhat of the same discipline as his friend Chillingworth, without taking the same extreme course: for his mother being a Papist and anxious that her son should be of the same religion, he was early incited to a close study of the controversy between the Romanists and the Protestants.

What his religious opinions ultimately became, it is not easy to decide. That he always retained his faith in Christianity, there is no doubt. From the temper of the men who

---

[1] Farindon's Letter, prefixed to Hales's Golden Remains.
[2] Life of Edward, Earl of Clarendon, written by himself, vol. i. p. 33.

joined in these friendly conferences under his roof, we may not unreasonably infer, that, while they possibly differed from each other in their conception of points of doctrine, they agreed in the acknowledgment of certain broad fundamental principles affecting the heart and life. This, indeed, was the true spirit of Latitudinarianism. It was at Lord Falkland's house, after frequent debates on the leading points of the controversy, that Chillingworth conceived and executed his celebrated work on the Religion of Protestants. Falkland, Hales and Chillingworth have been called Socinians; but the term is employed in so loose a way, (the same individual, for example, being charged at once with Popery and Socinianism,) that no great stress can be laid on the statements of such a mere retailer of anecdotes as Aubrey. His account of Falkland's first becoming acquainted with the works of Socinus, is, however, probable in itself, and rests apparently on good authority. Cressy of Merton College Oxford, an Irish dean, and afterwards a Benedictine monk, told Aubrey, in 1669, who mentions the place and other circumstances of the meeting, that he was the first person who brought over Socinus's books; and that Lord Falkland, coming to him one day and casting his eye on them, was so taken with them, that he borrowed them to peruse. Aubrey dates Falkland's conversion to Socinianism from that time[1].

Hales was of a reserved and cautious temper; always seeking some middle point between extremes; and never disposed to commit himself to any strong dogmatic opinion[2]. The evidence for the Socinianism of Chillingworth is more satisfactory, though it is still inferential and constructive[3]. We

[1] Aubrey's Lives, vol. ii. p. 348. Wallace's Antitrinitarian Biography, vol. iii. p. 154. On the whole, it is most probable, that Falkland's theology inclined to Socinianism; though the letter of the Earl of Sunderland in the 'Sidney Papers' (cited by Wallace) seems in its most obvious construction to imply the reverse.

[2] See his 'Confession of the Trinity,' and his sermon 'Of Dealing with erring Christians.'

[3] In the last edition of the Biographia Britannica (1793) it is admitted, that Chillingworth, in the latter part of his life, became a Socinian. In the passage from the 'Sidney Papers' (vol. ii. p. 669) referred to in the preceding note, he is mentioned as defending Socinianism against Lord Falkland. See Carpenter's Reply to Archbishop Magee, p. 101, note. Dr Edwards, the Calvinistic defender of the Church of England, quoted by Peirce (Vindiciæ Fratr. Dissent. in Anglia, p. 154) does not hesitate to class Chillingworth with the Unitarians. Tillotson says, he was considered a Socinian " for no other cause but his worthy and successful attempts to make the Christian religion reasonable, and to dis-

run no risk in trusting Clarendon's account of the principles
of these celebrated men, since he could have no inducement to
overcharge them with freedom and scepticism. Of Chillingworth he says, "that in some particulars he allowed himself
to be overruled by the judgment of his friends, though in
others he still adhered to his own fancy, which was sceptical
enough, even in the highest points." He notices his wonderful skill in argument, which excited the admiration of Hobbes,
with its retroactive effect on his own mind; "that his scruples were assisted with all the strength of his own reason,"
so that "he contracted a habit of doubting, and by degrees
grew confident of nothing, and a sceptic at least in the greatest
mysteries of faith." The mind of Hales had less fire and power,
but was equally prone to freedom of speculation. The same
author tells us of him, that "he had contracted some opinions
which were not received, and would often say, his opinions,
he was sure, did him no harm, but he was far from being confident, that they might not do others harm; and therefore he
was very reserved in communicating what he thought himself
in those points in which he differed from what was received[1]."

The dogmatic spirit of the later Unitarianism has raised
questions with respect to the divines of this school, which it
was not in the nature of their system to afford them the means
of answering. The last thing they thought of, was the propagation of a particular doctrine: what they chiefly desired, was
to establish certain principles as the basis of universal Christian communion. Nor was their theory wholly new. It had
been introduced into England fifty years before by Acontius,
a learned Italian, who put it forth in a work entitled, "Stra-
tegemata Satanæ," which he inscribed to Queen Elizabeth.
His plan, according to the representation of an adversary, consisted in reducing the Christian doctrine to so small a number
of fundamentals, that all sects might be admitted to mutual
communion. It was a complete anticipation of Latitudinarianism[2]. This system accepted Christianity as a divine institu-

---

cover those firm and solid foundations upon which our faith is built." Birch's
Life of Tillotson, p. 6. The term Socinian was applied then, as it is still, with
extreme vagueness. Cheynell, in his "Rise, Growth and Danger of Socinianism, etc.," London, 1643, charges Laud, Potter, Hales and Chillingworth,
with favouring Arminianism, Socinianism and Popery. Des Maizeaux, "Historical and Critical Account of the Life and Writings of Chillingworth," p. 275.

[1] Clarendon's Life, vol. i. p. 32, 42, 44.
[2] Huic homini scopus fuit, ut ex toto libro apparet, ad tam pauca necessaria

tion, sustained by an external authority from the miraculous evidence which attested its origin; but as Jesus Christ had appointed no authorized interpreter, it left each man to follow his own judgment, and regarded all as Christians, who acknowledged the rule and obeyed the precepts of Scripture. This was the final conclusion of Chillingworth, expressed in the well-known aphorism; "The Bible, and the Bible only, is the religion of Protestants." The Latitudinarians, therefore, **took a** different ground from the High Church, the Puritans, **and the Deists.** From the two former they differed, in denying that there was any test of orthodoxy for the inquiring mind within the limits of Scripture, once ascertained by the unbroken testimony of ages to be the authentic word of God; from the latter, in asserting that there was, external to the Christian doctrine itself, such proof of miraculous demonstration in its behalf, as clearly established its divine authority. Hales for example makes the final test of a revelation to consist in miracles[1]. This was a new mode of reasoning, different at least from that which had been current among the Puritans. It is in strong contrast with the argument of his contemporary, Dr. Owen, on the same subject, who maintains, that the self-evidencing power of Scripture truth, is a surer test of divine authority than is afforded by miracles[2].

doctrinam Christianam arctare, ut omnibus sectis in Christianismo pateret aditus ad mutuam communionem." Rivetus (quoted by Bayle, Acontce). The learned Joseph Mede, who in point of time connects Acontius with Chillingworth and his contemporaries, belonged to the same school. He was anticalvinistic; desirous of peace by not insisting on non-essentials; and friendly to a union among all Protestants by keeping only to fundamentals. His life has been written by a Latitudinarian divine, Dr. John Worthington, Master of Jesus College, Cambridge, under the Protectorate.

[1] See among his "Miscellanies," the article, "How we come to know the Scriptures to be the Word of God."

[2] "Of the Divine Original, Authority, Self-evidencing Light and Power of the Scriptures. With an Answer to that Inquiry, How we know the Scripture to be the Word of God." Oxford, 1659. Owen has here argued the point with uncommon force and boldness. We trace in his views the strong Puritan hatred of tradition under any form. The substance of his reasoning may be thus stated. "The miracles alleged on behalf of Christianity, are reported in Scripture; Scripture is the medium through which we receive them; we must therefore have evidence on other grounds, that Scripture is the Word of God, before we can build our faith on the miracles which it reports." "For the proof," says he, "of the divine authority of the Scriptures, unto him or them, who as yet on no account whatever do *acknowledge* it, I shall only suppose, that by the providence of God, the Book itself be so brought unto him or them, as that he or they be engaged to the *consideration* of it, or do attend to the *reading* of it. This is the work of God's *providence* in the government of the

The position taken by Hales and the Latitudinarians of his school, was an approach to the rationalistic view of Christianity which gradually prevailed, and which acquired **ascendency** after the Revolution. One effect of it was the development of a branch of theological inquiry, called the Evidences, which

world; upon a supposal hereof, I leave the *word* with them; and if it evidence not itself unto their consciences, it is because they are *blinded by the God* of this world, which will be no plea for the refusal of it at the last day; and they who receive it not *on this ground*, will never receive it on any, as they ought." (Sect. 15.) " Abstracting then from the testimony given in the Scriptures to the *miracles* wrought by the prime revealers of the mind and will of God in the Word; and no *tolerable* assurance as to the business in hand, where a foundation is inquired after, can be given that ever any such miracles were wrought." (Sect. 17.) "Many writers of the Scripture *wrought no miracles*, and by this rule their writings are left to shift for themselves. Miracles, indeed, were necessary to take off all *prejudices* from the persons that brought any new doctrine from God; but the doctrine still evidenced itself. The Apostles converted many, where they wrought no miracles, Acts xvi. xvii. xviii.; and where they did so work, *they* for their *doctrine*, and not the doctrine on their account, was received. And the Scripture now hath no less evidence and demonstration in itself of its divinity than it had when by them it was preached." (Sect. **18.**) In the fifth article of the first chapter of the Westminster Confession of **Faith** ("Of the Holy Scriptures") it is declared, that while the testimony of the Church and the intrinsic excellencies of the sacred books are concurrent proofs of the divinity of Scripture, yet the full persuasion and assurance of its infallible truth and divine authority are derived "from the inward work of the Holy Spirit bearing witness by and with the word in our hearts." " I am now," says Baxter, "much more apprehensive than heretofore of the necessity of well-grounding men in their religion, and especially of the witness of the indwelling spirit: for I more sensibly perceive, that the *Spirit* is the great witness of Christ and Christianity to the world: and though the folly of fanatics tempted me long to overlook the strength of this testimony of the Spirit, while they placed it in a certain *internal assertion*, or enthusiastic inspiration; yet now I see that the Holy Ghost in another manner is the witness of Christ and his agent in the world: the Spirit in the prophets was his first witness; and the Spirit by miracles was the second; and the Spirit by renovation, sanctification, illumination, and consolation, assimilating the soul to Christ and heaven, is the continued witness to all true believers." Reliquiæ **Baxterianæ** (Part I. p. 127). Chillingworth's view is like that of Hales, and differs from the Puritan in laying more stress on tradition and miracle. Advising an inquirer, he says: "Tradition being such a principle as **may** be rested in, and which requires no other proof," he "would counsel him to rely upon it, and to believe that the book which we call Scripture, was confirmed abundantly by the works of God to be the Word of God." Answer to Charity maintained by Catholics (Ch. iv. § 53).

There were differences, however, among the **Puritans themselves.** Owen and the Independents generally were more rigid Scripturalists than Baxter **and the** Quakers. One other extract from Owen will set his view of Christian evidence in the clearest light. (Sect. 27.) "Though I should grant, that the Apostles and *penmen* of the Scriptures were persons of the greatest *industry, honesty, integrity, faithfulness, holiness* that ever lived in the world, as they were; and that they *wrote* nothing but what themselves had as good assurance of, as what men by their

is almost peculiar to modern Protestantism. From the proof of the genuineness and authenticity of the Sacred Books, and the inferred reality of the miracles and prophecies recorded in them, an external argument is derived for their divine authority, which is supposed to compel the assent of the mind to their doctrinal and preceptive contents. A tract by Hales 'On Schism and Schismatics' gives us an insight into the principles of his school. It was drawn from him, in consequence of a conversation with a friend on the improper use of the terms heretic and schismatic, and was only intended for circulation among his acquaintance in manuscript. Hales, while he freely communicated his ideas in private circles, was averse to publication; so that his great reputation, which procured him the title of the 'ever-memorable,' rests now rather on tradition and the deep impression which he made on his contemporaries, than on any extant monuments of learning and ability, at all proportionate to his extended fame. In this tract he argues, that "they are schismatics who by insisting on unnecessary terms of communion, not prescribed by Scripture, force others conscientiously to separate from them; and that all liturgies and public forms of service should contain only such matters as all Christians are agreed in; there would then be no schism."

The rise of Latitudinarianism is an interesting and significant phenomenon. It was plainly the effort of enlarged and contemplative minds, soaring above the narrow aims of the factions which encompassed them, to find a just medium between the divergent extremes of public opinion, and to reconcile mental progress with the preservation of institutions. The founders of the school were amiable, virtuous, and highly

---

senses of seeing and hearing are able to attain; yet such a knowledge and assurance is not a *sufficient foundation* for the faith of the Church of God: if they received not every word by *inspiration*, and that *evidencing* itself unto us, otherwise than by the authority of *their integrity*, it can be no foundation for us to build our faith upon." (Sect. 27.) Calvin had already taught the same doctrine: "Quod autem rogant: unde persuadebimur, a Deo fluxisse scripturam, nisi ad ecclesiæ decretum confugiamus? perinde est, ac si quis roget: unde discemus lucem discernere a tenebris, album a nigro, suave ab amaro." "Altius petenda est hæc persuasio, nempe ab arcano testimonio spiritus." "Sicuti Deus solus de se idoneus est testis in suo sermone ita etiam non antea fidem reperiet sermo in hominum cordibus, quam interiore spiritus testimonio obsignetur." "Idem spiritus qui per os prophetarum locutus est, in corda nostra penetret necesse est, ut persuadeat, fideliter protulisse quod divinitus erat mandatum." Instit. I. vii. 2, 4, quoted by Strauss, 'Christliche Glaubenslehre,' I. p. 134.

intellectual men. We are not conscious of injustice to their memory, in questioning the fitness of their principles for any deep and lasting influence on society, or in refusing them a place in the first rank of the guides and instructors of mankind. Their system, by seeking the evidence of divine authority, that which binds the reason and the conscience, in *outward* sanctions, placed it at too great a distance from common apprehension amidst the researches and conclusions which only the learned could pursue and entertain—at the end of a long series of historical testimonies and logical deductions. At the same time the very latitude of opinion which it allowed *within* the bounds of Scripture, however acceptable to the indolent indifference of speculative men, failed to arrest attention particularly on any one point of belief and endeavour as specially Christian, and acted with no strong and impulsive effect on the general mind. It was adapted to scholars, but unsuited to the multitude. The Latitudinarianism of these remarkable men was a step in the right direction towards a fuller discovery of religious and social truth; an important link in that chain of successive developments, on which the human mind is borne along towards some grand and comprehensive result which has yet to come : but as conceived by them, it can never be considered a final and complete adjustment of the civil and spiritual relations of society. The influence of the system on the minds of its most distinguished adherents, supplies no argument in its favour. They wanted that clear perception of the right in action, that strong faith and decision of purpose, which constitute the truly great character. The irresolution of Falkland, the timid caution of Hales, and the disingenuous compromise by which Chillingworth sullied the brightness of his early fame, appear to great disadvantage, as we look back on them through the rectifying light of time, in contrast with the high-souled enthusiasm of Milton, and the simple-minded, intrepid honesty of Baxter.

SECTION V.

EFFECT OF PHILOSOPHICAL THEORIES AND SCIENTIFIC DISCOVERIES.

The influence of the earliest Latitudinarians belongs to the first part of the seventeenth century, previous to the war; but their principles survived the troubled times which ensued, and gained new force from the intellectual tendencies that were developed in the midst of social disorganization. I have noticed, in a former chapter, the prosperous state of learning and the commencement of the Royal Society at Oxford, under the rule of the Independents. It was at Oxford that Hales, Chillingworth, and Falkland had formed their minds: and to the meeting in one centre of principles so apparently discordant as Independency and Latitudinarianism, neither of which could however be without effect on the adherents of the other, we may perhaps ascribe a portion of the mental vigour which distinguished the period, and which is so conspicuous in Wilkins and Locke. During the same time, a new spirit, itself the result of previous influences, broke out in the sister University. Here, as it has already been shown, before the end of the sixteenth century a reaction against Calvinism had set in; and this movement, though checked for the moment by Whitgift, continued silently to gather strength. Latitudinarianism spread from Oxford to Cambridge, where its principles were zealously espoused. In both places indeed it must be considered as a natural working of the time, strongly expressing itself through particular minds, rather than properly originating with them. Dr. Whichcote, Provost of King's College, Cambridge, a man of great reputation and influence in his day, disgusted with the dry, systematic divinity which had been hitherto in fashion, took a wider view of the nature of religion, and directed the attention of his students to the philosophical writers of antiquity, Plato and Cicero, not excluding the later Platonists[1]. A new species of theology, less confined by dogmatic particularity, free and all-embracing, and deeply tinctured with Platonism, began now to flourish at Cambridge,

---

[1] The spiritual affinities of the time, which it is so important to notice during this most interesting period, are indicated in the fact of John Goodwin, the Independent Arminian and republican, dedicating to Whichcote his famous work 'Redemption Redeemed,' in which he attempts to reconcile the doctrines of Calvin with Arminianism.

and bore its fruits in the writings of Cudworth and More. Glanville, a kindred spirit, was at Oxford. Cudworth applied his rich lore and speculative genius to **reconcile the doctrines of the Church with his favourite philosophy, and to fix the principles of morality on an immutable foundation.** Of his religious views early in life, and of the large, spiritual sense in which he embraced Christianity, we have a noble specimen, **teeming with a** latent poetry that continually breaks out into **passages of** genuine eloquence, in a discourse which he preached **before** the House of Commons in 1647. His object, he tells **us** in the dedication, "was not to contend for this or that opinion, but only to persuade men to the life of Christ, as the pith and kernel of all religion[1]." **More** embodied the doctrines **of** this philosophical school in **verse.** **His** Song of the Soul, "a Christiano-Platonical Display of Life," which, in the midst of mysticism and extravagance, is still **richly** fraught with beauties, conveys perhaps a better idea **of the religious** influences then predominant in the minds of many **speculative** men, than productions of a graver character, and is a complete outpouring of the Latitudinarian spirit, breathing a religion "full of charity,"—

"———— Free, large, e'en infinite,
Not wedged in strict particularity,
But grasping all in her vast active spright[2]."

[1] His great work 'On the Intellectual System of the Universe,'—the fruit of the studies of his life,—was not published till 1678, when he had reached an advanced age. It was designed as a confutation in the Platonic spirit of Atheistical necessity and materialism. Its doctrine of a plastic nature, gave rise to a controversy (see the Bibliothèque Choisie, V. iv. VI. vii.) between Bayle and Le Clerc. In 1733 it was translated into Latin by Mosheim, with copious illustrations from the treasures of his own neo-platonic lore. From a passage in Cudworth's preface to this work, we gather the fundamental principle of his Christian belief. "Scripture faith is not a mere believing of historical things, and upon inartificial arguments, or testimonies only; but a certain higher and diviner power in the soul that peculiarly correspondeth with the Deity."

[2] Book II. canto iii. 6. It was published in 1647. It has been remarked by one intimately acquainted with the literature of this period, that the noblest specimens of More's poetry are to met with in his **prose writings.** (Note of Mr. **James** Crossley to his edition of Worthington's 'Diary **and** Correspondence,' in the thirteenth **volume of the** Chetham Society's publications, p. 306.) Almost against himself, Mr. Crossley has quoted in the same note two exquisite specimens of More's English and Latin verse. His general remark is however fully borne **out** by the 'Divine Dialogues,' which, in their delightful **interspersion** of the subtlest disquisition with occasional touches of the richest **and** sweetest fancy, carry the mind back to Plato and forward to Berkeley. **How** delicious is his description (p. 138, 2nd edit. London: 1713) of the 'fresh evening air, wafted through the sides of the arbour, and steeped in the cooling

Tillotson was a student at Cambridge, when these men were in the vernal freshness of their powers, and lived in familiar intercourse with them: but his calmer temperament, intent on the practical and useful, and well disciplined by a close study of the works of Chillingworth, imbibed their large spirit of charity, without partaking of their poetry or venturing on their flights of Platonic speculation, and gave promise from the first of that quiet and moderate rationalism which marked the era of the Revolution[1].

beams of the moist moon, whose strained light through the shadow of the leaves casts a tremulous chequer on the table'! Compare another passage, p. 144. One of the most characteristic of More's works is his 'Treatise on Immortality,' 1659, of which Mr. Crossley gives an interesting account, with extracts, in another note to Worthington's 'Diary and Correspondence,' p. 121.

[1] Burnet's 'Own Times,' I. pp. 187–9. Birch's Life of Tillotson, p. 6. Latitudinarianism had several phases; it had its prosaic and its poetical side. In some it was severely rationalistic; in others it was highly spiritual and inclined to mysticism. An account of the 'Principles and Practices of the Latitudinarians in a Free Discourse between two intimate Friends' (known to be the work of Fowler, who was made bishop of Gloucester after the Revolution, 1st edit. 1670, 2nd 1671), exhibits the former aspect of this school; has more of Chillingworth than of Cudworth in its composition; and in the unrelieved flatness of its style, suggests an unfortunate comparison with the 'Divine Dialogues' of More. The writer indicates his theological position by refusing the witness of the Spirit, and denying the self-evidencing light of Scripture (pp. 55, 65), though his exceptions should perhaps be understood as applying only to the exaggerated statement of those doctrines. To the list of Platonizing Latitudinarians who belonged at this time to the University of Cambridge, must be added the names of George Rust and John Smith. Rust obtained preferment in Ireland after the Restoration through the interest of Jeremy Taylor, whose funeral sermon he preached. Smith's 'Select Discourses' were arranged and put together after his death from a confused mass of papers and edited by Dr. Worthington, a divine of the same school. Smith's conception of the prophetic spirit is highly characteristic. 'When we have once attained to a true sanctified frame of mind, we have then attained to the end of all prophecy, and see all divine truth that tends to the salvation of our souls in the divine light, which always shines in the purity and holiness of the New Creature, and so need no further miracle to confirm us in it' (Of Prophesie, p. 266). More in a beautiful passage of the 'Divine Dialogues' tells us in the same spirit, that amidst the "high noise and tempest of prophetic phrases and iconisms rattling about our ears and beating on our fancies, we are to lie low and couch close, and to listen to a more still, soft and intellectual voice, conveying a more inward and frugal instruction with it;"—and "sweetly charming our attention to her more calm and still whispers, while she more safely instructs us in the most true and useful meaning of the prophecies, as much as is sufficient to encourage us to side with truth, and faithfully to adhere to the interest of the kingdom of Christ,' p. 390. Penington, the Quaker, expresses substantially the same truth as these Latitudinarian divines, Smith and More, when he says, that "the Scriptures of the New Testament were written to the saints, and cannot be truly or rightly understood or made use of, but as men come into their spirit and state." (Letter lxxiv. from Reading Gaol, 1670.)—Mr. Crossley informs us in a note to

Although there is little affinity between the theories of Platonism, and the cautious induction leading to solid and practical results, which the new philosophy was now beginning to employ in the fields of natural science, for a time the two tendencies concurred in their effect on the mind. They joined in a determined revolt against the old Aristotelian despotism; in an effort to free the intellect from a superstitious reliance on mere abstractions, and induce it to open the living fountains of knowledge. There was much in the Baconian interrogation of nature to allure the Platonic appetite for the occult and the mysterious, and to confer a new interest on pursuits which explore the relations of the seen with the unseen. Among the first revivers of learning in Italy, were some enthusiastic Platonists. Chemistry, Astronomy and Physiology, the most advanced of our modern sciences, emerged, it is well known, from those twilight realms of thought, amidst which still flitted the shades of the later Platonism. A system may have value, simply from the new direction which it gives to the mind. The intellectual movement excited by Des Cartes and Gassendi on the continent, spread into England, and aided the effect of Lord Bacon's eloquent exposition of the true principles of scientific investigation: and this again contributed to the increase of knowledge and became the most glorious monument of the time, less perhaps from any positive result which it immediately yielded, than from the new spirit with which it impregnated the minds of all inquiring men.

Nor was it an age of speculation only. Every day the resources of the inductive system were developed by fresh achievements in art and science. If the sixteenth century had produced a vaster erudition, the seventeenth unfolded a clearer appreciation of principles and more efficient powers of original research. The profound philologists who had dug into the past, and brought up out of its depths the buried wisdom of antiquity, were succeeded by workmen of another order, who threw light into the darkness of the future, and marked out the regions which coming generations were des-

Worthington's Diary (p. 214) that he possesses a MS. of Glanville in continuation of Bacon's fragment 'The New Atlantis,' which concludes with a series of characters of the great divines of the day, Cudworth, More, Rust, Smith, Whichcote, etc. Everything relating to the Latitudinarianism of this time is so interesting, that it is to be wished so accomplished an editor would give the MS. to the world.

tined to possess and cultivate. The triumphs which the awakened intellect of man had gained over time, it was now preparing to carry into the boundless empire of space. And what splendid auguries of success presented themselves on every side! The discoveries of Kepler, Galileo and Harvey, and the inventions of Otto Guericke and Huygens, were so many outposts secured in the advancing conquest over nature, from which still bolder excursions could be made in every direction.

Thoughtful men, living in the midst of religious and civil discord, could not fail to contrast the quiet, steady progress of physical science with the hopeless logomachies of divines and political enthusiasts. For two centuries Europe had been the theatre of ceaseless revolution. France, Germany and England had been desolated with intestine war; Church and State were convulsed and torn asunder: and yet the questions for which men had fought, were neither settled nor understood; and the controversies of the theologians seemed as far from a solution as ever. Attention was therefore naturally directed to first principles. The true theory of government and society became a subject of deep and earnest study. In the speculations of Hobbes we discern the effort of a cold and subtle intellect to solve the embarrassing problems of the time. Filmer's patriarchal theory and the republicanism of Sidney's Discourses on Government which were written to confute it, are a manifestation in opposite directions of the same deep-felt want. The Oceana of Harrington addressed to Cromwell, which shadows forth the ideal of the true British constitution in Church and State, and Milton's Letter to Monk on the Means of a Free Commonwealth, though produced under very different circumstances, since the former was the fanciful production of learned leisure, and the latter called forth extemporaneously by the strong emergency of the times, alike bear witness to feelings universally predominant, and show with what earnestness men's minds were then exercised on the first principles of social organization.

In such theories the subject of religion could not but have a part; and their tendency was to simplify and rationalize the conception of it. The mind cast about for some firm ground of reason and moral feeling, on which it could take refuge from the vortex of incessant controversy. A sense of this want gave a wide diffusion to Latitudinarian principles. Glanville, imbued as he was with Platonic spiritualism, embraced nevertheless with great ardour the principles of the **inductive system** and associated them with Christian **theology.** He developed these views in various discourses; and for his endeavours to establish the harmony of reason and religion, he received the thanks of the Royal Society[1]. The Lecture **founded** by Boyle, that zealous cultivator of natural philosophy, was conceived in a similar spirit: it was not to enter into any controversies among Christians, but to defend their common religion against the objections of unbelievers. Bentley who preached the first course in 1692, applied the Newtonian theory of the Universe, then a novelty in the scientific world, to demonstrate the folly of Atheism. Even Baxter's views of the ground and measure of religious faith, were modified by these influences[2].

Harrington both in civil **and** in ecclesiastical **matters was** a great worshipper of "right reason," which **had become already** the accepted phrase. In his Oceana and other writings he attempted to reconcile a national religion with freedom of conscience. He took his general idea from the distinction between the priestly and the prophetic office in the Hebrew commonwealth; both which offices, he contended, were necessary and ought to be combined in a well-constituted **state.** Setting **out from** the threefold assumption; that the Scriptures cannot yield a national religion without a body of learned **men skilled in** the original languages, to interpret them; that such a body cannot permanently exist without an assured **maintenance and** well-appointed Universities **for their**

---

[1] Biographia Britannica, Glanville.

[2] "My certainty that I am **a** man, is before my certainty that there is a God; *quod facit notum est magis notum.*" He then proceeds through successive propositions with diminishing degrees of certainty down to the truth of particular doctrines and the canonicalness of certain books; and concludes thus: "They that will begin all their certainty with that of the truth of the Scripture, as the *principium cognoscendi*, may meet **me at the** same end; but **they** must give me leave to undertake to prove to a heathen or infidel, the being **of a** God, and the necessity of holiness and the certainty of a reward or punishment, **even while** he yet denieth the truth **of** Scripture, and in order to his **believing** it to be true." **Reliquiæ** Baxterianæ, § 212. 5.—This passage compared **with the extracts in note** of sect. iv. exhibits in strong contrast the different **character of** the minds **of** Owen and Baxter. Scripture was a self-evidencing *principium cognoscendi* with Owen. Baxter admitted to a large extent the principle of rationalism. The same contrast explains, why Owen's object was to gather a number of *pure* churches; Baxter's, to form a *comprehensive* one.

education; and that the majority of a nation have a right, without oppressing others, to satisfy their **religious wants** in their own way[1]; he proposed, that provision should be **made** for the support of public **worship and religious instruction in** every parish, out of the **national funds, whether** arising from tithes or from **any other source;** that on a benefice becoming vacant, **the elders of the parish should** apply to the University for **a successor to it, and after due** formalities should elect **him their** minister, this popular choice conferring on the **clergy their** sole ecclesiastical authority; and that while the national worship should be conducted according to a directory enacted by Parliament, the clergy should be left at full liberty to interpret the Scriptures for themselves. Thus was the Levitical or priestly element provided for, on which order, learning and civilization were supposed to depend: but along with this was conceded the full activity of the prophetic element, and the right to gather independent congregations, the members of which should enjoy **the same** civil privileges with those of the national religion, and be empowered to elect magistrates for the settlement **of** disputes among themselves, **or** for bringing their affairs, **if they thought** fit, before the Council of Religion **appointed** by **Parliament** for the defence **of** liberty **of conscience.** No Popish, Jewish, or idolatrous assemblies were to be tolerated[2]. Such was the ideal of a religious society conceived by an English scholar and gentleman in the time of the Commonwealth[3].

Among the remains of the poet Cowley, is a "Proposition

[1] "A commonwealth is nothing else but the national conscience; and if the **conviction of** a man's private conscience **produces his private religion, the** conviction of the national conscience **must produce a national religion."** Oceana, fol. p. 58. 3rd edit.

[2] Oceana, pp. 87, **127, 179.** Art of **Lawgiving, book iii. ch. ii.** p. 449. Political Aphorisms, pp. **505 and 516.**

[3] Harrington largely introduced the ballot **into the** working of his imaginary commonwealth, and thought it an indispensable **instrument** of pure and good government. He was a great admirer of the Venetian republic, and expressed his belief, that it would endure for ever. Some **fine** sentiments occur in his Aphorisms; e. g. " Man **may rather** be defined a **religious** than a rational creature; in regard that in **other** creatures, there **may be** something of reason, but there **is** nothing **of** religion." p. 516. In 1659 Baxter wrote his " Political Aphorisms or a Holy Commonwealth," to confute Harrington's " Oceana," and Sir H. **Vane's "** Endeavours **for a** Commonwealth." He thought Harrington's scheme heathenish, and that **Vane's** encouraged fanaticism; and was convinced that neither of them would take. In 1670 Baxter recalled his book, thinking it led to misapprehension **and** only did mischief. Reliquiæ Baxterianæ, part iii. **pp. 71, 72.**

for the advancement of Experimental Philosophy," by the establishment of a College, from which divines were to be as carefully excluded, as poets from the republic of Plato. Only the chaplain was to read prayers once a-day and preach and catechize on the Sunday; with the express understanding, however, "that he should not trouble himself and his auditors with the controversies of divinity, but teach God in his just commandments, and in his wonderful works[1]." It must have been feelings allied to these, weariness with the vain jargon of a technical theology, the want of a religion more pure, and loving, and spiritual, and perhaps some leaning towards mysticism, also a characteristic of the age, which urged men so highly cultivated and refined as Barclay and Penn, to embrace the principles of the Quakers. These tendencies were experienced by numbers who did not make the same outward profession. I have already alluded to the known predilections of Whitlocke, as evinced by his posthumous writings, and of that remarkable woman, Lady Conway, the patroness of Van Helmont, and the pupil of More. Of another learned lady of this age, the princess Palatine Elizabeth, granddaughter of James I., we are told that she had many conferences, and maintained a correspondence, with the founders of Quakerism[2]. The anecdotes which Aubrey has preserved of the poet Davenant and Hales of Eton, both men who had had extensive intercourse with the world, contain curious revelations of the secret working of the public mind. It was the private opinion of Davenant, that a hundred years after his time, religion would come to a settlement "in a kind of ingeniose Quakerism." Hales loved to read Stephanus, one of the Familists, whose tenets closely resembled those of the Quakers, and was accustomed to say, "that some time or other, these fine notions would take in the world[3]."

[1] Hartlib, to whom Milton addressed his 'Tractate on Education,' entertained a similar design of establishing a philosophical college. He alludes to it in his correspondence with Worthington, and still more frequently to a grander idea which he had conceived of a comprehensive society, quaintly designated by him Macaria (the Blessed), that was to combine in one connected scheme of operation, all the friends of science and religion. Evelyn was smitten with the same idea, and in a letter written to Boyle in 1659, draws out a plan. Worthington's Diary and Correspondence, with the editor's notes, pp. 149 and 163. These various projects are highly significant of the spirit of the age, and must be regarded as manifestations of the working of the new philosophy. The only permanent result of these efforts was the Royal Society.

[2] Worthington's Diary and Correspondence, p. 210, note.

Aubrey's Lives, II. pp. 310, 362. The significance of this period of our

SECTION VI.

FIRST SCHOOL OF ENGLISH UNITARIANISM.

While the Latitudinarian spirit was thus spreading among numbers of the learned and philosophical, opinions more positively dogmatic and Scriptural, but equally opposed to the received ecclesiastical theology, had taken root in various quarters among the people. When the Bible was first delivered to the multitudes in their native tongue, it is not surprising—so clear and distinct is the monotheism of both Testaments, and so beautifully human Christ's character and intercourse as described in the New—that, in spite of the efforts of their teachers to impress a particular doctrinal system on their

religious history, and the obvious tendency of the Latitudinarianism which so extensively pervaded it, have never yet been adequately appreciated. There was at that time a deep religious awakening of the human spirit, and a disposition in the best minds on all sides to coalesce in a broad and noble Catholicism, such as had never existed before, and of which there has been no revival since. It was the momentary gleam of a better day, soon darkened over again by a cloud of bigotry and intolerance thicker than ever. It was one of those lost opportunities of the past, of which history furnishes so mournful a catalogue. Baxter thus writes to Dr. Bates: 'On this occasion, Mr. Baxter becoming acquainted with the bishop (Usher), at last he treated with him about the necessary terms of concord between the Episcopal Divines and the Presbyterians, and such other Nonconformists: for you must know that in Worcestershire they had before attempted and agreed upon an Association, in which the Episcopal, Presbyterians, Independents, and the disengaged, consented to terms of love and concord in the practising of so much of discipline in their parishes as all the parties were agreed in (which was drawn up) and for bearing each other in the rest. Westmoreland and Cumberland and Essex and Hampshire and Wiltshire and Dorsetshire, quickly imitated them, and made the like association; and it was going on, and likely to have been commonly practised, till the return of the bishops after broke it. Mr. Baxter at the same time treated with bishop Browning and Dr. Hammond about the terms of the desired concord. But bishop Usher and he did most speedily agree.' From the Baxter MSS. in Dr. Williams's Library, London. Extracted in the Monthly Repository, vol. xx. p. 287. Adam Martindale, in his very curious and instructive autobiography, speaks of the year 1659 as a season 'When moderation was growne in fashion,' and he tells us, that Mr. Heyrick, at that time Warden of the Collegiate Church of Manchester, declared himself, at a much earlier period, somewhere about 1646, on coming down from the Westminster Assembly, "so perfect a Latitudinarian as to affirme that the *episcopall presbyterians*" (this expression should be noticed) "and independents might all practice according to their owne judgements, yet each by divine right." Chetham Publications, vol. iv. pp. 63 and 70.—One of the objects in which Hartlib and his friend Duræus (whose daughter married Oldenburgh, the secretary to the Royal Society and a correspondent of Spinoza) at this time took the deepest interest, was an attempt to unite all Protestants in one Church. Duræus, a Scotchman by birth, whose proper name was Dury, was almost a fanatic in this cause.

minds, not a few who were wholly unacquainted with the controversies of the learned, from merely studying the Scripture and following the dictates of their native sense and feeling, should have renounced the established system, and embraced the principles of Unitarianism. Traces of such views occur at a very early period of the Reformation, and are constantly associated with the tenets of Anabaptism; the same strict and simple Scripturalism, without any regard to the refined theories of theologians, leading naturally to both conclusions.

In the reign of Edward VI. a Dutchman, George Van Paris, was burnt to death in Smithfield at the instance of Cranmer, for denying the proper divinity of Christ. Under Mary when the control of the Protestant bishops was suspended, many heresies of a kindred nature broke out among the humbler class of reformers: some denying the godhead of Christ; some, his manhood; some, the godhead of the Holy Spirit; others, original sin. Arianism, Pelagianism and Docetism, were not unfrequent among the Anabaptists of this time. The orthodox Protestants were greatly scandalized at the prevalence of these errors, as affording the Catholics an argument against the Reformation. Hence we find strong protests against heresy, put forth with great sincerity, no doubt, but with equal inconsistency, by several of the Marian martyrs[1]. Some who were believers in the simple humanity of Christ, appear to have been loosely designated Arians. This was the case with Bartholomew Legate, whose tenets are recited at length by Fuller, and who was burnt alive at Smithfield for avowing them in March, 1612. Legate was admirably versed in the Scriptures, a ready disputant, and of unblemished character; on which the historian remarks, in his peculiar style, that "the poison of heretical doctrine is never more dangerous than when served in clean cups and washed dishes[2]." In the following month, according to Fuller, Edward Wightman, after sentence by Neile, bishop of the diocese, underwent a similar fate at Lichfield, for a complication of heresies which are all enumerated in the warrant for his burning, and among

---

[1] See Hutchinson's 'Image of God, or the Layman's Book,' dedicated to Cranmer; and Philpot's 'Jesus is God with us,' an Apology for spitting upon an Arian. Both these works are among the recent publications of the Parker Society. Compare also Strype's Eccles. Mem. II. 114, 348. V. 69–70. Neal, I. p. 41. Wallace's Antitrinitarian Biography, Historical Introduction, vol. i. pp. 3–31.

[2] Church History, Book X. Sect. iv. 6.

which are included the incompatible doctrines of Ebion and Arius[1].

The prosperous condition of the country during the half century which preceded the civil wars, its intercourse with Holland, and the universal interest in theological questions, aroused and opened the public mind, and stimulated to freedom of thinking even those classes which had no direct participation in the discussions of the learned. Influences escaping through a thousand apertures from the study and the university into the world at large, create in it a certain moral and intellectual atmosphere, by which the mass of ordinary minds is unconsciously affected. Indications are abundant, that during this period opinions at variance with the orthodoxy both of the hierarchy and of the Puritans, were spreading under the names of Socinianism and Arianism, among the people. The fourth of the canons that "were treated and agreed upon in the synods of London and York" in 1640, is expressly directed against Socinianism, and prohibits the importation, sale, or dispersion of books infected with this "damnable and cursed heresy," except in the case of certain privileged members of the Church and the Universities, who are specially described. As the learned were thus allowed the use of Socinian books, the prohibition must have been designed for the general public, and would never have been framed, had not books of this description been generally sought after. The poet Suckling, whose sphere was the world, and not the circle of the learned, included an article on Socinianism, in his "Discourse of Religion[2]." These heterodox opinions were not suppressed by the intolerance of the more powerful sects. Under the Long Parliament the doctrine was openly preached in the city, that "Christ was a prophet, and did miracles, but not God;" and Nye, we are informed, told some divines of the Assembly, that "to his knowledge, the denying of the divinity of Christ was a growing opinion." Edwards says, that tenets of this description found an entrance into some even of the Independent churches[3]. It was the belief of foreigners at this time, that the Socinian doctrine was widely spread through

---

[1] The Commission and Warrant are given in the Appendix to Crosby's History of the English Baptists, vol. i. No. 1.

[2] I have never seen Suckling's book, but I learn the fact from the twofold allusion to it, by Aubrey, vol. ii. pp. 548, 550.

[3] Gangræna; Letters and Narrations, pp. 26, 31, 32; Part II. pp. 13, 14.

the English nation. Dr. Owen writing against it in 1655, warns his reader, that "the evil is at the door, that there is not a city, a town, scarce a village in England, wherein some of this poison is not poured forth[1]." In April 1652 the sheriffs of London and Middlesex were directed by a resolution of the Parliament, to seize all the copies which they could find of the Racovian Catechism (drawn up originally for the use of the Polish Socinians and published at Racow), and cause them to be burned at the old Exchange, London, and the New Palace, Westminster[2].

These facts supply unquestionable proof of an extensive diffusion of Unitarian opinion; but as yet it had assumed no body and prominence. It was rather a latent element of thought silently circulated in books, than an open profession and worship; for no individual of eminent learning and high character had arisen, to preach it boldly in opposition to the general persuasion of the Christian world. Such an one at length appeared in the person of John Biddle, who to sound scholarship, and an acquaintance so intimate with the original Scriptures, that he could repeat in Greek almost the entire New Testament, united not only a clear and firm belief in the Unitarian doctrine and a dauntless zeal in its behalf, but also a strong persuasion, that he had a mission from heaven to propagate it in the world. He gave himself therefore to the work with all the courage and devotion of a martyr, and sought every opportunity of proclaiming and defending his views[3]. His zeal subjected him to persecution and imprisonment, and even his life might have been in danger from the intolerance still ascendant in the national councils, had not Cromwell interposed for his protection. Nevertheless he made many converts especially among the Anabaptists, and gathered a separate church in London. He appears to have been unacquainted with the works of the foreign Socinians, and had been led to his conclusions solely by private study and constant meditation on the Scriptures. We may almost describe his system as rudely scriptural. In his strict adherence to the biblical letter, he goes the whole length with

[1] Vindiciæ Evangelicæ; preface to the reader, p. 69.
[2] Dr. T. Rees has prefixed the parliamentary votes to his translation of this Catechism.
[3] See his "Letter to Sir H (arry) V (ane), a Member of the House of Commons" 1647, (in which he prayed to be heard before Parliament) in the first volume of the Old Unitarian Tracts.

Milton in his Treatise of Christian Doctrine, and betrays far more sympathy with the principles of Puritanism than of Latitudinarianism. In two Catechisms, published by him in 1654, he maintained that God is confined to a certain place; that he has a bodily shape; that he has passions; and that he is neither omnipotent nor unchangeable[1]. He admitted a Trinity of three divine persons, Father, Son, and Holy Spirit, but denied their equality or that these three persons were one God. The Father alone he acknowledged as God, in the highest and proper sense. Jesus Christ he regarded as our brother, and having no other than a human nature, " but also our Lord, yea, our God;" and in consequence of his divine sovereignty over us, entitled to a subordinate worship. The Holy Spirit also he considered to be a person, " the one principal minister of God and Christ, peculiarly sent from heaven to sanctify the Church, who by reason of his eminency and intimacy with God, is singled out of the number of the other heavenly ministers or angels, and comprised in the Holy Trinity, being the third person thereof." The doctrine of Christ's satisfaction to divine justice, and that of the two natures in Christ, on which the former doctrine is built, he rejected, as " a mere device of men, neither expressed in Scripture, or capable of being solidly deduced from it[2]."

Biddle had a great contempt for the scholastic subtleties of the popular theology. He says, his opponents " endeavoured to delude both themselves and others with personalities, moods, subsistences, and such like brain-sick notions, that have neither sap nor sense in them, and were first hatched by the subtilty of Satan, in the heads of Platonists, to pervert the worship of the true God[3]." The publication of such opinions caused a great sensation. When the two catechisms appeared, the Provincial Assembly of London, to counteract their effect, issued particular instructions for the education and catechizing of youth; and the Council of State thought them of sufficient importance to direct Owen, the most eminent of the Independent divines, to prepare a reply to them. Owen obeyed the summons; and his Vindiciæ Evangelicæ came out in the

---

[1] I make this statement on the authority of Neal, II. p. 470.

[2] A confession of Faith, touching the Holy Trinity according to the Scripture, 1648. Reprinted in the first volume of the Unitarian Tracts, 1691.

[3] Letter to Sir H. V., p. 18.

following year, 1655[1]. Biddle did not long survive the Restoration, but died in 1662, the victim of a close and very severe imprisonment; during which he often comforted himself with the remark, *that the work was done;* that the truth which God had raised him up to profess, was now sufficiently brought to light; so that there only needed ingenuousness in men, to induce them to embrace and acknowledge it[2]. Among those who attended on Mr. Biddle's ministry, after he had formed a separate congregation, was a young London apprentice who had been already converted to Arminianism by the preaching of John Goodwin, and whose zeal for his new instructor was so great, that he ventured, young as he was, to apply to Oliver Cromwell for his release from Newgate. Cromwell, pretending surprise but really tolerant at heart, said to him half jocosely, as the story goes, "You curlpate boy, do you think I will shew any favour to a man, who denies his Saviour and disturbs the government[3]?" This youth was Thomas Firmin,

[1] The title of Owen's book is "Vindiciæ Evangelicæ, or the Mystery of the Gospel vindicated, and Socinianism examined, in the consideration, etc., of a Scripture Catechism of J. Biddle; and also of the Catechism of Valentinus Smalcius, commonly called the Racovian Catechism; with a reply to Grotius's annotations on the Bible, etc., by John Owen, D.D., etc., Oxford, 1655. Dedicated to the Council of State and his Highness." In the epistle dedicatory to the Heads of Houses and other students of divinity at Oxford, Owen states, that Biddle's Catechism had spread into Holland, where it was replied to by several learned men, Arnoldus of Franeker and Maresius, professor at Groningen. The latter had charged the English nation with a general infection of Socinianism. Owen had corrected him in a private letter; although in the present work he seems to admit, as is evident from a passage already quoted, that there was some pretext for the charge. Owen remarks of Grotius, that he was suspected of Socinianism, though he leaned in some things to the Romanists; and observes of many who were in outward communion with the Church of Rome, that they were suspected of being privately Socinians. What he says of the execution of Servetus, deserves notice, as showing how ill he understood, with all his zeal for the rights of gathered churches, the true nature of religious liberty. "He is the only person in the world that I ever read or heard of, that ever died upon the account of religion, in reference to whom the zeal of them that put him to death may be acquitted. But of these things God will judge." p. 44.

[2] Short Account of the Life of John Biddle, M.A., sometime of Magdalen Hall, Oxford, in the first volume of the Old Unitarian Tracts.

[3] Birch's Life of Tillotson, p. 293, who quotes Kennet's Register and Chronicle, p. 761, as his authority. Godwin (History of the Commonwealth, IV. p. 325) treats the story as a pure fiction, partly from its internal improbability, partly from its inconsistency with chronology. As Firmin was born in 1632, if with Godwin we place this incident under the year 1655, just before Biddle's banishment to Scilly, it is no doubt exceedingly improbable. But if the imprisonment referred to be a previous one (for Biddle was several times imprisoned), at the beginning of the Commonwealth, early in 1650, the incident is

who afterwards acquired celebrity among his contemporaries, as an Unitarian and a philanthropist.

Few lives and characters present a greater contrast than those of Biddle and Firmin, though they entertained the same principles, and were devoted to a common cause. Biddle was a laborious scholar who wrought out his persuasion from assiduous study. Firmin was a simple citizen, wholly unacquainted with the learned languages, who embraced his opinions, because he felt them rational, and was convinced by his master's instructions. Biddle thought he served mankind by bearing fearless witness to the truth, and encountering reproach and persecution for its sake. Firmin spent his days in acts of practical benevolence, lived on terms of friendship with the clergy, and never separated himself from the communion of the Church. Poverty and opprobrium, the noisome dungeon, and the lonely rock of exile were the portion of one : while the other accumulated wealth, and enjoyed general respect and influence, and passed his leisure in the quiet retreats of pleasant gardens. Biddle's high conscientiousness required men to come out of the churches which he regarded as corrupt, and to renounce all outward conformity to the profession of error. The gentle and sanguine temper of Firmin led him to hope, that he could more effectually disseminate the truth by continuing where he was. If one had the courage of a martyr; the other glowed with all the zeal of a propagandist.

Firmin was charged by those who disliked his principles, with disingenuousness and timidity for remaining a conformist; and considering the decided nature of his opinions, it would doubtless have been more consistent to take another course. But allowance must be made for the influences by which he was surrounded, and the hopes which men of his cast of mind often allow themselves to entertain, of some possible change in the public service of the Establishment. He might shrink from the origination of new societies: and for one with his views, there was little to invite sympathy in any section of the Nonconformists, among whom orthodoxy was yet harsher and more intolerant than in the Church. In his days Tillotson, Patrick, Fowler, and other moderate divines of the same school, were popular preachers in the metropolis; and he enjoyed their

---

clearly within the limits of possibility, and agrees very well with the characteristic humour of Cromwell. If not true, it is at least *ben trovato*.

friendship, and was **admitted into** their society. He was a man, moreover, of the most extensive benevolence, **and** raised and contributed large sums for employing and improving **the** poor, and preventing mendicity[1]. No doubt he persuaded himself, that by setting up as a sectary, he should **at once** lose his greatest means of influence, and be deprived **of much** valuable co-operation. His charity was confined **within no** limits of sect or party. He set on foot a subscription **for the** relief of the deprived Non-jurors, and was only deterred from prosecuting it, by the assurance that he was aiding the enemies of government. When **the** Protestant refugees came **over from** France in 1680 and 1681, **he** collected the funds, **and** arranged the **plan,** for their reception and assistance. For this gratuitous **kindness of an Unitarian,** some of the French ministers afterwards **made an ungrateful return,** by giving secret information to **the civil and ecclesiastical courts of** unlicensed books and heterodox opinions[2]. Though **he did not** write himself, he was very active and liberal in **procuring and** circulating the productions of others, in defence of his **doctrinal** views; and to him, in this sense, it has been often supposed, that many of the old Unitarian tracts are ultimately due. To justify his continuance in the Church, he was accustomed to give a vague Sabellian interpretation to the language of its **public** formulary. Towards **the close** of his **life,** however, he became dissatisfied with **his conduct, convinced** perhaps by the proceedings **of Convocation, how vain** it was to look **for** any change in the liturgy; and **he** was preparing, it is said, to establish **congregations for the** open profession of Unitarianism, not by way of **schism,** but only as fraternities in the Church, when death intercepted his design[3].

Firmin's was not a solitary case. Milton's posthumous Treatise on Christian Doctrine, contains ample proof that he too must be classed with the Unitarians of this period. There

---

[1] In 1681 he published a Letter on this subject, **in which** he gave an account of a workhouse that he had established in London. Birch's Life of Tillotson, p. 293.

[2] Reflections on Two Discourses by **La Mothe, Unitarian Tracts, vol. ii.**

[3] Life of Firmin, written by an intimate acquaintance, 1698; with an account of Mr Firmin's religion appended, **p. 51.** Of Best, Webberley, Lushington and others who lived about **this time, and** belong **to the first** school of English Unitarianism, accurate notices will **be found** in the third volume of Wallace's Antitrinitarian Biography. The chief publisher of Unitarian works and others of similar character, during the Commonwealth, was Richard Moone, at the Seven Stars, St. Paul's Church Yard. Wallace, vol. i. p. 156.

is clear evidence, that from the accession of Charles II. to the Revolution, in spite of High Church doctrines and the professed Calvinism of most of the Dissenters, a strong and deepening under-current of theological rationalism was bearing some of the most influential minds of the period in an opposite direction. The Latitudinarianism so prevalent among the clergy, was believed by many on very plausible grounds, to be only a cover for heterodoxy. Edwards, a Calvinistic defender of the Church of England, boldly asserted, that a large body of the clergy were fast lapsing into Socinianism; and that they were providentially rescued from it by the imprudence of the Unitarians, whose fearless promulgation of their doctrine in all its strength, occasioned a reaction against it[1]. William Penn openly attacked the doctrines of the Trinity, Satisfaction, and Imputed Righteousness, and brought his arguments from Scripture testimony and right reason[2]. This was the very ground taken by Unitarian writers. Penn was answered by one formerly of his own persuasion, who charged him with Deism. The supposed affinity of these views with Deism, was hinted at in a very early stage of the controversy. Those who disliked them, affirmed that they necessarily led to that system; while those who embraced them, maintained that their general adoption would supersede it in the minds of all good men.

The anxieties which accompanied the first reign of James II., absorbed every other consideration; but when the Revolution was once settled, the Unitarian controversy broke out with great activity, giving birth to an immense number of tracts on all sides, and continued to engage the attention of the theological world during the last ten years of the seventeenth century. A new interest was imparted to it at the first, by King William's appointment of a commission to consider alterations in the rubric and liturgy. In 1693 a treatise in confutation of the Trinity was widely dispersed, and copies of it sent under cover to members of both Houses of Parliament. It was voted by the Lords an infamous and scandalous libel, and ordered to be burnt by the common hangman; and the Attorney-General was directed to prosecute its author,

[1] Peirce, Vindiciæ Fratrum Dissentientium in Anglia, p. 155.
[2] The Sandy Foundation Shaken, by William Penn, a builder on that Foundation which cannot be moved. London, printed for J. Johnson and Co. 1812.

printer, and publisher. The question was evidently regarded as one of vital importance, from the number of distinguished churchmen who took part in it, and who published explanations of the Trinity. Of these, the two most remarkable, as exhibiting the opposite points of theory, were Wallis, Savilian professor of geometry at Oxford, who sacrificed the trinity to preserve the unity, and Sherlock, afterwards Dean of St. Paul's, who for a contrary reason fell into actual tritheism. When Sherlock's treatise first appeared, it was applauded as a master-piece; but it was soon after attacked with much acuteness and great bitterness by South, the celebrated High-Church wit, who though really adopting the views of Wallis, seemed to avoid the extreme errors of both sides, and vindicated a theory which from the time of its acquiring authority in the Middle Ages, had been generally received as orthodox in the Church[1]. The dispute between South and Sherlock was carried on with so much heat, excited such vehement dissensions in the Church itself between the Nominalists and Realists, as those who supported the opposite views were called, and drew forth so many sarcastic observations from those who stood by and witnessed the affray, that it became a downright scandal to religion[2]. At length Tenison who had succeeded Tillotson at Canterbury, thought it necessary to interfere, and prohibited all allusion to the Trinity in sermons and discourses, except in Scripture language or terms already recognized by the Church, without any attempt at new modes of explanation. Howe, the Nonconformist, engaged in this controversy, and adopted almost the identical idea of Sherlock; but as they differed in the subordinate details of their theory, close agreement in essentials did not prevent some exchange of angry feeling between them. In 1695 Sherlock's exposition of the Trinity was condemned in a solemn decree of Convocation at Oxford, as false, impious, and heretical[3].

[1] He admitted that the three divine persons have "no real existence of their own, but are modes, habitudes, or affections of the divine substance—being such in spiritual and immaterial beings, that a posture is to a body." Quoted by Wallace, I. p. 264.

[2] It was ridiculed in a well-known ballad of the time, called the Battle Royal; which is given at length by Wallace, I. p. 351.

[3] Toulmin's Historical View of the State of the Protestant Dissenters from the Revolution to the accession of Queen Anne, Ch. II. sect. ii. A very full and accurate account of the Trinitarian controversy in the last ten years of the seventeenth century, derived from contemporary documents, is contained in Wallace's Historical Introduction to his Antitrinitarian Biography.

This controversy is important from its effects on the general progress of theological opinion. The Unitarians skilfully used the opportunity which it afforded, of calling attention to their views, and kept the press constantly in action with their publications, though the state of the law still rendered it necessary to write anonymously. Their tracts fill several volumes and nearly exhaust the Scriptural argument on the side of the Unitarians, abounding with proofs of learning and acuteness, conveyed in a clear, condensed and forcible style[1]. Reason and Scripture, the true grounds of a Christian's belief, are declared to give no support to the doctrine of the Trinity; which is traced under all its modifications to the principles of some philosophical school, and so has its roots not *in* Scripture, but *out* of Scripture. Thus Wallis's theory is called the Ciceronian Trinity, because justified by an expression found in the writings of the Roman philosopher; Sherlock's, the Cartesian; Cudworth's, the Platonic; South's, the Aristotelian or Peripatetic: while the Trinity of the multitude is resolved into their simple love of mystery[2].

These tracts show, that Unitarianism had now become a proper English opinion; since the writers are careful to insist on the several points in which they differed from the foreign Socinians. Socinus and Crell had questioned God's certain foreknowledge of contingent events: the English Unitarians believed in his absolute omniscience. The foreigners thought he was present every where only by knowledge and power: the English affirmed his essential, personal omnipresence. We see the effect of charges brought against them, in purifying their doctrine. They were accused of ascribing the same power and knowledge, and offering the same worship, to Christ, a mere man, as to Almighty God; but they replied, that they did not pay to Christ the same homage as to God, but something very inferior, no more than what most Trinitarians themselves paid to the human nature of Christ. They

---

[1] These tracts fill five or six volumes in small quarto. The three first are the most important; in the publication of which Firmin is supposed to have been largely concerned. It is indicative of the state of the times, that some of these volumes have no date on the title-page, no printer's or publisher's name, and no mention of the place of publication. The bibliography of these tracts for those who are curious in such matters, will be found in the Appendix to Wallace's Antitrinitarian Biography, No. XXIII. Compare the same work, I. p. 358.

[2] Considerations on the Explications of the Doctrine of the Trinity, etc., written to a Person of Quality. 1693. Tracts, vol. iii.

professed to follow, not the Polish Socinians, but Mr. Biddle, whom they looked up to as their acknowledged head[1].

Contemporary with this controversy about the Trinity, were discussions on other disputed points of theology, especially on those of Satisfaction and Imputed Righteousness. These had been first excited in the Church by the appearance of Bull's Harmonia Apostolica[2]; but they were soon warmly agitated among the Nonconformists, the Presbyterians generally taking one side and charging their opponents with Antinomianism, the Independents the other and accusing the Presbyterians of a tendency to Socinianism. A division in the Lectureship which they had hitherto jointly supported, was the consequence[3]. In 1690 after the passing of the Toleration Act, a plan of union had been proposed between Presbyterians and Independents, drawn up chiefly by Howe. It was designed, "not as a measure for any national constitution, but for the preservation of order in congregations," and was based on the simple knowledge of Scripture as the perfect and only rule of faith, to which the Articles of the Church of England and of the Westminster and Savoy Confessions, should be admitted to be agreeable. This measure was defeated by doctrinal jealousies between the two parties[4]. Questions of this description were not confined to the clergy, but largely interested the laity; and the discussion of them acted strongly on public opinion and confirmed its rationalistic tendency.

In the midst of these controversies most of the Protestant Dissenting meeting-houses were built, and the congregations assembling in them, acquired for the first time a permanent form and constitution. On the whole, Socinian opinions were more prevalent in the Church than among the Dissenters[5]. Firmin himself was an Episcopalian, warmly attached to the

---

[1] Before the close of the century, the Unitarians appear to have had separate places of worship of their own in London, the ministers of which were heretical offshoots from the Presbyterians. Wallace, i. p. 252, who cites as his authority, Leslie's "Socinian Controversy Discussed: London, 1708." Firmin towards the close of his life designed, as we have seen (p. 225), the setting up of a public meeting-place in the metropolis for the Unitarians.

[2] It was an attempt to reconcile the doctrinal views of Paul and James.

[3] Nelson's Life of Bull, pp. 257–276. In these disputes the Dissenters applied to Stillingfleet as an arbitrator.

[4] Howe's Life by Calamy, pp. 59–60.

[5] Pierce's Vindiciæ Fratrum Dissentientium, etc., P. II. ch. ii. De Socinianismo Ecclesiæ Anglicanæ attributo. p. 137. The statement is confirmed

idea of one Catholic indivisible Church, and had contracted from his Latitudinarian acquaintance a strong aversion to separation.

It may be taken, however, as a proof of the wide and deep influence of the Unitarian and kindred controversies, that the Presbyterians, with a wise foresight, not wishing to anticipate the issue of a question that was yet under examination, for the most part left the trusts of their meeting-houses quite open, providing simply for the public worship of God and the teaching of his Holy Gospel: or if any limitations were introduced, admitted such only as were necessary to bring the trust within the benefits of the Toleration Act. This was by no means an unimportant phenomenon, to mark the close of the century and accompany the first workings of the Revolution. It showed that the experience of the last age had not been without its effect.

SECTION VII.

INFLUENCE OF THE WRITINGS OF LOCKE.

In every period remarkable for a critical change in human affairs, some one mind may usually be singled out, that in a more peculiar manner expresses its spirit and embodies its results. If we take Cromwell and Milton as representing, one the civil and military, the other the spiritual, element of the Commonwealth; we may consider Locke as the intellectual symbol of the age of the Revolution. Not indeed that he represents the Revolution itself: for it was not brought about by his influence; and his chief works, including his political tracts, appeared subsequent to it; and as a fact it fell very far below his principles. But his mind in its various forms of religious and philosophical manifestation, supplies the spiritual links which connect the great movements of the seventeenth, with the tranquil progress of the eighteenth, century. His cautious, thoughtful, practical understanding drew a deep moral from the exciting drama of which he had

by Palmer in his Vindication of Dissenting Academies from the attacks of Samuel Wesley. He speaks of "troops of Unitarian and Socinian writers, and not one Dissenter is found among them." This was in 1705.

witnessed the closing scenes; and delivered it to the world in short unpretending treatises filled with wisdom, popular and attractive at once from their marvellous clearness and simplicity and from their ready applicability to the most important of human concerns. It is perhaps the chief praise of the Revolution, that it furnished an immediate and assured, though a limited, stage for calling out and exhibiting in progressive expansion, the fruitful principles condensed in the writings of Locke. He was the genius that watched over and guarded the critical period of transition—the solemn " breathing moment on the bridge of Time." His education, the materials from which he reasoned, and the influences which directed his inquiries, all belong to the age that was then passing away: but his results, his conclusions, and the powerful sway he was destined to exercise over the human mind, connect him with a new age of very different character, of which he was permitted to behold only the commencement.

His great works, those by which he moulded the opinions of posterity, were the fruit of his latter years. The principles of civil and religious freedom which his writings disseminated, if, in passing through his masculine intellect, they lost something of the poetic beauty and speculative grandeur of their original conception in the minds of his predecessors, were stripped of useless adjuncts, reduced to clearness and precision, and put into a shape for being dealt with by practical men in the actual affairs of the world. The subjects of his various works announce the character of his mind, and the kind of service which he was fitted to render to his contemporaries and their descendants. They treat of government, of religion, and of the foundations of knowledge in the constitution of the mind. They propose to settle on a rational basis without assumption or theory, those great questions of human well-being, lying at the very foundation of society, conflicting views of which had caused the strife and bloodshed of the preceding century. This was the governing idea of his life; and in reference to this, we must estimate and interpret his works. Their influence on the progress of religious opinion, is the immediate object of our present inquiry.

Locke's history and early connections throw light on the formation of his mind, and the growth of those views which he has developed in his Letters on Toleration, his Essay on the Human Understanding, his Reasonableness of Christianity, and his Commentaries on the Epistles of Paul. He was born of Puritan parents; and after completing his school education, was entered of Christ Church Oxford, where Penn was his fellow-student, at the time when Owen was Dean, and the University under the rule of the Independents. At Oxford he applied himself to the philosophy of Des Cartes; but his inclination led him peculiarly to the study of physic and natural philosophy; and while the Royal Society was yet in its infancy, we find him interested in the researches of Boyle, and making observations on the properties of air[1]. In after life he was brought much under Latitudinarian influence. Whichcote was his favourite preacher; and the friend of his age, at whose house he breathed his last, was the daughter of Cudworth[2]. His connections with Shaftesbury, to whom he continued steadily attached through all changes of fortune, introduced him to public affairs, and gave him an insight into the secret springs and working of government. At the request of Shaftesbury, he sketched out a form of constitution for the province of Carolina, in the religious part of which he adopted the principles afterwards more fully expounded in his Letters on Toleration, granting equal favour, protection and civil rights to all who acknowledged a God, whether Christian, Jews, or Heathens. In this bold suggestion he was before his time; and the clause which contained it, was against his own judgment expunged[3]. In 1682 he accompanied his patron into Holland; and there he remained till after the Revolution. During his absence he fell under the suspicions of the English Court, and at the King's command was deprived of his studentship at Christ Church. In Holland he cultivated an intimate acquaintance with Le Clerc and Limborch, divines of the Remonstrant school, distinguished for their learning and freedom of thinking, and held weekly conferences with them at Amsterdam. Under these influences he completed his Essay which he had commenced many years before, and wrote his first Letter on Toleration. In 1689 he returned to England in the same fleet with the Princess of Orange; and the fifteen last years of his life, spent chiefly in rural retirement, he devoted to study and composition, in

---

[1] His observations were published at the end of a posthumous work of Boyle's entitled, "A General History of the Air."
[2] Lady Masham, the wife of Sir Francis Masham, of Oates in Essex.
[3] Biographia Britann. Locke, note G.

which religion occupied an increasing share. His Reasonableness of Christianity and his Commentaries on Paul were written during this period. The latter did not appear till after his death.

The mind of Locke was thus trained up by a rare union of various influences, such as only an age of Revolution could supply, to survey in the broadest and clearest light the great subjects to which he devoted his powers. His native genius at once prudent and sagacious, bold without any tendency to extravagance, and imbued from early years with a deep sense of religion, derived from the different schools of the Independents and the Latitudinarians, precisely those elements of opinion hitherto uncombined, which enabled it to apprehend the true idea of Toleration; so that in him tendencies apparently discordant blended in harmonious action and found a common issue. On the other hand, his travels and acute observation of men and things, his intercourse with foreign divines and his large experience of affairs, raised him far above the narrow vision of a mere theologian of the closet; placed religion before him in its actual relation to society; and tempered his speculations on Church and State with the comprehensive views and practical wisdom of a statesman and man of the world. It is not often that such qualifications for judging rightly on moral and social topics, meet in one individual.

His celebrated Essay was the first undertaken of all his works, and grew from small beginnings, by successive accretions in the course of many years, to the form in which we now possess it. He has told us himself, that its origin was accidental, and arose from his being made to feel, in a discussion on another subject, the necessity of ascertaining the grounds, and determining the limits, of knowledge within the mind itself[1]. The importance of a rational foundation for our opinions was the suggesting principle of his inquiry: and this idea followed him into all his other speculations; so that in this sense, the Essay on the Human Understanding may be regarded as the matrix of his subsequent works. In the pursuit of this object, he swept away the entire system of innate ideas, that accumulation of assumptions, in which the philosophy and theology of the past age had taken refuge from the penetrating attacks of reason. He sought for the ultimate source of know-

[1] In his Epistle to the Reader.

ledge and ground of certainty, not in abstractions—which he treated as gratuitous figments of the mind—but in facts of a twofold order, which admitted no dispute; the impressions of sense, and the suggestions of consciousness. The mind came into the world, he contended, a mere *tabula rasa,* and derived the ideas which furnish the materials of all its knowledge, exclusively from this twofold experience. It may be questioned whether this view, called out by strong resistance to error in the opposite direction, embraces the entire subject of the mind, and does not rather limit itself to one side of it; whether it allows enough to the action, not indeed of *innate ideas,* but of *inherent tendencies,* some common to the race, some peculiar to individuals and giving birth to all the varieties of genius and character, which control the associations and determine the conclusions of the mind independent of external influence, and on some subjects yield a higher kind of certainty than is attainable by logical deduction from the simple facts of experience. Whether this be so or not, such was not the specific object of the mission of Locke. His business was to expose the pretensions of long-established error; to dissipate a baseless philosophy; and to clear away the ground for the unencumbered operations of a practical reason. Nor ought he to be blamed, because he saw nothing before him but the work which the age immediately required, and without exceeding the terms attached to it, executed it with great courage and singleness of purpose. The practical result of his Essay was this: that knowledge with the dispersion of the false appearances which usurp its name, is only to be gained, by forming clear and determinate ideas in the mind; distinctly apprehending the relations between them; and always designating the same idea, once defined, by the same term.

The bearing of these principles on certain theological controversies of the day, was soon perceived. Toland availed himself of them in his "Christianity not Mysterious." The Unitarians at once saw the new strength thus brought to their cause; and Stillingfleet in his Vindication of the Trinity, charged "this new way of ideas," as he contemptuously called it, with undermining the certainty of the greatest truths of religion[1].

---

[1] A controversy between Stillingfleet and Locke was the consequence. The substance of it is inserted in the margin of the Introduction to the Essay, in some editions.

Locke's own faith in Christianity was sincere and rational. In his Essay he has clearly distinguished the provinces of faith and reason; and fully admitted the possibility of a revelation attested by supernatural sanctions, coming in aid of the discoveries of our natural reason, on subjects which lie beyond the limits of experience. The times through which he had lived, filled him with great distrust of the pretensions of enthusiasm. He has a strong chapter on the subject, in the later editions of his Essay[1]. It was this feeling which led him to insist the more earnestly on miracles and the completion of prophecy, as outward signs necessary to establish the certainty of a revelation from heaven[2]. But while he thus conceded the need and the value of that external sanction, he still maintained, that not only the proof of its having been actually given, but also the credibility and the worth of the doctrine so attested, must be decided in the last resort by reason: since no accumulation of outward testimony could be so convincing as the sense of right and truth within, still less compel assent to any doctrine opposed to it[3]. He even goes beyond this, and makes the internal, the final criterion of the external, evidence, referring among other passages, for confirmation of this view, to Deuteronomy xiii. 1–5; and he says distinctly; "Even in those books which have the greatest proof of revelation from God, and the attestation of miracles to confirm their being so, the miracles are to be judged by the doctrine, and not the doctrine by the miracles[4]."

It was in truth the very rationalism of Locke, which attached him so strongly to the belief of a particular revelation miraculously witnessed. Only with extreme caution would he admit the possibility of any direct communication between

[1] Book IV. Ch. xix.
[2] Locke justifies Moses for not hearkening to the inward impulse to go to Pharaoh, till the miracle warranting it had been confirmed by another. Essay, IV. xix. § 15. In a posthumous Discourse on Miracles, (London, 1706,) he admits the possibility of other beings than God, and even beings hostile to God, exhibiting appearances which men cannot distinguish from an immediate act of divine power. He makes the evidence of a proper miracle, fitted to prove a divine revelation, consist in its superiority to every other demonstration of knowledge and power, confronted with it, as when the miracles of Moses overpowered the signs of the Egyptian magicians. It is proper to notice this; as Schlosser, in his History of the Eighteenth Century, has misrepresented Locke's opinions respecting miracles, and so classed him with the Christian deists.
[3] Essay, Book IV. Ch. xviii. xix.
[4] Locke's Journal, August and September 1681; February 1682. Life, etc., by Lord King, pp. 123–25.

the human soul and God; and every alleged instance of it he subjected to the most rigid scrutiny of reason and Scripture[1]. At the same time he was profoundly conscious of the immense importance of a positive religious sanction to human motives and hopes: and under these opposing considerations, that belief in divine influence and interposition which his philosophy all but excluded from the general providence of God, was concentrated by his deep and earnest piety with a redoubled interest in the special dispensations of Moses and Christ, which he regarded as the only certain media of supernatural communications to the human soul. The divine authority, therefore, of these two religions he laboured to establish, internally by a display of the beauty and excellence of their doctrine, and externally by the proof of miracles and prophecy, on the sure basis of reason. Locke was not the first to promulgate this view of the authority of Christianity. Hales had already encountered the pretensions of enthusiasm on the same ground[2]. But from his having so clearly laid down the first principles of reason in his Essay, and submitted Christianity to the same rational test as all other truths, almost to the denial of any witness of the spirit within, as well as from the wide diffusion which his great name gave to this conception of revealed religion among the divines of the eighteenth century —Mr. Locke may justly be pronounced the Father of English Rationalism.

He applied these principles in his celebrated apologetic treatise, the Reasonableness of Christianity. It was designed to shew, that all who receive Jesus Christ as the Messiah, whatever also they may hold in conjunction with that fundamental tenet, are Christians; and that Jesus is proved to be that high personage, as well by the sublimity and perfection of his doctrine and character, as by his miraculous powers and the fulfilment in him of ancient prophecy. Thus the question at issue between the Christian and the Deist, was reduced to the proof of the outward facts on which these exalted claims were advanced. This was taking a broad view of the case, hitherto unusual among theologians, and wonderfully simplified the definition of a Christian. Whether all difficulties were thus completely surmounted, and the ultimate ground of faith was put in the right place, may be open to question; but this is

[1] Essay, Book IV. xix. § 16.
[2] "How we know the Scriptures to be the Word of God:" in his Miscellanies.

not the place to pursue such an inquiry. Mr. Locke's views are noticed here as a sign of the age, as an indication of the bias by which its best minds were beginning to be swayed. We see in them a clear expression of the Latitudinarian spirit which his mind had so freely imbibed, no longer left vague and fluctuating as in the more imaginative speculations of Cudworth, but brought down into a definite form and reduced to a plain proposition by his direct and simple understanding. The temper of the Church had been recently excited by the Unitarian controversy; and our author's book, divesting Christianity of mystery, and annihilating at a stroke the exclusive pretensions of orthodoxy, could not expect any cordial reception among those who had arrayed themselves in defence of the Trinity and its associated doctrines. It met the fate of all books which exceed the measure of contemporaneous liberality. The worst designs were imputed to it; and Edwards made it the object of a direct attack in his "Socinianism Unmasked[1]."

Locke's Discourse on Toleration was probably a fruit of his close intercourse for several years with the Remonstrants of Amsterdam[2]. It was in Holland, 1689, that his first letter appeared, written in clear and fluent Latin, and addressed with initials to Limborch[3]. He afterwards translated it into English for the benefit of his countrymen. Its principles being assailed, he found it necessary to vindicate and still further develope them in two other letters, which greatly ex-

---

[1] "A Discourse, shewing the unreasonableness of a late writer's opinion concerning the Necessity of only one Article of Christian Faith," etc. London, 1696.

[2] In 1687, Locke formed a society with Le Clerc, Limborch and other friends in Amsterdam, for weekly discussions, "pour lesquelles," says Le Clerc, " on s'assembleroit tour à tour, tantôt chez les uns, et tantôt chez les autres, et où l'on proposeroit quelque question, sur laquelle chacun diroit son avis dans l'Assemblée suivante. J'ai encore les loix, qu'il souhaitoit qu'on observât, écrites de sa main en Latin." Bibliothèque Choisie, t. vi. p. 376.

[3] 'Epistola de Tolerantia ad clarissimum virum T·A·R·P·T·O·L·A· Scripta a P·A·P·O·I·L·A; i. e. Theologiæ apud Remonstrantes Professorem, Tyrannidis Osorem, Limburgium, Amstelodamiensem; Pacis Amico, Persecutionis Osore, Joanne Lockio, Anglo.' This singular title-page indicates the caution with which he still thought it necessary to write. The work appears to have been composed in the autumn of 1685, when he lay concealed in the house of a M. Veen at Amsterdam, for fear of being delivered up to the King of England. It was first printed at Tergou in 1689. Two impressions of the English translation appeared at London, in the course of 1690. Bibliothèque Choisie, VI. p. 375. Le Clerc is good authority for that part of Locke's life which was passed in Holland.

ceed in length the first. These again were followed, after an interval of twelve years, by a fourth. But his whole theory, stated with remarkable force and clearness, is contained in the first. He begins with an analysis of the ideas of Church and State; and on the distinction which he makes between religious and civil societies, as well in their ends as in their means, he founds his theory of their mutual independence and necessary separation. Its seminal principle is contained in this proposition: "That there is absolutely no such thing, under the Gospel, as a Christian Commonwealth[1]." The State, as such, knows nothing of religious differences; it is not a person; it has no conscience; and consequently it can have no religion. In these views, we trace the influence of Locke's philosophy. He loved the concrete in all things; and abhorred those personified abstractions in which folly and intolerance are wont to shroud themselves. It followed at once from his fundamental principle, that the magistrate has no right to control, or to notice in the way either of favour or of discouragement, any religious opinions and practices whatever, so long as they do not interfere with the civil order of society. Hence not only all Christian sects, but Jews, Mahometans and Pagans, while they keep within the limits of civil obedience, are equally entitled to the rights of citizens. To make his argument the more striking, Locke ingeniously supposes the case of Christians living under a Turkish government. In meeting the objection furnished by the Hebrew commonwealth, he argues, that the case of the Jews was a special one, arising from the intermixture and mutual assimilation of civil and religious elements in their theocracy; and that even with them the dependence of political rights on the worship of Jehovah, applied only to their own citizens, in whom apostasy involved treason. To this large toleration Locke admitted only two exceptions; in the case, first of Atheists, whom he considered unfit for citizenship, as incapable of obligation by oaths and promises; and secondly of those (he had no doubt the Papists in view) whose principles made them necessarily intolerant of others, and who owed allegiance to a foreign power.

It must be obvious on reflection, that in this scheme of toleration, Locke by excluding Atheists from its benefits, has

---

[1] Sub Evangelio nulla prorsus est respublica Christiana.

failed to establish the complete separation of **Church** and State, and admits the indispensableness of **some religion** for securing the ends of civil government. He takes for granted, that a sense of moral obligation cannot exist without a **distinct** religious belief; and invests the State with the very questionable power of penetrating to the inner sanctuary of the soul, and inferring a man's conduct from the assumed absence of a principle necessary to virtue. He requires the State to see that a man has some religion, though he will not allow it to decide which is the true religion, and to establish it. No one, in fact, can doubt, that religion does yield a great support to government **and law.** When **we have** resolved the ideas of Church and State into **their primitive elements,** however necessary it may be in **the present divided state of the** Christian world to keep them distinct, **we at once perceive,** that there is a close affinity and ready sympathy between **them; that they** pre-suppose each other's existence; and **are essential to each** other's completeness. Never yet, however, has it been possible to regulate their true mutual relation by any outward bond. It would seem, therefore, the most obvious course, to abandon all attempts to fix it by premature legislation; to release the two principles from a constrained and unnatural **alliance;** and to let them, each pursuing immediately its own ends without **encroachment on** the other's province, grow up into that state of full and healthy development which must impel them from **a sense** of common need, to enter spontaneously into a living and cordial union. The apparent impossibility of reconciling and combining in one system, the endless diversities of religious belief and religious practice, has driven most men who have any respect for the rights of conscience, to the negative result of separating Church and State.

A sense of these difficulties doubtless influenced the conclusions of Locke. In his invaluable treatise, the religious problem which had distracted the mind of Europe since the Reformation, most nearly reached its practical solution. "Narrowness of spirit on all sides," to use his own noble and vigorous language, "has undoubtedly been the principal occasion **of our miseries** and confusions. But whatever have been the occasion, it is now high time to seek for **a** thorough cure. **We have** need of more generous remedies than what have yet been made use of in our distemper. It is neither DECLARATIONS OF INDULGENCE, nor ACTS OF COMPREHENSION, such as have yet been practised or projected amongst us, that can do the work. The first will but palliate, the second increase, our evil. Absolute liberty—just and true liberty—equal and impartial liberty—is the thing that we stand in need of[1]."

It was fortunate for the progress of public opinion, that the appearance of Mr. Locke's works so generally involved him in controversy. This gave a wider dissemination to his principles, and caused them to be more thoroughly discussed; and excited an interest and an attention which their intrinsic worth might not else have occasioned. Their influence on the academies and churches of the Protestant Dissenters, then first settling down into a fixed state and constitution under the shelter of the Toleration Act, must have been incalculably great. This effect of them I shall presently notice again. An ardent enthusiasm for religious truth and liberty, was a striking feature in the character of Locke. He loved the simplicity of the primitive Gospel, and wished to see it restored. We discern this spirit in some rules which he drew up for a society of Pacific Christians in Holland on the principles of his own Letters on Toleration[2]. Among his papers, was found an unpublished Defence of Nonconformity, in reply to Stillingfleet's Unreasonableness of Separation[3]: and although to the end of his life, he never dissolved his communion with the Church of England, yet while he resided at Oates, as if to show his total indifference to the sacerdotal sanctions of religion, he generally attended the services of a lay-preacher in the neighbourhood[4].

In his latter years, Locke devoted himself to a close examination of the New Testament. Watts, in his Horæ Lyricæ, has alluded with evident satisfaction to the circumstance, in some lines addressed to Mr. Shute, afterwards Lord Barrington, on a dangerous sickness which threatened the philosopher's life[5]. It is to this period of Scriptural study, that

---

[1] To the Reader; prefixed to the First Letter concerning Toleration.
[2] Life by Lord King, p. 273.   [3] Ibid. p. 341.
[4] Editor of the Letters on Toleration, 1765, on the authority of persons then living.

[5] Reason at length submits to wear
   The wings of Faith; and lo, they rear
   Her chariot high, and nobly bear
   Her prophet to the skies.
                                    June, 1704.

we are indebted for those Commentaries on the Epistles of
Paul, with the Essay for the right understanding of the Apostle by comparing him with himself, which have furnished a
model to so many subsequent interpreters, and stimulated the
kindred labours of Peirce, Hallett, Benson, and Taylor. A
mode of exegesis was introduced by Locke, wholly different
from that which had prevailed among the Puritan divines of
the preceding century, who looked immediately to edification, and neglected the principles of rational criticism and exposition. With them every text of Scripture was as a voice
from heaven, speaking directly to the soul; and they interpreted it by the feelings which it spontaneously awakened.
The requirements of the context, the purpose and circumstances of the writer, and the influences of age and country,
entered comparatively little into their judgment of the signi-
fication of a passage, and were absorbed by the far deeper
consideration of their own spiritual state. They threw open
their Bibles with as little care or selection, as if they were
consulting the *sortes sacræ;* for their eye could not alight
amiss. Wherever it fell, it met with some expression, literal
or symbolical, of the eternal verities of the Christian faith.
The clear and simple reason of Locke perceived at once the
source of endless error that was opened by this mode of
proceeding, especially in a writer so broken and irregular in
his trains of reasoning, so full of latent meaning only to be
detected by a thoughtful survey of the general bearing of his
discourse, and so fraught with allusions to his age, and country, and situation—as Paul. He constructed his own Commentary, therefore, on the principle which he has fully explained in his Essay—of endeavouring to throw himself back
into the circumstances and feelings of the writer; apprehending from this point of view his particular line of argumen-
tation; and bringing all separate phrases and detached observations into connection by their common relation to it.
This was rationalizing the Bible. It was putting the interpretation of it on the same footing with that of other ancient
books. It was employing the aids of history, and the ordinary rules of grammar and logic, to find out what the Bible
actually said; where mere feeling and imagination, and notions
already in the mind, had been hitherto allowed to decide.
These principles were taken up and applied by the most eminent English divines of the eighteenth century; and borrowed

originally from them, gave the first impulse to that system of historical exegesis, which has been cultivated with such immense learning, and carried out to such bold results, by the great theologians of Germany.

It must not, however, be supposed, that this free employment of reason on the contents of Scripture, either weakened the faith or chilled the devotion of Locke. On the contrary, all his latest expressions of thought are tinged with a tender and earnest piety, as if they came from one who was living in the presence of God, and waiting for eternity. His death-bed confession of the vanity of life, though it has incurred the sarcasms of less religious philosophers, was the beautiful and solemn farewell of a resigned and devoted spirit, losing all sense of its own brief services to truth and humanity in the absorbing thought of God and the vast prospects of immortality[1]. It may be compared with the touching humility of Newton, as he gazed with childlike awe on the infinity of the universe whose deepest secrets he had brought to light, and spoke of his own discoveries in it as but the picking up of a few shells and pebbles on the shore of a boundless ocean. In an age of great intellectual excitement, when old opinions were fearlessly cast aside and the freest stimulus was given to the pursuit of truth, it is an impressive fact not lightly to be disregarded, that its two greatest philosophers, one leading on the van of moral science, the other conducting discovery with unexampled triumphs through the physical creation—should have stood firmly and devotedly by the religion of Jesus Christ; not simply paying it the respectful homage which is due to a venerable and beneficent belief, but subjecting its history and documents to a thoughtful scrutiny, and consecrating their high powers to its illustration and defence.

Locke has left behind him no explicit statement of his doctrinal views. He was too cautious to commit himself to a positive opinion, where there was still room for hesitation;

---

[1] Shaftesbury's Characteristics, vol. i. p. 302. Shaftesbury's sentiment is adopted by Conyers Middleton, in a letter to Warburton. Works, 4to, vol. ii. p. 475. Locke expressed the sentiment of his death-bed at the close of a letter which he addressed to Anthony Collins in 1704, the year of his death, to be delivered after his decease: "All the use to be made of it is, that this life is a scene of vanity that soon passes away, and affords no solid satisfaction but in the consciousness of doing well, and in the hopes of another life. This is what I say on experience, and what you will find to be true, when you come to make up the account. Adieu."

and his Latitudinarian spirit made him averse to creeds. But his Reasonableness of Christianity furnishes conclusive evidence, that he attached no importance to what is usually called orthodoxy. We may safely infer, that he was neither a Calvinist nor an Athanasian. In some of his controversies, he disowned the name of Socinian. Watts who in the fervour of youthful orthodoxy, though filled with admiration for his genius, had almost hesitated to give him a place in heaven, from the supposed tendency of "that unhappy book," the Reasonableness of Christianity,

"Where glimmering Reason with false lustre shines,"

felt relieved from his perplexity by the commentary on 2 Cor. v. 21, which gave him reason to believe, that Locke was no Socinian[1]. It is not improbable, that with his characteristic freedom from all party bias, he kept his judgment in suspense on some controverted texts. From his Adversaria Theologica[2], which were commenced in 1694, during the heat of the disputes about the Trinity, we may collect some idea of the tendency of his opinions. Here we find arguments and texts weighed against each other in parallel columns, with a preponderance almost uniformly against the orthodox view, and a continual reference to the writings of Biddle. Of his illustrious friend, Newton, there seems no reasonable ground to doubt, that his sentiments were simply Unitarian. Such facts are of importance in the history of opinion: but it was the large charity of these eminent men, their love of truth and virtue, and their freedom from a narrow dogmatism, which have given such a value to their example, and entitled them to lasting veneration[3].

Locke's close and rigorous mode of reasoning on topics, where assumption and dogmatism had been allowed a predominant sway, produced a wide and lasting effect. It operated

---

[1] Lines on Mr. Locke's Annotations, etc., left behind him at his death. Horæ Lyricæ, p. 140, with the note. The commentary referred to, has no decisive bearing on the question.

[2] Preserved in Lord King's Life of Locke, p. 337.

[3] The evidence of Sir Isaac Newton's Unitarianism in the stricter sense, rests on the explicit statement of an intimate friend, who was in office with him at the Mint, Hopton Haynes Esq., himself of the same opinion. See Lindsey's Sequel to the Apology on resigning the vicarage of Catterick, pp. 18–19; also his Historical View of the Unitarian Doctrine, etc., ch. vi. sect. v. The materials at present accessible for forming a judgment on the doctrinal views of Locke and Newton have been collected by Wallace in the third volume of his Antitrinitarian Biography, pp. 399–468.

both within and without the limits of the Scriptures. In the former case, it created a school of Christian Rationalism, acknowledging the reality of a divine revelation; in the latter, it called forth a remarkable display of Deism, or, as it was then called, of Freethinking. Deism professing itself unconvinced by the external evidence for the divine authority of the Bible, took its stand on the truths of natural religion; and from that point of view, pronounced a judgment on the origin, history and records of Christianity. Locke himself was not involved in the Deistical movement. Religiously conservative in all his habits of thought, he saw in the Gospel a positive aid and sanction to all the highest aspirations of man, which Deism destroyed without substituting an equivalent[1]. To the vindication of Scriptural theology on the principles of reason he devoted the closing labours of his life: but having inculcated and exemplified the freest exercise of the mental powers in the pursuit of truth, it was no more than he might expect, that some of his disciples should turn his own principle against doctrines which he himself revered as true and of the utmost importance. Each of these tendencies, the Christian and the Deistical, which arose out of the new impulse imparted by Locke to moral and religious inquiries, claims a separate notice. Between them they nearly embrace the whole spiritual history of the first half of the eighteenth century.

SECTION VIII.

CHRISTIAN RATIONALISM AFTER THE REVOLUTION: DISSENTING ACADEMIES: CHARACTER AND POSITION OF DODDRIDGE.

It has already been shown, that it was the effect of the Revolution to elevate, and bring into immediate connection

[1] " Mr. Locke disliked those authors that labour only to destroy, without establishing anything themselves. A building, said he, displeases them; they find great faults in it; let them demolish it, and welcome, provided they endeavour to raise another in its place, if it be possible." Costi's Character of Locke in a Letter to the author of *Nouvelles de la République des Lettres*. Feb. 1705. Locke's Works, fol. vol. iii. p. 658. 1759. Le Clerc has devoted an article to the memory of his illustrious friend, in the sixth volume of the Bibliothèque Choisie: *Éloge de feu Mr. Locke*.

with the government, that party in the Church which was latitudinarian in sentiment, and inclined to a liberal policy towards Dissenters. With these men there was a large party outside the Church, quite ready to sympathize; willing, in fact, to meet them half-way; and by the term Presbyterian which vaguely designated it, expressing little more than its Catholic spirit, and its disposition to own all practical Christians of every persuasion as brethren. This temper had been introduced among the Presbyterians by Marshall and Baxter; it was prolonged into the eighteenth century, by Howe and Calamy and Peirce. Between these two parties there was scarce any intelligible distinction but this; that the one was established, and the other not. Tillotson and Howe, Hoadly and Calamy, Burnet and Peirce, might almost have changed places, without finding it necessary to modify in any essential point their views of Christianity and the Church: except indeed, that among the Nonconformists, partly, no doubt, in consequence of their position, there was a closer adherence to the forms and phrases of the old Puritanic Calvinism; and that Hoadly's Latitudinarianism, with all his zeal for the Establishment, far exceeded that of his contemporaries. "I know many," says Calamy, "that the world calls Presbyterians, that are of no party." Still more explicitly he remarks on another occasion: "Those, (whether in or out of the Church) whose principles and spirit are against narrowing or straitening the terms of Christian communion, by adding to what our Lord has plainly appointed, are a very considerable and increasing number. Let such persons be in the Church, nay, and dignified in it too, and they shall yet be called Presbyterians[1]." The Tory fox-hunter in Addison's Freeholder, whose religion "consisted in hating Presbyterians," and who loved his spaniel, because "he had once like to have worried a Dissenting Teacher," thought the neighbouring shire very happy, for having "scarce a Presbyterian in it, except the Bishop[2]."

Such being the relation of a large body of the Dissenters to the most eminent personages in the Church, it may be asked, how it was that no union took place between them. There was an invincible obstacle; they differed about the lawfulness of the terms of conformity; the Low Churchmen not scrupling to make the subscription which in the actual state of

[1] Calamy's Defence of Moderate Nonconformity in reply to Hoadly and Ollyffe; 1703, p. 259, Part I.: also Postscript to P. I. p. 250. [2] No. 22.

parties, they could not hope to remove or qualify; the Dissenters objecting to it as unscriptural. With the most entire agreement, therefore, in their general views, they could not practically approximate: and the Revolution which strengthened the foundations of the Establishment, only increased their mutual alienation. The Churchmen thought the Dissenters unreasonable and scrupulous; the Dissenters charged the Churchmen with laxity. Constituted as the Church of England was, and encumbered with such a load of secular interests, the Presbyterians seem at a very early period to have abandoned all expectation of a comprehension. It was an object which they had earnestly desired; but they now looked upon it as only among the possibilities of a distant future. There is a remarkable coincidence in the language of their leaders, in referring all hope of such an event to some powerful effusion of the divine spirit on men's hearts, which should break up existing parties and re-constitute the Christian world.

The main controversy between the Church and the greatest part of the Dissenters, related now not so much either to doctrine or to government, as to the terms of Christian communion. These, it was contended by the Presbyterians, should be simply Scriptural. Calamy has thus stated the principles of Nonconformity, as they were then conceived: "That all true Church power must be founded on a divine commission" (*i. e.* derived from a Scriptural precept); "that where a right to command is not clear, evidence that obedience is a duty, is wanting; that more ought not to be made necessary for an entrance into the Church, than is necessary to the getting safe to heaven; that as long as unscriptural impositions are continued, a further reformation in the Church will be needful, in order to the more general and effectual reaching the great ends of Christianity; and that every man that must answer for himself hereafter, must judge for himself at present[1]." Of the ministers of this date in London, scarcely any one but Dr. Daniel Williams, the founder of the library which bears his name, is said to have been an assertor of the *jus divinum* of Presbyterianism. In Scotland Calamy found that doctrine generally abandoned. The Presbyterians had now taken broader ground.

[1] Dedication to Protestant Dissenting Ministers, p. xv., prefixed to the Continuation of the Account etc., 1727.

The spirit prevalent among them, is well illustrated by the case of Dr. Edmund Calamy, one of their most distinguished writers and preachers at the beginning of the last century; who was descended through his father and grandfather from the old Puritan divines of the Commonwealth, and connected them through his son in a line of unbroken filiation with the Dissenting Minister of modern times. On completing his studies in Holland, he settled privately at Oxford, that he might thoroughly master the question at issue between the Church and the Dissenters, and read attentively the great authorities on both sides. In spite of worldly allurements he deliberately took his lot with the Nonconformists, and avowedly in consequence of their freedom from those impositions that were attached to the ministry in the Establishment[1]. Before he assumed the pastoral office, he would willingly, he tells us, have received ordination from a bishop; "could he have found any one that would not have demanded a subscription and engagement to conformity and a subjection to the present ecclesiastical government[2]." His contemporary, Peirce of Exeter, though maintaining the validity of Presbyterian ordination, still for the sake of peace would not have objected to a modified Episcopacy, and a partial, well-regulated, use of liturgies[3]: nor would he, on the other hand, have disowned the ministry of those whose ordination he considered less regular, as derived simply from the popular choice, if they gave evidence of suitable qualification in other respects, and showed that Christ was with them[4]. In this healing spirit he published a sermon, entitled, "An useful Ministry, a valid one." These concessions indicate a latitude of principle that would have embraced a moderate Episcopacy and a sober Independency within the limits of the same Church.

As circumstances prevented the Presbyterians from putting their form of church government in practice, they soon ceased to attach much importance to the subject, and in their actual usage became Independents. Thus the whole of their attention was attracted exclusively to the other grounds of their separation from the Church; especially to their demand of a

---

[1] Life and Times, Vol. I.
[2] Defence of Moderate Nonconformity, Part I. p. 213.
[3] Vindication of the Dissenters, Part III. ch. iv., and ch. i.
[4] Defence of the Dissenting Ministry and Presbyterian Ordination. London, 1717.

faith and worship more strictly in accordance with the Scripture rule. This led to their general abandonment of all religious tests, beyond a simple acknowledgment of the divine authority of the Bible. A subscription to the doctrinal Articles of the Church of England was indeed required by law, to secure the benefits of the Toleration Act; but we learn from Calamy's example, how even that might be avoided; for he told a friend, he had never signed them himself, and recommended him to take the same course[1]. Events marked the progress of opinion. Towards the close of the Socinian controversy at the end of the preceding century, in the very year of Firmin's death, 1697, the Dissenters with Dr. Bates at their head, requested King William, in an address presented to him, to shut the press against the Unitarians[2]. The early part of the eighteenth century also was signalized by proceedings against Emlyn in Dublin, Peirce and Hallett at Exeter, and others of inferior note[3], for expressing antitrinitarian opinions. Yet in 1719, when the Exeter case was brought before the London Ministers, we find at their first meeting a majority of four, and at their second a minority of fifty to sixty, refusing to sign a declaration of belief in the Trinity[4]. Bradbury, a leader of the Independents, was the great promoter of subscription: the Presbyterians generally were opposed to it. Pamphlets swarmed on the occasion, which exhibited the question under all its aspects, and accelerated the progress of liberal ideas.

The effect of these discussions was not to establish any one doctrinal system, but to assert the exclusive authority of the Scriptures and the right of a free interpretation. The opinions of the great majority of the Dissenting Ministers were still probably orthodox, with a leaning in some towards antitrinitarianism: but the bond of union among the Presbyterians who still formed the largest and most powerful section of the Nonconformists, was the acceptance of the Bible alone as a rule of faith and practice for Christians. Thus a soil was prepared, in which Mr. Locke's philosophy struck a deep root and brought forth a harvest of rationalistic theology.

---

[1] Fox's Autobiography, quoted in the Historical Illustrations of the Hewley case, p. 36.
[2] Lindsey's Historical account of the Unitarian Doctrine, etc., p. 302.
[3] Tomkins of Newington, and Elwall the Quaker.
[4] Wilson's Dissenting Churches, III. pp. 517-20.

The Presbyterian theology of this period was in fact the offspring of an alliance between the new philosophy of Locke and the Scripturalism of the old Puritans. Scripture was accepted absolutely as a divine record, and rested on as an ultimate fact in the researches of the theologian. Locke himself would not have objected to this statement[1]. One of the most learned works produced among the Presbyterians at this time, is an elaborate proof of the canonical authority of the New Testament[2]. On that divine record, reason was to be exercised with the greatest freedom and impartiality; not only in eliciting its contents, but also in establishing their coincidence with those natural truths which the same reason as clearly affirmed. For the prosecution of such studies the Academies of the Dissenters were well adapted.

When the Act of Uniformity passed, many of the ejected ministers opened Academies for the teaching of University learning. This was done, not out of rivalry to the old seats of learning, but as a temporary resource; in the belief, that better times would come, and the restrictions on admission at Oxford and Cambridge, be taken away. It was not unusual for students at these private Academies to enter themselves also at some college in the Universities, where they still hoped, that they might hereafter with a change of times take a degree, and have their years of study passed elsewhere duly allowed. This was the advice frequently given to young men by Dr. Owen, who had once filled a post of high dignity at Oxford. Graduates moreover at the old Universities had taken an oath, prescribed by a very ancient statute[3], that they would not set up any other schools of the higher learning; and were prevented, therefore, as well by conscientious scruples, as by the troubled state of the times, from giving to their Academies a public character. Nevertheless, persons of great

---

[1] The profound Scripturalism of Locke, the fruit in part of his Puritanical education, is strongly expressed in the words, so often quoted, which occur in a letter to his cousin Richard King, written in 1703, only a year before his death 'Study the Holy Scriptures, especially the New Testament; therein are contained the words of eternal life; it has God for its author; Salvation for its end; and *Truth without any mixture of error for its matter.*' Biographia Britannica, Locke [B.B.], where this letter is referred to, as printed in Des Maizeaux's Collection.

[2] The posthumous work of Jeremiah Jones on the Canon.

[3] It had reference to the incipient Universities of Northampton and Stamford in the thirteenth century, and was now brought up against the Nonconformists.

eminence for learning and abilities engaged in these undertakings, and their lectures were often attended by pupils of rank. Harley afterwards Earl of Oxford and the celebrated St. John, Lord Bolingbroke, both so conspicuous in the councils of Queen Anne, received a part of their education in the Seminary of Mr. Woodhouse at Sheriff-hales in Shropshire[1].

After the Revolution Protestant Dissenters were recognized by the laws, and their institutions assumed of course an air of greater permanence and stability. Those of their youth who did not resort to the Universities of Holland and Scotland, continued to pursue their theological studies in the domestic establishments of the more learned of their ministers; of which there were many both in the provinces and in the immediate vicinity of London. Partly the force of usage, partly the old feeling of unwillingness to compete with the Universities, and a still lingering persuasion, that they were not for ever separated from the Church, deterred them from entertaining wider views and combining their resources to found a public College for the general education of their youth. The Institution at Warrington, celebrated by the muse of Barbauld, and adorned by the names of Taylor, Aikin, Priestley, and Wakefield among its teachers, was opened soon after the middle of the last century, and exhibits the first stage of the transition from the old private Academy to the Dissenting College of modern times, with its professors in various departments corresponding to the great divisions of the field of knowledge, and qualified at length through its incorporation with a national University, for the exercise of proper academic functions.

Looking back on the private Seminaries of our forefathers from our present advanced position, we naturally conclude, that their system of instruction must have been very limited and defective. We cannot conceive, how one tutor could efficiently embrace so many branches of instruction; while their insulation from the world in some remote province, the smallness of their libraries, and their want of an adequate philosophical apparatus, would seem to have withheld from the student some of the most essential requisites for the due enlargement and cultivation of his mind. These were undoubtedly great defects, but they were then of less relative

[1] Toulmin's Historical View of the State of Protestant Dissenters, etc., p. 230, and Appendix, No. V.

importance than they would be now; and they were counterbalanced by many advantages, especially in the actual circumstances of the Dissenters. It must not be overlooked, that their Academies were specially designed for the education of ministers. The attention of the pupil was carefully directed to the pursuits which were to qualify him for his sacred vocation in life; and with these pursuits, the whole spirit of the establishment and all its domestic arrangements were in unison. The Tutor was always among the most eminent in his denomination for learning and character; one, who had prepared himself for his task by long previous studies, and had reflected deeply on the chief subject of his lectures. Acting on his own responsibility and fettered by no code of academic restrictions, he was at liberty to introduce into his instructions all the new ideas of the time, and to examine them with perfect freedom. The very range and variety of the topics on which he was obliged to treat, though it involved much superficiality in detail as compared with our standard, had its use in widening and liberalizing his views; in opening before him a philosophical survey of the general relations of the field of knowledge; and infusing into his lectures a spirit of earnest and genial inquiry.

In these small establishments the personal influence of the Tutor was powerful and direct. Where he was able and popular, his mind became the actuating impulse of the whole society; and under his influence deeper religious impressions and a more ardent devotion to truth and liberty, were often imbibed, than could have been acquired in the promiscuous intercourse and general discipline of a great University. We possess from different sources, a pretty full account of the ordinary course of instruction in these Seminaries[1]. Logic, metaphysics, ethics and natural philosophy, with a due admixture of mathematical and classical reading, prepared the pupil for the higher studies of theology. Though less accurate and profound in certain kinds of learning, this course was favourably distinguished from that of the old Universities, in being more diversified and liberal, and keeping a more equal pace with the general progress of knowledge in the world. When Sir W. Jones was a student at Oxford in 1764, there

[1] Besides the information contained in the Diary and Correspondence of Doddridge, Butler and Secker, both of whom were brought up among the Dissenters, have left behind them notices of their early Academic studies.

was a fellow of the same college, who in reading Locke with his pupils, passed over all the passages where the philosopher attacks the old system[1]. It may be doubted, whether a parallel instance could have been produced from a Presbyterian Academy at a much earlier period. On the most important subjects, the Tutor systematized his instructions under brief heads drawn up by himself, with copious references to works for private study; so that the lectures of the Tutor were a sort of guide to the reading and reflections of the pupil. The object was less to impart a mass of information, which might be obtained from books, than to awaken inquiry and incite the mind to think. Speculative studies involving the fundamental questions of ethics and theology, usually predominated over the historical and purely philological, in the early Dissenting Academies. Doddridge gives us a very good idea of the usual mode of instruction, in describing the course of his own tutor, Mr. Jennings. He encouraged, we are told, the greatest freedom of inquiry, not according with the system of any particular body of men, but taking sometimes the Calvinistic, sometimes the Remonstrant, sometimes the Baxterian, sometimes the Socinian view, as truth and evidence might determine him; his care being to inspire his pupils with sentiments of catholicism, and to warn them against a zeal not according to knowledge[2]. Collins' famous Discourse on Freethinking was at that time openly circulated in the Academy, and "was agreeable enough," we are informed by Doddridge, "to some of his companions." These Seminaries did not consist exclusively of candidates for the ministry; young laymen intended for the professions and the higher walks of civil life, were often sent to them in preference to the Universities. Even the Church benefited by their fruits. Secker and Butler, two of its most eminent prelates in the eighteenth century, were educated in the Academy of Mr. Jones at Tewkesbury.

No institutions at present exist in England, which in their character and general influence can be altogether compared to the old Dissenting Academies. With a strictness of internal discipline, and a regular apportionment of hours to study, almost resembling the conventual system, they combined the amenities and sanctities of domestic life. The pu-

---

[1] Life, by Lord Teignmouth. 8vo, p. 55.
[2] Doddridge's Correspondence and Diary, vol. i. pp. 155, 198–199.

pils were the inmates of their Tutor's family, who presided over them as a gentleman in the midst of gentlemen. Not unfrequently the heads of these Academies were persons of good family, who had enjoyed extensive intercourse with the higher classes of society, and who tempered the severe character of the scholar and the divine with the courtesies and accomplishments of the man of the world. Considerable numbers of the gentry and a few of the nobility still adhered to the Presbyterian and Independent denominations; and this circumstance had its effect on the manners and bearing of those who looked forward to exercising their ministry among them. Young men dedicated themselves to the sacred profession under a profound sense of its importance and inherent dignity, and with that devotional fervour and those strong religious convictions which distinguished the early Nonconformists. These feelings accompanied the student to the Academy, where they were cherished in him by the habitudes and influences of the place, and entered deeply into all his studies and speculations. Religious exercises formed a large part of the ordinary discipline of the Academy. The Tutor and his pupils, not occupying the cold and distant relationship of professor and student at an University, felt themselves daily drawn towards each other by those sacred bonds of prayer which hold together the peace and unity of a Christian household.

It was in these retired seats of learning and piety, that the character of the old Protestant Dissenting Minister was formed. Here it acquired that union of intellectual freedom with spiritual earnestness, that catholicity of temper, that devotion to the cause of religious truth and civil liberty, and that ardent zeal for the promotion of knowledge and education, which were so widely disseminated by its influence through the middle class of the last century, and gave so strong an impulse to the progress of civilization in the chief centres of provincial life. In many of the principal towns of England there are schools and libraries, now exerting very powerful influence on society, which date their origin from the early and unbefriended efforts of the Nonconformists. The very insulation of their Academies which was in one sense an evil, contributed to uphold in full activity the principles which separated them as a peculiar people from the world, and which would have been overpowered at the old Universities by the superior attractions of the Establishment. Even High Churchmen were not blind to the advantages of such a course of discipline, for the future ministers of religion. Nelson in his Life of Bishop Bull, recommends the establishment of Seminaries distinct from the Universities, for the special training of candidates for holy orders[1].

Dissenting Academies were naturally an object of suspicion and dislike to the Church, as cherishing an interest in opposition to itself. Even Tillotson advised archbishop Sharp to withhold a license from Mr. Frankland's Seminary in the north of England, on the ground that he was violating the oath taken on graduation at the University[2]. At the beginning of the last century there was a sharp controversy on the subject of Academies, between the Rev. Samuel Wesley and the Rev. Samuel Palmer. The former, who was the father of the more celebrated man of the same name, had deserted the ranks of the Nonconformists, and now attacked with extreme bitterness the constitution and influence of their Seminaries[3]. The latter, who was a Dissenter, vindicated them. The controversy involves matters which are now completely forgotten; and has little interest for the modern reader, beyond indicating the social weight of the Dissenters at that time, and the strong apprehension of danger from their Academies, in drawing away great numbers of youth that would else be educated at the Universities[4].

The Protestant Dissenting Ministry never, perhaps, stood higher in public estimation for learning and general accomplishment, than during the period that the system of private Academies was in its greatest vigour. The first half of the last century was pre-eminently the age of learning among the Nonconformists. Nor was this distinction confined to one denomination; it applied to the Independents and to the Baptists, as well as to the Presbyterians. Among the Baptists, Dr. John Gale, who had studied in Holland with high repute under eminent divines and philologers, brought home with him from Leyden and Amsterdam, a great fund of critical

---

[1] Life, etc., p. 19.   [2] Birch's Life of Tillotson, p. 271.
[3] Letter from a Country Divine to his Friend in London, concerning the education of the Dissenters in their Private Academies, etc., 1703.
[4] This paper war spread over several years. On the question of the obligation of the University oath, see Calamy's Continuation, vol. i. pp. 177–197; vol. ii. pp. 731–735. Toulmin's Historical View, etc., ch. iii. sect. i., and Appendix, No. V. Toulmin has availed himself of MSS. in the possession of old Dissenting families.

learning; and while yet a young man, distinguished himself by a display of extensive acquaintance with Christian antiquity, in his answer to Wall's History of Infant Baptism. For some time he was chairman of a society for promoting the knowledge of the Scriptures, which met at Whiston's house in Hatton Garden. Liberal opinions must at this time have been making great progress in the Baptist body. Gale himself was decidedly anticalvinistic; and in the discussions at Salters' Hall in 1719 about the Trinity, we find him in the majority of 73 against subscription. His auditory at Paul's-alley, Barbican, is said to have been one of the most numerous and learned in London. We may conclude, therefore, that many of the intelligent and educated inquirers of that day were attracted and impressed by his representation of the doctrine and practice of the primitive Church. This we know, was the case with Whiston, who joined the Baptist church under the ministry of his successor, Dr. James Foster, whose pulpit oratory has been celebrated in a well-known couplet of Pope[1]. The piety, learning and accomplishments of Watts, are alone sufficient to confer honour on the Independents.

There was a general disposition among the leading men of the Three Denominations, to merge these sectional distinctions in the comprehensive title of Protestant Dissenter. It was a period of earnest eclecticism, in which men brought their learning and thoughtfulness to find out that common truth, which was believed to be dispersed and variously expressed among them all. In spite of the strong hold which the popular orthodoxy had early taken of his poetical temperament, Watts was deeply imbued with this Catholic spirit; and we have the authority of Lardner for stating, that his views in his closing years partook of the general tendency of the age towards Unitarianism[2]. The governing principle of

---

[1] Crosby's Hist. of English Baptists, vol. iv. pp. 366 et seq.; Wilson's Hist. and Antiquities of Dissenting Churches, vol. iii. p. 247. Pope's Epilogue to the Satires, 131.

[2] Belsham's Life of Lindsey, p. 219, note. Dr. Lardner in a correspondence with the Rev. Samuel Merivale of Exeter (the particulars of which were communicated by the latter to Dr. Priestley, then of Leeds, and to the Rev. Dr. Aikin, of Warrington), stated, that Dr. Watts's opinions on the Trinity, at the close of his life, were known to very few; that he had seen some of his papers, and that his last thoughts were completely Unitarian. From works published during his life-time, it is evident, that Watts deviated from the orthodox doctrine of the Trinity; and his notions on this subject embroiled him with Bradbury, the

his mind, which gathered strength as he advanced in life, was the love of all good men, whatever their doctrinal persuasion; and of this spirit he gave a beautiful instance in the directions left behind him at his death, that his remains should be borne to the grave by two Independent, two Presbyterian, and two Baptist ministers[1].

This truthful, catholic spirit of religious inquiry, was not limited to divines. The contemporary controversy with the Deists aroused the interest of all earnest minds, and quickened the desire to place the authority of Christianity on a basis of right reason. Many distinguished laymen, Sir Peter King, a kinsman of Locke, and ultimately Lord Chancellor, Shute, afterwards Lord Barrington, Sir Joseph Jekyll, Master of the Rolls, and Haynes, the friend of Newton, and a decided Unitarian—warmly participated in the learned and enlightened labours of the Nonconformist ministers, patronized and encouraged them, and sometimes employed their own pens with great effect in the same cause. Rationalistic preaching was decidedly in vogue with a large and influential portion of the public. On this ground we must partly account for the extraordinary popularity of Dr. James Foster just alluded to, whose discourses though distinguished rather by a clear and forcible reasoning than by what would now be called eloquence, were eagerly listened to by a "confluence of persons of every rank, station, and quality — wits, free-thinkers, and clergymen[2]." Even Doddridge whose genius was of a very different stamp, betrays various signs, particularly in his earlier correspondence, of the spirit of the times. He was suspected of verging towards Presbyterianism, (which was already considered less orthodox than Independency) and thought orthodoxy and good sense not always the most intimate friends. In arguing with a Deistical friend, he took the broad rationalistic ground, and admitted that "the perfections of God are the very basis on which the proof of any revelation must be built, and that, therefore, any pretended revelation which is contrary to these perfections, does in effect contradict itself, and subverts its own foundation[3]."

Independent, who was rigidly Trinitarian. Wilson's Dissenting Churches, vol. i. p. 306, note A.; III. p. 526.

[1] Doddridge's Correspondence, vol. v. p. 84.
[2] Dr. Caleb Fleming's Sermon on his Death, p. 15, quoted by Wilson, Dissenting Churches, II. p. 274.
[3] Correspondence, etc. I. p. 169; II. p. 311, 430.

The general object of the predominant theology was to establish the coincidence of Christianity with the principles of natural religion and reason : and the position to be maintained against the Deists was twofold—the evidence from history of the divine authority of the Scriptures, and the intrinsic beauty and reasonableness of their contents. This direction of the public mind introduced a calm, broad, ethical view of the Christian system, as an exposition of divine morality—with little to excite the feelings and act on the imagination. Doctrinal views held no very prominent place in the ordinary style of preaching, and possessed rather a negative than a positive influence—alluded to, if at all, chiefly to disown or explain the harsh and repulsive features of the old orthodoxy. Any strong expression of dogmatism, as the rallying-point of a party, was neither consistent with the unsettled and progressive state of theological opinion, nor with that pervading catholicity of spirit which distinguished the age. The Socinian controversy had nearly died away. In the Church, as well as among the Dissenters, the belief of great numbers of the learned might be described as Arian; a vague designation, which precluded the necessity of coming to a decision on some ambiguous texts, and embraced every gradation of opinion, from the confines of Athanasianism on the one hand, to the very verge of Socinianism on the other. To the prevalence of this doctrinal system the high name of Dr. Samuel Clarke, the conscientious sacrifices of Whiston, and the martyr-like renown which attached to the characters of Emlyn and Peirce, must doubtless have contributed.

There is much in the religious condition now described, to excite our sympathy and command our approval. It is a refreshing spectacle—not often witnessed in the history of Christianity—to see men of different denominations agreeing to lay aside their party names, and to assist each other in the pursuit of a common truth. And if churches were schools of philosophic discussion, or the Gospel were intended to promote abstract speculation, or men generally had leisure and inclination to engage in it—nothing could be imagined more consonant to the ends of such a dispensation, than the spirit which at this time pervaded the theological world. But such a spirit was not adapted to the wants of the multitude; it was not in harmony with a true conception of the nature and office of religion. Full of reverence for the new philosophy, and confounding religion with science, it applied to the one, without due discrimination, processes that belonged to the other. Men were to be reasoned into faith. A certain state of the affections, it was assumed, must inevitably ensue as the result of a logical deduction. Demonstration was the great ambition of the divine. He was to put down by the strong arm of argument the turbulent ebullitions of an insurrectionary understanding. From a simple postulate, the celebrated Dr. Clarke attempted to deduce, *à priori*, with mathematical certainty, the natural and moral attributes of God[1].

Two great deficiencies disqualified the theology of this period for producing any deep effect on the popular mind. It did not take sufficient note of those spontaneous suggestions and aspirations—that consciousness of frailty and transgression, and that inherent sense of something more pure and elevated, to be struggled after by prayer and a resolute will—which form the *matériel*, if we may so call it, of the religious sentiment in the human heart: and secondly, it did not present an object sufficiently distinct and interesting to the faith and spiritual affections of the great mass of men. It was too constantly employed upon the outworks of religion, proving to people *why* they ought to believe, and showing them the legitimate way to arrive at the faith; instead of producing the faith itself in their hearts, by appeals to their inmost conviction and deepest sympathies, and teaching them from the witness of their personal experience, what religion is. How could unscholastic minds derive any spiritual nutriment from abstract discussions on the divine attributes and the foundations of morals, or from elaborate proofs of the genuineness of the books of Scripture, and of the reality of miracles performed, and prophecies fulfilled, ages ago? They were craving for something which their imaginations could firmly grasp; to which their affections could cling; which they could realize in their daily experience, and verify in their habitual intercourse with the world. This, the smooth, unimpassioned style of preaching, which had now taken the place of the rugged but earnest oratory of the old Puritans, could not give. It wanted reality and application; it did not come home to the soul; it did not meet the demands of the inward life; and therefore in its

---

[1] 'Demonstration of the Being and Attributes of God, in answer more particularly to Hobbes and Spinoza.' Warburton supposed his *demonstration* of the Divine Legation of Moses " very little short of mathematical certainty." Book I. Sect. i.

general results it was not successful. **Such was** its predominant character. There were of course exceptions. Doddridge, for instance, was plain, earnest, and forcible in his pulpit addresses, much followed, well understood, and thoroughly relished by the humbler classes. But then Doddridge was remarkable for resisting in this respect the tendencies of the time. He was a student and a great admirer of the Puritan divines.

What has been said of the Dissenters, applies even more strongly to the Church during this period: and in both cases it was followed by the same effects—a decline of fervour and zeal, diminished attendance on the public services of religion, and a loss of hold on the popular affection. Before the middle of the century we hear complaints from all quarters of the general decay of religion, and in terms far too precise, in forms far too special, to admit of our understanding this as merely the ordinary exaggeration of religious rhetoric. As early as 1730, Doddridge gave to the world his 'Free Thoughts on the most probable mode of reviving the Dissenting Interest;' and pamphlets of similar purport and design were put forth about the same time by his contemporaries[1]. The growing wealth and prosperity of the country under the two first Georges, encouraged a general license of manners which the predominant forms of religion (for Methodism was yet in its infancy) were not strong enough to control. Infidelity and indifference to religion widely prevailed; and this " dissoluteness and contempt of principle in the higher part of the world," with the " profligate intemperance, and fearlessness of committing crimes in the lower[2]," excited the serious apprehensions of reflecting men. During the closing years of the reign of George II., we find Secker and Butler, in charges to their Clergy, and in occasional Sermons—and among the Dissenters, Dr. Leland, in his 'Letter on the Public Fast,' 1756[3], Towgood, in his 'Serious and Free Thoughts on the Present State of the Church and of Religion[4],' and Dr. Chandler, in his 'Case of Subscription, etc.,

---

[1] 'Free and Serious Remonstrance to Dissenting Ministers, on Occasion of the Decay of Religion,' by Nathaniel Neal, son of the Historian of the Puritans. Neither this pamphlet nor that of Doddridge have I been able to see.

[2] Expressions in a charge of Archbishop Secker's.

[3] Printed in the Supplement to his Review of the Deistical Writers.

[4] Humbly addressed in a Letter to the Right Rev. the Bishops, by a Christian. It was first published in 1755, and is appended to his work on Dissent from the Church of England.

impartially reviewed[1]'—all uniting, with a remarkable coincidence in their representations, to deplore the moral and spiritual condition of the country, and suggesting different remedies for the evil[2]. It is worth notice, that these publications allude to the efforts of Catholic emissaries in all quarters, to recover the people to the ancient faith of Europe[3].

Of the fact of wide-spread irreligion and great spiritual destitution at that time, more than half a century from the settlement of the Revolution, there cannot be a doubt; though different parties imputed it to a different cause. Churchmen generally ascribed it to the influence of the Freethinkers; the Freethinkers, to the Church itself. Some attributed it to the laxity of principle and latitudinarian spirit introduced and recognized by the Revolution; others, and especially the most eminent men among the Dissenters, to the failure of the Establishment to carry out the fundamental principle of its Protestant constitution, the restrictions on conscience which fettered it, and the general suspicion of hollowness and hypocrisy which attached to the clerical office and character[4]. The Ca-

---

[1] It appeared in 1748.

[2] To these Tracts, so strongly attesting the general irreligion and licentiousness of the age, may be added the conclusion of Dr. Hartley's 'Observations on Man,' written about the same time, which solemnly predicts the ruin of the existing states of Christendom from the prevalent corruption of manners.

[3] A few years afterwards, in 1774, Mr. Lindsey expresses his apprehensions on the same subject, in his Farewell Address to the Parishioners of Catterick.

[4] The spirit of the leaders of the Presbyterians in the first half of the eighteenth century, was moderate, conciliatory and liberal. It is well expressed by James Peirce in his 'Defence of the Dissenting Ministry and Presbyterian Ordination,' p. 60 (London, 1717): "Though I do not think it indifferent what party a man is of (for he certainly ought to be of that which he believes in his conscience is in the right), yet little stress do I lay upon this, in the matter of eternal salvation; being fully persuaded, that, 'as in every nation,' so in every party, 'he that fears God and works righteousness is accepted of him.' And I can truly say, with the excellent Archbishop Tillotson: 'I had much rather persuade any one to be a good man, than to be of any party or denomination whatever.' So essential do I esteem charity, moderation, and peace to Christianity, that I should very much dislike the Dissenters, if I saw as little of these among them, as I do among the High Churchmen."

The *principle* of an Establishment, conceived in a liberal, comprehensive spirit, was still maintained among them. As with Baxter, reform, not destruction, union rather than separation, was their aim. In Dr. Samuel Chandler's 'Case of Subscription to Explanatory Articles of Faith, etc.' (1748), he holds up the example of the Church of Geneva, as worthy of imitation, and quotes with high approval the speech of J. A. Turretin to the Lesser Council, on the abolition of all subscription. His doctrine is, that submission to Christ as the sole Head, is the only bond of union for Protestant Churches, and one much called for by the growth of infidelity on one hand, and the intrigues of Popish emissaries on

tholics, profiting by **the dissensions** among Protestants, threw the blame of all these **evils on the** Reformation itself, and maintained that they **were** a necessary consequence **of the** original **separation from Rome.** There was perhaps a portion of truth in all these representations—the last not excluded; but as none of them embraced the whole evil, none could suggest a sufficient remedy. In the meantime, large masses of society were estranged from religion and given up to vice: and this was enough to prove, that there must be something defective, something unsuited to the feeling and conception of **the multitude, in** the **doctrine or** the administration of the predominant religion, or perhaps in both.

At the time when the rationalistic tendency was widely dif-

the other. Acknowledging the genius of the **English and Genevese** Churches to be so **distinct,** that the **one** cannot **in all things furnish a rule for the other,** he still contends, that the former may remove **some** of her **enclosures,** without shaking her foundations, and open her bosom to receive many now excluded, into her communion and ministry—" by only altering things really alterable, and exceptionable in themselves, and only taking away a few others, that are inconsistent with true Protestantism, and prejudicial to religion and virtue **in** the midst of us." p. 179.

Towgood himself, whose work on 'Dissent from the Church of England' was long regarded as a standard authority, takes the same ground, and declares that the Dissenters, whose views he represents, are no enemies to the Church, but sincerely desirous of a coalition with it, if it were thoroughly reformed; and he **seems, moreover, to approve of** the Protestant Establishments of Scotland and **the Continent.** "The destruction of the Church of England," says he, "is what **we by no means wish" (p. 79); and** again (p. 245), "I verily believe, that, if such **concessions as a great part of our governors,** both in Church and State, would, I presume, **think it not unreasonable to make,** were made **to the Dissenters, there would be no unbecoming stiffness or aversion shown by the most** considerable part of them." **Such were the principles of what was then called** "Moderate Dissent." Since **that** time, Nonconformity has begun to assume a different ground. It either turns, as with the late Mr. Belsham, chiefly on *doctrinal* differences with the Church of England, or, as with many Unitarian, and nearly all orthodox, Dissenters, it rejects the principle of an Establishment **under** any modification. Thus latter ground of separation was not, however, **entirely** disregarded during the period of which I am speaking. In 1737 a **Tract** appeared under the title of ' Conscientious Nonconformity to every civil Establishment of Religion whatever, and to the English Establishment thereof in particular, considered and defended.' It is in the form of a dialogue between a clergyman and his **son who had become a** Nonconformist at the University. **The** Tract **is curious, as indicating the** contemporaneous state of opinion, and showing, **that the best known and most** influential of the Dissenters had abandoned their **Calvinism,** and become friends to a general Toleration, and were against submission to **human** tests and **standards** of Divine Truth. They are described **as** preaching **up** morality and practical religion, and distinguished from the Church by laying perhaps more stress on love to Christ, as a principle of action. The author ascribes the decline of their numbers and influence, which was already perceptible, to the great secular attractions of the Establishment.

fused, Watts earnestly contended for a different mode of preaching Christianity, and placed the consummating evidence of its divine authority in the testimony of man's own conscience and personal experience[1]. "A statue," says he, "hung round with moral sentences, or a marble pillar with divine truths inscribed upon it, may preach coldly to the understanding, while devotion freezes at the heart." He eloquently vindicates ". the movements of sacred passion," "life and zeal in the ministry of the word," though they may be "the ridicule of an age which pretends to nothing but calm reasoning;" and he tells us, that he has made it his aim to rescue appeals of this sort "from the charge of enthusiasm, and to put them in such a light as might show their perfect consistence with common sense and reason[2]."

[1] See his Three Sermons on the Inward Witness of Christianity, or, an Evidence of the Truth of the Gospel from its Divine Effects. 1720.

[2] Dedication to his Sermons. The following extracts from Watts's third Sermon on "The Inward Witness to Christianity," contain an element of valuable truth, and resemble passages in the writings of Cudworth and Channing. "Every true Christian has a sufficient argument and evidence to support his faith, without being able to prove the authority of any of the canonical writings. He may hold fast his religion, and be assured it is divine, though he cannot bring any learned proof, that the book that contains it, is divine too, nay, though the book itself should even happen to be lost or destroyed."—"In the first ages of Christianity, for several hundred years together, how few among the common people were able to read! How few could get the possession or the use of a Bible, when all sacred as well as profane books must be copied by writing! How few of the populace, in a large town or city, could obtain, or could use, any small part of Scripture, before the art of printing made the Word of God so common! And yet millions of them were regenerated, sanctified, and saved by the ministration of this Gospel. The sum, and sense, and substance, of this divine doctrine, communicated to the nations in various forms of speech, and in different phrases, made a divine impression on their minds, being attended by the power of the blessed Spirit; and while it stamped its own sacred image on their souls, it transformed their natures into holy and heavenly, and created so many new witnesses to the truth of the Gospel, for it began eternal life in them. Consider, then, Christians, and be convinced, that a Gospel has a more noble *inward witness* belonging to it, than is derived from ink and paper, from precise letters and syllables, etc." pp. 48–50. (Watts's Sermons, Vol. I. London, 1772.) The whole of this Third Sermon, though the author does not keep back his strong orthodoxy, is full of religious wisdom and Christian eloquence. I cannot refrain from bringing into comparison with it some beautiful passages in Cudworth's Sermon before the House of Common, 1647. "Though there be never such excellent truths concerning Christ and his Gospel set down in words and letters, yet they will be but unknown characters to us, until we have a living spirit within us that can decypher them; until the same spirit, by secret whispers in our hearts, do comment upon them which did at first indite them. There be many that understand the Greek and Hebrew of the Scripture, the original languages in which the text was written, that never understood the language of

Had more of this spirit remained among the Dissenters, associated with sound Biblical learning and general cultivation and guided by **good** taste, it would have preserved the religious life inherited from their forefathers; retained **the** affection and sympathy of their people; prevented the decline of **their** congregations; and superseded the **extravagance which** accompanied the revivals of Methodism. Had the Church also encouraged a religious ministration which met the spiritual necessities of the age, she might have guided and tempered it, and kept within her pale thousands that have now perhaps irrecoverably escaped **from** her control. But such would seem **to** be the **mysterious** condition of human

the Spirit. There is a caro and a spiritus, a *flesh* and a *spirit*, a body and a soul, in all the writings of the Scriptures. It **is but the flesh** and body of divine truth that is printed upon paper, which many **moths of books and** libraries do only feed upon,—many walking skeletons of knowledge, that bury and **entomb** truths in the living sepulchres of their souls, do only converse with; such as never did anything else but pick at the mere bark and rind of truths, and crack the shells of them. But there is a soul and spirit of divine truths that **could** never yet be congealed into ink, that could never be blotted upon paper, which by a secret traduction and conveyance, passeth from one soul unto another, being able to dwell or lodge nowhere but in a spiritual being, in a living thing, because itself is nothing but life and spirit." "Though the old **law** work us **into some outward** conformity to God's commandments, and so hath a good **effect upon the** world,—yet we are all this while but like dead instruments of music, **that sound** sweetly and harmoniously when they are only struck and **played upon from without** by the musician's hand, who hath the theory **and law of music** living within himself. But the second, the living law of the Gospel, the law of the Spirit of life within us, **is as if the soul** of music should incorporate itself with the **instrument and live in the** strings, and make **them** of their own accord, without any touch or impulse **from** without, **dance** up and **down**, and warble out their harmonies."—The secret **of all** religious influence seems to lie in the contagion of deep earnestness and genuine conviction. I know few things finer in the records of the spiritual life, than Penn's description of George Fox in prayer. "The *inwardness* and *weight* of his spirit, the *reverence* and *solemnity* of his address and behaviour, and the *fewness* and *fulness* of his words **have** often struck even *strangers* with *admiration*, as they used to reach others **with** *consolation*. The most *awful, living, reverent, frame* I ever felt or beheld, I **must** say was his in prayer. And truly it was a testimony he knew and lived **nearer** to the Lord than other men; for they that know him most will see most **reason to** approach him with reverence and fear." 'A brief Account etc. of the People called Quakers,' p. 108. London: 1708, 4th edition. See also a most solemn and affecting prayer, breathed forth **on** his deathbed by another simple and unlearned Quaker, a true follower **of** George Fox—in the 'Journal of the Life, Gospel Labours and Christian Experiences of John Woolman, etc.' Warrington: 1840, p. **172.** On reading such passages as these, one feels how eloquent beyond all human utterance, is the language of genuine faith, as it issues pure and fresh from the inmost depths of the subjected and trusting heart. With *facts* like these before him, no man can doubt that religion is a *reality*.

progress, that whenever two elements of thought and action are indispensable to it, they do not act together and quietly check each other, but operate alternately. They draw off into independent spheres, and carry on what should be their joint work by action and reaction. Of our country at least it is eminently characteristic, to separate rather than combine, for prosecuting the different, but related and mutually-essential, objects that are embraced in the general weal. Rational and critical inquiry was as necessary as the preservation of the devotional sentiment, to the growth and health of the religious life; and there is no reason in the nature of things, why the two tendencies might not have been associated, so as beneficially to stimulate and qualify each other. But the Church and the old Nonconformists were attached to their hereditary system and rationalistic style of instruction, and would not meet as they might have done the strong demands of the popular mind for more nourishing spiritual food. They kept themselves coldly and proudly aloof, full of alienation and distrust. The consequence was, that a new spirit arose, which infected all ranks with a contagious enthusiasm, and absorbed a large portion of the vital strength both of the Dissenters and the Church. Rationalism striking into a narrower dogmatic path, was content to gather to itself a small band of earnest and devoted followers, and to live on its own convictions in the hope of better days.

The first strong working of these divergent tendencies coincides with the most active period of Doddridge's ministerial life; and his tender, susceptible spirit, full of devotional enthusiasm and all the poetry of religion, yet withal learned and highly accomplished—was perplexed and embarrassed by the incompatible claims they made upon him. He had spent his early years amidst rationalistic influences; and in passing through the usual discipline of a Dissenting Academy, had entered freely into the religious and philosophical controversies of the time. His temperament, however, had more sympathy with Watts than with the generality of the Presbyterian divines; and that eminent man appears to have exercised great influence over his mind. It was at the instance of Watts, that he composed one of the most popular of his works, "The Rise and Progress of Religion in the Soul," which was conceived in a spirit quite at variance with the prevailing rationalism, and placed the seat of religion in the conscience and the heart. With strong affections and a fervent piety, he united that love of human praise and sympathy which is incident to such a character, and which prevented him from exhibiting on all occasions the clear decision and fixed purpose essential to the highest form of usefulness. He was himself too learned and too enlightened, not to be fully aware of the value of the contributions that were made by the rational school, to the cause of sacred criticism and pure Christianity; and yet personally he felt perhaps a deeper interest in the movements of more enthusiastic and even mystical religionists. Count Zinzendorf, Mr. Wesley, and Lady Huntingdon, were among his correspondents; and he did not scruple to open his pulpit to the Calvinistic Whitfield. He seems, in short, to have clearly seen, that there was work to be accomplished in society, to which the existing means of religious agency were altogether inadequate, and on which he was willing to assist earnest minds, out of his own denomination, in bringing to bear a new force and a better adapted instrumentality. For these friendly relations with the Methodists, he incurred the displeasure of his old Nonconforming friends, and amongst them of Watts himself. On the other hand, his intercourse with the most eminent of the clergy was highly flattering. Warburton constantly wrote to him in terms of the greatest cordiality, and asked his advice on points of literature and criticism. He had correspondents at Oxford and Cambridge, and among the bishops. Doddridge's was not a mind to be insensible to such distinctions. Perhaps this influence on him interfered a little with perfect simplicity and directness of action. He was anxious to maintain his high position, and tried to keep a middle way between all extremes. Of this character was his suggestion to Archbishop Herring, that in place of a complete comprehension, there should be a recognition of the Dissenting Churches as unschismatical, with an occasional exchange of pulpits between the clergy and the Nonconformist ministers[1].

Doddridge's religion consisted so much in feeling, that it is not surprising, it should have placed him, at different times, in positions which to every one but himself seemed inconsistent. His great work on which he bestowed the best years of his life, the Family Expositor, reflects the character of his mind, and represents the two elements which it was the con-

---

[1] Correspondence, vol. v. p. 76.

stant effort of his life to combine and reconcile—the critical or rationalistic, and the orthodox or sentimental. In his notes and paraphrase, he discovers the well-instructed scholar and divine; in his reflections and improvement, he too often sinks into the declamatory preacher. His character, as a whole, is amiable and estimable, full of fervour and zeal; interesting to look back upon, as expressing with vividness and prominence the spirit of his age; but deficient, it must be confessed, in the higher attributes of mental and moral greatness. Yet in Doddridge, the Protestant Dissenting ministry reached its culminating point of worldly influence and respectability. Never, perhaps, before or since, did a Nonconformist divine enjoy so extensive a reputation, or meet with such universal respect. He flourished just at that juncture, when parties pretty nearly balanced each other in the religious world; and his courteous, sympathizing spirit won honourable opinions from them all. From the time of his death, the old form of Protestant Dissent began to decline, and change its character; and principles which his position and influence had enabled him to keep together in tolerable union, soon after diverged into irreconcileable hostility.

The religion of feeling, crushed by formalism and rationalism out of the Church and the old Dissent, was taken up and embodied in Methodism. The origin of this vast sect is entirely due to the imperfections of earlier religious bodies. It represents no great idea; it expresses no principle, like Puritanism or the Church; it is a mere outbreak of feeling that was pent up, and wanted free expression; it was an irregular effort to compensate the deficiencies of existing institutions. Attached to the liturgy and discipline of the Church, and expressing in its two great sections, the Arminian and Calvinistic interpretation of the Articles, it is a reflection, an echo, of the hierarchy among the people. It shows clearly what the hierarchy might have done, and, to retain its place as a national religion, ought to have done. With Dissent it had little in common, but the freedom of its original action, and its appeal to the popular heart. When spiritual life was everywhere languishing, Methodism arose with a new blessing to society in the fresh outpouring of its missionary spirit over the dry and waste places of the earth. Its continuance as an institution, is less perhaps due to the unabated energy of its moral power, than to the skilful organization of its separate societies, and their union under a strong and central authority. As it represents a fact rather than a principle, it becomes difficult to form any conjecture as to its ultimate destiny. Should the Church ever undergo some great reform, and bring its ministrations into harmony with the wants of the people, it would appear most natural, that Methodism should be re-absorbed into the womb that gave it birth. But should this not be—as Methodism rests on no great historical tradition, and embodies no distinct principle—it is hardly to be conceived, how in its present form, it should be able permanently to maintain its ground in the midst of a growing spirit of intelligence and freedom, diffused through those classes to which it must chiefly look for its support. But we must now direct our attention to a very different phenomenon.

SECTION IX.

CHARACTER AND TENDENCIES OF ENGLISH DEISM, OR FREETHINKING.

The name Deist is said to have been first assumed by the deniers of revealed religion in France and Italy, about the middle of the sixteenth century[1]. In the great unsettling of previous opinions, occasioned by the Reformation, it is probable, that deistical principles early took possession of some speculative minds, though they were not enough diffused, nor excited sufficient interest, nor possessed perhaps in themselves sufficient power, to form the bond of a sect. Lord Herbert of Cherbury, already alluded to, was the first in our own country to give these principles in a systematic form to the world. Built on the assumption of certain innate notions of religion in every human mind, his theory was fundamentally opposed to the philosophy afterwards introduced by Locke. The views of Lord Herbert were taken up at the latter end of the seventeenth century, by Charles Blount, the second son of Sir Henry Blount, a person of some celebrity in the civil wars[2]. The son was a young man of ardent, romantic temperament,

[1] Leland's View of Deistical Writers, vol. i. p. 2.
[2] Aubrey's Lives, II. p. 241.

not devoid of religious feeling, but wild and extravagant in the indulgence of it. Having conceived a hopeless passion, he deliberately destroyed himself, in the belief that his spirit would pass at once to the bosom of God. He published a variety of pieces, which indicate the tendency of his opinions: a translation of part of the Life of Apollonius Tyanæus, by Philostratus, in the notes to which he draws some comparisons between that sophist and Jesus Christ; "Religio Laici," which is said to be little more than a translation of Lord Herbert's treatise with the same title; "Anima Mundi," or an account of the opinions of the ancients concerning man's soul after this life; and the "Original of Idolatry," in the preface to which he speaks reverentially of Christ and his religion. The work by which he is best known, is a collection of pieces by himself and others, entitled the "Oracles of Reason," published after his death by a friend, who justifies in a prefatory account of the life and death of the author, the act by which he terminated his existence. This posthumous work was printed in 1693[1].

Another deistical writer of the same time, was Toland, a man of extensive reading and considerable ingenuity, but paradoxical and vain, who unnecessarily excited odium, to enjoy the notoriety it procured. He was of Popish extraction; but early embracing the Protestant faith, he joined the Dissenters, some of whom contributed to his support at the University of Leyden. In 1695, during the height of the Socinian controversy, he published his "Christianity not Mysterious," intended to show, that there is nothing in the Gospel contrary to reason, nor above it; and that no Christian doctrine can be properly called a mystery. In this last view he certainly differed from Locke, whose new philosophy was made responsible for all the startling theories that were now promulgated, but who says distinctly in his first letter to Stillingfleet, "I shall always hearken to Scripture, as containing infallible truth, relating to things of the highest concernment; and I wish I could say, there were no mysteries in it; I acknowledge there are to me, and I fear always will be[2]." Toland was raised into undue importance by the attacks upon his book. It was presented by the Grand Jury of Dublin, where he was then residing, the

---

[1] Remains of C. Blount, and Leland's View, vol. i.
[2] Quoted in the View of Bolingbroke's Philosophy, (ascribed to Warburton,) p. 330.

Dissenters being great promoters of these intolerant proceedings. The book was ordered to be burned by the Irish Parliament; and the Attorney-General commenced a prosecution against the author, who made a timely escape into England. Some of his subsequent pieces, such as his Amyntor, his Origines Judaicæ, and his Nazarenus, impugned the canonical authority of the books of Scripture, and called forth a series of learned works in defence of it. Jeremiah Jones's work on the Canon, and Lardner's on the Credibility of the Gospels, were only more remote results of the inquiries which his bold scepticism was the means of exciting. Notwithstanding the apparent tendency of Toland's productions, it should in justice to him be stated, that he professed himself sincerely attached to the pure religion of Christ and his Apostles, and declared it was his only wish to exhibit it free from the additions and corruptions of later times. But he was one of those men who are urged towards scepticism, more by the love of singularity than by the simple desire of truth, and who therefore lose the credit of whatever ingenuity and originality there may be in their opinions, and incur the reputation of more extreme views than they actually entertain. Toland died in 1722[1].

Blount and Toland stand distinct from the school of Locke: but there were men of a far higher order, intellectually and morally, formed by his instructions, and largely imbued with his spirit of truthfulness, who went beyond their master's conclusions and did not with him recognize in Scripture a divinely constituted limit to the researches of human reason. Such men were Lord Shaftesbury and Anthony Collins. Shaftesbury was a highly accomplished and virtuous man, whose early education had been entrusted to the care of Locke[2]. He used the mental freedom in which he had been educated, to adopt a very different philosophy from his instructor. When Locke's Essay appeared, he expressed his dissent from its unqualified repudiation of all innate tendencies in the mind—a doctrine which he thought as objectionable as that of Hobbes[3], taking

---

[1] Memoirs prefixed to a collection of his Pieces, 1726. Compare Leland, vol. i.
[2] Locke had been for years attached to the person of his grandfather, the celebrated Chancellor, immortalized in the verse of Dryden.
[3] See two letters of his, addressed to Locke. King's Life of Locke, pp. 183–89.

away all natural foundation for moral and religious ideas, and destroying the security of social order. The same views were further unfolded in some "Letters addressed by a Nobleman to a Young Man at the University," published without his name in 1716; which are now ascertained to have been written by him to the son of a domestic, whom he was educating for the Church. The mind of Shaftesbury was earnestly directed to moral and religious speculation. His earliest publication was a volume of select sermons by Whichcote, Locke's favourite preacher, which he was at the trouble of collecting from different parties who had taken them down in shorthand, and which he introduced with a preface full of respectful feeling towards Christianity.

It is curious to notice the different influence of the philosophy of Shaftesbury and of Locke. The religious deficiencies of Locke's psychological system urged him to seek a compensation in full reliance on the external proofs of divine revelation; Shaftesbury's firmer trust in an immutable principle of faith and duty within the breast, left him more open to scepticism about historical testimony, and made him quicker to perceive any discrepancy between doctrines held by Christians and that implanted sense of right which he revered as the voice of God. These tendencies which naturally drew him away from a traditional religion enforced by outward sanctions, were confirmed by his dislike of the prevalent character of Christian theology. It was studied in a spirit, and placed on grounds, with which his whole cast of thought was at variance. It was too literal and too systematic; it aimed at demonstration through the medium of historical facts. The Characteristics, his principal work, revised by him for publication in the last years of his life, betray undoubted alienation from Christianity as usually conceived. He admired the pure and benevolent spirit of the simple Gospel; but he could not find certainty in the historical proof of miracles, and was disgusted with the dogmatic and contentious spirit of divines. Yet he seems to have felt the importance of a fixed and definite system of faith for the multitude, and thought with Harrington, there should be a public leading in religion, conjoined with a general toleration[1]. This conflict between what he imagined to be necessary, and what he felt to be true, has occasionally had an unhappy effect on his language—mingling expressions of profound reverence

[1] On Enthusiasm, p. 17.

for whatever is established, with covert insinuations against its sense and reasonableness[1]. There runs indeed through all his observations on Christian institutions and theology, a tone of latent sarcasm, which one would gladly exchange for a healthful expression of simple-hearted doubt. With this exception, however, an elevated spirit of morality and natural religion pervades the writings of Shaftesbury; and the amiable Mr. Lindsey, in his Conversations on the Divine Government, has ventured to claim him as, in reality, notwithstanding some free notions, a believer in Christianity[2].

Anthony Collins was the chosen friend of Locke in his declining years. To him the aged philosopher addressed those memorable words, preserved in his correspondence:—"Believe it, my good friend, to love truth for truth's sake, is the principal part of human perfection in this world, and the seed-plot of all other virtues; and if I mistake not, you have as much of it as ever I met with in anybody." For him, too, he left a letter of affectionate counsels, to be delivered after his decease. There must have been some noble qualities in the mind of Collins, to secure the confidence and esteem of so clear-sighted and experienced a judge. The works by which Collins acquired notoriety, did not appear till some years after the death of Locke. The love of truth which Locke had remarked in him, not tempered by the conservative caution and judgment of his venerable friend, took the form of an extreme freedom of speculation, mingled with a great dislike of the priesthood.

When a particular tendency of thought is strongly excited by the condition of society, it spreads like an epidemic; becomes a ruling passion in many minds; and vents its favourite ideas in certain cant phrases which pass for axioms. Such is the history of all sects; and when the Freethinkers became a sect, they exhibited sectarian weaknesses. In 1713, Collins published without his name, a "Discourse of Freethinking, occasioned by the rise and growth of a sect, called Freethinkers." Its object was unobjectionable and excellent, being simply to assert, in the most unrestricted sense, the right of every man to use his own judgment in the pursuit of truth. But in his self-abandonment to a favourite sentiment, the author has not altogether escaped that spirit of sect which I have described. His language is often declamatory; his state-

[1] Miscellaneous Reflections, p. 71. [2] Conversation II. p. 39.

ments want precision, and are tinged with prejudice; and he laid himself open to animadversion by frequent inaccuracies, misapprehensions, and hasty conclusions. These were exposed with unsparing severity, in a reply by Dr. Richard Bentley, written in the character of a Lutheran divine, under the assumed name of Phileleutherus Lipsiensis. It is impossible not to admire the caustic wit, the masculine vigour and exuberant learning, of this celebrated piece; but, with all its intellectual excellences, it is not a fair and candid reply. The author runs down his adversary, instead of properly answering him. He destroys his credit, by exhibiting his errors and ignorance in detail, without once encountering the principle of his main argument, and imputes to him opinions and motives which, it was evident from his book itself, that he would disavow. There was enough to condemn in it, without the gratuitous inference of bad intentions. Collins was a man of probity and talent, a sincere theist, led into error by his very passion for speculative truth; and it was an unworthy resource of controversy, to hold him up to opprobrium as a fool and an atheist.

In 1724, Collins published anonymously a "Discourse on the grounds and reasons of the Christian Religion." His general argument was this: that the New Testament being founded on the Old, as the prophecies contained in the latter, had reference to events near the time of their delivery, they must have been fulfilled in Christ, not literally but mystically and allegorically; and that only on this principle of interpretation which had long prevailed among the rabbis, could Christianity be shown to be true. These views so contrary to received opinions, called forth a multitude of animadversions and replies; which induced the author still further to develope his idea in the "Scheme of Literal Prophecy Considered," accompanied by a review of the preceding controversy. In the preface to this last work, he observes, that many of the answers to him were "written with a temper, moderation, and politeness, unusual in theological controversies, and becoming good, pious, and learned men;" and that their authors, allowing the subject to have its difficulties, and to be proper for free and public debate, depend only on the force of argument, appeal only to the reason of men for a determination, and disclaim all force and other application to the passions and weakness of men, to support and maintain the notions they **advance**[1]." This was in 1727; **and** the fact alluded to indicates the progress of **more** liberal sentiments, and shows that good had resulted from the bold suggestions of the Freethinkers. Men who wish to examine a **subject** thoroughly on every side, sometimes propose a view *tentatively*, **to see** how far it will carry them, and what result it will yield; and the conclusion which they adopt for the time, in developing that view, must not always be considered as the expression of their settled convictions, nor can be tried by the same standard as the judgments of the practical divine. Some allowance, therefore, must be made for the speculations of such Freethinkers as Collins. They may, on the whole, be very extravagant, and yet offer valuable suggestions to the thoughtful inquirer. Their suppression **at least would be fatal** to the interests of truth. The philosophy of Collins differed **much** from that of Shaftesbury, and had more affinity with **the principles** of their common master. He defended the doctrines of necessity and materialism. In all the social relations of life, Collins is admitted to have been a man of great worth. During many years, he filled the responsible office of Treasurer for the county of Essex, with a high reputation for integrity and abilities.

As Collins denied a **literal prophecy,** so Woolston whose writings **attracted notice between the years** 1726 and 1730, allegorized the miracles **of Jesus, and treated his** history, contained in the New Testament, as an emblematical representation of his spiritual life in the souls of men[2]. He attacked particularly the evidence for the resurrection, and gave occasion to Sherlock's well-known piece, the "Trial of the Witnesses." His fanciful notions appear to have been contracted from a study of Origen, and other mystical writers; and, as he always declared he was a Christian, some have considered him as a mere enthusiast. He chiefly rendered himself ob**noxious** by his abuse of the clergy. Whatever his offences against good manners, his punishment, **if** intended for his libel **on** persons, was unreasonably severe—**if** for his opinions, in entire contradiction **to the** spirit of Christianity. He was condemned to **one year's** imprisonment, and a fine of a hundred **pounds.** The controversy which his writings **occasioned,** is memorable for having **drawn from** Lardner an **express** disapproval **of** pains and penalties **in** support of religion. That

---

[1] Preface, etc., p. 4.   [2] Leland's View, etc., Letter VII.

mild and candid apologist would have tolerated great freedom in the manner of an attack upon it, rather than have recourse to the arm of the civil power for repelling it.—He has stated these views, partly in the preface to his Vindication of Three of Christ's Miracles against Woolston's objections[1], and partly in a correspondence with Dr. Waddington, bishop of Chichester, on the subject[2].

The two main supports of the external evidence of a divine revelation—prophecy and miracles—had been thus exposed to successive attacks. The controversy was pursued, on somewhat different grounds, by Tindal and Morgan, both of whom classed themselves with the Christian Deists, though their views in other respects were unlike. Tindal, in a work published by him anonymously in 1730, and entitled, "Christianity as old as the Creation, or the Gospel a republication of the Religion of Nature"—admitted no distinction between natural and revealed religion, but contended that they are, and must be, in all things entirely coincident. The former he regarded as the *internal*, the latter as an *external*, revelation of the same immutable will of God; but he denied, in fact, that there can be any external revelation distinct from, still less opposed to, the internal revelation of God's law in the hearts of all mankind[3]. It is the leading idea of his book, that God cannot change, and that his law from the first was perfect, being the expression of that unalterable and eternal truth and right by which he governs his own acts, and which is obligatory on his rational creatures throughout the universe, and in all states of existence. He repudiates the authority of a traditional religion, and denies the possibility of religious progress and development. In some points, the views of Tindal resemble those of Shaftesbury; both indicate the same reverence for an ideal of faith and duty, set up by God in the inner sanctuary of the human mind, which nothing outward can change or qualify.

In 1737 appeared the "Moral Philosopher," by Dr. Morgan, who called himself a Christian on the footing of the New Testament—a Christian Deist, as contradistinguished from the Christian Jews. His object was to separate the religion of

---

[1] First published in 1729, and inserted in the 11th volume of the octavo edition of his works, 1788.
[2] Given in the Appendix to Kippis's Life of Lardner, No. I.
[3] Christianity as old as the Creation, ch. vi.

the New Testament from that of the Old, by which he thought the minds of Christians generally were too much possessed. He admitted the possibility of an immediate communication of truth from God, in other words, of divine inspiration; though he argued, that the test of its being such must be sought in the reason of the individual inquirer. He acknowledged that this divine light might be traditionally conveyed, with great benefit, to subsequent generations; since the natural strength of the human reason was, in his opinion, greatly over-estimated. He thus made a distinction between *immediate* and *traditional* revelation. While Tindal therefore contended, that the divine law was as fully revealed in the Creation as in the Gospel, Morgan conceded the possibility of religious growth and development, in the occasional access of fresh measures of spiritual light and influence direct from God. In his hostility to the Old Testament, he was as bitter as Marcion himself; and his attacks upon it drew forth some learned defences of the institutions of the Hebrews[1].

The Deistical controversy was still carried on in various pamphlets, which from time to time issued anonymously from the press[2]. But the greatest sensation was produced by the appearance, nearly about the same time—the middle of the last century—of the posthumous works of two men widely separated from each other by rank and character. One belonged to the humbler class of society, had no learning, and was of quiet, exemplary life. The other was a nobleman of brilliant powers and elegant accomplishments, restless, factious and unprincipled, who followed the excitement which he loved, with a wild and erratic vehemence at once in the pleasures of the world, in political intrigues, and in daring speculation. These were Mr. Chubb and Lord Bolingbroke.—Chubb's writings leave on the mind an impression of great sincerity. His love of truth was sensitively scrupulous. He would give nothing a place in his convictions, but in proportion to the evidence which he could persuade himself it brought with it;

---

[1] Among others, Lowman's Dissertation on the Civil Government of the Hebrews.—I have taken this account of the "Moral Philosopher" from Leland's View, Letter IX., which bears, however, internal marks of uncandid interpretation. In the Appendix to Kippis's Life of Lardner, No. IV., there is a correspondence between Lardner and Morgan, on the difficulties in the introductory chapters of Matthew and Luke, written in a friendly and respectful spirit on both sides.

[2] Leland's tenth and eleventh Letters.

and from this high conscientiousness of intellect, stimulated by the rationalism which then so generally pervaded religious inquiries, he has laid himself open to the suspicion of doubt respecting some truths, with which there is every probability, that his inward **nature was** wholly **in** unison. He revered Christianity **as a moral system, and** inclined to the opinion, that it **was a** revelation from God; though he still referred the **test of its** truth and divinity to its agreement with the law **written on the human** heart. In the progress of his views, he **removed** to a greater distance from the ordinary notions of Christianity, and took up a strong prejudice against **the** doctrine and character of Paul. His mind appears to have wanted comprehensiveness; he was incapable of seeing things under more than one point of view. He had no sympathy with religious enthusiasm, and his metaphysical views disqualified him for doing justice to any character that was under its influence. Inclined to the doctrines of materialism and necessity, he denied the influence of the Spirit and the direct efficacy of prayer, and described virtue as a simple conformity **of mind and** life **to that eternal rule of** righteousness which **God has immutably** fixed. As his character was much respected, his writings exercised a wide influence in their day. **Their moral tone is admirable.** In his Farewell to his Readers, he expresses a hope, that he may be "a sharer with them of the divine favour, in that peaceful and happy state which God has prepared for the virtuous and faithful in some other future world." His Advice to Believers and Unbelievers is written in the same amiable spirit—earnestly pleading **the** cause of seriousness and truth, and entreating both **parties to abstain** from reproaches **and** the imputation of motives[1].

In his Letters on the Study of History, Lord Bolingbroke had, during his lifetime, thrown out opinions which impugned the credibility of the Scriptures, especially of the Old Testament, or at least put it on such grounds, as indicated more suspicion than belief. But it was not till after his death, that the whole extent of his alienation from the system of revealed religion, was made known. He wrote so much from impulse, and was so unsettled in many of his views, that it is difficult to obtain a **clear** and connected insight into his principles. Warburton maintains[2], **that it** was his great object to sub-

---

[1] Chubb's Essays; Leland, Letters XII. and **XIII.**
[2] View of Bolingbroke's Philosophy, p. 48.

stitute for the different systems of religion recommended by divines, a First Philosophy, or Naturalism, quoting, in support of this statement, the noble author's own words: "a self-existent Being, the first Cause of all things, infinitely powerful and infinitely wise, is the God of natural theology: and the whole system of natural religion rests on it, and requires no broader foundation." From Leland's very full analysis of his philosophical writings, illustrated by copious extracts, we may distinguish the chief points of his system under the following heads:—(1.) a belief in a Supreme Being, as described in the foregoing passage, to the exclusion of any distinct apprehension of his moral attributes, except as involved in, and necessarily flowing from, his infinite wisdom and power; (2.) the government of the world by general and unvarying laws, established at the beginning of creation, without particular providences for individuals; (3.) the probability, that body and soul are modifications of the same substance, and the consequent doubt whether there be a future life,—an assumption not needed to justify and explain the present constitution of things, since whatever is, is right; (4.) a law of duty founded in human nature, so clearly and sufficiently discoverable by reason, though obscured by philosophers and divines, as to supersede the necessity of any supernatural revelation; (5.) gratitude and resignation, the fittest expressions of that natural worship which is due to the First Cause of all things; (6.) that it is blasphemous to ascribe the Jewish Scriptures to God, since they contain statements and doctrines inconsistent with his perfections; (7.) that the religion taught by Christ, in its genuine simplicity, is a pure and benevolent system, usefully confirming by its few and simple institutions, the law of nature; worthy of God, and conducive to the well-being of mankind; but that it must be distinguished from another Gospel, contradictory to it, that was preached by Paul[1].

In common with many of the Freethinkers, Bolingbroke had conceived a strong dislike to that apostle, and expressed his surprise that Locke whom he greatly admired, should have written a commentary on his Epistles[2]. In the course of his discursive speculations he took up, at various times, such opposite ideas, that it is often impossible to say what was his

[1] Leland, vol. ii. pp. 136–139.
[2] Philosophical Works, vol. ii. p. 132.

real opinion: but if he was sincere in the following sentences, he differed from most other Deists, who professed like himself a great respect for the moral worth of Christianity, in urging divines to neglect the internal evidence, and to bend their whole attention on the proof furnished by testimony. "It seems to me," says he[1], "that divines should rest the authority both of the Old and New Testaments on the proofs they are able to bring of their divine original, and of the uncorrupt manner in which they have been conveyed down to latter ages, solely." "Reason has been too much employed, where it has nothing to do, and too much neglected where it has most to do. Men have believed implicitly when they should have reasoned, in laying the grounds of faith; and they have reasoned dogmatically when they should have believed implicitly, these grounds being once laid."

In his metaphysical views he had an evident leaning towards materialism, and professed a great contempt for the reveries of the Platonic school respecting the intrinsic divinity of the human soul[2]. Bolingbroke was in favour of a national religion, supported by a test and accompanied by a toleration—"rejecting alike," to use his own words, "the principles of Latitudinarians and Rigidists." "To make government," he says, "effectual to all the good purposes of it, there must be a religion; this religion must be national; and this national religion must be maintained in reputation and reverence; all other religions and sects must be kept too low to become the rivals of it[3]." He had early imbibed intense disgust at the scholastic pedantry of the old theology; but he professed himself quite as little satisfied with the rationalizing theories of the modern divines. When Whitfield commenced his career, Bolingbroke was smitten with the fresh earnestness and native power of his preaching, and was often to be found among his select audience at Lady Huntingdon's. Indeed the good Countess fully reckoned on making a convert of him before his death, and had far better hopes of him than of some graver men[4].

With Bolingbroke, the school of English Freethinking, which excited so much attention in the first half of the last

---

[1] Works, vol. ii. pp. 211, 212.
[2] See the second Essay in his Philosophical Works.
[3] Works, vol. iii. pp. 330-1. Essay IV.
[4] See Memoirs of her Life and Times.

century, may be said to terminate. Hume and Gibbon who continued the attacks on Revelation in the same covert way, are connected by their influence, and the character of their writings, rather with the general spirit of scepticism which had begun to infect the contemporaneous literature of Europe, than with the series of writers just described, whose peculiar views stood in the closest relation to the religious and philosophical controversies of England. The influence of French literature is strongly reflected in the writings both of Hume and of Gibbon.

It is clear from every indication of the times which we have been considering, that the principles of the Freethinkers were widely diffused through society. Lord Barrington, in his Essay on the Divine Dispensations, speaks of the increase of virtuous and serious Deists, which he imputes to the prevalence of narrow and false views of Christianity; and he observes, with a concession which marks the spirit of his age, that the religion of Deists is a true religion, though it wants the motives and sanctions of Revelation. The many works which appeared in answer to the Deists, attest the high importance that was attached to the controversy. Leland, a learned Presbyterian minister of Dublin, has devoted three octavo volumes to an analysis and refutation of their different writings. It is an elaborate performance, but written from the rigidly scriptural point of view, and deficient in candour and openness of spirit. Warburton also entered the field against the Deists, with the tone of bold defiance that was peculiar to him. His "Divine Legation of Moses" was designed with a special reference to their theories, and in the prefixed dedication to the Freethinkers, he has attacked with more insolence than charity their principles and their proceedings. In some animadversions on a reply by Waterland to Tindal's "Christianity as old as the Creation," Dr. Conyers Middleton gave a specimen of what he thought would be a more satisfactory mode of dealing with the Freethinkers. He shows from history, the inadequacy of the simple religion of reason to the necessities of the multitude; and that in every civilized community there has always been a traditional system of popular faith and worship, distinct from the speculations of philosophical minds; that where such a system is already established, though mixed with much superstition and folly, it would be wrong to attempt its overthrow, without being prepared to put something better fitted for the purpose, in its place; that Socrates and the wisest of the heathens always acted on this principle; and that consequently it must *à fortiori* be much more absurd and mischievous to endeavour to substitute the simple inferences of reason for a belief in Christianity, which is the best of all traditional religions, "the best contrived to promote public peace and the good of society," and acknowledged by Deists themselves "to come the nearest of all others to their perfect law of reason and nature[1]." Middleton's line of argument leaves it doubtful, whether he himself admitted, in any sense, a supernatural sanction to Christianity: but he seems at all events, to admit as a fact, that some other principle than reason is needed, to furnish the motives and consolations of the mass of mankind. In their modes of reasoning, and in their general conception of religion, the Deists and the rationalist Divines of this time had much in common. The line must have been vague and arbitrary indeed, which kept such writers as Middleton and Wollaston[2] *within* the limits of Christianity, and put Shaftesbury, Morgan, and Chubb *without* them.

The influence of the English Freethinkers was not limited to their own country. Their writings were read and translated by the French Encyclopedists; they passed with the literature and philosophy of France into the rising monarchy of Prussia; and disseminated that spirit of theological rationalism which was encouraged by Frederic the Great, and the remote effects of which are still working in the mind of Germany. At the very beginning of the eighteenth century, Toland accompanied the Earl of Macclesfield on a mission to the princess Sophia at Hanover, and was afterwards introduced to the Queen of Prussia at Berlin, where he disputed in her presence with the celebrated Protestant divine, Beausobre, on religion[3].

In looking back on the Deistical controversy, a regret arises, that it was not conducted in a better spirit and on broader grounds. There was narrowness and prejudice on both sides. The fundamental conditions of the question were corrupted by the prevailing Rationalism; since on both sides it was assumed, that religion must have its source in the assent of the understanding to a logical conclusion. In their views respecting

---

[1] Middleton's Works, 4to, vol. ii. p. 166–177.
[2] Author of 'The Religion of Nature Delineated.' Lond: 1726.
[3] Calamy's Life and Times, vol. i. p. 429, editor's note.

the religion of nature, **both the Deists and the** believers in
Revelation went completely together up to **a certain** point; it
was in their judgments **on** the evidence **for a** supernatural
origin of Christianity, that they moved widely apart. But the
Christian divines, by submitting **the question** to free inquiry,
implied that there was room for the entertainment of different
opinions, and ought not therefore to have condemned, as necessarily involving moral obliquity, any conclusion honestly
arrived at. For the dispute was not, whether the moral principles of Christianity were pure and excellent, its doctrine of
life and immortality full of consolation and holy influence, and
the character of its founder **worthy of the** highest admiration
and love (for this, most, **if not all,** of the Freethinkers were
fully prepared to admit); **but whether the** external evidence
accompanying the books **of** Scripture, was **such, as to compel**
every honest mind, to receive all **their statements as histo-**
rically true, and all their doctrines as of divine **authority.**
Throughout the controversy, the opponents of the Deists too
generally assumed their own conclusions on this matter of
evidence, not only as right and certain, but as *so* right and *so*
certain, that any dissent from them indicated a corrupt heart,
a biassed will, and an hostility to what was moral and spiritual
in Christianity. The two parties occupied a different mental
position, and could not understand each other. One party had
reached their conclusion, and were astonished that all who
were looking for truth, had not come to the **same; the others**
were **still in search of theirs,** and admitted, perhaps too readily, that only prejudice **or self** interest could have enabled
their adversaries to find one so soon. They stood, therefore,
to each other, in the relation of dogmatists and sceptics; and
between such parties, we know, there can be little sympathy.

Men who are in pursuit of truth, pass on from one view of
things to another, and support each of them for the time with
such evidence as they can command; but these transitions,
which are necessary steps toward a final result, wear the appearance of criminal inconsistencies to those who have defini-
tively fixed their own opinions. A state of doubt is indeed in
itself objectionable, and should be tolerated only as a condition **of wise** and thoughtful determination at last; **but there**
are circumstances, in which doubt implies as high moral **feel-**
ing as faith, and the *animus* **with** which it is entertained,
ought always to be taken into account. What right have

we to assume, that Shaftesbury, Collins, Morgan, and Chubb, were not as sincere in their desire of truth, as Leland and Warburton? If it be affirmed, that their intellectual constitution was less fitted for the clear and firm apprehension of truth; that is no ground for moral imputation, unless it can be shown, that this infirmity resulted from the wilful indulgence of passion or prejudice. A still greater wrong has been often done to the Freethinkers, by ascribing their caution and reserve in the expression of their opinions, to a secret malice and base disingenuousness. A thoughtful, serious man may question the truth and reasonableness of some opinions, which he perceives, nevertheless, to be closely bound up in the minds of multitudes, as things are at present constituted, with many valuable practical convictions. Where he is himself but an inquirer, cautiously stretching out his mind on every side to feel after truth, it may be no more than a justifiable consideration of his circumstances and his future peace, not to expose himself needlessly to that storm of prejudice and misrepresentation, which an unreserved utterance of all that he regards as probable, would be certain to bring down. But mark the injustice constantly perpetrated by those who have the public feeling on their side! They make the honest expression of opinion penal, and then condemn men for disingenuousness. They invite to free discussion, but determine beforehand, that only one conclusion can be sound and moral. Where they should encounter principles, they impute motives. They fill the arena of public debate with every instrument of torture and annoyance for the feeling heart, the sensitive imagination, and the scrupulous intellect,—and then are angry, that men do not rush headlong into the martyrdom that has been prepared for them.

The writings of the old Freethinkers have left no very deep impression on the public mind, and are now seldom referred to, except by the studious and inquisitive. They are unfitted for strong popular influence by the same qualities which distinguished the general theology of the period. They are too cold, abstract and philosophical in their form; they do not interest the affections; and the views promulgated in them, lie remote from the familiar conceptions and practical concerns of mankind. The awful events which convulsed Europe at the close of the last century, alienated the thoughts of the higher classes from all speculations of this kind. Paine clothed the Deistical argument in a more popular dress; nor were his strong sense and forcible style without their effect: but his writings owed much of their influence to political enthusiasm, and that hatred of priests and religious establishments, which pervaded large portions of the middle and lower classes at the time of their appearance. The Deistical controversy had worked powerfully in the general fermentation of ideas which followed the Revolution of 1688, and left behind it results that reappeared in other forms, and secretly influenced the future progress of opinion: but its direct effects do not appear to have extended through the latter half of the eighteenth century. Public opinion has been so deeply affected by the wonderful scenes that have been exhibited on the theatre of the world, within the last sixty or seventy years, that abstract speculations on religion and government have fallen into comparative disrepute. An historical spirit has sprung up in their place. Inquiry now takes its departure on all subjects from something concrete and actual. Perhaps we may be even going too far in that direction: but we can hardly be mistaken in asserting, that the views of society and its prospects, which now carry with them the approval and sympathy of the greatest number of intelligent and instructed men, assume the existence of some positive religious system, as the basis of a true civilization.

There is an inherent deficiency in simple Deism, which must for ever preclude it from becoming the prevalent religion of the world. Deism is the religion of the individual reason, isolated and self-relying; arriving by its own efforts, through the contemplation of second causes, at the idea of a Supreme Intelligence; disdaining the traditions of the past, and taking its independent stand on the knowledge of the present. Such a religion, though many wise and virtuous men have entertained it, is essentially anti-social; for it is remarkable, that while the most extravagant enthusiasm has often given birth to extensive sects, Deism has never yet coalesced into a permanent religious society. It sets out from false data. It seeks the primary element of the religious life in an inference from external phenomena, and admits into its belief only so much as can be deduced, in regular logical sequence, from that fundamental proposition. Faith, therefore, in the proper sense of the word, is excluded; and religion becomes only another name for the chain of inference which is drawn out, link after link, silent and solitary, by the reflecting mind. We might as well make a theorem of Euclid, a bond of communion and sympathy among men, as a religion so conceived. Such is not the true genesis of religion. Religion springs up within us, a spontaneous feeling, an instinctive aspiration, a deep, indestructible consciousness of spiritual power and presence encompassing us on every side, as surely and as necessarily in the unfolding of our moral nature, as the sense of right and truth and beauty. All these sentiments—the religious, the moral, the æsthetic—are ultimate facts in our constitution. We cannot go beyond them. We must take them as they come to us, conditions attached to the exercise of our faculties. They arise, because they are destined to arise. Reason may show *how* they have arisen, and explain the *mode* of their operation, and clear them from pernicious adhesions, and present them with their proper objects. But their *origin* does not depend on an act of reasoning. They come into operation in obedience to deep-seated and immutable laws, which reasoning may pervert or obscure, but can never wholly annihilate.

Feeling and affection, whatever their nature, require an object and ask for sympathy, long before reason interposes its doubts and suggests its cautions. Reason's office is to guide them to their worthiest objects, and to restrain the intercourse they seek, within the limits of mental and moral health. The objects of religious feeling and the forms of religious communion, are brought to men's minds, in the first instance, traditionally. So brought, however partially corrupted by superstitious influences, they probably furnish some elements of religious faith corresponding to the spiritual want within, which the mind, unaided by external stimulus, could not have produced from itself. Out of these materials, a conscientious reason selects what is purest and best for the inward nutriment of the soul; and as nobler objects are brought one after another within its view, it successively directs to them the homage of the religious affections. But an object there must be—for most, perhaps in some moments for all, minds—externally presented, to raise and quicken their spiritual aspirations, to fix and realize their dim and fluctuating sense of human communion with God. Rites and symbols have aimed at producing this effect in the ancient religions, and in the less perfect forms of Christianity; but in the simple Gospel, the end is accomplished by the exhibition of a pure and heavenly humanity, by inviting men to repose their trust and sympathy in Christ, as the moral image of the invisible God. Transcending far the ordinary standard of human morality, the embodied love of God comes forth in the character of Christ to meet our aspirations; no humanity ever equalled his: yet it holds out to us a virtue that wins the affections, an excellence that is conceivable and imitable. We meet, then, in Christ with an object which is fitted above every other to satisfy our strongest religious affections; to associate them with the highest of our moral aims; and to furnish a bond of the holiest communion between all good minds. In this harmony of all our powers, resulting from faith in him—in this correspondence between what our nature craves and what the Gospel offers—there is an evidence of divine appointment, on which the mind may practically rest. From this, as from a fixed datum, well secured in the experimental convictions of the heart and the conscience, we may proceed, as opportunity offers, to consider such points in the external evidence, as occasion more difficulty or demand a prolonged suspense of impartial judgment.

These elementary wants of our spiritual nature are overlooked by Deism. It does not provide for them. It labours under deficiencies, which only an historical religion can supply. It wants a visible head; it has no Christ. It needs some link for the human soul, through human sympathies, with the unseen God; a centre of living union; a bond of universal brotherhood. It has no usages, no institutions, no cherished remembrances; no light from the past, shedding its hallowed lustre on particular spots and recurring seasons, and consecrating our daily life with the spirit of a sacred poesy. Its doctrines are airy and unsubstantial; fading away into dim abstractions; remote from the sympathies of warm, living, suffering humanity. True, "it is the spirit that quickeneth"—the spirit, that creates the kingdom of God within us: but the Church united with its risen and glorified Head, the Church with its social offices and its common voice of thanksgiving and prayer—preserves and cherishes that spirit, and institutes an outward medium of spiritual communion among men. It is no small presumption against Deism's possessing the whole truth and meeting the entire demands of our nature, that it has shown itself incapable hitherto of generating and sustaining a Church.

SECTION X.

INFLUENCE OF HARTLEY'S PHILOSOPHY: REVIVAL OF THE UNITARIAN CONTROVERSY BY DR. PRIESTLEY.

Some of the ablest defenders of Revelation had ascribed the prevalence of Deistical principles to false and narrow views of Christianity, which obscured its true character, and raised a prejudice against it in the minds of reflecting men. It was observed, that the simplicity of the Gospel had been overlaid by the constructions of human creeds; and it was believed not without reason, that if the religion of Jesus could be shown to be, in all essential points, coincident with that of nature, only giving clearness and a divine authority to some truths which nature left dim and uncertain, the controversy might be brought to a satisfactory issue, and all honest inquirers reclaimed to the faith. This feeling contributed, with other causes, to the revival of the Socinian, or rather Humanitarian, Doctrine, proper Unitarianism; which had not been made a subject of general discussion since the close of the preceding century. It has already been noticed, that the opinions of Watts respecting the object of worship and the person of Christ, underwent a change in the latter years of his life; and Lardner, the great champion of the credibility of the Gospel history, had become an Unitarian, or believer in the simple humanity of Christ[1], as appears from his Letter on the Logos, as early as 1730. In the meantime, the other side of the orthodox system, in its two principal doctrines of original sin and vicarious satisfaction, was attacked with sound biblical learning and a most powerful intellect, by Dr. John Taylor, a Presbyterian minister, first at Norwich, and afterwards professor of Divinity and Morality in the Academy at Warrington[2].

---

[1] Henceforth the term Unitarian will be used in this restricted sense, as contradistinguished from Arian.

[2] Taylor's principal works were his Paraphrase etc. on Romans, with a Key to the Apostolic Writings, a Scheme of Scripture Divinity, and two volumes of Tracts on several important subjects. Taylor's style even in handling critical matters, is singularly impressive and even eloquent. The work on which his fame chiefly rests, is his Hebrew Concordance in two volumes folio. It is a proof of the spirit which then prevailed in the Church of England, that in the list of subscribers to this learned work, are found the names of great numbers of the clergy, as well as of the bishops and archbishops of England and Ireland. The work indeed is dedicated to the metropolitans and prelates of the two Churches, in grateful acknowledgment of their generous encouragement of the

But the circumstance which, **above all others,** gave a peculiar turn to theological inquiries in the latter **half of** the eighteenth **century,** was the influence of the philosophical system **of Dr. Hartley,** who was born in the same **year** that Locke died[1], **and whose** Observations on **Man were published rather more** than fifty years after the first appearance of **the** Essay on Human Understanding. Divines are in the habit of repudiating all connection with philosophy; but the sympathy between theological and philosophical theories is too close and too **obvious** ever **to escape notice.** The two philosophers just **mentioned gave a character not to** be mistaken, to the theo-

undertaking; and the dedication concludes with the expression of a wish, that 'the Churches of England and Ireland may always be happy in prelates of the same excellent disposition.' Yet it appears from several letters in Doddridge's correspondence, that Taylor's writings from their supposed heretical tendency, were viewed with suspicion and alarm by many of the Dissenters of that time. Among others, John Wesley was much scandalized by Taylor's account of the doctrine of Original Sin. In a letter dated July 3, 1759, Wesley wished to draw him into controversy on the subject. He addressed him, however, with extraordinary respect, 'as a person of uncommon sense and learning,' and says that to engage in controversy with him, would humanly speaking be *formica contra leonem*. He adds: 'Take away the Scriptural doctrine of redemption or justification, and that of the new birth, the beginning of sanctification, or, which amounts to the same, explain them as you do, suitably to your doctrine of Original Sin: and what is Christianity better than Heathenism? Wherein (save in rectifying some of our *notions*) has the religion of St. Paul any pre-eminence over that of Socrates or Epictetus?' Again, 'Either I or you mistake the whole of Christianity from the beginning to the end. Your scheme has gone through all England, and made numerous converts. I attack it from end to end: let all England judge whether it can be defended or not.' Wesley's Journal, No. X. 1758–1760. In the 2nd vol. of Dr. Taylor's Tracts, is a posthumous reply to Wesley's Remarks on Original Sin. Wesley however was not wanting in discretion, and knew how to adapt himself to his audience. We learn from his Journal (1770–1773) that on preaching in Warrington, when he observed the young men from the Academy (where Taylor had been Tutor) among his audience, he discoursed very pertinently on the use of Reason in relation to Religion. One other characteristic notice in this curious Journal, must not be omitted. In speaking of the Octagon Chapel, then recently erected in Norwich for Taylor, as one of the handsomest meeting-houses in Europe, Wesley 'wonders how the plain, simple Gospel can be preached in such a place!' The late Dr. Parr, in a Latin inscription to the memory of Dr. Taylor, has delineated his character with more discrimination than he always displayed in compositions of this kind.

VIRO . INTEGRO . INNOCENTI . PIO
SCRIPTORI . GRAECIS . ET . HEBRAICIS . LITTERIS
PROBE . ERUDITO
VERBI . DIVINI . GRAVISSIMO . INTERPRETI
RELIGIONIS . SIMPLICIS . ET . INCORRUPTÆ
ACERRIMO . PROPUGNATORI.

[1] 1705. *Parr's Works, vol.* iv. *p.* 565.

logy of the two periods at the head of which they respectively stand. Both were earnest and devout Christians; both continued through life in communion with the Church of England; though their principles were most eagerly imbibed and applied by Dissenters. What Locke was to the school of undogmatic rationalism which prevailed till the middle of the last century; Hartley became to Priestley and his associates or followers, who found in the principles of the Hartleian philosophy, a support and defence of their peculiar modification of Unitarianism.

The system of Hartley was a further simplification of that of Locke. The tendencies to materialism and philosophical necessity, and the suggestion of the association of ideas, which had appeared in the writings of the last-named philosopher, as pregnant hints and mere germs of thought, were developed by Hartley into an ampler doctrinal form, and assumed a prominent place with a more definite value in his theory of man. Of the two sources to which Locke had traced back all ideas, one was now given up, and all the materials of human knowledge, belief and sentiment were resolved into the elementary impressions on the senses, out of which, it was maintained, the most refined and disinterested affections of benevolence and piety could be successively evolved, through the transforming processes of the all-pervading law of the association of ideas. According to this system, all that enters into men's mental and moral constitution, is originally external; and the evidence for the most important truths rests primarily on the depositions of the senses, taken up by the great organic law of association, and wrought out by it mechanically to a given result. It is obvious, how readily such principles coalesce with those views of religion which, distrusting the impulsive suggestions of the mind within, look for assurance in the testimony of historical facts alone, and place the main hope of a future life on the attested resurrection of Jesus[1]. The psy-

---

[1] It ought to be observed, that Hartley, whose excellence of character and exalted piety are worthy of all veneration, has disclaimed the necessary connection of his philosophical system with materialism. He would not be so interpreted as to oppose the immateriality of the soul. He seems to have left the question an open one, affirming that the immateriality of the soul has little or no connection with its immortality. Observations etc. P. I. Conclusion. On the Mechanism of the Human Mind. In Part II. ch. iv Sect. 3, he gives a calm and dispassionate, but very satisfactory and encouraging, summary of the natural indications of a future life, showing evidently that he was deeply impressed

chological tendencies were confirmed by the taste of the age for physical research, to which the rapid progress of chemical discovery and the new powers developed by mechanical science gave a peculiar stimulus. Fascinated by the unprecedented phenomena which were daily opening upon them with new wonders, the most educated minds of the time discovered generally a strong aversion to spiritual contemplation and religious enthusiasm. This is attested by all contemporary records. A reference to the literary history of that period, would, I believe, show that principles allied to those which Hartley embraced, were widely diffused among reflecting and philosophical persons, who took no part in theological controversies. As more directly affected by such principles in his whole conception of Religion and Christianity, may be mentioned an eminent and liberal-minded prelate, Dr. Edmund Law, bishop of Carlisle, who was in habits of friendly intercourse with some of the learned and philosophical divines among the Dissenters[1]. But the individual who adopted them with the greatest ardour, and allowed them the most direct influence on his entire range of moral and religious speculation,

by their combined force. In the interval between death and the resurrection he held it probable, that the soul would remain in a state of inactivity, though not perhaps of insensibility. He thought, that the Christian revelation gives us absolute assurance of a future state, and regarded all the miracles recorded in Scripture, and all the prophecies that have been accomplished, as so many 'pledges and attestations of the truth of this doctrine.' Prop. lxxxvii. and xc.

[1] Law's principal work is his 'Theory of Religion.' He was also the first to give to the world (prefixed to his translation of Archbishop King's Essay on the Origin of Evil) the Dissertation by Mr. Gay, "On the Fundamental Principle of Virtue;" to which Hartley modestly attributed the first suggestion of his own theory. Dr. Law edited the works of Locke, with a preface and a Life of the Author. This edition appeared in 3 vols. 4to, about 1777. Chalmers's Gen. Biogr. Dict. Law. All the writers of this school, including Hartley, combined with their peculiar philosophy, a great reverence for the simple doctrine of Scripture supernaturally confirmed by miracle and prophecy. See Hartley's Observations on Man, Part II. ch. ii. Of the Truth of the Christian Religion. The opinion for which Law is most remarkable, that of the natural mortality of man and of his re-creation at the last day by the power which God has bestowed on Jesus Christ, though no doubt favoured by his philosophical tendencies, was an inference, as appears by his copious induction of passages from both Testaments, from his interpretation of Scripture language. It appears, that Dr. John Taylor who was one of his correspondents among the Dissenters, acceded to his views on this subject. Protestant dislike of the Catholic doctrine of Purgatory, had something perhaps to do with their adoption of these views. See the Discourse on the Nature and End of Death under the Christian Covenant, subjoined to the Theory of Religion, with the Appendix and Postscript.

O

was Dr. Priestley, to whom the second school of English Unitarianism owes its origin.

In the same degree that the rationalizing process has been applied to the contents of Scripture, we may observe, there has often been a proportionate effort to draw tighter the outward sanctions of **miracle** and prophecy; **and** that the strongest minds have sometimes exhibited the greatest tenacity of this extrinsic **support to their faith.** Never perhaps was the endeavour **to reconcile the** antagonist principles of reason and authority, **by** keeping the former within, **and** putting the latter without, the limits of the written word, carried to a greater extent than in the school of Unitarianism founded by Priestley. He differed from the earlier Rationalists of his country, in the more dogmatic **cast of his mind**[1]. It had been the main object of his predecessors in this field of inquiry, to guard the boundaries of Scripture with **such** bulwarks, as **the** learned and conscientious toil of Lardner **had** enabled them to pile up on **every side**; but every **mind which once** found itself safely entrenched within them, **was left** to be as reserved or as explicit **as it chose**, in the declaration of doctrinal belief. The old **Presbyterian warfare of the last century,** was with creeds of human devising. Its animating spirit was a broad ethical eclecticism **and tolerance.** Its watchword was, the Bible only. But **the mind of** Priestley was too earnest and inquisitive, **to** rest in this vague and negative state. He wanted more positive results. Having convinced himself, that only one view of religious truth could be exhibited **in the** different **books of** Scripture, and that **this was** simple Unitarianism, he claimed for his own conclusion, all the certainty and authority of divine revelation.

He has thus stated the result of his inquiries, in an Essay on the Inspiration of Christ[2]. "If there be any truth in history, Christ wrought unquestionable miracles, as a proof of his mission from God; he preached the great doctrine of the resurrection from the dead; he raised several persons from a state of death; and, what was more, he himself died and

---

[1] Under the name Rationalist, I include all those who place the first principle of *religious* belief in a logical inference from data *external* to the mind, rather than in a spontaneous suggestion which springs up *within* the mind through the organic working of its original constitution, and which precedes and underlies every act of proper reasoning; in one word, who lay the *foundation* of faith in *ratiocination*, instead of *intuition*.

[2] Theological Repository, vol. iv. p. 456.

rose again in confirmation of his doctrine. The belief of these *facts* I call the belief of Christianity." He adds, "I think that a great deal is gained by carefully excluding from the *essentials* of the Christian religion every other opinion whatever except that of Christ being the Messiah." It appears from these last words, that he regarded his own view of Christianity, as identical with that of Locke, whose language is: "saving faith consists in believing only that Jesus of Nazareth is the Messiah[1]." But Locke's definition is more general and comprehensive, and therefore more spiritual. Its terms would embrace all who, whatever their opinion respecting the external facts of Christ's recorded history, provided it imply no imputation on his mental soundness or moral purity, are prepared, in full sympathy with the mind, the spirit, that dwelt in him, to accept him as their Messiah—the King and Lord of their moral being[2]. It is not asserted, that Locke had any doubt of the reality of those facts, or that there is any philosophic objection to the admission of them, as miraculous, provided we take them in the proper order; *i.e.* if we proceed from a faith in what our spiritual consciousness recognizes as holy and divine, to the acknowledgment of the outwardly miraculous which an honest historical criticism proves to be inseparably blended with it, instead of setting out from the miraculous, as a mere subject of human testimony, with a view to the original production of faith. Dr. Priestley's statement confounds *belief* as an intellectual act, with *faith* as a spiritual affection. By making the decided acceptance of certain historical facts, which no accumulation of testimony can bring within the limits of absolute certainty, the indispensable condition of becoming a disciple of Christ, he excludes, as it appears to me arbitrarily and harshly, from the Christian brotherhood, many sensitive and conscientious minds that best understand its spirit and would nobly fulfil its duties[3].

[1] Reasonableness of Christianity Works, vol. i. p. 166.

[2] I think I am justified in making this distinction between the Christianity of Priestley and of Locke, on a comparison of the former's assertion, that the belief of certain miraculous facts is the same thing as the belief of Christianity, with the declaration of the latter in his Journal, already referred to, (Life by Lord King, pp. 123-25) that 'even in those books which have the greatest proof of revelation from God—the miracles are to be judged by the doctrine, and not the doctrine by the miracles.'

[3] If one thing be clear in the New Testament, it is, that the conversion to which Christ summoned men, as the beginning of the Christian life, was a change

Brought up among the Independents, Priestley inherited through them from the old Puritans, a profound sense of the value of Revelation and of the authority of Scripture, which through all his changes of opinion remained with him unabated to the last, and combining with the singular boldness of his philosophical speculations, gave a very composite character to the general structure of his opinions[1]. Like Faustus Socinus,

wrought on their wills and affections. When this is accomplished, through faith, in other words, though deep sympathy with the spirit of Christ, it is altogether a matter of secondary importance, what view be taken of those purely *external* facts which have no value, but as subservient to the moral effects that are anticipated from a belief in them. Otherwise, the question may reasonably be asked, whether the Jewish rulers who witnessed the miracles, and had proof of the resurrection, of Jesus, (who had therefore the required *preliminaries* of belief in their minds, though they did not draw the proper inferences from them,) or those devout persons of the present day who, unable to assure themselves of the reality of these facts, still acknowledge with their hearts the intrinsic divinity and holiness of Christ's doctrine, person, and work, would be considered by Christ himself as standing nearest to the end of his great mission to the world. The former possessed at least the *data* which, according to the usual theory, are indispensable to belief; the latter, from their intellectual inability to grasp them, must, if Dr. Priestley's view be correct, remain necessarily *unchristianized* for ever. Rammohun Roy and the late Blanco White would come within the last description of persons.

[1] There was a singular mixture of the literal and the boldly speculative in Priestley's view of Christianity. The Puritan and the philosopher were never completely assimilated in him. Nothing could be freer than his notions about inspiration and prophecy, and of Christ's peccability and liability to prejudice and ignorance. (See his Evidence of Divine Revelation, Disc. ix. Rutt's edit. of his works, vol. xv. p. 309, and especially the articles on Inspiration in the fourth vol. of the Theological Repository, signed Pamphilus, more particularly pp. 208, 436, 442, 445 et seq.) Nothing could be more arbitrary than his occasional treatment of statements in the Scriptures, which opposed his own views; as when he told his friend, Dr. Price, that even if it could be shown, that the Apostles had taught the doctrine of Christ's being the Maker of the world, he would not have received it (Letters to Price, Works by Rutt, vol. xviii. p. 388). Yet in one of his conversations with Mr. Belsham, just before his departure for America, he expressed his belief, that the second advent of Christ would occur within twenty years. Belsham's Life of Lindsey, p. 375. It was his firm persuasion, that those passages in the prophets which speak of the restoration of the Jews to their native land, would be literally fulfilled, and that the Law would be set up anew with restored splendour and authority in Jerusalem. See his Letters to the Jews, Works vol. xx. especially pp. 230 and 249, and the remarkable papers in the v. and vi. vols. of the Theological Repository, signed Hermas, on the perpetual obligation of the Jewish Ritual. For the indication of the passages in his works containing this singular opinion, referred to perhaps too vaguely and generally in the first edition of this volume, I am indebted to a respected friend and former tutor, the Rev. W. Turner, junr., Christian Reformer: New series, vol. i. p. 762. To be consistent, Dr. Priestley should have gone farther, or not so far. The line is not drawn with sufficient distinctness between what is authoritative and what may be left to the free decision of reason.

he was disposed to regard a special revelation as the main source of all **positive** religious **belief; laid too** little stress on that universal sentiment of dependence on spiritual power and of reverential trust, which is co-extensive with humanity itself; and, **I must think,** undervalued the natural arguments **for a future life**[1]. The opinion repeatedly **occurs** in his writings

---

[1] On this subject, it has been objected, that I have exaggerated Dr. Priestley's views in the first edition. Yet it is evident from a paper communicated to the first volume of the Theological Repository, p. 236, (Literary Memoirs, relative to a future state, etc., written in the year 1768, by John Buncle, Esq.) where his opinions are represented under the person of Clemens, that at an early period of life he had adopted views not materially different from those imputed to him in the text. The following passage will furnish a proof. 'This would not do with Clemens. His *cry* was, *all-sufficient revelation*,—the *books* —the *books*,—it is in them only we can learn the doctrines which accord with the attributes of the Deity. In them only we can acquire just notions of a Being omnipotent, **infinite** in wisdom and goodness; by them only we are screened from pernicious errors, and can be fully *satisfied* that *immortality* and *glory* is to be the *reward* of those who faithfully obey the gospel. The *book of nature* is *nothing*. If that was all we had for a life everlasting, I should never think of a remove from the clods of the valley.' In sect. 5, ch. ii. **of the first Part of his Institutes** of Natural and Revealed Religion, ' Of the future expectations of mankind,' he has followed pretty closely Dr. Hartley's summary **of the natural** arguments for a future life; but he has stated them with far less geniality of feeling, and it is **quite** evident, that he does not himself attach any great value to them. What else can be inferred from such expressions as the following? '**It** must be acknowledged, **that considering only what we know of the constitution of the body** and mind **of man, we see no reason to** expect **that we shall survive death.**' He admits in an ensuing sentence, that if the divine attributes require it, God can easily revive **mind and body, or continue** the same consciousness in some other way. p. 95, vol. i. (4th edit.) London : 1808. In another place, he says : '**Upon** the whole, **I cannot help thinking, that there is something in the arguments above recited, which shows that a future life is very agreeable to the appearances of this, though I do not think them so striking, as to have been sufficient of themselves to have suggested the first idea of it.**' '**If we had never heard of a future life, we might not have expected it.**' p. 97. In ch. iii. sect. i. of the third Part of the same work, he remarks, that while the light of nature is tolerably clear as to the *duty of man* **in** this life, it leaves us under great uncertainty whether we shall survive the grave or not, and sums up his observations in the following **terms:** ' Such is the substance of what we were able to collect from nature concerning a future state, *provided there* **were** *any such thing*. From revelation we learn the *actual certainty* of a future state, and have an *absolute assurance* of its being a state of **exact retribution.**' Vol. ii. p. 238. In the 8th **of the Letters to a** Philosophical **Unbeliever,** the evidence for the future existence of man does not go beyond the concession of its possibility. **No faith could be** founded on such premises. **Our minds are very** differently **constituted for the** apprehension **of truths respecting the invisible. Dr.** Priestley's **firm belief in** the bodily resurrection of Christ was **the** circumstance which first gave value and significance to those natural indications of immortality, which would else have carried little weight to his mind. There are some (I must confess myself of the number) with whom it is quite otherwise. **It is** their natural belief in immortality as a

and is strongly urged as an argument for Christianity, that the rejection of revelation draws after it, if not logically yet as a usual consequence, the abandonment of all deep sense of natural religion. The character of his mind and the direction of his favourite pursuits, led him to seek outward and, as it were, tangible proofs of every doctrine he embraced, and created a distrust in all appeals to feeling and the interior sense of spiritual truth. He asked for demonstration in things which, from their very nature, are incapable of it; nor was he perhaps sufficiently prepared to admit, that a state of mind, far short of the certainty produced by demonstration, which relies on great spiritual tendencies, and gives itself up with entire trust to God, is favourable to moral culture and discipline, and constitutes the proper element of faith[1]. His mind was direct and simple, but had little power of adapting itself to the views of other minds, variously modified by the influence of age and nation. He was, therefore, ill-fitted to become the historian of religious opinion; for he interpreted the monuments of the past by his own philosophical ideas, and seemed unable to conceive, that truth could manifest itself under more than a single form. It was an arbitrary limitation of the design of Christianity, to assert as he did, that it consisted essentially in the revelation of a future life, confirmed by the bodily resurrection of Jesus.

For the stress which Priestley laid on miracle as the only conclusive proof of direct communication from God, the way had been prepared by the writings of his contemporary, Mr. Farmer. That learned writer had completed on another side, the argument from the New Testament for simple mono-

great law of God's spiritual creation, which renders credible to them the fact of Christ's resurrection, and the supernatural evidence of it enjoyed by his disciples. Apart from this natural trust, the historical testimony would not suffice for their conviction. They cannot but think, that the tacit influence of this trust, as an essential part of the deep religiousness of Priestley's mind, lent an authority to mere human testimony, which, left by itself, it would never have been felt to possess.

[1] It has been questioned (Christian Reformer for November, 1845, p. 761,) whether Dr. Priestley ever demanded *demonstration* in matters of religion; and a passage has been adduced from his Letters to a Philosophical Unbeliever (P. I. Letter i.) to prove the contrary. But in the very next sentence to the passage quoted, as much is stated as seems to me necessary to justify my representation of the case. 'In some of the cases, his *persuasion* (resulting from the evidence laid before him) shall hardly be distinguishable, with respect to its *strength*, from that which arises from a demonstration properly so called, *the difference being, as mathematicians say, less than any assignable quantity*.'

theism, by showing that the passages usually supposed to authorize a belief in Satanic and demoniacal agency, admitted another interpretation, and by arguing from these premises, against the opinion up to his time usually maintained, that well attested and real miracle could only be referred to the immediate agency of the one true God[1].

It is worthy of notice, that while the internal evidence for Christianity, and the experimental test of its divine origin, have remained the same through all time, and have even required fresh force with the progress of society, the external evidence has undergone continual modification, and been exhibited sometimes under one aspect and sometimes under another. Prophecy was the great argument employed by the Apostles and early Apologists. Miracles were also appealed to; but they were less insisted on, because it was believed that evil spirits could perform them: and prophecy was sometimes brought to the aid of miracle, to show that it really came from God[2]. This order of proceeding was reversed by Dr. Priestley. Without rejecting the evidence of prophecy (for in some cases he almost fanatically clung to it) he yet felt it weakened at so many points, that his great reliance was on the proof of miracle, especially the great miracle, Christ's resurrection from the dead.

With remarkable steadfastness and independence of mind, Priestley adhered to his religious principles and his Christian faith, amidst the almost universal unbelief of the philosophical world. What importance he attached to them, is evident from the unwearied activity of his pen, under all the discouragements of exile and the growing infirmities of age, to defend and explain the pure religion of Jesus, and to point out the mischievous influences of infidelity. Yet his later writings abound with complaints of the prevalence of unbelief. Some of his most intelligent and virtuous friends remained unconvinced by his reasonings[3]. If Christianity contain, as we be-

---

[1] See his Dissertation on Miracles, and Essay on the Demoniacs of the New Testament.
[2] Justin Martyr, Apolog. I. c. 30.
[3] In some observations on the importance of faith, (Theological Repository, vol. iii. p. 242, 3,) Dr. Priestley thus expresses his opinion respecting unbelievers in Christianity:—"For my own part, I must acknowledge that, with respect to the generality of modern unbelievers, I have no charity for them, except goodwill; and their condition fills me with concern; because I cannot

lieve it does, a truth from God, there must have been something defective in his mode of representing it, to account for the small effect of so much virtue and piety and ability employed in its behalf. With the purest purposes and most sincerely religious feelings, it must, perhaps, be confessed, that he surveyed Christianity in too limited a point of view, and defined it by too rigid an outline; that he looked at it too much through the philosophy of a particular school, and not sufficiently in the entire breadth of its relations to every part of our complex nature. Hence, he could not comprehend the various points of access it might have to minds differently constituted from his own; and by restricting to one particular avenue its legitimate approach to them, he might, in not a few cases, throw up a barrier against their receiving it at all:—and yet he was astonished at their unbelief.

The most successful advocates of Christianity have taken broader ground, and appealed directly to the moral consciousness of the universal heart. Baxter acknowledged "the indwelling spirit" as "the great witness of Christ and Christianity to the world[1]." "The great mystery of the Gospel," says Cudworth, "doth not lie only in Christ without us, (though we must know also what he hath done for us,) but the very pith and kernel of it consists in Christ inwardly formed in our hearts. Nothing is truly ours, but what lives in our spirits. Salvation itself cannot save us, as long as it is only without us[2]." Channing too has spoken truly and elo-

help thinking, that a very wrong state of mind, a state of mind to which Christianity holds out nothing but a *fearful looking-for of judgment*, is the cause of their unbelief; and that nothing is requisite to make them see and rejoice in the evidences of Christianity, but a truly virtuous and ingenuous disposition. It is with equal truth and much more pleasure, that I must acknowledge, that I cannot think so uncharitably of all my acquaintance among unbelievers. Some of them, I have all the reason in the world to think, are men of excellent dispositions, and want nothing but a firm belief of Christianity to make them as perfect as humanity will admit." His concluding observation gives perhaps the true view of this interesting subject, and suggests an excellent rule for our judgment and conduct respecting unbelievers:—"As it is expressly asserted, that Christ came 'to bless mankind, in turning them away from their iniquities,' Acts iii. 26, I think I am authorized to consider the Christian religion as *a means to an end;* and therefore, if the great end of it, viz. the reformation and virtue of man, be, in fact, attained by any other means, the benevolent author of it will not be offended, but rejoice at it, and say, 'He that is not against us, is on our part,' Mark ix. 40."

[1] Reliquiæ Baxterianæ, Lib. I. P. i. § 213. 4.
[2] Discourse before the House of Commons, March 31, 1647, p. 26.

quently of that "conviction of the divine original of Christianity, which results from the consciousness of its adaptation to our noblest faculties, as the evidence which sustains the faith of thousands who never read, and cannot understand, the learned books of Christian apologists, who want perhaps words to explain the ground of their belief, but whose faith is of adamantine firmness, who hold the Gospel with a conviction more intimate and unwavering than mere argument ever produced[1]."

Dr. Priestley stretched the principle of combining the free exercise of reason on the contents of Scripture, with the recognition of an outward authority, which made its acceptance as a divine rule obligatory on every unprejudiced mind—to its utmost point. Further progress in that direction was impossible. In his system we witness the last results of the rationalistic spirit in its application to the New Testament. The point had been reached, at which, unless the mind chose to remain immoveably where he had left it, one only of two alternatives was possible; either to go on into simple Deism, or to fall back on a broader and more spiritual conception of Christianity. That the latter has been almost universally adopted among the churches, which were most deeply affected by his principles, is to be ascribed chiefly to the very seasonable influence of the writings of Dr. Channing.

I am anxious that the purport of these observations should not be misapprehended. In common with many who hold the distinguishing tenet of Dr. Priestley's theology, the simple unity of the great Being who is revealed to us in the Gospel as our Father, I am unable to accept as *alone* conclusive, the grounds on which he placed the divine authority of Christianity; nor can I persuade myself, that he either fully embraced its whole design, or rightly apprehended its relation to the human mind and to the expectations excited in us by the constitution and visible tendencies of the Universe. Yet it must not be imagined, that this expression of dissent from some of his views, implies any insensibility to the magnitude of his services in the cause of religious truth, or to the great and heroic qualities of his character. It is a strange fallacy to assume, that we must agree in all things with those whom we most profoundly revere as men. In steadfastness of Chris-

---

[1] Dullcian Lecture on the Evidences of Revealed Religion.

tian principle, in ardour for truth, in purity of life and simplicity of purpose, and in genuine magnanimity and disinterestedness of spirit, Dr. Priestley stands pre-eminent, and almost without a rival, among the philosophers and men of science whose names shed such a lustre on the close of the eighteenth century. His opinions on some points may be considered as a natural result and expression of the times in which he lived—supplying a link in that chain of connected thought which binds together with a mysterious affinity the successive generations of civilized men. His place was assigned him by Providence. It is his highest praise to have filled it nobly—to have lived for what he believed to be truth, and to have sacrificed wealth and ease and worldly reputation in its defence and pursuit[1].

The theological opinions of Dr. Priestley were adopted with no important modification by Mr. Belsham, a man of clear and vigorous intellect, of warm affections, and of a very up-

---

[1] Strong aversion to many of Priestley's speculative tenets, and especially to the peculiar philosophy which he so closely interwrought with his theology, has prevented the deeply religious character of his mind, and the excellent practical tendency of many of his writings, from being duly appreciated. An Unitarian divine of a very different school, who does not conceal his entire dissent from him on several important points, the late Dr. Henry Ware, jun., of Boston, Massachusetts, has done justice to his memory in these respects, in a small volume, entitled 'Views of Christian Truth, Piety, and Morality, selected from the writings of Dr. Priestley,' Cambridge: 1834. On the influence of these estimable qualities in another field of activity, exhibiting the man of science in the same light as the theologian, a most competent judge has thus expressed himself: "In all those feelings and habits that connect the purest morals with the highest philosophy (and that there is such a connection no one can doubt) Dr. Priestley is entitled to unqualified esteem and admiration. Attached to science by the most generous motives, he pursued it with entire disregard to his own peculiar interests. He neither sought, nor accepted when offered, any pecuniary aid in his philosophical pursuits, that did not leave him in possession of the most complete independence of thought and action. Free from all little jealousies of contemporaries or rivals, he earnestly invited other labourers into the field which he was cultivating; gave publicity in his own volumes to their experiments; and, with true candour, was as ready to record the evidence which contradicted, as that which confirmed, his own views and results. Every hint which he had derived from the writings or conversation of others, was unreservedly acknowledged. As the best way of accelerating the progress of science, he recommended and practised the early publication of all discoveries; though quite aware that, in his own case, more durable fame would often have resulted from a delayed and more finished performance." An Estimate of the Philosophical Character of Dr. Priestley, by William Henry, M.D., F.R.S., etc., read at the first Meeting of the British Association for the Advancement of Science, at York, 1831.

right and truthful spirit, the most eminent representative of his school in the last generation of English Unitarians[1]. Towards the close of the eighteenth, and at the commencement of the present, century, the controversy excited a very general interest.

Unitarianism in the last age was maintained in various forms by men of learning and ability. Among these were the meek and conscientious Lindsey, whose gentle spirit was sometimes disquieted by the startling suggestions of his great philosophic friend[2]; the devout and contemplative Cappe, who made the Gospel consist of two parts, the restoration of natural religion by the abolition of the law, and the assurance of a future life by the fact of Christ's resurrection from the dead, and whose theological system, based on the religion of nature, differed therefore materially from that of Priestley[3]; and several men connected by birth and education with the Church and the Universities, such as Jebb and Tyrwhitt and Wake-

---

[1] At the end of his commentary on the Second Epistle to the Corinthians, Mr. Belsham has exhibited, in a condensed form, his views of the evidence and authority of Christianity. Having given a summary of the contents of the Epistle, he adds: "When we take all these things into consideration, it seems almost impossible to avoid coming to the following conclusions:—First, that this Epistle is *genuine*; that it was written by Paul himself, and not by an impostor assuming his name: and therefore, Secondly, that the facts stated in this Epistle are *true*, and consequently that the *Christian Religion is of divine original*; that the Apostle Paul was fully authorized and amply qualified to publish this heavenly doctrine to the world, that he justly challenges the most serious and attentive regard to his instructions, and that *they who reject his testimony, reject it at their peril*."—In this statement, faith in Christianity is identified with the intellectual act, that assents to the inference from a logical deduction. First, we have the genuineness of the book established; then, as a consequence, the truth of the facts contained in it; then, as another, the authority of the Apostle; lastly, as a result of the whole, the divinity of the religion and the danger of rejecting it. The whole process is external: Faith is founded on authority and enforced by fear.—We are so differently constituted, that it is impossible for one man to say, how the same statement may affect another; but I find it difficult to conceive, how such an argument could reach the *moral* and *spiritual* in man. The views of Watts, Cudworth, Baxter, and even of Owen, when reduced to their essence—seeking the true source of faith in inward feeling and conviction, which external facts only serve to call forth—seem to me to imply a profounder and more experimental acquaintance with human nature.

[2] Belsham's Life of Lindsey, ch. viii.

[3] See his Christian Principles deduced from Scripture, in the Critical Remarks, II. pp. 403-433. "All the *doctrines*, properly so called, the truth of which is supposed or admitted, or incidentally taught in Christianity, are doctrines of natural religion, and should stand entirely upon that ground. They are all supposed to be known or knowable, before the promulgation of Christianity. All that it *reveals*, is *fact*."—p. 421.

field, who relinquished the hope of preferment, that they might by their writings and example more effectually serve the interests of religious truth[1]. The great and good Dr. Price retained to the last his Arianism; but he was connected by many ties of sympathy and co-operation with the confessors and champions of Unitarianism. The distinguishing quality of all these men, who were the contemporaries and associates of Dr. Priestley, and shared in the intellectual and moral activity which he created around him—was a certain simplicity and ingenuousness of mind, which sought for truth as the most valuable of human possessions, and believed that under its purer and stronger influence a new era of virtue and happiness would arise on mankind. With such convictions, the feelings of hope inspired by the bright dawn of French liberty, naturally allied themselves, and gave birth to an enthusiasm, not always void of some extravagance, which was a new feature in the calm and intellectual faith of Unitarianism. But excellent and true-hearted were the men of those days; and ever honoured be their memories! They lived in a generous faith; and their bosoms glowed with the purest love of mankind.

SECTION XI.

ORTHODOX DISSENT: POPULARITY OF CHANNING: INFLUENCE OF GERMANY: POWERFUL ORGANIZATION OF INDEPENDENCY.

The bold development of Unitarianism in that section of the Dissenters with which Dr. Priestley had connected himself, produced some reaction towards a more decided orthodoxy among those Nonconformists who adhered to their traditional theology. Their condition, moreover, had been influenced by other causes, which drew them still further aside from the rationalistic tendency. The vehement and pathetic preaching of Whitfield and the two Wesleys had spread its contagion into the churches of the Establishment and the Dissenters. Among the Independents and the Baptists, the constitution of whose societies was readily susceptible of any popular impulse from without, a spirit of zeal and earnestness

---

[1] Biographical notices of these men will be found in vol. ii. of the 'Lives of Eminent Unitarians,' by Rev. W. Turner, jun., M.A., London: 1843.

revived, sometimes bordering on fanaticism, which dissipated the scholastic coldness and formalism of their predecessors, and preserved their churches from the decline already beginning to affect them. Learning for the time was less cultivated; but a strong hold was gained on the popular mind, which gave those denominations a new strength, and is the source of their numbers and influence at the present day. Religious sympathies attracted towards each other the orthodox Dissenters, the Methodists, and the Evangelical members of the Establishment. Partly in conjunction, and partly by separate efforts, these different bodies organized those vast associations for the conversion of the heathen and the distribution of the Bible, which have produced such extensive effects, and impressed so peculiar a character on our modern civilization[1]. Great also were the energy and perseverance of these same parties, effectually aided by the benevolent Society of Friends, in promoting the measures which put down the slave-trade, and, in the British colonies, finally abolished slavery. In achievements of practical philanthropy, inspired by deep religious enthusiasm, the power of the Evangelical body, both in and out of the Establishment, has been conspicuous. One pleasing feature distinguished the grand movement against the slave-trade, as if the spirit of Christ had converted for once the gall of theology into the milk of human kindness :—its leaders were of all religious persuasions, and yet acted together in perfect harmony and with mutual esteem. The Evangelical Churchman and the Unitarian fought side by side against oppression, on the floor of the House of Commons; and in the intervals of the strife, Clarkson and Wilberforce and Smith, Macaulay, Thornton and Stephen took righteous counsel together in the communion of private friendship.

While such were the aims and endeavours of the religious world, studies of a novel character, springing out of the researches of Adam Smith or the theories of Bentham, were beginning to engage the attention of thoughtful and earnest

---

[1] The Baptist Missionary Society was founded in 1792; the London, in 1795; the Church, in 1800; the British and Foreign Bible Society, in 1804. Two earlier Societies—for Promoting Christian Knowledge, 1698, and for the Propagation of the Gospel in Foreign Parts, 1701—originated with the Church; the latter, founded on a Company that had been constituted under the Long Parliament. But the operations of these two Societies have not equalled in extent those of later date. See Toulmin's History of Protestant Dissenters, ch. iv.

men. An enlarged and noble-minded benevolence mingled in the zeal which these and kindred pursuits inspired, and concentrated it on objects of practical good. But if the mind was thus delivered from the entanglements of vain speculation and unfruitful controversy, there was wanting, on the other hand, the attraction of a high moral and spiritual interest, to exclude a certain taint of utilitarianism. It is startling, at least, to observe the indifference of such men as Romilly, and Horner, and Mackintosh, to the religious questions of their day, and while they conformed to the established worship of the country, the cold reserve with which they abstained from identifying themselves with any great religious interest. There must, one would think, have been something deficient or repulsive in the contemporaneous theology, to account for the alienation of pure and elevated minds from a subject, which its close affinity with morals and jurisprudence must else have rendered so attractive. A clergy who would have expounded the truths of Christianity, like the late Sydney Smith, in a spirit of manly wisdom and benevolent application to the actual wants of society, without enthusiasm, priestly pretension, or doctrinal refinements, would have best met the wishes and satisfied the demands of this order of minds[1].

During the protracted and anxious struggle with France, which interrupted all intercourse with the Continent, theology made no visible progress in England. With few exceptions, original research was abandoned. Even the learned Marsh derived a very large portion of the materials of his valuable writings from German sources. The current divinity of the time was chiefly maintained out of the accumulated treasures of past generations. Old controversies kept their ground. To the same objections repeatedly advanced, the same answers were repeatedly given, year after year, with no very marked result. The various sections of the religious world retained pretty nearly the same relative position and influence, with an occasional exchange of members amongst each other. About the return of peace, the writings of Channing began to be known in this country. His Dudleian Discourse on the Evidences of Christianity, from its luminous exposition of the argument, the condensation and precision of its language, and the deep

---

[1] A prayer found among the papers of Romilly, and inserted in his Life, shows that in his mind a spirit of the sublimest theism was not wanting. Memoirs and Correspondence, vol. iii. p. 76.

religious feeling which pervaded it, produced a very strong impression. From that time till the lamented death of this eminent man, the public expectation which had been raised so high by the character of his earliest performances, was continually excited and fulfilled by a succession of essays and discourses on themes which come intimately home to men's business and bosoms—on religion, government and literature in their widest sense and application, and on the prospects which futurity holds out of a happier constitution of society.

Channing was not distinguished by profound acquirements or original research. His strength lay in the purity and fervour of his moral feeling, guided by a taste of exquisite delicacy, with such an infusion of the poetical faculty, as made him keenly alive to all the influences of beauty, and qualified him vividly to conceive, and warmly enter into, the most varied situations of the human character and heart. Indifferent to the outward distinctions of sect and party, he embraced the whole family of God in a spirit of comprehensive benevolence, and owned the Gospel as a law of universal love. Full of mercy and compassion for error and frailty, he could still even amidst the ruins of guilt, sympathize with the humanity which he revered and loved, and hope in the possibility of its final restoration. With exclusiveness, intolerance and persecution, inveterate malignity and hopeless sensuality, he was alone implacably at variance. It was from this inner fountain of love—this fresh spirit of humanity ever active in his heart—that Channing's literary productiveness gushed freely forth, in a style pure, fluent and copious—so beautifully translucent that it reveals the lightest thought which stirs the depth of the writer's mind—and if sometimes chargeable with turgidity, only betraying that stronger impulse of moral earnestness which lifts it for an instant above the smooth surface of our conventional phraseology.

It has been urged against Channing's fame, that he produced no great work. His writings were, indeed, all occasional; but for that reason they made a profounder impression on his contemporaries. Addressed to present feelings and interests, and eagerly absorbed by them, they only infused the principles of which they were the vehicle, more deeply into the heart of society. Such has ever been the literary character of men who have acted most powerfully on the general mind of their time: it was that of Wesley; to a large extent, it was that also of Baxter and Luther. Channing's function was rather that of the prophet, than of the scholar or philosopher. He explored no fresh mine of learned inquiry; he broached no new theories; he has not suggested, so far as I know, any one principle for the clearer solution of those difficulties which still embarrass the more recondite questions of morals and theology. But he gave utterance, in tones of such deep conviction and thrilling persuasiveness, to sentiments and aspirations which lie folded up in every human breast—that he called out a wide response of sympathy, and made thousands experience, as a fresh communication of religious life, through the kindling medium of his affectionate spirit, the awakened consciousness of principles which had long been slumbering in their hearts, but to which they had become almost insensible through the mechanical inculcation of a dead traditional form. He drew forth from its depths the hidden man of the heart; asserted its worth, its nobleness, its inherent capabilities of good; and with a prophet's influence, making all things new, brought back Christianity from words and phrases and doubtful disputations, in which it had wellnigh perished, to become a living power for the renovation of humanity. His scattered pieces have gone out into the world, like so many oracles of the indwelling spirit; the words of a soul that lived in close communion with God, and saw all things in the light of his truth; spoken with immediate reference to particular times, and seasons, and persons, and having no common unity but the strong interest which they all express, for the improvement and happiness of mankind. In their collected state, they will witness to future generations the first fresh outpouring of that pure spirit of religion which is destined to raise at last, out of the dry dust of antiquated creeds, the fair and blooming garden of the united family of God.

The minds of Priestley and Channing were so differently constituted, that neither perhaps could have fully understood the other; and the latter certainly did not, at one time, render full justice to the great merits of his predecessor, as a theologian and a man. Priestley delighted in the clear and definite results of physical science, and unreasonably expected the same in very different regions of inquiry; Channing loved the grand and vague speculations of general philosophy, and was fitted by nature for the refined and delicate studies of literature and the arts. Priestley was a materialist and a necessarian, and had a feeling of contempt, which he never disguised, for the abstractions and reveries of the Platonic school; Channing was as enthusiastic in defence of the doctrines of free-will and spiritualism, which appeared to him essential to the preservation of morality and religion, and was allied by the imaginative cast of his genius, to that order of minds which feel themselves irresistibly attracted towards the "lofty visions" of the philosopher of the Academy. Priestley was disposed to underrate the value of natural religion, and found, as he thought, in a few well-attested statements of the New Testament, the only evidence worth consideration of a life beyond the grave; while Channing saw in the implanted affections and tendencies of our moral being, a natural ground and assurance for the principles and hopes, which it appropriates, as with a kindred feeling, when presented to it in their purest form by the religion of Christ. In Priestley, religion was a conviction of the understanding; in Channing, it was more a sentiment of the heart. They had only one point of agreement and sympathy; their common acknowledgment of the sovereign, unapproachable unity and the infinite goodness of the Supreme Father.

Channing's writings discover rather an intimate familiarity with the spirit of Christianity, than learned skill in the interpretation of its letter. It is not often, and only when driven to it by the necessities of his subject, that he enters minutely into doctrinal questions; nor is he perhaps the most satisfactory authority to consult, on purely controversial points. His learning was not deep; his mind lived in the present rather than the past; and he had evidently no natural taste for critical disquisition. In most of his discourses, after he has once announced his text, he soars away into the regions of general thought, and, except in an occasional reference, never allows his reader to get a second glimpse of Scripture. Indeed, the relation of his religious system to the Bible, which he sincerely and fervently reverenced as a vehicle of divine revelations, was somewhat vague and indistinct. With a feeling of sensitive conservatism for whatever he had once regarded as sacred, and accustomed to look more *within* for the evidence of divine authority, than among the testimonies of a remote age—he appears to have rested in the general conclusion, that the writings of the Old and New Testament convey to men the teachings of the Spirit of God, and that he was fully justified in employing reason fearlessly to establish the agreement between them and his own inherent sense of right and truth. So far as I know, he has never attempted to settle the fundamental question, how far our individual feeling of what is right and true, must give way to the clearly ascertained purport of the doctrine of Scripture. The earnest and devotional character of his mind was wholly adverse to the wild and gratuitous scepticism, which has infected so much of the theology of the Germans. Nevertheless he had a quick and ready sympathy with the free and open spirit, and the readiness to appreciate every sincere and pure-hearted manifestation of humanity, whether in literature or in religion, which pervades the studies of that learned and contemplative people. He does not appear to have been acquainted with their language, or in any instance to have drawn directly from their stores of erudition and philosophy; yet his writings—perhaps in his own country—certainly among the Unitarians of England—have contributed to prepare the public mind for more truly estimating the scholarship, and comprehending the intellect, of Germany, and furnished a medium of transition from the school of Priestley, which on nearly every point is at war with them.

It is interesting to trace the mazy windings of the stream of opinion. The principles of English Freethinking penetrated into Germany, as I have already remarked, at an early period of the eighteenth century. They were in harmony with the views of the most distinguished of its sovereigns, Frederick II. of Prussia, under whose influence the *Deutsche Bibliothek* became a similar receptacle for the free discussion of religious questions at Berlin, with the *Encyclopédie* at Paris. As yet however the theology of the Germans maintained in general its orthodox and conservative character. To uphold it in this position by the aid of solid learning, was one of the objects contemplated in the foundation of the University of Göttingen by George II. in 1735. Mosheim and J. D. Michaelis, two of its earliest ornaments, were essentially orthodox. Semler was one of the first who threw a bolder spirit of doubt into sacred criticism and ecclesiastical history. Before the close of the century, two very remarkable men produced a deeper and more lasting impression on the state of religious opinion in Germany. These were Lessing and Kant.

The former was an elegant scholar and a man of the world; the latter a recluse philosopher, who began and ended his days in Königsberg, but from that remote quarter exerted an influence which pervaded for a time every realm of German thought. Kant passed through the moral law, which he accepted as a positive, ultimate fact in human nature, to the belief of a God as a necessary influence required for its completion. His belief was in fact, therefore, *à priori;* or at least a corollary from an intuitive proposition. Religion with him grew out of, and finally resolved itself into, an immutable and absolutely perfect moral law. How these views must have modified his conception of Christianity, will occur to every one. Yet he had a strong sense of the practical value of Christianity; and thought its historical origin and scriptural form well fitted to act beneficially on the great mass of minds. It ought, however, he contended, to be so interpreted and administered, as to make it yield with increasing clearness the higher principles involved in it, and render it a discipline of preparation for the religion of pure reason. To any miraculous sanction of a divine truth Kant attached no weight. The only evidence of its heavenly origin was its accordance with the eternal law of reason. These views he has developed in a treatise entitled ' Religion within the limits of simple Reason[1];' which he undertook, as he informs us in his preface, from a persuasion, that such a course on the Philosophy of Religion was very desirable at the close of a theological education. In accordance with this idea, his whole work exhibits an ingenious effort to convert the chief articles of the orthodox belief into a corresponding series of philosophical equivalents. Many of these attempts are very far-fetched, and the questionable principle of accommodation is pushed to a great extent. The predilection of the German mind for traditional forms, combined with extraordinary freedom and subtlety of speculation, is conspicuous throughout. Everything must come out of the past, through gradual historical development. His whole procedure was in striking contrast to that of his philosophical contemporaries in France. It is an obvious defect in this system of Kant, that he altogether overlooks the existence of the religious principle as an original element and spontaneous impulse of our mental constitution, which, however it may grow

---

[1] Die Religion innerhalb der Gränzen der blossen Vernunft. Königsberg: 1793.

up by the side of the moral law, and ought always to subsist in perfect harmony with it, is still entirely distinct.

From this imputation the less systematic views of Lessing are free. With a deep feeling of what was beautiful in the pure religion of Christ, he would have left it very much as feeling. He disliked all attempts to rationalize it; and in full agreement with a well-known aphorism of Lord Bacon, he strongly protested against the modern practice of amalgamating theology and philosophy. He thought Christianity had become too much a matter of intellect and speculation. "We are angels in knowledge," he says, speaking of the philosophical Christianity of the eighteenth century, "but devils in our lives[1]."

He had no belief in the old orthodox system[2]; but he was of opinion, that it should either be preserved in its entireness, the compact and subtle consequentiality of which he admired, standing on its own basis and holding no communion with philosophy, or else be swept away completely and a new edifice be erected in its place. What he objected to, was patching up an old and ruinous edifice with a stone here and there, taken from the quarry of the philosophers. In a remarkable letter to his brother, he has expressed himself very freely on this subject. "We have pulled down," he says, "the old wall of separation, and under pretence of making rational Christians, we have made most irrational philosophers[3]." In speaking of the effect produced on him by defences of Christianity and attacks upon it, he recalls what many others must frequently have experienced, and betrays at the same time the religious tenderness, which in spite of scepticism was ever present in the depths of his soul[4]: "It has often seemed to me, as if these gentlemen, like Death and Love in the fable, had exchanged their weapons. The more closely one presses me with the proofs of Christianity, the more I am filled with doubts. The greater the insolent triumph with which the other would trample it in the dust, the more disposed I feel to

---

[1] 'Der Erkenntniss nach sind wir Engel, und dem Leben nach Teufel,' Gedanken über die Herrnhüter, in his Theologischer Nachlass.

[2] 'Darin sind wir einig, dass unser altes Religionssystem falsch ist.' In a letter to his brother.

[3] 'Man reisst deise Scheidewand nieder, und macht uns, unter Vorwande uns zu vernünftigen Christen zu machen, zu höchst unvernünftigen Philosophen.' Lessing's Leben, von K. G. Lessing, Berlin: 1793, pp. 351–2.

[4] Bibliolatrie, p. 73. Theolog. Nachlass, III.

sustain it erect, at least in my heart." One of the means by which Lessing most powerfully stimulated the fearless search and theological doubts of his contemporaries, was the publication of the celebrated fragments of Reimarus, deposited in the ducal library at Wolfenbüttel, which contained the boldest assault yet made on the received faith of the Christian world, and particularly on the credibility of the resurrection[1].

But another mind of earlier date and remoter influence was working perhaps more deeply still in the formation of German opinion, than either Lessing or Kant; I mean that of Spinoza. While the theology and philosophy of England were yet obeying the impulse originally given to them by Locke, the speculative intellect concentrated in the Universities of Germany, was silently imbibing the spirit of the Jewish pantheist. Herder, Lessing, Eichhorn, Paulus, Schleiermacher—all names which mark successive steps in the development of German theology —indicate in their writings and opinions the sway exercised over their thoughts by this subtle and meditative thinker. Perhaps to no circumstance can the different direction which theological inquiry has taken in England and in Germany, be so immediately ascribed. In the two countries the mixture of a philosophical system with a yet unbroken rigidity of Scripturalism, produced different but analogous results. In England the miracle was retained, to invest with a divine authority the religious and ethical wisdom which the letter of the primitive record was made to yield. In Germany where miracle was not reconcilable with the prevalent philosophy, while the letter of Scripture was still accepted with reverence, it was so interpreted as to bring miracle within the limits of natural law. In both there was a straining of Scripture language; in both an exegesis was tolerated that would have been considered admissible in no other book; but it was in a different way and for a different purpose in the two countries. The system of antisupernatural interpretation is seen to perfection in the works of Paulus. Its hollow, unsatisfactory character was easily detected. It could hardly have convinced those who had recourse to it. Divines of a higher order, De Wette, Lücke, Schleiermacher, and the great Orientalist, Ewald, while universally regarding miracle as no evidence of divine truth, have been more generally disposed to leave the miraculous of Scrip-

[1] Fragmente des Wolfenbüttelschen Ungenannten. Herausgegeben von G. E. Lessing. Berlin: 1835. 4te Aufl.

ture undetermined, or to look for its origin rather in the conception of the narrator than in the nature of the fact. The pretensions of this shallow system of antisupernaturalism were completely dispelled by the school of Schleiermacher. In his Discourses[1] addressed to the educated classes, who, at the beginning of the present century, under the influence of the French philosophy, had sunk into a complete state of moral relaxation and spiritual apathy, he eloquently called attention to the fact, that religion is an independent and original element of human nature, and distinguished it from mere knowledge on one hand, and from simple morality on the other. In this respect, by developing a new and fruitful principle, with the germ of which he had perhaps been furnished by Jacobi, Schleiermacher rendered great service to the religious life of his country, and was always spoken of by the late excellent and pious Neander, as having made quite an era in theology. Yet Schleiermacher's philosophy which betrays itself very decidedly in all his scientific productions, excluded belief in a personal God and individual immortality. It is difficult for an English mind to conceive, how such opinions could be honestly reconciled with the retention of an office in the Evangelical Church and the professorship of Christian theology. Nevertheless, though I cannot adopt the view on which his great work, 'The Christian Faith according to the principles of the Evangelical Church,' is written, where he endeavours to bring all these principles into harmony with his philosophical system, and even goes so far as to assert the doctrine of man's total incapacity for good previous to his redemption in Christ[2]; there was certainly in Schleiermacher, as any acquaintance with his writings will prove, a deep religiousness of spirit combined with great reverence for the person and work of Christ, and a sustained and disinterested effort through his whole life, to renovate the Christian Church and make it more conducive to the purification and ennoblement of human nature. On several points he expressed himself so ambiguously, that it was a question at his death, what his real opinions were, and different parties claimed him as their own. The philosophical schools of Fichte, Schelling, and Hegel, which succeeded one after another that of Kant,

---

[1] Ueber die Religion. Reden an die Gebildeten unter ihren Verächtern. The first edition appeared in 1806.
[2] Christliche Glaube, § 70.

each in their turn exercised an influence on the contemporaneous state of theology; but of these that of Hegel which is admitted to be essentially pantheistic, has made by far the deepest impression, and seems likely to leave behind it the most enduring effects[1]. While the disciples of Schleiermacher preserved a moderately conservative character and still maintained Christianity on its historical basis[2]; the influence of the Hegelian philosophy found an expression in the freer and bolder theology of the Tübingen school, from which the celebrated Strauss came forth. In his Life of Jesus two distinct elements are to be noticed: first, the mythical principle, which he has carried to the utmost length, and fairly exhausted, in his attempt to account for the origin of the supernatural in the narratives of the New Testament; and secondly, the pantheistic spirit in which he conceives the whole subject of religion and Christianity. Of the first of these elements the influence can never again be overlooked in the interpretation of the primitive records of the Gospel, though a more cautious and reverential criticism will doubtless reduce it within far narrower limits. The second, whose effects are of a much more serious and lamentable character, is only to be overcome by a philosophy more powerful than itself, and truer to the unchangeable principles of human nature, which shall have its source not in the abstractions of the intellect, but in the living realities of the spiritual consciousness: and such a philosophy can only arise under the favouring shelter and stimulus of civil and religious freedom[3].

[1] A theological professor of Heidelberg, Daub, is remarkable for having passed through all these different philosophical systems, and for having reconciled with each in succession his Christian faith. Critical History of Rationalism, etc., by Amand Saintes, ch. xiii. p. 228, Engl. transl.

[2] The principles of this school were represented in the *Theologische Studien und Kritiken*; a journal set on foot by Schleiermacher himself, and continued up to this time by the most eminent of his followers.

[3] In the preface to his countrymen, prefixed by the Chevalier Bunsen to the *German* edition of his Hippolytus, are some very wise and seasonable remarks on the necessity of uniting practical life with science, for the sake of science itself. "Ich bin überzeugt, dass auf dem kirchlichen Gebiete das sittliche Leben als Selbstzweck, als die eigentliche Religion, vor allem anderen anzustreben sei, und zwar von den Wissenden insbesondere. Ich bin ferner überzeugt, dass die innigste Verbindung des Gedankens und der Forschung mit der religiös kirchlichen Verwirklichung als einem Theile des öffentlichen Lebens, uns jetzt mehr als je nothwendig ist, damit wir nicht auf dem Gebiete des Denkens und Forschens selbst rückwärts gehen, sondern das Begonnene würdig vollenden."—The 'History of Rationalism' by Amand Saintes, already referred to, does not come up to its subject, and is written from a narrow point of view. A really

The intercourse between England and the Continent for the last quarter of a century has been so constantly on the increase, and so many of the present generation of ministers among the Dissenters, have received a part of their education in the Universities of Germany, that the new views of sacred history and criticism suggested by its profound and original learning, and the bolder tone of its philosophical speculation, could hardly fail to produce some effect on that portion of the Nonconformist body, which from hereditary principle, the previous state of opinion, and ardent sympathy with the spiritual tendencies of the school of Channing, is most open to receive any new impulse in the direction of free inquiry. The result has undoubtedly been, some division of opinion among them. In all communities there are men, equally intelligent and estimable, who in consequence of the different complexion of their minds, naturally arrange themselves, during the great crises of social development, in the two classes of the *conservative* and the *progressive*. Whenever there is clear evidence of earnestness and mental purity, mutual respect and forbearance is the great duty of such periods. Some Unitarians of the present day, those especially whose opinions have been long formed, are disposed to adhere to the position in which theology was left by Dr. Priestley and his contemporaries. Others dissent from his view of the human mind, and its relation to God and the universe; consider his Scriptural system as deficient in strict self-consistency; and are persuaded that the whole theological truth cannot yet have been discovered. They are anxious, therefore, to pursue and develope such views, as shall more effectually remove admitted difficulties, and help to place religion generally, and Christianity, its purest and most exalted expression, on a broader and more secure foundation in the spiritual nature of man. But of those who are disposed to go farthest in this new direction, it may be asserted, that they deny neither the metaphysical nor, in duly attested cases, the historical possibility of the miraculous. Only in their estimate of Christianity and their access to it, they set its *internal* far before its *external* evidence. With diminished interest, except as matters of history, in many of the doctrinal ques-

philosophical history of German theology has yet to be written. It is too soon for such a work to appear. The whole influence of such writers as Lessing, Schleiermacher and Strauss on the future development of Christianity and the Church, only coming generations will adequately appreciate.

tions which most warmly excited the last generation, they have an increased love and reverence for the life and person of Jesus Christ, an increased sympathy with his great and holy work; and they shrink with instinctive pain and disgust from every interpretation of his history, that would impair his spiritual influence and authority over their hearts.

Upon other classes of English Dissenters the learning of Germany has not been without its effects. The most eminent writers among the Independents are well acquainted with German theology; and their young men are imbibing more and more of its spirit[1]. But the power of the great body of Evangelical Dissenters, whether Independents or Baptists, is shown now, as it has ever been, rather in practical life and extensive social movements, than in learning and speculation. Its whole strength has been called out against the high sacerdotal tendencies manifested of late years by the Church. The revival of the spirit of Laud has revived once more its old antagonist—the spirit of Puritanism;—with this difference, however, resulting from the progress of society, that, whereas the old Puritans would have set up their own church government in place of Episcopacy, the modern Puritans, asking no preference for themselves, would level all ascendency, and put every denomination on the same footing of freedom and self-reliance. Independency, perhaps the most popular organization of the religious life at present in existence, defies and encounters the Church at every point. Whatever the Church attempts, Independency, conscious of its strength, meets with a counter-attempt. It multiplies schools; founds colleges; establishes lectureships; circulates tracts[2]; institutes a society for the publication of old Puritan writings[3] and centralizes its energies in a National Union[4]. If any of its cherished principles are encroached upon either by the Government or the Hierarchy, the assault is at once resisted by a vast and simultaneous manifestation of public opinion from the press, the pulpit, and the platform, and by the systematic exertion of a powerful influence on all the springs of parliamen-

---

[1] The work of Mr. J. D. Morell (once an Independent Minister) on the Philosophy of Religion, has been obviously influenced by the spirit of Schleiermacher's theology.
[2] Congregational Union Tract Series.   [3] The Wycliffe Society.
[4] The Congregational Union of England and Wales, formed in 1829. See Bright's Apostolical Independency, p. 20.

tary action. Among the religious phenomena of the time, not the least remarkable is the strength and organization of Independency.

From the association which the more ardent of the Independents and Baptists and some other religionists have organized for the dissolution of the Establishment, under the title of the Anti-State-Church Union, the majority of the Unitarians have kept aloof. Some of them, in common with their Presbyterian ancestors, would much prefer the reform and the purification of that which exists, to complete revolution. Others who admit in the abstract the inexpediency of religious establishments, experience so strongly the difficulties which historical conditions attach to the present realization of their views in England, that they are inclined to pause, and feel their way step by step towards a more just and equal constitution of religious society. Nor can it be denied, that the spirit too often displayed by those who are most eager for the separation of Church and State, has caused no unreasonable apprehension, that the liberty of the individual mind might not be increased by the event, and that the tyranny of a fanatical public opinion would prove more intolerable than the ascendency of a favoured Church.

Every one who comprehends the spirit of Christianity, must wish to see perfect freedom of conscience established, and all civil distinctions removed from diversities of religious profession. Many accept the voluntary system as the most direct means to this desirable end. But to the progress of truth and the healthful development of individual conviction, other assistances must concur besides the simple independence from civil control of the particular bodies in which men associate for worship and edification; and among these, are repose of mind, leisure for inquiry and meditation, and some security against the impatient, and at times ignorant, interference of the popular will. I do not say that the voluntary system may not be so organized, as to secure effectually all these ends; but this must depend on the quality of the minds, to which the organization is entrusted. The voluntary system, it should be remembered, is not in itself an end, but only a means to an end. The present day but adds another to the many instances of that bewilderment of the public sentiment, in which a great end is postponed and almost sacrificed to a fanatical predilection for a favourite means. In the wish to see religious ascendency abated, and religious equality put in its place; in the desire, that all religious communities should stand in the same relation to the laws of their country, and be permitted, under the stimulating influences of sound education, to develope healthfully and vigorously their inherent tendencies and views; there is, so far as I am aware, no difference of opinion whatever among Unitarians. To religious justice and religious freedom they cling as sacred principles. But with regard to the best method of reducing those principles to practice, and the most direct course for approaching their realization—they feel, there is room for an honest and intelligent diversity of opinion, which must not be put on the same ground with a fundamental principle.

CONCLUSION.

On completing this brief survey of the Religious Life of England, it is natural to ask, what impression it has left upon the mind, and what indications it offers of the probable direction of its future course. In each of the three manifestations of it, which have been here noticed—the Church, Puritanism, and Free Inquiry—though all have contributed in turn to the general progress, it is impossible for a candid mind not to be aware of a deficiency and a one-sidedness, which forbid our regarding any one of them, taken apart, as an expression of the whole truth, or a solution of all the difficulties entering into the religious constitution of society. They seem rather to furnish the different ingredients which, mixed in due proportions, and qualifying each other, might compose a universal Church.

We have, for instance, in our national hierarchy the principle of tradition, modifying the conception and outward expression of the primitive religious elements, contained in Scripture. Tradition in the Anglican Church has acquired an undue force; it has stifled the power of inward growth, and closed up the religious life in a mass of fixed and rigid forms. Instead of casting out what is withered and dead, and, through the absorption of fresh influences from contemporaneous ideas and interests, lengthening out a continuous identity from generation to generation, it clings superstitiously to the decisions of a particular period, and drags after it the cumbrous adhesions of ages less instructed and enlightened. Notwithstanding these abuses, Tradition is still a principle of indispensable application in all the social arrangements of religion. It secures the peaceable evolution of the present out of the past; it cherishes a healthful feeling of nationality; it prevents the destructive outbreaks of ignorant caprice and passionate self-willedness; it furnishes a broad base on which practical wisdom can erect its plans, and adjust them calmly and deliberately to the advancing demands of social progress; and by fixing provisionally men's **outward relations to** each other in the offices of public worship, it **constitutes** the only attainable bond of extensive religious **communion.** Viewed as the recognized symbols of internal feeling, forms and **usages** which no one would at present think of originating, **find a** sufficient justification in the fact of their established existence; provided they are **at war with** no fundamental **conviction,** and express with **fitting** solemnity the innate religiousness of the soul. The **acceptance of** them on such grounds, is to acknowledge **so far the** principle of Tradition. Tradition is the natural vehicle of a progressive civilization.

Scripture, on the other hand, brings into immediate contact with the individual soul, **the fresh intuitions of** religious truth, as they descended, under the influence **of the** Spirit of God, into the minds of holy men and prophets, **and** thus renews from their original source, convictions and feelings which are always latent in the conscience and the heart, but which the use of mere traditional forms tends to benumb. Of this important element of the religious life, Puritanism is the great representative in our national history. But Puritanism unfortunately took under its defence rather the letter, than the spirit, of Scripture; **and it has** therefore distorted and exaggerated the principle of which it is the symbol.

A **third** element of spiritual progress has been furnished by Rationalism **or** Free Inquiry—the **exercise of a speculative intellect**: but this again has been cultivated **in the same partial** and exclusive spirit as the former two, as if **religion were** wholly the product of reason, instead of being simply measured and estimated by it. There must be something given **and** positive, for reason to set out from: independent of such data, it loses itself in vague theories, and wanders on without coming to a conclusion. Proofs of this abound in the history of every civilized community. Yet if reason be not invested with the fullest right of free examination, Tradition will infallibly degenerate into a dead formalism, and Scripture only engender fanaticism.

These three principles, then, seem **intended to check** and balance each other: and that they have each been **so** powerfully developed in our own country, at once attests the vigour and activity of the national mind, and may be accepted as an omen of future good to be worked out under their joint influence. It is no mere accident, that they have stood out so prominently in the history of England, for they are deeply interwoven with the religious constitution of Christendom. As early as the third century, while the idea of Catholicism was advancing towards its realization, we find them distinctly expressed in the three great centres of patriarchal authority: Tradition upheld with conservative stiffness at Rome; Scripture studied with a critical fidelity at Antioch; and Speculation flourishing among the followers of Clement and Origen at Alexandria.

To produce the best fruits of which they are each capable, these tendencies should not be shut up in insulated schools and sects, but kindly recognize each other, and carry on a free and open intercourse. Some union of this kind was in preparation among the leaders of the different sections of the Church, under the Protectorate; and the hope of it never completely abandoned many excellent men who survived those times—Baxter and Howe and some Episcopalians of a kindred spirit. But the exclusive ascendency of one party so violently effected at the Restoration, and the legalization of the distinction between Dissent and the Establishment introduced by the Revolution, have settled the boundary lines of different Christian communions with a fixedness and a permanence, as obstructive to large views of truth, as to all genuine exercise of the spirit of the Gospel. The great landmarks then set up, have remained unmoved to the present day, and are protected with a religious veneration: so that, unless a man will voluntarily excommunicate himself, he must take his position in some clearly defined section of the fold of Christ, and by this act virtually declare his approval of particular doctrines and usages, as alone conformable to the eternal standard of truth and right. There are no Churches which do not rest more or less on this sectarian basis: and the fact is painful and perplexing to some minds of a high order, full of religious feeling and sighing for religious sympathy. So many prejudices and so many interests are bound up with this constitution of things, that it seems vain to expect any improvement, till it is dissolved by some external change, which shall once more unfetter the primitive elements of the religious life, and put them again into free circulation. Such a change might possibly afford an opportunity of so tempering and combining these elements in practice, as to prevent the exclusiveness which has hitherto prevailed, and unite all Christian minds, if not in one habitual communion, at least in a bond of mutual recognition and in a friendly interchange of religious offices. To anticipate any definite plan amidst the possible contingencies that may hereafter arise, would be rash and presumptuous. The particular mode of approximating to the desired result, must of course be determined by circumstances which no individual can foresee. It is sufficient for one who reasons from the past to the future, to point out the historical tendencies that lie deep in our national life, and to suggest the probability of their finally issuing in some harmonious result.

Such a comprehension of different religious forms in a general Christian union, so far as it is attainable in this world, would be more in harmony with the character and history and insular position of the English nation, and at the same time more directly conduce to the ends of the Gospel, than the endless multiplication and reciprocal exclusiveness of sects prevalent in America, which only tends to exasperate the spirit of schism, by making it a point of honour and consistency, if not a matter of interest, for each religious society to lay the greatest stress on the dogmas and rites which distinguish it from others. On this subject, it is more easy to feel what is wrong, than to prescribe its cure. We can only throw ourselves on our faith in God, and labour to diffuse the *spirit* of Christianity; believing that, as it spreads and takes a stronger hold of the heart, it will guide all sincere Christians to a clearer perception of the means that should be adopted for attaining the end which they all ardently desire. The change "must be effected,"—to adopt the impressive language of Howe—"not by mere human endeavour, but by an almighty spirit poured forth, which, after we have suffered awhile, shall put us into joint, and make every joint know its place in the body; shall conquer private interests and inclinations, and overawe men's hearts by the authority of the divine law, which now, how express soever it is, little availeth against prepossessions. Till then, Christianity will be among us a languishing, withering thing. When the season comes of such an effusion of the Spirit from on high, there will be no parties. And amidst the wilderness desolation that cannot but be till that season comes, it matters little, what party of us is uppermost[1]."

In the meantime, some important changes must first take place, to render such a union feasible. In the present divided state of opinion about the essentials of salvation, it is not even approachable. Either, therefore, mankind must come to an agreement respecting the doctrines which are taught with a divine authority, as necessary to be believed, in Scripture—an event which there is no reasonable ground to expect, since the progress of criticism seems rather to increase, than to lessen, differences of mere opinion; or else the Christian mind must take a new direction, and, renouncing a dogmatic theology, look for salvation in the *spirit* of Christ himself, wrought into the believing soul, and becoming the inward principle of a higher moral life. This spirit of Christ involves three elements: subjection of will and endeavour to the will of the everlasting Father; affectionate sympathy with humanity in all its stages of development; and the sure expectation of a more glorious futurity both for the individual and for the species. All these elements are expressed and embodied, with a surpassing beauty and power, in the life of Christ: and to sympathize with that life, to baptize our hearts into its redundant spirit of faith and love, to look up to Christ as our spiritual helper and guide to a higher world,—is belief unto salvation, an entrance into the kingdom of God. It is difficult to conceive how any pure minds could decline this sympathy with the life of Christ; how any minds in which the moral sense was not wholly extinct, should not be awakened, by having it held up before them, to a deeper consciousness of that which is divine and immortal in the human soul. In this sympathy of the will and affections with Christ; in this acknowledgment of him with the heart, as the head of his Church, the first-born of the spiritual family of God; there seem to exist the only indispensable conditions of a comprehensive union among Christians. On this simple basis individuals and societies may ground whatever forms and usages they find expedient for the culture of their spiritual affections, and may associate with it any exposition of doctrinal views which they need for the satisfaction of the specu-

---

[1] Quoted by Calamy, in the Dedication to the Protestant Dissenting Ministers, prefixed to his Continuation, p. xliii.

lative intellect; if only prepared, amidst their many varieties of opinion and worship, to own as a brother-disciple of Christ, every one whose life is conformed to his divine example, and whose heart is filled with his heavenly spirit.

An intellectual discipline is also necessary to facilitate the consummation desired. The reciprocal influence of religion and philosophy has been alluded to. But their relation to each other is indistinctly apprehended. It is a very unhappy circumstance, that religion, which belongs to our moral rather than our intellectual nature, and is wanted as the steady monitor and unchanging comforter of our daily life, should be carried through all the vicissitudes which mark the course of its more adventurous companion. We should define, therefore, more distinctly the line of separation between religion and philosophy. For this end a more exact psychology of religion is required. We ought also to possess a good natural history of religion. Both processes—a careful analysis of the mental elements involved in the various states of religious feeling and conviction, with an elimination of the fortuitous adjuncts of philosophical opinion—and secondly a comprehensive review of the historical development of the religious principle, with a comparison of its various outward manifestations in the rites and dogmas of nations most widely separated in character and institutions—are indispensable, to give us a clear insight into the working of the interior sense which connects us with the invisible and the infinite, and to place in the fullest light the worth and beauty of Christianity, by exhibiting its adaptation to our nature, and the freedom of its essential idea from the elements which have engendered superstition, and led to priestly domination in other religions. A valuable contribution towards the history of religion in this large sense, is furnished by the desultory, but eloquent and suggestive, work of Benjamin Constant[1]. But the task is too laborious and too vast for any one man at present to undertake. The materials for it must in the first instance be freely accumulated by deep and conscientious research into the religious monuments of the most celebrated nations, carried on without theory, and with a perfect readiness to admit the unbiassed results of faithful criticism. The records of heathenism have been too generally

---

[1] De la Religion, considérée dans sa Source, ses Formes, et ses Développements.

approached under the preconceived notion, that their examination could yield nothing but unmixed error and revolting impurity. What interest must attach to a full, dispassionate and unprejudiced account of the forms and influences of the religious principle, as it existed among such a people as the Egyptians, the ancient Greeks, or the old Scandinavians! It is evident that the study of theology, properly understood, is far from having reached its limits; and that it seems to be stationary, only because its field is arbitrarily limited, and reason is sent into it, unfurnished with the proper implements, and deprived of the free use of all its powers.

To aid the religious progress of society, the province of theology, as a science, must not be confounded with that of religion, as a spiritual influence. The same man may be, and often is—to a certain extent he always ought to be—at once a theologian and a preacher; but he should not often exercise both his functions at the same time. The theology of the preacher should be a hidden source of light, lying deep in the mind, and mingling as a general radiance with the full flow of the spirit to his lips, to make distinctly visible the ideas which he wishes to convey, and guide them to their destined effect in the convictions of his hearers. Learning must often be employed to undo its own work; to help a preacher to separate the living spirit of the Divine Word, from the incrustations which a misplaced erudition has gathered round it. What he should chiefly seek as the proper aim of his studies, is the power of throwing himself back into the spirit of the holy men whose mind and life are reflected in the sacred books. Having once possessed himself of this, he must forget, when he addresses his contemporaries, all that is antique in the thought, or inappropriate in the phraseology of the text, through which he imbibed it; and try to speak, under the sole consciousness of present, living interests, just as Paul or John would now speak, if from our point of view they were looking out with their own deep heart of faith and warm impulse of human sympathies, on the still enduring strife of man with doubt and sin and woe. That theology has been so generally brought into the pulpit, rather than religion, is probably one reason why most churches have lost their hold on the popular feeling. The masses are more attracted by the earnest fanaticism which comes under however rough and unshapely an exterior from the genuine heart of man, than by the cold light which streams from the polished intellect, and plays with a graceful indifference round the ingenious theories of learning and philosophy. Nevertheless, it is in the highest degree undesirable, that the popular religion should be left to the direction of ignorant and vulgar minds. The mental food which has been prepared by the highest intelligence of the time, will ever be found the most palatable and the most nutritious for the masses. Refined and elevated influences, when mingled with Christian simplicity and real benevolence, are the most certain of a cordial welcome and a beneficial effect, even with those who are themselves simple and uncultivated.

There must be something fundamentally wrong in the religious organization of society, when it is the fashion for the genteel and the educated to throng to places of public worship, while vast multitudes of the ignorant wander abroad, reckless and unreclaimed, without an instructor or a guide. This is in strange contrast to the merciful doctrine which the Gospel originally taught. We think of the Church of Christ as the natural shelter and refuge of the poor. The great work which its ministers have now to accomplish, the main direction which religious institutions must hereafter take,—is the adaptation of Christian principles and influences to the want and capacity of those vast industrious classes who are daily growing in strength and intelligence, and to whose future happiness and healthful progress it is indispensable, that their whole moral being should be brought under the control of a clear, firm, rational faith in Christ and God. Instead of being mocked with a technical phraseology which neither satisfies the understanding nor reaches the heart, the useful results of theological research should be popularized, made level to their comprehension, and blended with practical applications to their daily life. The grand poetry of the Bible should be brought home to their feelings, and rendered additionally impressive by the blended recommendations of solemn music and holy song. The true theory of their present existence should be clearly laid open before them, that they may understand its duties, and feel its worth, and perceive its connection in the great order of Providence, both with what has preceded them in the history of this world, and with the nobler futurity which awaits them after death. That Church alone is secure, and will yield good fruit, which has its roots deep and wide in the attachment and veneration of a virtuous and instructed people. Only such a Church fulfils the end of its institution. Every other praise is equivocal. Learning, refinement, intelligence, enlightened views, and a liberal spirit, however valuable in themselves, exist to little purpose, if they do not spread beyond the narrow circle in which they first arose, and flow over into the world with a quickening influence, to ennoble and purify and bless the whole family of man.

INDEX.

Acontius, his anticipation of Latitudinarianism, 205.
Adam Martindale's autobiography, quoted in proof of prevalent Latitudinarianism, 218, note.
Albigenses, 3.
Anabaptists, 125.
Andrews, Dr. Lancelot, cultivator of Greek theology, 68.
Anglicanism, spirit of, 58-9; periods of development of, 61; principles of, 172-77; contrasted with Puritanism, 183.
Antonio de Dominis, 68, note.
Arminianism, rise of, in the Church, 67; sign of prelatical tendencies, 112.
Articles, forty-two, 54; thirty-nine, 54 and 55; twentieth article, 55, note; statute of 1571 confirming, 57; petition for release from subscription to, 85.

Baptists, origin and principles of, 159; Burnet's testimony to them, 160; their eminent men, 161; their confessions of faith, 161.
Barclay, account of his Apology, 163.
Barrowe, 118.
Bates, Wm., his character, 152; Pepys's admiration of his preaching, 152, note.
Baxter, his character and influence, 147-51, with notes; comparison of, with Owen, 156-58, 215, note; his *principium cognoscendi*, 215.
Becket, 5.
Bentley, Dr. Richard, his Phileleutherus Lipsiensis in reply to Collins, 272.
Berkeley, bishop, his character and principles, 80 and note.
Biddle, John, his peculiar doctrines, 222; contrast with Firmin, 224.

Blount, Charles, account of his writings, 268.
Bolingbroke, Lord, partly educated among the Dissenters, 250; his character, account of his writings and opinions, 276-78.
Book of Sports, 113, note.
Bradshaw's English Puritanism, 119.
Bramhall, archbishop, his views of the Church, 71.
Brownists, 118.
Burnet, bishop, his character, 77; examination of his charge against the Nonconformists, of being bribed to silence on the subject of Popery, 150, note.
Butler, bishop, educated among the Dissenters, 81.

Calamy, Dr Edmund, his reasons for Nonconformity, 247.
Calvinism, predominant in the church under Elizabeth, 63; later, the sign of Puritanism, 112.
Canons and Convocation, 52-3.
Cappe, Newcome, his conception of Christianity, 299.
Cartwright, his controversy with Whitgift, 105; his high church principles, 106; more moderate in his latter years, 109.
Cathari, 3.
Channing, Dr., his character and the influence of his writings, 303-4; contrasted with Priestley, 305; his treatment of the Scriptures, 306; medium of transition to German thought, 306.
Charior, Dr. Benjamin, first introducer of Anglo-Catholicism, 65.
Chillingworth, his Socinianism, inferential and constructive, 205; his skill in argument, 205.
Christian Man, Institution of, 33;

Q

Necessary Doctrine and Erudition of, 34.
Chubb, his character and writings, 276.
Church, headship of, transferred to the Crown, 14; discipline of, 51; subjection of, to the State, 53; three distinct elements in, 87.
Churches, foreign, in London under Edward VI., 44.
Communion Service, Mr. Hallam's judgment on, 45; influence of Bucer on, 46.
Civilians, alliance of, with high church doctrines, 66; jealousy between, and common lawyers, 66, note.
Cranmer, his first advice to Henry, 31, note; refusal to vote for the Six Articles, 33.
Collins, Anthony, a friend and disciple of Locke, 271; his writings and opinions, 272.
Confessional by archdeacon Blackburne, 85.
Conforming clergy, contempt for, among the aristocracy of the 17th century, 115.
Cowley's Philosophical College, 217.
Cromwell, ecclesiastical vicegerent of Henry VIII., 32.
Cromwell, Oliver, an embodiment of Puritanism, 139; his comprehensive toleration, 141; his projected college at Durham, 188, note; general encouragement of learning, 188.
Cudworth, Ralph, his view of Christian Faith, 211.

Deists, Lord Barrington's judgment of them, 279; their affinity of thought with rationalist divines, 280; their influence on the Continent, 280; unjust treatment of them, 282.
Deism, its inherent deficiencies, 283; neglects the need of a Christ, 285.
Directory of Worship, 132.
Dissenting Academies resorted to by men of rank, 250; their character and system of studies, 251-4.
Dissenting, Brethren, Apologetical Narration of, 122-3, note; Meeting-houses, their original type, 169.

Doddridge, his character and wide social influence, 264-66.
Donatists, 3, with note.
Dort, Synod of, 67.

Eighteenth Century, character of, 82; influence on religion and the Church, 83.
Elizabeth, freedom of religious thought at the Court of, 198.
Engagement under the Commonwealth, 138.
Episcopacy, attachment of the Long Parliament to a mitigated, 128, with note.
Erastianism, origin of the name, 18, note; prevalent among the bishops under Elizabeth, 18, 62.
Establishment, principle of an, not repudiated by the early Dissenters, 260, note.
Evangelical party of the Church of England, 84.
Evidences, Christian, different views of, 206-8, note.

Fairfax, Sir Thomas, his Independency, 21, note.
Falkland, Lord, his religious earnestness, 203; charged with Socinianism, 204, note.
Farmer, his view of miracles and demoniacal agency, 295.
Fifth Monarchy men, 125; their outbreak under Venner, 146.
Firmin, Thomas, his character and principles, 224-5; contrast with Biddle, 224.
Frankfort, Troubles of, 95, note.
French literature, influence of, on Hume and Gibbon, 279.

Gale, Dr. John, his learning and numerous auditory, 255.
Glanville, his latitudinarian spirit and scientific zeal, 211-13 note, 215.
Grindal, his Puritanic tendencies, celebrated by Spenser, 95, note.

Hales, John, his aversion to dogmatism, 204; his view of the Christian Evidences, 206.
Hariot, companion of Raleigh, his Deistical tendencies, 199, note.

Harley, Earl of Oxford, partly educated among the Dissenters, 250.
Harrington, the doctrines of his Oceana, 215–16.
Hartley, his influence on the religious opinions of his day, 288; takes the place of Locke in an earlier generation, 288.
Herbert, Lord, of Cherbury, his opinions, 200.
Hoadly, his character, 77, with note; contrasted with Berkeley, 80, note.
Hobbes, in outward communion with the Church of England, 200; his theoretical approval of Independency, 200, note.
High Church doctrines, rise of, 66; their prevalence after the Restoration, 71; supported by Clarendon, 71.
High Commission, Court of, instituted by Elizabeth, connecting link of Church and State, 17.
Homilies, twelve, published by Cranmer and Ridley, 40; Second Book of, 56.
Hooker's Ecclesiastical Polity, 63; Hooker and Travers contrasted, 107, note.
Howe, his character, 152–154; interview with Richard Cromwell in his last illness, 154; his anticipation of future union among Christians, 319.
Huntingdon, Countess of, 84, 85.

Independency, earliest professors of, put to death, 119; power and organization of modern, 313.
Independents, their conformity to the usages of the world, 187, with note.
Irreligion, prevalence of, in the middle of the eighteenth century, 260.

Jacob, pastor of the first Independent Church in England, 120.
Jacobitism, its prevalence among some of the more extreme Dissenters, 168, with note.
Jewel's Apology for the Church of England, 56.

Kant, influence of his philosophy on theology, 307.

Kettlewell, 79, note.
Keys, power of the, 124.
Kiffin, William, account of, 161.

Latitudinarianism, bishop Fowler's account of, 212, note; its extensive diffusion and significance in the middle of the seventeenth century, 217, note.
Latitudinarians, rise and principles of, 73; eminent as preachers, 74; estimate of their character, 209; chief writers, 212, note; their cultivation of modern science, 213.
Laud, conference with Fisher, 67; his Protestantism, 70.
Law, Dr. Edmund, his view of man's natural mortality, 289, note.
Law, William, his character, 79; influence on Wesley and Venn, 83.
Lay impropriations, Society for the purchase of, 113.
Lay preachers in Mary's reign, 97.
Lecturers, influence of, 114, note.
Lessing, his dislike of Christian rationalism, 308.
Liturgy, use of by Episcopalians, connived at by Cromwell, 21; after the Use of Sarum in Henry VIII.'s time, 36; three principal parts of, 42; successive revisions of, 49, note; character of, 50.
Lobb, the Jacobite Independent, 168.
Locke, John, intellectual symbol of the Revolution, 230; various influences in the formation of his mind, 232–3; fundamental principle of his philosophy, 234; grounds of his belief in Christianity, 236; his Discourse on Toleration, 238–9; principles of Scriptural interpretation, 241; attachment to Revelation, 242; suspected of Socinianism, 243; influence of his Christian Rationalism, 244.
Lollardism, affinity of, with Independency, 90.
Lollards, origin of the name, 6; deterioration of their condition under the house of Lancaster, 12; spared during the wars of the Roses, 13; persecuted again under Henry VII., 14.
Low Church principles, influence of,

after the Revolution, 75; promote a plan of comprehension and reformation of the Liturgy, 75; character of Low Church clergy, 76.

Martin Marprelate, tenets of, 19; printing-press which circulated them, discovered and broken up at Manchester, 19.
Mary, effect of her reign on Protestantism, 60.
Mass, its relation to English Liturgy, 48; canon of, 48.
Methodism, rise of, 83; a compensation of deficiencies in the Church and the Dissenters, 266.
Middleton, Conyers, his mode of dealing with the Freethinkers, 279.
Millenary petition presented to James I. by the Puritans, 111.
Milton, the growth of his religious opinions, 127.
Ministers, ordination and induction of, under the Commonwealth, 137; under the Protectorate, 138, with note.
More, Dr. Henry, character of his writings, 211.
Morgan, the fundamental idea of his "Moral Philosopher," 275.

Newton, his humility and attachment to Revelation, 242; a Unitarian, 243.
Nonconformist, Churches, origin of, 147; Preachers, their activity during the plague and after the fire of London, 168.
Nonconformity, local distribution of, 98, note; persecution of, in the reigns of Charles and James the Second, 165–6; account of Indulgences for, during the same period, 166, note.
Non-jurors, their character and principles, 79.

Oath, *ex officio*, 63, note.
Owen, Dr. John, his character and principles, 154–6; comparison of, with Baxter, 156–8; his great learning, 185, note; his attention to dress and manners, 187, note; his doctrine of the self-evidencing light of Scripture, 206, note; confirmed by that of Calvin, 208, note; his writings against Unitarianism, 221; reply to Biddle's Scripture Catechism, 223.

Paine, Thomas, Deistical argument revived by him in a more popular form, 283.
Parker, the primate, his learning, inclined to High Church principles, 62; bishop of Oxford, renegade from Independency, his sycophancy, 72.
Parliament, its sympathies with Puritanism, 109.
Parliamentary leaders, opposed to High Church principles, but not hostile to Episcopacy, 116.
Penn, his character, 26, note.
Philosophical College, idea of, entertained by Cowley, Hartlib, and Evelyn, 217, note.
Presbyterianism, liberalized by persecution, 24; not a proper English growth, 110; high, mitigated after the time of Elizabeth, 117; established in London and in Lancashire, 137, note.
Presbyterians, their suspicions of James II.'s Declaration for liberty of conscience, 26; after the Revolution, in usage Independents, 247; averse to subscription, 248; influence of Locke's philosophy on their theology, 249.
Presbytery, first English, at Wandsworth, 1572, 102.
Priestley, Dr. Joseph, his adoption of Hartley's philosophy, 289; his view of Christianity contrasted with Locke's, 291; his estimate of natural religion, 293 and note; his complaint of the prevalence of unbelief, 295; carried Scriptural Rationalism to the furthest point, 297; his character, 298 and note.
Prophesyings, 100.
Puritan, ministers practise exorcism, 111; their practical and expository works, 186, note; gentlemen, 188.
Puritanism, its predominance in the north of England, 7; its conflict with the hierarchy still in pro-

gress, 28; fundamental idea of, 88; its spirit embodied in Cromwell, 140; its essential principles in contrast with Anglicanism, 177–84; its influence on literature, 189–91.
Puritans, doctrinal, 68; their extinction, 71; conformable and nonconforming, 101; their love of fasts, and the length of their public services, 182, note.

Quakers, 125–6; persecution of them by Owen at Oxford, 140, with note; their system attracts persons of high mental refinement, 162; scientifically expounded by Barclay, 163; its leading principles, 164; charged with Popish tendencies, 164; their principal writers, 165, note; diffusion of their principles in the middle of the seventeenth century, 217.

Raleigh, Sir Walter, his religious sentiments, their affinity with those of Shakspeare, 199, note.
Rationalism, after the Revolution, its character and deficiencies, 258; definition of, 290, note.
Reformation, reaction against the doctrines of the, in Arminianism and Socinianism, 202.
Religion, influence of economic and social theories on, 302.
Religious life, its three elements, 318.
Religious parties in England, history of, divisible into three periods, 6.
Revolution, moderation in and out of the Church after the, 245.
Robinson, the father of Independency, 120 and note; his farewell address to the pilgrims, 121, note.
Romilly, Sir Samuel, prayer found among the papers of, 302, note.

Savoy, Confession, 142–3, with note.
Scriptures, account of early translations of, 37, note; Lollard zeal for reading the, 97.
Secker, archbishop, brought up among the Dissenters, 81 and note.
Sectaries, free notions prevalent among the, under the Commonwealth, 194, note.
Selden, a Christian, 199.
Service Book, first, 43; second, 45; second restored on accession of Elizabeth, 48.
Shaftesbury, Lord, a pupil of Locke, 269; dissents from Locke's doctrine of innate ideas, 270; his feelings towards Christianity, 271.
Schleiermacher, his combination of religious and philosophical principles, 310.
Slave trade, union of all religious parties against the, 301.
Solemn League and Covenant, analysis of, 129, note.
Spinoza, extensive influence of his system on German theology, 309.
Stillingfleet, his early liberality, 72; change of views after the Restoration, 72.
Strauss, elements involved in his Life of Jesus, 311.

Taylor, Dr. John, impugns the orthodox system, 286; his principal writings and high reputation, 286, note; Wesley's respect for him, and opposition to his doctrines, 287, note.
Theology, character of Greek, 68–9; its relation to religion, 322.
Tillotson, his relation to the Latitudinarians, 212.
Tindal, his Christianity as old as the Creation, 274.
Toland, his character and writings, 269; disputes with Beausobre at Berlin, 280.
Toleration, opposition of the Presbyterians to, 136, note.
Toleration, Act, 27; Acts of Parliament developing the principle of, 170, note.
Tractarianism, origin and principle of, 86.
Tradition, its value in the religious life, 316.
Travers, his Directory of Church Government, 102; analysis of it, 103–4.
Treaty of Westphalia, 4.
Trinity, controversy of South and Sherlock respecting the, 227–8.

Triers under Cromwell, 138.

Unitarians, Milton and Penn to be classed with, 225-6.
Unitarianism, early, connected with Anabaptism, 219; its first martyrs, 219; its extensive diffusion under the Protectorate and previously, 220; English, distinguished from Polish Socinianism, 228; older and newer school of, 312.

Venn, founder of Evangelical party, 83-5.
Voluntary principle, estimate of the, 314.
Watts, his early orthodoxy, 255; Unitarian tendencies of his latter years, 255, note; his catholic spirit, 256; his protest against the Rationalism of his day, 262; compared with Cudworth, 262, note.
Waldenses, 3.
Warburton, his theory of the alliance of Church and State, 82 and note.
Westminster, Assembly, description of, 130; incompatibility of its objects, 132; Confession, 133.
Whiston, his honesty, 78 and **note**.
Wilson, bishop, his character, **79**.
Wightman, Edward, connected with the **early** Baptists, 159.
Witchcraft, 111, note.
Witchfinder-general, 111, note.
Woolston, his attack on the evidence for the resurrection, 273; fined and imprisoned, 273; persecution of him condemned by Lardner, 274.
Wycliffe, Puritanism begins with him, 5; his mind formed by the writings of Augustine, 7; his zeal against the preaching friars, 8; patronized by John of Gaunt and the Queen of Richard II., 8; anticipates the principles of the Quakers, 9; circulates translations of the Scriptures, 9; called the Gospel Doctor, 9; supposed friendship with Chaucer, 10; his peculiar tenets, 10, note; wide diffusion of **them**, 11; his gloomy spirit, 93.

www.ingramcontent.com/pod-product-compliance
Lightning Source LLC
Chambersburg PA
CBHW030348230426
43664CB00007BB/578